THE CITIES BOOK
A Journey Through the Best Cities in the World

MELBOURNE | OAKLAND | LONDON

Best Cities 01-10

The heart of this book was set beating by our travellers who provided us with the list of 200 cities for inclusion in the book, via a survey we ran on www.lonelyplanet.com asking travellers (and our staff) to nominate their favourite cities.

The top five held no major surprises – Paris, New York, Sydney, Barcelona and London – although a quick glance at the top 25 cities certainly speaks to the adventurous spirit of our travellers. In the top 10 we have Cape Town and Bangkok, and the top 25 features Kathmandu, Buenos Aires and Jerusalem. In the 200 cities selected, we were able to display the great diversity of city life as it is experienced all over the globe: in the classic Western European cities such as Paris; ancient South American cities such as La Paz and Quito; island cities such as Apia in Samoa; trading centres such as Nairobi, hi-tech/futuristic cities such as Hong Kong and Tokyo; and those iconic cities like London, Florence or Rome, where time appears to stand still and accelerate in the same moment. The incredible diversity of day-to-day life explored through these pages challenges our very notion of a consistent 'city lifestyle', and yet something about the energy, pace and commonality of experiences connects these cities.

We don't set too much store by the 'rating' of these cities, but it was interesting to see just how the city standard is set by Paris. There are several other cities in this book that claim the reputation by association: Budapest, as the Paris of Eastern Europe; Beirut, as the Paris of the Middle East; Buenos Aires, as the Paris of the South; and Melbourne, as the Paris of the southern hemisphere!

New York City

Sydney

London

006
Rome

San Francisco

Bangkok

Cape Town

010
Istanbul

Best Cities 011–70

Best Cities 071–135

Best Cities 136–200

Cities: Past, Present + Future

When you look at a city, it's like reading the hopes, aspirations and pride of everyone who built it. – HUGH NEWELL JACOBSEN

The Cities Book is a celebration. Of the physical form, in stone, glass, metal and wood, that is taken by these remarkable spiritual, cultural, political and technological bastions. Of the people whose energy spills out into the city, transforming itself into music, art and culture. Of the myriad sights, smells, sounds and other temptations awaiting travellers at the end of a plane, train or boat journey. By celebrating the majesty of cities on every continent we are pausing to marvel at the contribution they have made to the collective richness of humankind over more than six millennia.

Hence it made sense to us to begin this book with a look at the evolution of the city – the roots of cities in the first civilisations, the characteristics that we associate with the great cities of today, and the possible directions that they will take in the future.

Like so many other things, cities come to us as a gift from the ancients. Although capable of great foresight, our urban ancestors could not possibly have predicted the way in which cities were to change the world we live in. According to the UN, the urban populace is increasing by 60 million people per year, about three times the increase in the rural population. To get a sense of the impact that cities have made, try picturing the world without them. Imagine fashion without Milan, theatre without London's West End, hip-hop without New York, classical music without Vienna, or technology without Tokyo.

Former UN Secretary-General Kofi Annan summed it up when he said: 'We have entered the urban millennium. At their best, cities are engines of growth and incubators of civilization. They are crossroads of ideas, places of great intellectual ferment and innovation...cities can also be places of exploitation, disease, violent crime, unemployment, and extreme poverty...we must do more to make our cities safe and livable places for all.'

Past

The story of how cities evolved is the story of civilisation. The link is encoded in the words themselves: 'civilisation' comes from the Latin *civitas*, meaning 'city'. We can catch a glimpse of the past in the preserved walls of castles, palaces and places of worship that have survived, albeit haphazardly, for centuries, and which influence the colour and flavour of our present-day cities. Cuzco in Peru is the perfect example. The city's strongest walls remain those constructed by the Inca who, unfathomably, erected enormous stone monoliths carved by hand and laid the blocks so precisely, without mortar, that it is impossible to slide paper between them. Following the Spanish conquest, the ancient Inca stones were used to build palaces and cathedrals, but the stones were so mighty that many could not be brought down and so continue to make up the streets and foundations of newer buildings to this day.

Paradoxically, with the advent of the first sedentary settlements, where people flocked together to settle in large groups instead of roaming the countryside as small bands of hunter-gatherers, came the advent of inter-city travel. Initially people travelled (as they still do) for trade and business, war, or religious pilgrimages, but eventually cities gave birth to the leisured classes who could travel for curiosity and pleasure. Even in ancient times there were hoteliers who ran a roaring trade for prototypal backpackers and travel writers and historians who made their livings from the fantastical tales of their wanderings.

Sumerian Cities

Divine Nature gave the fields, human art built the cities.
– MARCUS TERENTIUS VARRO

Current archaeological records indicate that the oldest cities are those found scattered along the banks of the Tigris and Euphrates Rivers in Mesopotamia, modern Iraq.

Five thousand years ago merchants travelling upriver from Egypt would have entered the great Sumerian capital of Uruk by boat, sailing swiftly past the fertile shores lined with irrigation ditches that had been dug centuries before. These ditches, filled with water from the Euphrates River, had allowed the Sumerians to begin farming the land, producing surpluses of food that were used to feed an army of construction workers, possibly slaves, to raise the first cities the world had ever seen. The most ancient of these was Uruk and with its construction the door was firmly closed on the prehistoric epoch.

The city of Uruk was famous for its giant defensive walls, luscious gardens and the sophistication of its ruling elite, chief among them the god-king Gilgamesh, who became the subject for the world's oldest epic, the *Song of Gilgamesh*, which is still in print today. Excavation of the vast site where the city once stood, an area covering 450 hectares, has yielded astonishing finds. In the 1900s a cuneiform tablet found at Uruk happened to contain what is regarded as the best and most accurate description of the legendary Tower of Babel, an architectural feat referred to in the Bible.

But the real fascination is with the form of the city itself. In 2003 Jorg Fassbinder, part of a German-led archaeological team conducting excavations at the site, said that in its heyday Uruk must have been 'like Venice in the desert'. The dig covered more than 100 hectares, uncovering extensive gardens as well as an extremely sophisticated network of canals by which the Sumerians swanned around their idyllic city in absolute luxury.

RIGHT INCA CITY WALLS IN CUZCO.

It is incredible to think that after more than 5000 years the legacy of Sumerian culture could still remain potent. Not only did they invent the wheel and come up with the world's first written language (Sumerian cuneiform script, which emerged around 3500 BC), but they also dreamt up the sexagesimal number system, which we still use to measure time. Every time you count down the minutes to an event, you have the Sumerians to thank.

What we know of ancient Sumer has been deduced through careful analysis and interpretation of the discoveries made by archaeologists. These include stone tablets inscribed with ancient stories (the first ever recorded); gold necklaces inlaid with lapis lazuli that were once worn by Sumer's elite; weathered fragments of beautiful vases depicting the conquest and subjugation of rival cities; and the broken outlines of once-feared cities that stretched for kilometres. Interpreting these finds with a little imagination only whets our appetite and makes us want to learn more about these strange worlds that have been lost in time.

Rome – Antiquity's Great Melting Pot

A great city, whose image dwells in the memory of man, is the type of some great idea. Rome represents conquest; Faith hovers over the towers of Jerusalem; and Athens embodies the pre-eminent quality of the antique world, Art.
– BENJAMIN DISRAELI

Sicilian writer Vincenzo Salerno said that despite everything that came after it, the blueprint for Western civilisation was the society of ancient Rome. The Romans gave us our alphabet (minus *u* and *w*), and many of the words we still use are derived from ancient Latin. They gave us the 12-month lunar calendar; the rudiments of classical architecture; the pope; straight roads; a system of government; literature; public-ablution facilities; and endless subject matter for Shakespearian plays and even movies, such as *Gladiator* and *I, Claudius*. The Romans came, saw and conquered, and left enough behind that they would never be forgotten. And at the heart of the mighty empire was the imperial capital, a monolith of power carved in brilliant marble, home of the Senate and generations of megalomaniac emperors. Ancient Rome's former pagan glory is still visible if you take a stroll around the modern city, notably the remains of the Roman Forum, the Pantheon and the Colosseum.

Quite clearly, the Romans were a pretty remarkable bunch. But they were not the first people to become civilised, and nor did they develop in a vacuum. They were great assimilators, subsuming the skills, knowledge, literary conventions and even deities from neighbouring or past civilisations – a process hastened through conquest. From afar Rome admired in particular the Greek and Egyptian civilisations, centred on the capitals of Athens and Alexandria, which were already melting pots of ideas, racial groups and culture.

Alexandria the Great

It was in Alexandria, during the six hundred years beginning around 300 BC, that human beings, in an important sense, began the intellectual adventure. – CARL SAGAN

In 332 BC Alexander the Great thrashed the Persians and then conquered Egypt for the Greeks. The following year, after being crowned pharaoh, he ordered the construction of a fortified port which he named, in a moment of egotism, Alexandria. The city was to replace Memphis as the capital of ancient Egypt and, had Alexander not died of fever during the conquest of Babylon, would have become the capital of his enormous empire. As it happened, the empire was carved up by Alexander's generals following his death and Ptolemy Soter took over as pharaoh and king of Alexandria.

During antiquity the Egyptian capital was famous for its wonderful papyrus and had a reputation for producing great medicines, perfume, jewellery and gold work. But most of all, the city was, and still is, legendary for the Pharos Lighthouse, one of the Seven Wonders of the Ancient World, and for its library, established under Ptolemy III. It is alleged that he composed a letter 'to all sovereigns on earth, requesting them to send him works by every kind of author, including poets and prose-writers, rhetoricians and sophists, doctors and soothsayers, historians and all the others too'. Such was his zealousness in collecting knowledge that he gave orders for any books on board ships calling at Alexandria to be copied, and only the copies were returned to the owners. As a secure port city, an industrial and manufacturing base, and a hub of knowledge, Alexandria had a celebrated liberal system of governance that championed diversity.

Less than 500 years after Ptolemy Soter had ascended the throne, Alexandria was reduced to smouldering rubble, destroyed through a combination of Caesar's aggression, petty-minded Christian rebels, earthquake and flood. The coastal Egyptian city we know today as Alexandria bears almost no trace of its amazing history. But through the advanced system of trade and communications that existed throughout antiquity, at least some of the knowledge contained in the library (such as details of the Archimedes screw, a pump that Archimedes invented while staying at the Mouseion, the city university), was not completely lost. Then as now, the great powers adopted and adapted the successful tricks and strategies of their contemporaries and in so doing ensured that the legacies of civilisations dating back countless millennia would be recorded.

Lost Cities – Atlantis to Great Zimbabwe

Towered cities please us then,
And the busy hum of men. – JOHN MILTON

For thousands of years fabled lost cities have had a vicelike grip on our imagination. Even such a wise philosopher as Plato would get excited thinking about how these advanced civilisations could just be mysteriously wiped out. His fascination with lost cities has trickled down hundreds of generations and given us the most tantalising and well-known mysterious lost city of all, Atlantis.

The legend of the lost city of Atlantis has captivated scholarly and public imagination since it was first recorded over two millennia ago. The source of the great legend stems from an account written by Plato (427–347 BC) in *Critias* and *Timaeus*. Plato's account was originally derived from Solon (640–560 BC), the great lawmaker of Athens. It is alleged that Solon was told of the disappearance of a vast and worldly island civilisation by Egyptian priests while he was visiting the Nile delta. This story was told to Plato by Critias (a poet, philosopher and controversial political figure), via his great-grandfather, who had learned the story with Solon. In *Timaeus*, Plato quotes Critias' account of the legend:

> *Now in this island of Atlantis there was a great and wonderful empire which had ruled over the whole island and several others, and over parts of the continent... But, there occurred violent earthquakes and floods, and in a single day and night of misfortune...the island of Atlantis...disappeared in the depths of the sea.*

Right now there are still people out there trying to find the site of this ancient Utopia. Based on the scant detail in Plato's account, it is highly unlikely we could identify Atlantis even if it were to be discovered. But there has been no shortage of possible candidates. Over the past few years a spate of potential Atlantises have been found in waters off India, Cuba and Japan.

In May 2001 underwater archaeologists at India's National Institute of Ocean Technology detected signs of an ancient submerged settlement in the Gulf of Cambay, off Gujarat. Acoustic-imaging analysis identified a 9km-long stretch of what had once been a river now lying 40m beneath the waves. Evidence retrieved from the site, including pottery, beads, broken sculpture, wood and human teeth, has been carbon dated, and a conservative estimate of the age of the site puts it at around 7500 BC. It is not clear whether the Cambay site represents a city or a smaller type of settlement. If it is a city, then the belief that the Sumerians built the first city would be proved wrong, and the whole theory of the origin and spread of ancient civilisations would need to be revised.

But wait, it gets better. In December 2001 another lost city was discovered, this time off the west coast of Cuba in the Yucatán Channel by scientists innocently engaged in sonar imaging for a Canadian company that was hoping to discover sunken ships laden with Spanish treasure. The fact that some of the buildings alleged to be part of the city appear to be shaped like pyramids got dozens of internet Atlantean hopefuls extremely fired up.

Although the jury is still out on whether this Cuban discovery is a lost city or just an anomaly that showed up on the radar, there is no doubt that a strange megalithic structure discovered in Japanese waters off the island of Yonaguni is genuinely man-made. The huge stone structure, which is over 100m long, was discovered by a diver in 1985. By itself the megalith isn't enough to signify the existence of a whole civilisation or even a city, but the estimated age of the structure, put minimally at 6000 years, represents another spanner in the works for those attempting to piece together the chronology of ancient human civilisation.

Each new archaeological find is a puzzle, and as much likely to inspire fear and prejudice as it is joy. Nowhere is this tenet illustrated more plainly than at the site of one of Africa's great lost cities, Great Zimbabwe. The first rumours of a magnificent lost city began circulating around the Portuguese colony of Mozambique during the 16th century. However, the spectacular ruins, with their massive curved walls, were not discovered by Europeans until nearly the end of the 19th century, when a young German explorer named Carl Mauch was directed to the site by a German trader who told him of some large ruins 'that could never have been built by blacks'.

It was almost another 20 years before a full exploration of the site was conducted by J Theodore Bent, an amateur archaeologist at best, bankrolled by British imperialist Cecil Rhodes. Despite unearthing masses of evidence that pointed to the indigenous origins of Great Zimbabwe, Bent concluded that the impressive curved-walled enclosures, which stretched over 40.5 hectares and were over 9.1m high, were the work either of Phoenicians or Egyptians who had travelled down from North Africa.

The inability of conquering civilisations to appreciate the achievements of those whom they have conquered has added significantly to the numbers of lost cities and ruined sites on all continents save Antarctica. The ruins of the World Heritage–listed site at Machu Picchu, picturesquely perched among the clouds high in the mountains of Peru, were once the spiritual capital of the Incan population that was decimated by the Spanish conquistadors, and are now an enigma. With the Inca gone and their knowledge lost, the ruins they left behind can never be interpreted with any certainty. But perhaps that only adds to the allure of the lost city. And the dim, irrational thought that perhaps, upon spending time wandering the ruins with the ghosts of our spiritual ancestors, it is possible to catch a glimmer of understanding in these sacred places.

Present

In the days of the European Grand Tour of the 19th century, it was fashionable for young aristocrats to complete their education by travelling to the great cities of the Continent to study their history and art. These 'tourists' are the origin of our modern word. But travel was still time-consuming, difficult and expensive and therefore only really available to the privileged classes. Today, modern transport means that we can travel between cities in hours, not days. The world is becoming smaller while correspondingly people's interests are becoming broader, thanks to our greater access to the world through the media. Recent travel trends show that short-break city trips are one of the most popular kinds of travel, and that the main motivators are education and exploring other cultures, escaping the stresses of everyday life for a while, and a sense of adventure. Travellers claim that travel has had a considerable impact on their lives, helping define a social conscience and positively impacting personal goals and values. Today, the most difficult part of city travel is deciding which city to visit next.

Plan for Living

The chief function of the city is to convert power into form, energy into culture, dead matter into the living symbols of art, biological reproduction into social creativity.

– LEWIS MUMFORD

The quality of life survey of the world's leading cities has become a regular feature of magazines such as *The Economist* and *Monocle*. For their mobile, business-savvy readers, a city's 'livability' is not just a matter of tax rates but embraces more subjective metrics: the amount of green space, the quality of schools, trains, bike paths and restaurants. Looking at a decade of such surveys and it's obvious that the top 10 is dominated by Northen European cities such as Copenhagen and New World centres in Australia and Canada. In particular, over more than three decades, the idyllic Canadian city of Vancouver has earned accolades through the introduction of a simple yet revolutionary approach to city planning and design.

In 1972 Vancouver's planning office took a bold step often feared by public servants scared of opening a Pandora's box. They decided to look beyond the computer models, livability indicators and programme plans they had created and ask the public what they thought would make the city most livable. The more they tried to answer the question 'what is livability?', the more they realised they didn't have the answer. So they decided to phone a friend – millions of friends.

The city's public discourse about livability eventually led to a plan that recognised the city as an organic entity in itself. A discussion paper on Vancouver prepared by the Vancouver-based International Centre for Sustainable Cities stated:

The brain and nervous system of a livable city refers to participatory processes by which a city develops visions and plans, monitors the implementation of its plans and adjusts to changing circumstances. The heart is the common values and public space of a city that define its essential identity. The neighborhoods, industrial clusters, downtown, parks and other hubs form the organs of a city. Similar to the circulatory system and neural networks that weave connections

RIGHT CANOEING IN ENGLISH BAY, VANCOUVER.

within a living organism, transportation routes, infrastructure, waste disposal, communication lines, water flows, and green space connect these nodes.

The essence of livability was found to be about quality of life, which is tied to the ability of citizens to access food; clean air; affordable housing; infra-structure (transport, communication, water and sanitation); meaningful employment; and green parks and spaces, and is also determined by the access that its residents have to participate in decision-making to meet their needs. These are criteria that favour mid-sized cities in countries with low population densities.

The *Economist* survey, published annually, ranks living conditions in 140 cities around the world by looking at stability, health care, culture and environment, education, and infrastructure. The most recent survey placed Melbourne in the top spot, followed by Vienna and Vancouver. A further two Canadian cities (Montréal and Toronto) rank highly. Alongside Canada, Australia has some of the most livable places in the world, with Perth, Adelaide and Sydney doing well.

Elsewhere in the Asian region, cities in Japan, New Zealand, Hong Kong, South Korea, Singapore and Taiwan all offer a good standard of living, and it is only a humid climate that brings scores down slightly.

Higher crime rates and a greater threat of terror put US cities below those of Canada, the most livable coming in around 25th place. Africa and the Middle East fare the worst of any region. Instability, the threat of terror and many cultural restrictions bring the ratings down, although strong anticrime measures in many Arab states are a stabilising factor, and in Israel the negatives are offset by a generally high level of development that makes Tel Aviv generally the best destination surveyed in the region.

Rapt in Wander

We all become great explorers during our first few days in a new city, or a new love affair. – MIGNON MCLAUGHLIN

Cities are places to wander, without a map, relishing the freedom that comes of being lost in a strange new world. Whether you're taking a leisurely stroll along the wide, cobblestone pathways of Antigua or letting a doe-eyed dog lead you aimlessly round the busy streets of Bangkok, exploring on foot or bicycle can easily be the highlight of any trip around a city.

The best thing about walking is that you have control. Whenever you come across something interesting you can stop and check it out, take your time and really savour the experience. Often the most ancient cities are the most rewarding ones to walk through. Perhaps it's because they were built for walking, in a time before cars were invented and carriages and horses were reserved for a small elite. Small cities also lend themselves to walking, as it is easy to learn your way around and to get a feel for their human scale. The slow pace of walking allows us to meditate and absorb the ambiance of a place, particularly in holy cities.

Passing along the decorated walls of the streets of Varanasi in India, winding through the hustle and bustle, can be a dreamlike experience. The myriad temples and sumptious buildings of the place nicknamed 'the eternal city' may help you to understand the Hindu belief that anyone who dies and is cremated in the city automatically ends the cycle of death and reincarnation and ascends immediately to nirvana. Lost in thought, wandering slowly, meandering like the Ganges as it flows through the centre of the city, you might feel as if your sins have been washed away and your mind made clear. In Mecca, a city where you are required to walk, the sense of renewal and rejuvenation comes from the river

ABOVE ANCIENT TRADITIONS CONTINUE ON VARANASI'S GHATS.

of humanity you will find yourself caught up in in the haj pilgrimage. Every year well over two million Muslims perform the sacred pilgrimage, forming a human mass that has to be seen to be comprehended. The focal point of Mecca is the Kaaba, the 'House of God', believed by Muslims to have been built by Abraham (peace be upon him) and his son Ishmael (peace be upon him), and which is covered in a large black- and gold-embroidered cloth. The pilgrims who have made the journey to Islam's holiest city wait patiently to circle the Kaaba seven times before they try to touch or kiss its cornerstone, the Black Stone, which is believed to be a meteorite. The process can take several hours simply due to the unbelievable numbers of pilgrims. This is one walk you won't forget in a hurry.

Tasty Travel

To be tempted and indulged by the city's most brilliant chefs. It's the dream of every one of us in love with food.
– GAEL GREENE

Food is the foundation of city and human life and a trip to any city would be much the worse for not savouring the flavours favoured by the locals. The quality of a city's restaurants can reveal much about its inhabitants – the importance of their traditions and their openness to new ideas.

Cities around the world, and many in this book, would all claim to be top or near the top of the epicure food chain. New York, Paris, London, Toronto, Melbourne, Montréal would certainly stake a fierce claim, as would San Francisco. Some cities have nice weather, others have nice beaches, but San Francisco has both (most of the time) and great food to boot. Whether you're sampling the city's best seafood with the leather-clad crowd in the Castro, chewing on dim sum (yum cha) in one of the world's biggest Chinatowns, going Mexican in the Mission District or dining sophisto in California's oldest restaurant, Tadich Grill, this is one city that demands you eat, and eat well.

But of course sampling a city's cuisine isn't always about eating the very best. The locals in any city have their own peculiar favourites, often in marked contrast to all the grand fare served up by gastronomic wizards in the finest restaurants at the fashionable end of town. In Chongqing, a searingly spicy hot pot of meaty slivers and noodles has a cult following among the locals, while the *porteños* of Buenos Aires prefer snacking on *empanadas* (turnovers) and *lomitos* (steak sandwiches). Sometimes it's all about discovering the local secrets, trying something a little different that you wouldn't find at home.

When you're in Minsk and need something to help keep your strength up against the Belarusian wind, make sure you gobble down a couple of fish in jelly. They're a lot tastier than you might think.

In Lahore it pays to explore the full range of Pakistani delicacies and there is no better place to achieve this goal than at the conveniently dubbed 'Gawalmandi food street'. The whole street is cordoned off to traffic, and from where you sit you can order whatever appeals from any of the stalls. Balti and tandoori dishes are most popular, but the more adventurous can tuck into *karai kaleji* (chicken livers), *gurda* (kidneys), *kapureh* (testicles) and *magaz* or *bheja* (brains).

In Celebration of Diversity

This is the most happening place in the city, and it happens to be gay. I don't think it's a coincidence. – PAUL COLOMBO

There's something about Sydney's Mardi Gras and Rio's Carnaval that makes it hard to picture them taking place in a tiny, sleepy country village with a population of 50 where everyone knows your name and if you go back far enough the inhabitants are all blood related. One of the great opportunities cities offer new residents is the chance for people to be themselves. Sharing a living space with millions of others is often regarded as a profoundly liberating experience. Anonymity allows for freedom and the chance to become the person you want to be.

Cities have a long history of attracting people who are seeking a fresh start or need to outrun the demons of prejudice and intolerance more common in villages and rural areas. During medieval times throughout Europe, peasants, not to mention thieves and vagabonds, would escape the attentions of despotic landlords by fleeing to the cities, hence the old expression 'city air is free air'. In 19th-century England, following the abolition of slavery in the British Empire, slave ships bound for the Caribbean continued to dock in port cities such as Liverpool. Occasionally slaves would be helped to escape and would hide among the throng of the busy city before eventually being integrated into society. Cities are also centres of migration, from rural areas and from abroad. The relative peace and stability that is enjoyed by people of different races, sexual orientation, cultural backgrounds and political views, who live together side by side in thousands of cities worldwide, is a wonderful advertisement for urbanisation.

The residents of Tbilisi in Georgia take pride in their city's reputation for multiculturalism. It is home to more than 100 ethnic groups, including Georgians, Russians, Armenians, Azeris, Ossetians, Abkhazians, Ukranians, Greeks, Jews, Estonians, Germans and Kurds. On the other side of the world in Puerto Vallarta (Mexico), locals celebrate the city's rich cultural diversity by eating out at the famous mix of restaurants.

Meanwhile, in the 'gayborhoods' of San Francisco, Sydney, Paris, New York and London, predominantly gay, lesbian, bisexual and transgender trendsetters continue to make a vital contribution to their city's economy by attracting curious tourists keen to hang out in a cool part of town. The Chueca barrio in Madrid is one of the city's best-known gay areas, with a totally chilled atmosphere where gay and straight people intermingle, and same-sex kissing and hand-holding is commonplace.

Endless Nights

Cities, like cats, will reveal themselves at night.
– RUPERT BROOKE

No matter how many natural, cultural or culinary charms a city may have, it is often judged by the quality of its nightlife. And having explored the delights of your chosen city by day, it's only natural that you should want to check out what happens between dusk and dawn, just to make sure you haven't missed anything.

Often the best nights out are those that are unplanned. Similarly, some of the best nightlife can be found in the cities where you'd least expect to find it.

Take Belgrade for example. Along the Danube you will find dozens of *splavovi* (floating raft clubs) blaring out funky, folksy Balkan beats as they slide out of view. In contrast, you expect New York to deliver – and it does. Whenever, wherever, whatever, however you want it, the world's most extravagant city has it all, 24/7. To maintain its pole position, the city has even spawned the New York Nightlife Association (NYNA), an orderly gang of owners, managers and staff from many of the city's top establishments, who in their own words believe New York City is the nightlife capital of the world and want to keep it that way.

Future

Having lured us out of the wild and into homes that for many are packed with creature comforts, fridges, hot water, electricity, heating, ADSL connections, telephones and the rest, what more does the city have up its sleeve? One thing is certain and that is that there will be change.

The challenges for the future faced by cities mainly revolve around sustainability and managing growing populations. Among the UN's Millennium Development Goals is a target to 'significantly improve' the lives of at least 100 million people living in urban slums by the year 2020. At the same time, cities must also plan to be less enviromentally damaging. Economic factors and the desire for unparallelled luxury are also motivators for city planners of the future. Technology moves ahead in leaps and bounds, and ultimately the only thing that can limit a city is the imaginations of the people who are building it. And today, perhaps more than at any time in history, ordinary people are nearer to turning their own city daydreams into something real.

New Real Estate

In a real estate man's eye, the most expensive part of the city is where he has a house to sell. – WILL ROGERS

In an essay entitled 'The Rise of the Ephemeral City' published in Metropolis Magazine, Joel Kotkin has suggested that we are witnessing the emergence of a new urban environment populated by 'non-families' and the nomadic rich whose needs are attended to by a subservient service class. He calls it the ephemeral city and suggests that it prospers merely through its ability to provide an 'alternative' – and one suspects extravagantly decadent – lifestyle for the wealthy few who can afford it. Even though Kotkin wasn't referring to the city of Dubai, he might well have been describing the playground for the nouveau riche.

Often the difference between the possible and the impossible is someone brave enough to have a vision. In the coastal city of Dubai, part of the United Arab Emirates, Sheikh Mohammed bin Rashid Al Maktoum is such a man. Following Dubai's decision to diversify its oil-based economy, the sheikh ordered the construction of a number of unprecedented projects to help transform the city. The Burj Khalifa topped out as the world's tallest tower (829m) in 2010, and is the centrepiece of a mixed-use complex known as Downtown Dubai. Other mammoth landmarks here include the Dubai Mall (the world's largest, including an aquarium and ice-skating rink) and the Dubai Fountain (also the world's largest). In total, the complex covers two square kilometres and is expected to cost around US$20 billion.

Not all of Dubai's real-estate projects have been so successful, however. Although construction began on three spectacular palm-shaped islands off the Dubai coast in the mid-2000s, the economic recession of 2008 brought development to a halt, with no date set to resume construction.

Less glamorous is the new district of Pudong, now part of Shanghai. Once a flat expanse of boggy farmland located across the river from the city, it was only in the 1990s that construction began here. One-and-a-half times larger than central Shanghai, in the space of just two decades Pudong's skyscrapers have become China's signature skyline. The speed at which Shanghai achieved its grandiose vision of the future – a car-based megacity of glass-and-steel office blocks and sprawling identikit residential towers – is very impressive, though its lack of a human scale poses questions about its sustainability.

RIGHT DUBAI'S MANMADE ISLANDS HAVE BEEN BESET BY PROBLEMS.

Raising the Dream

The city is a fact in nature, like a cave, a run of mackerel or an ant-heap. But it is also a conscious work of art, and it holds within its communal framework many simpler and more personal forms of art. Mind takes form in the city; and in turn, urban forms condition mind. – LEWIS MUMFORD

Some city planners have a more environmentally sustainable vision than the property developers. In the Arizona desert, north of Phoenix, a revolutionary city has been under construction since 1970. Its founder, Italian architect Paolo Soleri, hopes Arcosanti will inspire a change in the prevailing culture. Arcosanti is said to resemble the modernist urban Utopian designs of Le Corbusier and Sant'Elia. However, the principles of design are based on Soleri's concept of 'arcology' (a fusion of architecture and ecology). His vision is for an organic sustainable city that fits into the ecological system rather than imposing itself upon it: greenhouses beneath residential buildings generate solar energy for heating, as well as producing food. Soleri insists that when people come to Arcosanti they will be inspired and that when they leave they will begin to insist that genuinely sustainable principles start being applied to the development of their own cities.

Arcosanti is on too small a scale to provide the technical solutions for the challenges that face the world's major urban centres. However, Soleri fulfils the role of a visionary in that he believes that cities must become confluent with the example set by nature if they are not to be destroyed by the same forces that give them life. He writes:

In nature, as an organism evolves it increases in complexity... Similarly a city should function as a living system... The city is the necessary instrument for the evolution of humankind.

Citizen City

I have an affection for a great city. I feel safe in the neighbourhood of man, and enjoy the sweet security of the streets. – HENRY WADSWORTH LONGFELLOW

While old-school realists take a deep breath and get on with it, dreamers continue to dream. Anyone who has played Sim City knows the allure of being able to construct your own metropolis. Deciding whether the citizens have a greater need for a new university or a high-security prison can be fun, but for an increasing number of ordinary folk the fun is turning into reality.

Constructing cities started off as the sole preserve of warrior god-kings, then it passed into the hands of elected politicians, and now it seems anyone with enough passion and perseverance can give it a go, though finding financial backing has proven difficult.

For Florida-based Freedom Ship International (FSI), getting its city off the ground and into the ocean has been far from smooth sailing. FSI has plans to construct a 1371m-long, 228m-wide, 106m-tall, ocean-going vessel known as the *Freedom Ship*. The structure is billed as 'an international, cosmopolitan, full-spectrum, residential, commercial, and resort city that circles the globe once every three years'. If the project ever finds serious investors, the mobile modern city with its 518,160-sq-metre floor-space will have 18,000 living units; 3000 commercial units; 10,000 hotel units; a casino; world-class medical facilities; schools; an international trade centre; and more than 40 hectares of outdoor park, recreation and community space for residents to enjoy when they are not flying to the mainland in the ship's aircraft.

So far Norman Nixon, FSI's CEO, has reported the project has been inundated with offers of finance from bogus investors. But he hasn't given up hope of finding someone real who can turn the dream into reality. If only he could team up with Dubai's Sheikh Mohammed bin Rashid Al Maktoum, perhaps it would be full steam ahead for the world's first mobile floating city.

Clearly if you're looking to set up your own city it would be helpful to have loads of money. Then you could just buy a ready-made city like the one in Wiltshire sold off by Britain's Ministry of Defence. With an asking price of only UK£5 million, 'Burlington', with its 97 hectares, 100 miles of roads, private railway station and even its own pub, the Rose and Crown, seemed like a bargain. The catch is that the Cold War relic, built during the 1950s to house the government, British Royal family and 4000 civil servants in the event of a Soviet nuclear attack, is located underground on the site of a disused and rather dangerous stone mine. However, as an added incentive to prospective buyers, the city came fully furnished with government-issue ashtrays, lavatory brushes, tea sets and office chairs unpacked from 1959.

Paying Your Part

Man's course begins in a garden, but it ends in a city.
– ALEXANDER MACLAREN

As the evidence about the impact of climate change mounts there is a growing awareness among city-dwellers that something needs to be done.

The British Council estimates that over 75% of energy consumption is directly related to cities and that in many cases cities are highly vulnerable to the effects of climate change. At the same time, it says that cities have a great potential to 'instigate innovative solutions to the impacts of climate change'.

Feeling guilty? Try this then. The UK's ClimateCare Trust offers organisations and individuals a way to live guilt-free in the city by simultaneously selling carbon offsets while funding and managing projects that help to reduce further emissions elsewhere. How does it work? Simple. Using the trust's Car & Home Calculator, you can work out the amount of carbon dioxide emissions (which cause the negative effects referred to as climate change) for which you are responsible by entering how much electricity, petrol, gas and oil you use per annum. The calculator then works out how much carbon dioxide was ejected into the atmosphere as a result of the energy consumption you've admitted to, revealing a total in pounds that the environmentally conscious are then morally obliged to pay in the form of carbon offsets.

According to the Car & Home Calculator, an average one-car household uses about 9.5 tonnes of carbon dioxide, which would cost around £60 to offset. That £60 would in turn go towards funding worthy conservation projects such as disseminating efficient cooking stoves in Honduras or providing finance for renewable-energy cooking stoves in schools in India.

But the Climate Care Trust doesn't just work out your household and car emissions. To ensure guilt-free travel between cities, they have developed the Air Travel calculator that tells you how much carbon dioxide you are responsible for if you take a flight from, say, Boston to Delhi. Such a journey would emit 1.72 tonnes of carbon dioxide and would cost you £13 to offset. It may sound like a scam and critics ask why the organisation isn't run as a charity. The trust responds with this message: 'We do not believe that it should be left to the charitable sector to clear up pollution.' Whether or not you advocate the approach taken by the trust, the message that we have a responsibility to behave in a sustainable fashion to preserve the built heritage for future generations is one that is worth taking seriously.

Some examples of cities successfully finding ways to reduce emissions include: Berlin, where nearly all new buildings must include solar panels in their design; Toronto, where cold water pumped from the depths of Lake Ontario is circulated around the city as part of the Deep Lake Water Cooling Project to keep buildings cool, rather than using conventional air conditioners; and Chicago, where the government is trying to find new ways to encourage the use of rooftop gardens in order to keep buildings cool.

Fly Me to the Moon

In Rome you long for the country; in the country – oh inconstant! – you praise the distant city to the stars. – HORACE

Sometimes the only way is up. And when it comes to building the cities of the future, Professor Ouyang Ziyuan, author and member of the Chinese Academy of Sciences, couldn't agree more. He reckons that within our lifetime work will already be seriously underway to construct a lunar city, and it won't be made out of cheese.

Ouyang outlined his vision for a moon city in *Academicians Envisioning the 21st Century*, a book published in 2000 to encourage children to get interested in science. He predicted that by 2005 astronauts would have begun turning the moon into a 'natural space station' that would have pressurised modules, energy-generating facilities and groovy roving vehicles. By 2010 the completed and fully equipped station would allow human explorers to stay up there for weeks and in 2015, a small-scale but permanent moon base would appear. Humans living in the base would then start to build experimental factories and farms, gradually developing a fully fledged moon city before realising the dream of a self-sufficient 'earth village' by 2020.

Ouyang's predictions may have been a bit premature, as, in spite of claims by conspiracy theorists that NASA has already established colonies on the moon and Mars, there doesn't appear to have been much work in establishing a lunar base as yet. But those who can predict the future often seem to have a problem with dates – Nostradamus springs to mind – so perhaps we should wait a bit longer before giving the Chinese scholar's ideas the brush-off. After all, with China now investing billions on its space programme, maybe it won't be too long before Ouyang is proved correct. And we should hope so, because he also predicts that the moon city will feature a network of mining operations using solar power that will be able to generate enough surplus energy for it to be transmitted back to earth as a long-term, stable energy supply. Now that's got to be better than burning all that coal.

No two cities are the same. Some have great food, others great nightlife, some stunning architecture, some are rich with history and others have an eye on the future. Cities are individuals. Like a human being, a city is a mass of genes, chosen at random by forces beyond our control, fused together in a secret furnace, acted on by nature, reared through infinite probabilities of nurture before finally growing up and trying to make its own way in the world. Only by taking an interest in someone, spending time with them, observing their mannerisms, conversing with them, engaging with their likes and dislikes, strengths and weaknesses, learning their idiosyncrasies and funny habits, listening to them sing in the shower and snore at night, only by walking the path with them and imagining what it would be like if you were wearing their shoes, can you begin to realise how special someone is. And the city is the same, except maybe a little bit bigger.

The Cities

THE AL DAFRA CAMEL FESTIVAL – A BEAUTY CONTEST FOR CAMELS – BRINGS THE UAE'S VIPS TOGETHER.

ROGER GRESS / GETTY IMAGES

Abu Dhabi

DATE OF BIRTH 1760; NAMED BY THE FIRST SETTLERS, THE BANI YAS BEDOUIN TRIBE, MEANING 'FATHER OF THE GAZELLE' **ADDRESS** ABU DHABI, UNITED ARAB EMIRATES (MAP 8, F6) **HEIGHT** 27M **SIZE** 67 SQ KM **POPULATION** 613,500 **LONELY PLANET RANKING** 175

Oil rich since the 50s, the development of Abu Dhabi has closely mirrored that of neighbouring Dubai, only with slightly less glitz. Instead, like a mature and innovative older sibling, Abu Dhabi is stealthily emerging as the cultural hub in the UAE.

ANATOMY

Abu Dhabi is the largest and most senior of the seven emirates comprising the United Arab Emirates (UAE). It encompasses 80% of the UAE's total land area and the city itself occupies an island linked by three major bridges with the mainland. The seafront Corniche Rd is bookended by the *mina* (port) to the east and the Emirates Palace to the west. The Grand Mosque is midway between the two points, close to the main arterial road leading from the airport, Sheikh Rashid bin Saeed al-Maktoum St. The main bus terminal is on this road but private taxis (with air-conditioning) are a preferable way of getting around.

PEOPLE

Only one quarter of the population of Abu Dhabi is made up of UAE nationals; the majority are expatriates from India, Pakistan, Bangladesh, Sri Lanka, the Philippines, the UK and from across the Arab world. Although Arabic is the official language, English is widely spoken and understood.

TYPICAL ABU DHABIAN

Despite the stereotypical opinion, not all Emiratis are millionaires, not all are even wealthy. Most work in the public sector as the short hours, good pay, benefits and early pensions are suitably appealing. Wealthy or not, shopping is an important part of the lifestyle here, together with a deeply ingrained love of the desert and nature, as well as traditional culture and art.

DEFINING EXPERIENCE

Donning the stilettos, the slicked back hair, the high fashion outfit and, of course, the attitude and having a saunter around the extraordinarily lavish

THE FOUR-LEGGED COMPETITORS ARRIVE FOR THE AL DAFRA CAMEL FESTIVAL IN ABU DHABI.

Emirates Palace hotel. Linger for a moment at the world's only vending machine that sells solid gold bars, before enjoying a frothy cappuccino topped with real gold flakes (resist whipping out your tea strainer...).

STRENGTHS
- Louvre Abu Dhabi
- Saadiyat (Cultural) Island
- Beachside promenade
- F1 racing venue
- Major UAE concert venue
- Diverse cuisines
- Top shopping
- Falcon Hospital
- Grand Mosque
- Futuristic architecture
- Atmospheric souqs
- Easy-to-navigate grid system

WEAKNESSES
- Living and working condition of labourers
- Searing heat
- Lack of inexpensive nightlife
- No art-house cinema scene
- Media censorship

GOLD STAR
The spectacular Grand Mosque is not only the third largest international mosque and (unusually) open to the general public but also organise free 90-minute guided tours which culminate in a question and answer session with visitors sitting cross legged on the world's largest carpet under the world's biggest chandelier.

STARRING ROLE IN...
- *Syriana* (2005)
- *The Kingdom* (2007)

BLACK AND WHITE – A WOMAN REGARDS SHEIKH ZAYED GRAND MOSQUE; THERE ARE GUIDED TOURS THROUGHOUT THE DAY.

◢ *The Bourne Legacy* (2012)
◢ *Body of Lies* by David Ignatius

See Heritage Village and a glimpse of life here during the pre-oil days.

Eat a red-blooded quality cut at Marco Pierre White's steakhouse and grill.

Drink avocado smoothie topped with a sprinkling of pistachio nuts and honey.

Do rent a bike and cruise along the seafront Corniche .

Watch any of the musicians appearing at the annual F1 event.

Buy gold, it really is cheaper here.

After dark Head for one of the top hotels, like Intercontinental or Emirates Palace for the bars and clubs to see and be seen in.

TAKING A QUICK BREAK IN THE FIELDS.

Abuja

DATE OF BIRTH 1976: WHEN THE NIGERIAN GOVERNMENT KICKED OUT THE LOCAL GWARI INHABITANTS AND DECIDED TO UP-AND-MOVE THE CAPITAL FROM LAGOS TO ABUJA **ADDRESS** NIGERIA (MAP 6. G8) **HEIGHT** 360M **SIZE** 250 SQ KM **POPULATION** 1.9 MILLION **LONELY PLANET RANKING** 158

One of the newest cities on the planet, Abuja was imagined in the 1970s on the back of oil revenues, and building began in the 1980s at the geographical centre of Nigeria.

ANATOMY

The very character of this purpose-built city has been shaped by the two renowned rock formations around it – Zuma Rock, the 'Gateway to Abuja', and Aso Rock, located at the head of Abuja, with the city extending southwards from the rock. The rolling landscape is dotted with hills and plains, canopied with scenic greenery and virgin forests. As a new city, with a rapidly growing population, public transport provision is racing to catch up. It is serviced by a modern road system and the numerous cheap taxis and vans are the main method of getting around.

PEOPLE

Several indigenous groups live in Abuja, the largest among them are the Gbabyi (also known as the Gwari) and the Koro. Several smaller indigenous groups are the Gade, Egbura, Gwandara, Bassa and the Gana gana.

TYPICAL ABUJAN

A civil servant, a politician, a diplomat, or a member of the domestic staff of the aforementioned.

DEFINING EXPERIENCE

Meeting early at the International Conference Centre, going hiking in the hills around the city, playing a round of golf in the afternoon, then finding one of the local botanic garden–styled drinking spots in town and sampling some local fare before a spot of dinner at an international hotel.

FILING OUT OF THE NATIONAL MOSQUE FOLLOWING FRIDAY PRAYERS.

STRENGTHS

- Wide-open streets
- A good golf course
- The imposing Zuma Rock
- Aso Rock, the largest rock formation, nearly 400m above sea level
- The Dutse hill range, a sanctuary for baboons and other forms of wildlife

WEAKNESSES

- Domestic flights are unscheduled, as they are mainly charter flights, even to Lagos

GOLD STAR

Aso Rock, the city's spine, a granite monolith that towers over the gleaming green dome of Nigeria's National Assembly building.

STARRING ROLE IN...

- The plans of international architecture practices!

See the flowering bougainvillea and other exotic greenery that conceal the high walls and razor wire protecting the office towers, apartment buildings and villas dotting the landscape.

Eat *edikang ikong*, a rich, leafy delicacy from the southeast; probably Nigeria's most famous and most cosmopolitan meal, it's served in many restaurants and the biggest hotels.

Drink the popular traditional brew *brukutu* – a chocolate-coloured, faintly sour fermented drink made from sorghum.

Do attend Asofest in November, an annual festival of traditional arts and culture.

Watch baboons in the nearby Dutse hill range.

Buy music by Fela Kuti or King Sunny Ade – leaders of the West African music scene.

After dark have a drink at Elephant Bar in the Sheraton.

Addis Ababa

NICKNAME ADDIS ABABA MEANS 'NEW FLOWER' IN AMHARIC **DATE OF BIRTH** 1886; FOUNDED BY EMPEROR MENELIK ON LAND CHOSEN BY HIS EMPRESS, TAYTU, FOR ITS PLEASANT CLIMATE IN THE FOOTHILLS OF THE ENTOTO MOUNTAINS **ADDRESS** ETHIOPIA (MAP 8, B9) **HEIGHT** 2450M **SIZE** 250 SQ KM **POPULATION** 3.4 MILLION **LONELY PLANET RANKING** 186

Ethiopia has been called the 'cradle of civilisation': one of the few countries on the continent never to be colonised, its unique culture is vibrantly expressed in its teeming capital, which is one of Africa's largest cities.

ANATOMY

Addis lies over a series of folds in the hills, but these have little effect on its sprawling mass, clustered round the Piazza to the north and Meskel Sq to the south. High-rise blocks stand next to fields of thatched, wattle-and-daub huts, air-conditioned taxis ferry businesspeople and bureaucrats while the rest of the population crowds into the fleet of tiny minibuses.

PEOPLE

Addis' population speaks 80 languages: Galla from the south comprise almost half of the total population, Amhara are the second-largest group at around one third, and others include Tigrayans, the Somali, Gurage, Borana, Awi, Afar, Wolayta, Sadama and the Beja.

TYPICAL ADDIS ABABAN

Like the city itself, Addis' citizens are a strange mix of the ancient and modern: priests in medieval robes bearing ceremonial umbrellas mingle with diplomats from across Africa visiting the African Union; street kids in filthy football shirts play among Oromo warriors attending tribal conferences, their elaborate hairpieces representing their prowess as hunters.

DEFINING EXPERIENCE

Joining in the week-long celebrations of the Feast of the True Cross in September, when huge bonfires are lit in Meskel Sq, topped by crosses made of flowers, and the singing and dancing goes on long into the night.

ጀ አመራርና የሁሉም ዜጋ ተሳትፎ ወሳኝ ነው

By Artist Tesfami

GOING THE DISTANCE – ETHIOPIAN ATHLETES SPECIALISE IN MARATHONS.

STRENGTHS

◢ Warm, temperate climate
◢ One of the safest cities in Africa
◢ Friendly locals

WEAKNESSES

◢ Extreme poverty
◢ Corruption
◢ The lack of education, employment, decent housing...

GOLD STAR

Ethiopians really are among the most welcoming people around: sit down for a natter and a strong, sweet coffee in one of the numerous cafés around the Piazza and just try and get away in a hurry.

STARRING ROLE IN...

◢ *Shaft in Africa* (1973)
◢ *500 Years Later* (2005)

See the rest of Ethiopia while you're there: from the Great Rift Valley to the Central Highlands, and the 1700-year-old obelisks of Axum to the rock churches of Lalibela, Ethiopia is one of the most fascinating and least visited countries on earth.

Eat Ethiopia's delicious national staple of *wot* (a spicy stew) and *injera* (a soft, spongy bread) at the Addis Ababa Restaurant, housed in a former Ras (duke's) residence.

Drink a flask of *tej*, the powerful local mead brewed from honey, in one of the numerous *tej beats* (Ethiopian pubs).

Do visit one of our oldest ancestors in the National Museum: 'Lucy', an almost complete hominid, was discovered in northeast Ethiopia in 1974, and she's at least 3.2 million years old.

Watch a football match at Addis San Giorgis stadium in the centre of town, complete with barefoot players, live animal mascots, fire-breathing spectators and lashings of St George beer.

Buy anything you like at the sprawling open-air Merkato, the largest market in East Africa.

After dark head to the bars on the Bole Rd for music and dancing in all styles – everything from *azmaris* (traditional Addis tunes) to international stars such as the adored Gigi Shibabaw.

RICH AND VIBRANT, ADDIS ABABA IS A CITY BUILT ON CULTURAL DIVERSITY.

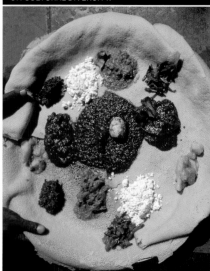

FOOD FOR THE MASSES – INJERA IS A UNIQUE DISH OF ETHIOPIA.

ETHIOPIANS LOOK FORWARD TO A BRIGHTER FUTURE.

PATIENT MOTHERS WAIT AT THE HOSPITAL.

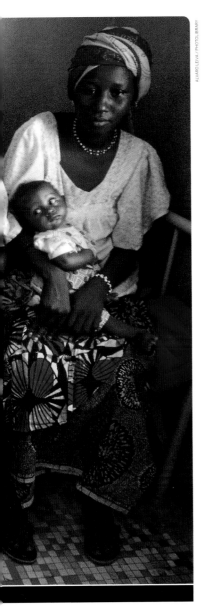

Agadez

DATE OF BIRTH AD 1100; STEMMING FROM ITS PRIME LOCATION ON THE TRANS-SAHARAN CARAVAN ROUTES **ADDRESS** NIGER (MAP 6, G6) **HEIGHT** 529M **POPULATION** 88,500 **LONELY PLANET RANKING** 152

Niger's premier ancient city, Agadez offers the romance of the Sahara and the allure of exotic mud minarets, swarming markets and nomadic culture.

ANATOMY

In Niger's central west sits Agadez. The centre of the city is taken up by the extraordinary Grande Mosquée, which affords spectacular views over the town and the surrounding desert. From here you can see the Old Town (Vieux Quartier) and to the south lies the main focus of town life – the Grand Marché (the main market). Head west for a good price on a camel or just to absorb the sights and sounds of the Tuareg Camel Market. Rising out of the Sahara to the north are the majestic Aïr Mountains, dotted with hospitable Tuareg villages, lush valleys and enough rough terrain to delight any budding mountaineer. A motley selection of minibuses, *taxis-brousses* (bush taxis) and Toyota 4WDs service the city's public-transport needs.

PEOPLE

The small but active nomadic Tuareg population has strong roots in and around Agadez, emerging from outlying areas to do business with the Hausa traders from the south at the city's Grand Marché. Pastoral populations such as the well-known Wodaabe also live in areas west of Agadez. Although French is the official language, some tribal languages are also spoken. Muslim dress is taken very seriously by Agadezers, and foreign women in particular should wear modest clothing.

TYPICAL AGADEZER

Agadezers are friendly and lively and are eager for tourism to take off in their city. They are traders, farmers and marketers – nomadic and agricultural. They are festive and as such, festivals thrive in Agadez. While they hold religion dear to their hearts and are Muslim in dress and belief, they readily indulge their liking for drinking, gambling and sport. The national obsessions of *la lutte traditionelle* (traditional wrestling) and table football are alive, well and flourishing thanks to Agadezers.

DEFINING EXPERIENCE

Wandering the labyrinth of narrow alleyways between the traditional single-storey *banco* (mud-brick) buildings of the Old Town to the small night market opposite Place de la Fraternité to eat and watch the bustle of the medicine men, food stalls and people while contemplating a game of table football or another brochette.

STRENGTHS

- Camel markets
- The nearby Aïr Mountains
- Ténéré Desert
- Camping
- Plentiful festivals and festivities
- Mud-brick architecture
- The Old Town
- Table football

WEAKNESSES

- Fierce competition (for the tourist dollar)
- The distinct lack of beer
- Occasional scams, thievery and armed hold-ups
- Requests for a *cadeau* ('gift' or bribe)

GOLD STAR

The Grande Mosquée – standing in the centre of Agadez, this stunning mosque is for many people the single most definitive image of Niger.

STARRING ROLE IN...

- *The Sheltering Sky* (1990)
- *Agadez* by Jonathan Bennet
- *Seven Words for Sand* by Allen Serafino

See the stomping bustle of the Tuareg Camel Market at sunset.

Eat homemade ice cream from a streetside counter.

Drink nomadic Tuareg 'desert tea', strong and sugared in small glasses, in one of the scattered Tuareg villages.

Do take a camel ride through the lush valleys and rough, stony Aïr Mountains.

Watch the artisans in action at the Centre Artisanal.

Buy *croix d'Agadez* at the Grand Marché.

After dark sit in the small night market opposite Place de la Fraternité eating brochettes and watching the world go by.

SOMETIMES OLD-FASHIONED MODES OF TRANSPORT ARE MORE RELIABLE.

INVESTIGATING THE NARROW STREETS BETWEEN MUD HOUSES IS A REAL TREAT.

A GROCERY-LADEN CYCLIST MAKES HIS WAY HOME.

Alexandria

NICKNAME THE PEARL OF THE MEDITERRANEAN **DATE OF BIRTH** 332
BC; WHEN ALEXANDER THE GREAT COMMISSIONED HIS ARCHITECT
DEINOCRATES TO CONSTRUCT A NEW CAPITAL CITY ON THE COAST
ADDRESS EGYPT (MAP 8, A2) **HEIGHT** 32M **SIZE** 300 SQ KM
POPULATION 4.4 MILLION **LONELY PLANET RANKING** 162

As much Mediterranean as Middle Eastern, Alexandria has stood the test of time. Although its early 20th-century European-influenced cosmopolitanism and decadence have faded, with Cleopatra's Palace and the ruins of the Pharos lighthouse emerging from the seabed and a dazzling new library, this confident city of cafés and promenades is making waves again.

ANATOMY

A thin, ribbonlike city, Alexandria runs along the Mediterranean coast for 20km without ever venturing more than 5km inland – a true waterfront city. The Great Corniche sweeps along the eastern harbour, with a string of city beaches. Trams travel at a snail's pace across the city, supplemented by buses and minibuses. The busy central area is small enough to walk around.

PEOPLE

Alexandria's citizens no longer include the prerevolutionary mix of Egyptians, Greeks, English, French and Italians that gave the city its 19th- and 20th-century vitality. Of the 300,000 people here in the 1940s, 40% were foreigners; today's millions are exclusively Egyptian.

TYPICAL ALEXANDRIAN

Alexandria is currently undergoing something of a regeneration, courtesy of an enlightened and free-spending municipality and the high-profile activities of a bunch of foreign archaeologists whose discoveries keep the city in the news. Its citizens are more laid-back than Cairenes, and have an immense pride in simply being Egyptian. Large extended families and close-knit neighbourhoods act as social support groups, strangers fall easily into conversation with each other, and whatever goes wrong, somebody always knows someone somewhere who can fix it.

TWILIGHT TRAFFIC FRINGES THE MEDITERRANEAN.

DEFINING EXPERIENCE

Breakfasting at Trianon before exploring the Roman amphitheatre, Pompey's Pillar and the Catacombs of Kom ash-Shuqqafa – creepy tombs out of a horror film set – then wandering along the Corniche to the Royal Jewellery Museum for a taste of excess before swimming at Mamoura, resting in the late afternoon, and dining at the 1950s-style Elite.

STRENGTHS

- ◢ Beautiful beaches
- ◢ Antoniadis Gardens
- ◢ Old-world cafés
- ◢ Creepy catacombs
- ◢ The Corniche
- ◢ The Mediterranean

WEAKNESSES

- ◢ Summer crowds, especially on the beaches
- ◢ Its rejection of cosmopolitanism

GOLD STAR

The Biblioteca Alexandrina recreates the repository for literature and history founded 2500 years ago by the Macedonian conqueror of the world. It resembles a giant discus embedded in the ground at an angle, representing a second sun rising from the Mediterranean.

STARRING ROLE IN...

- ◢ *Alexandria: A History & Guide* by EM Forster
- ◢ *Death on the Nile* by Agatha Christie (film 1978)
- ◢ *Alexandria Quartet* by Lawrence Durrell
- ◢ *Lawrence of Arabia* (1962)

See the ancient royal remains submerged in the surrounding sea (scuba-diving equipment needed).

Eat fresh fish from a seafood restaurant overlooking the Eastern Harbour.

Drink coffee at the classic and very elegant Trianon Le Salon.

Do visit the new Biblioteca Alexandrina, two millennia after the world's first library was founded here.

Watch the Alexandrians promenading along the Corniche overlooking the sea, enjoying the cool of the evening.

Buy leather goods in the shops south and west of Midan Saad Zaghloul.

After dark catch the belly dancing in the Sofitel Cecil Alexandria.

AN ALEXANDRIAN BAKER DELIVERS HIS WARES.

ZENKOV CATHEDRAL WAS BUILT IN 1904 AND SURVIVED THE 1911 EARTHQUAKE THANKS TO ITS WOODEN STRUCTURE.

Almaty

DATE OF BIRTH 1854; A RUSSIAN FRONTIER FORT ON THE SITE OF THE SILK-ROAD OASIS, ALMATU **ADDRESS** KAZAKHSTAN (MAP 9, B2) **HEIGHT** 775M **POPULATION** 1.4 MILLION **LONELY PLANET RANKING** 190

The honey pot of Kazakhstan, Almaty is a city so European you would think you were in a leafy part of London, where you can sift through eclectic markets, pomp it up in fine old hotels, or make like a Soviet speed skater on the massive ice rink.

ANATOMY

The Zailiysky Alatau Range rises like a wall along the southern fringes to form a superb backdrop to this clean, forested city. Almaty's long, straight streets are easy to navigate, running north–south and east–west, with mountains to the south and the city sloping upward from the north. There is a crowded network of *marshrutnoe* (minibus), bus and tram routes encompassing Zhibek Zholy, Almaty's pedestrianised shopping centre.

PEOPLE

Almaty's people are a mix of dozens of nationalities but, atypically for southern Kazakhstan, Russians and Ukrainians form the majority. To the ear, the sound of Russian, spoken even by most Kazakhs here, reveals the continuing hold of the colonising culture over the city. Several thousand Western and Asian expatriates, all after a foothold in the developing Kazakhstan economy, have also added to the mix in recent years, making Almaty Central Asia's most cosmopolitan city.

TYPICAL ALMATYAN

Almatyans are on the upswing. They are modern and European, having long moved away from rural Kazakhs in their dress, work habits and home life. Their former nomadic lifestyle, however, has bequeathed a certain attitude – laid-back and open – which separates them from their Russian brethren. Their middle-class incomes fuel the expansion of movie complexes, fashion shops, malls and amusement parks. While the rich build mansions in the valleys around Almaty, some typically Kazakh traits remain and many an Almaty home will still be decorated with colourful carpets and tapestries, a tradition inherited from the brightly decorated yurts in which they once lived.

ALMIGHTY ALMATY TRAIN STATION IS THE CITY'S LINK WITH RURAL KAZAKHSTAN.

DEFINING EXPERIENCE

Eating apples and *shashlyk* (kebab) in Central 'Gorky' Park before lazing on heated stone platforms at the Vostochnaya banya (Turkish baths) and then catching the infamous Otrar Sazy Kazakh Folk Orchestra and loudly discussing it afterwards.

STRENGTHS

- Zenkov Cathedral
- Altyn Adam (Golden Man)
- Eclectic museums
- Finest cafés and restaurants in Kazakhstan
- Arasan Baths
- Cosmopolitan

WEAKNESSES

- Prostitution
- Police shakedowns
- Taxi scams
- Waning national identity

GOLD STAR

Skiing – a hop, skip and jump from Almaty lies the powdered glory of the best skiing in Central Asia and the vertical 900m drop of Shymbulak ski resort.

STARRING ROLE IN...

- *The Racketeer* (2007)
- *The Place on the Grey Triangle Hat* (1993)
- *The Hiker's Guide to Almaty* by Arkady Pozdeyev

See the candy-coloured, tsarist-era Zenkov Cathedral, built entirely of wood (and apparently without nails) in Panfilov Park.

Eat from the menu at PBC (RVS), the restaurant for the retro Soviet.

Drink pints of beer at the Sunday festivities in Central 'Gorky' Park.

Do catch a cable car to the viewing platform at Kok-Tobe, the foothills of Zailiysky Alatau.

Watch *dombra* (a two-stringed instrument) recitals at Almaty's Philharmonic Central Concert Hall.

Buy traditional felt slippers and hats from the artisans in Sheber Aul.

After dark line up with the young A-listers for pints of beer at the teeming Soho urban bar.

JANE SWEENEY / GETTY IMAGES

Amman

NICKNAME AL-HAMAMA AL-BAYDA (WHITE PIGEON) **DATE OF BIRTH**
3500 BC; THE SITE OF AMMAN HAS BEEN CONTINUOUSLY OCCUPIED
SINCE THIS TIME **ADDRESS** JORDAN (MAP 8, B3) **HEIGHT** 777M
POPULATION 2.5 MILLION **LONELY PLANET RANKING** 101

More a modern Arab city than a great ancient metropolis, Amman comes to life in its earthy and chaotic downtown district, with its markets and men smoking *nargileh* (water pipes) and playing backgammon, and in the leafy residential districts of Western Amman, with trendy cafés and bars and impressive contemporary art galleries.

ANATOMY

Amman was originally built on seven hills but has stretched out beyond these and now covers around 19. The area around the King Hussein Mosque is referred to as *il-balad* (downtown). Memorise the major landmarks or you'll find navigating the city a near impossibility, particularly in a short time. Restaurants, big hotels and shops are located around the main hill, Jebel Amman. The impressive Citadel sits atop the city's highest point, Jebel al-Qala'a. You can catch buses around town.

PEOPLE

Most of Amman's residents are Arab, including Palestinian refugees as well as Iraqi and Kuwaiti refugees who arrived after the first Gulf War of 1990–91. Amman's population is also graced by a small number of Circassians, Chechens, Armenians and Bedouins. Around 50% of Ammanians are under the age of 18.

TYPICAL AMMANIAN

Ammanians, like all Jordanians, are a welcoming bunch, and Amman, like most cities, sees a great divide between the classes. The Bedouins, who have little, will give you the hair off their camel's back in the midst of all the gentrification.

THE IMPRESSIVE ANCIENT CITADEL TOWERS ABOVE THE CITY FROM ATOP JEBEL AL-QALA'A.

DEFINING EXPERIENCE

Wandering around the large Roman Amphitheatre, a remnant of ancient Philadelphia (as the city was known under the Romans) that was cut into a hill that once served as a necropolis, and later in the day crowding round a coffee-house TV in support of Amman's football teams.

STRENGTHS

- ◢ Roman ruins
- ◢ Proximity to Israel
- ◢ A convenient base to explore Jordan
- ◢ Jordanian hospitality

WEAKNESSES

- ◢ Drivers who insist that a white line down the centre of a road is just that, a white line

GOLD STAR

While Amman might be a sprawling metropolis with fewer signs of the area's ancient past than its Arab neighbours, a performance in the 2000-year-old Roman Amphitheatre will have you reaching for your toga and asking for directions to the Nymphaeum.

STARRING ROLE IN...

- ◢ *Story of a City: A Childhood in Amman* by Abd Al-Rahman
- ◢ *The Desert and the Snow* by Gertrude Bell

See the remains of a prehistoric Neolithic settlement near Ain Ghazal, which dates back to about 6500 BC.

Eat *mensaf* – a whole lamb, head included, on a bed of rice and pine nuts, eaten with *jameed* (sun-dried yoghurt).

Drink coffee – Ammanians are said to have a serious caffeine addiction.

Do experience the contemporary art space, Darat al-Funun.

Watch or participate in the annual Dead Sea Ultra Marathon.

Buy hand-woven Bedouin rugs.

After dark see a free art-house film (undubbed) at Books@Cafe.

LOCAL MARKETS OVERFLOW WITH INTERESTING TREASURES BUT ALL THAT GLITTERS IS NOT GOLD.

A WINTRY EVENING SETTLES OVER AMSTERDAM'S BIKES, BRIDGES AND CANALS.

Amsterdam

NICKNAME MOKUM, VENICE OF THE NORTH **DATE OF BIRTH** 1275;
WHEN THE COUNT OF HOLLAND LIFTED TOLLS FOR RESIDENTS ON THE
AMSTEL DAM **ADDRESS** THE NETHERLANDS (MAP 4, H8) **HEIGHT** 1M
SIZE 220 SQ KM **POPULATION** 821,000 (CITY); 2.3 MILLION (METRO AREA)
LONELY PLANET RANKING 024

Forget images of red lights, drug addicts and coffee shops – Amsterdam's truly liberal, laid-back atmosphere, beautiful watery setting, picturesque houses, excellent museums and infamous nightlife give it a unique appeal.

ANATOMY

The central area of Amsterdam is Centrum, home to Dam Sq, ace shops, and those notorious red lights. Heading east, you pass through the market of Waterlooplein, the museums of the Plantage, the Eastern Islands and the new residential district, IJburg. The main tourist spots are in the Southern Canal Belt, while the fashionable shops of Jordaan are west of Centrum. Not far from the Van Gogh Museum is the leafy haven of Vondelpark. Bicycles are the most popular way to get around.

PEOPLE

The Netherlands is one of the world's most densely populated countries. Almost half of Amsterdam's residents come from somewhere else, mainly Suriname, Morocco and Turkey.

TYPICAL AMSTERDAMMER

About 10% of Dutch people own their own homes, but nearly all residents of Amsterdam have a bicycle (the city has more bikes than cars). The unemployment rate is under 10%. As you would expect, Amsterdammers are a pretty relaxed bunch with liberal approaches to drugs, abortion, prostitution, euthanasia and homosexuality. That said, they say what they think and can come across as rude. They like a good time and don't take themselves too seriously. Like the English, queuing is a religion – woe betide anyone who tries to jump.

DEFINING EXPERIENCE

Taking a bike ride along the canals, then visiting the Van Gogh Museum and pottering in the antiques shops of Nieuwe Spiegelstraat, before enjoying a well-earned beer on one of the many café terraces.

STRENGTHS

- 160 canals and 90 islands
- 7000 historical buildings
- Bicycles everywhere
- Dutch-Renaissance architecture
- Dutch beer served frothy and cold
- Clubbing at Bloemendaal beach
- Golden Age painters
- Van Gogh Museum
- Rijksmuseum
- Anne Frank Huis
- Vondelpark
- Shopping in Negen Straatjes
- Beurs van Berlage and the Amsterdam School

WEAKNESSES

- Bicycle theft
- If the dams burst, 25% of the Netherlands would flood

GOLD STAR

Liberal attitudes abound in the city.

STARRING ROLE IN...

- *Ocean's Twelve* (2004)
- *Traffic* (1971)
- *The Acid House* by Irvine Welsh
- *The Diary of Anne Frank*

See Dutch art in the Rijksmuseum.

Eat spicy Indonesian cuisine to the sounds of the sax at Coffee & Jazz.

Drink in the sun at arty Finch on one of Jordaan's most attractive squares.

Do visit Anne Frank Huis and see the attic where Anne Frank hid.

Watch the city go mad on Koninginnedag (Queen's Day), with street parties, live music and endless beer.

Buy upmarket fashion and vintage clothing along the Western Canal Ring.

After dark hit Bitterzoet to get a fix of hip-hop, roots or Latin music.

SAY CHEESE – HOLLAND'S FAMOUS GOUDA LINES THE SHELVES OF A CITY SHOP.

LIKE A SCENE FROM A DREAM, BUILDINGS IN KEIZERSGRACHT TILT AT BIZARRE ANGLES.

TOURIST TRADE – THE FAMOUS RED-LIGHT DISTRICT IS A DIMINISHING CORNER OF THE CITY.

Anchorage

NICKNAME LOS ANCHORAGE; THE RAGE **DATE OF BIRTH** 1914; ANCHORAGE WAS FOUNDED WHEN IT SERVED AS A HEADQUARTERS AND WORK CAMP FOR THE ALASKA RAILROAD **ADDRESS** USA (MAP 1, B2) **HEIGHT** 40M **SIZE** 4396 SQ KM **POPULATION** 290,000 **LONELY PLANET RANKING** 175

Anchorage is an outpost of wilful humanity crafting more than survival from this unforgiving yet beautiful land. In this unparalleled urban wilderness polar bears take no notice of city limits and outdoor adventure is as easy to have as theatre, great food and a rocking nightlife.

ANATOMY

Sprawling across a broad triangle of a peninsula, the city is embraced by Cook Inlet and the 1500m-plus peaks of Chugach State Park, a backyard getaway to wilderness adventure. Anchorage's excellent public bus system shuttles you from the grid of flower-filled downtown streets where you'll find more than enough museums to keep you happy, and through the interesting Midtown neighbourhoods with their diverse eateries and lively nightlife. But get off the bus and explore the 196km of paved bicycle paths, the stunning tracts of green (or white, depending on the season) parkland and the lakes that dot the city.

PEOPLE

Fifteen years ago barely a quarter of Anchorage residents were born in Alaska but these days the city's population is a lot less transient. That said, the lure of the final frontier never diminishes, and the typical resident is young (average age is 32), mobile and often from the US West Coast. Ethnic communities are growing fast in this previously male and very Caucasian town, but Alaska Natives are the largest minority group.

TYPICAL ANCHORAGITE

Anchoragites have the frontier spirit of most Alaskans, but with the urban edge of big-city dwellers. They are independent, practical people who answer extreme weather with extreme living, whether it's

TAKING THE TIME TO CATCH UP ON CURRENT EVENTS AT PEGGY'S CAFÉ.

TROPHIES THAT WOULD HORRIFY RUDOLPH AT THE GENERAL STORE.

indulging in arctic diving, bear hunting and back-country snowboarding, or just drinking until the sun goes down. Looked down upon by rural Alaskans, Anchoragites can't wait to hit the mountains on the weekend, but they always get back in time to catch a local band.

DEFINING EXPERIENCE

Wandering through the Saturday market to the Snow City Café for a breakfast of Ship Creek Benedict and a Kaladi coffee while tossing up whether to bike the Tony Knowles Coastal Trail or hike the tundra in the Chugach State Park, then heading down to the Beer Tooth Theatrepub for an evening meal/movie/beer.

STRENGTHS

- Big, green parks
- Proximity to mountains, glaciers, lakes – this is a nature-lover's paradise
- Alaska Zoo
- Beluga whales in Cook Inlet
- Being able to catch an 18kg salmon from under a highway bridge
- A multitude of microbreweries
- Title Wave Books
- The aurora borealis – when you can see it!
- Good music scene

WEAKNESSES

- Winter
- No major league sports teams
- Ravenous summer mosquitoes
- One of the most expensive cities in the USA

BRIGHT MODERN ARCHITECTURE BRINGS A RAY OF SUNSHINE TO 4TH AVE.

GOLD STAR

Anchorage isn't simply a big city on the edge of the wilderness but rather a big city in the wilderness. It's a great base for outdoor adventures.

STARRING ROLE IN...

- *About Grace* by Anthony Doerr
- *Mystery, Alaska* (1999)
- *Sidney Laurence, Painter of the North* by Kesler E Woodward
- 'Anchorage' by Michelle Shocked

See the start of the Iditarod, the last great trail sled-dog race, charge up 4th Ave at the beginning of March each year.

Eat oconut-beer-battered Spam (or not).

Drink an ice-cold pint of Alaskan Amber on the deck of the Snow Goose and soak up the midnight sun.

Do hear ancient Alaskan songs, once thought lost forever, performed at the Alaska Native Heritage Centre.

Watch the *Whale-Fat-Follies*, a fun and raunchy musical about duct tape, spawning salmon and Alaska's official state fossil, the woolly mammoth.

Buy a Qiviut scarf or cap from the Oomingmak Musk Ox Producers' Co-operative.

After dark head to the 10 bars at Chilkoot Charlie's (Koot's) – the place for unbridled Anchorage debauchery for the last 35 years.

Antananarivo

NICKNAME TANA; LITERALLY 'CITY OF A THOUSAND' (WARRIORS) **DATE OF BIRTH** 1610; AFTER THE MERINA RULER, KING ANDRIANJAKA, CONQUERED SEVERAL VILLAGES IN THE AREA **ADDRESS** MADAGASCAR (MAP 7, H6) **HEIGHT** 1372M **POPULATION** 1.2 MILLION **LONELY PLANET RANKING** 193

Often eclipsed by the natural beauty of the rest of the country, Tana offers a glimpse into the edgy, urban side of Malagasy culture, plus the chance to indulge in fine French colonial cuisine.

ANATOMY

Renault 4 taxis whine up and down the cobblestone hills, belching blue exhaust fumes over the crowds of pedestrians. In spring, purple jacaranda trees blaze into life, raining nectar onto the heads of skipping children and strolling couples. Terracotta mansions are stacked on the hillsides, turning gold under the setting sun. Beyond the city sprawl, paddy fields glint in the pale sunshine.

PEOPLE

The majority group in Tana is the indigenous Merina community. They and the other indigenous groups of Tana are joined by a very few French descendants, with the languages of choice being Malagasy and French.

TYPICAL TANA CITIZEN

The typical Tana resident is rooted in traditions and community but flexible enough to make room for tourists and their beliefs. The people of Tana are proud of their illustrious history but a little reserved about sharing it. Your best understanding of the Malagasy will come from the locals you encounter in your travels – ladies selling embroidered tablecloths on the pavement, men hawking rubber stamps from improvised stalls, or taxi drivers sharing peanut cake bought from a roadside kiosk.

DEFINING EXPERIENCE

Breakfasting *à la française* with coffee and bread, spending the day shopping or selling wares at the markets, eating dinner at a *hotely* (local foodstall), sampling local rums at hotel restaurant Sakamanga with friends and, finally, dancing all night to contemporary Malagasy music.

LOCALS COME TO TRADE GOSSIP AND GOODS AT THE CITY'S MARKETPLACE.

STRENGTHS

◢ The zoo at Tsimbazaza
◢ Zebu-drawn carts
◢ Merina history, living and dead
◢ Rice paddies in the middle of town
◢ On-foot exploration
◢ The Marché Artisanal (Handicrafts Market) at La Digue
◢ Blended African and French heritage
◢ Access to the rest of Madagascar
◢ Views from the city down to the plains

WEAKNESSES

◢ Steep streets and steps
◢ Crowds, noise, pollution
◢ Train tracks that cross the runway of the airport
◢ Continual advances of beggars and street vendors
◢ The large portion of the population living below the poverty line

GOLD STAR

Having the most amazing names for people and places – the queen's palace at the Rova is called Manjakamiadana (A Fine Place to Rule). It was designed for Queen Ranavalona I, and is located next to a replica of the palace of King Andrianampoinimerina, founder of the Merina kingdom.

STARRING ROLE IN...

◢ *Madagascar* (2005)
◢ *Le Tricheur* (The Cheat) by Claude Simon
◢ *I Vola* by Andry Andraina
◢ *Fofombadiko* (My Fiancée) by Emilson Daniel Andriamalala

See the view from the Rova at sunset.

Eat at Chez Mariette – gourmet Malagasy cuisine based on the banquets served to Madagascan royalty.

Drink tea, coffee or hot chocolate at a *salon de thé* (tearoom).

Do stroll down the steep, narrow streets to the Avenue of Independence.

Watch a traditional Malagasy performance of acrobatics and music.

Buy handicrafts from the revamped Zoma markets.

After dark dance to a mixture of American hip-hop, Malagasy chart hits, and French soft-rock anthems at Le Pandora Station.

YANN ARTHUS-BERTRAND / CORBIS

AN AERIAL VIEW REVEALS TANA'S HAPPILY COLOURED ROOFTOPS.

THE END OF A SUNNY DAY MAKES FOR LONG SHADOWS IN ANTIGUA.

Antigua

DATE OF BIRTH 1543; WHEN IT WAS FOUNDED AND SERVED AS THE COLONIAL CAPITAL FOR THE NEXT 233 YEARS **ADDRESS** GUATEMALA (MAP 2, G6) **HEIGHT** 1480M **POPULATION** 35,000 **LONELY PLANET RANKING** 127

One of the oldest and most beautiful cities in the Americas, Antigua thrives as an eclectic arts hub and magnet for students of its many language schools.

ANATOMY

Nestled in the Ponchoy Valley, Antigua is dramatically set between three volcanoes: Volcán Agua to the southeast, Volcán Fuego to the southwest and Volcán Acatenango to the west. Antigua served as the capital until it was moved to Guatemala City following the 1773 earthquakes, and a few buildings remain from this era. The central point of the city is Parque Central and *calles* (streets) are labelled east and west of this point. Buses arrive at the Terminales de Buses, four blocks west of Parque Central.

PEOPLE

The majority of Antigüeños are of a mestizo (mixed Spanish and indigenous) heritage and are practising Roman Catholics. The region's indigenous Mayan people speak Cakchiquel and continue to practise their nature-based religion along with Roman Catholicism.

TYPICAL ANTIGÜEÑO

Antigüeños usually start the day early the same way they finish it – with a meal of eggs, beans, fried plantains and plenty of tortillas. A two-hour siesta follows lunch, the main meal. They are social, polite and refined in the arts, and enjoy the marimba and mariachi music played at frequent festivals and celebrations.

DEFINING EXPERIENCE

Visiting the museums and ruins strewn about town, studying Spanish while living with a Guatemalan family, summiting Volcán Pacaya, hiking or horse-riding to the Cerro de la Cruz vista point, buying vividly coloured, traditional handmade *traje* (clothing) in the market, and watching the passing parade during elaborate religious celebrations.

STRENGTHS

- Cathedral of San Francisco
- Elaborate religious celebrations during Holy Week

SPOILT FOR CHOICE – ANTIGUA'S FRUIT AND VEGETABLE MARKET.

JON ARNOLD IMAGES / ALAMY

- Intensive Spanish-language courses
- Climbing the stunning Volcán Agua
- Charming Spanish baroque architecture
- Parque Central
- Intricately beaded crafts
- *Huipiles* (embroidered blouses)
- Unique and weathered doorknobs and knockers
- Colourful cobblestone streets
- Shopping for Mayan crafts
- Volcanoes
- Mayan water-lily blossoms and vegetable motifs adorning the church of La Merced

WEAKNESSES

- Twisting ankles on cobblestone streets after a drink
- Leaving
- Pleading for accommodation in the busy season

GOLD STAR

Parque Central – the gathering place for locals and visitors alike. On most days the plaza is lined with villagers selling handicrafts to tourists; on Sunday it's mobbed and the streets on the east and west sides are closed to traffic. Things are cheapest late on Sunday afternoon, when the peddling is winding down. At night, mariachi or marimba bands play in the park.

STARRING ROLE IN...

- *Riotous Rhymes 'n' Remedies* by Sylvanus Barnes
- *Garden of Life* by LHC Westcott

See Samuel Franco Arce's photographs and recordings of Mayan ceremonies and music at Casa K'Ojom.

Eat the Sunday buffet in the Café Condesa.

Drink Zacapa Centenario (a fine Guatemalan rum).

Do enrol in an intensive Spanish-language and culture course.

Watch the afternoon handicrafts trade around the 1738 fountain in Parque Central, to the sounds of mariachi or marimba bands.

Buy colourful beaded and embroidered handicrafts, ceramics and carved wooden masks.

After dark explore Antigua's atmospheric bars and see if you can practise some of that new-found Spanish.

Apia

DATE OF BIRTH 1820s; WHEN THE RESIDENT EUROPEANS ESTABLISHED A SOCIETY IN APIA **ADDRESS** SAMOA (MAP 10, P3) **HEIGHT** 2M **SIZE** 1.2 SQ KM **POPULATION** 37,000 **LONELY PLANET RANKING** 142

With its run-down colonial buildings, big old pulu trees and easy-going pace, Apia retains a certain shabby and romantic charm.

ANATOMY

From the centre of town, Apia's neat villages spread west along the level coastal area and climb up the gentle slopes towards the hills and into the valleys. Travelling by public bus is the most common method of getting around. Taxis are also cheap and plentiful.

PEOPLE

The indigenous people of the Samoan islands are large and robust folk of Polynesian origin. Samoans account for the majority of the population and Euronesians make up the rest. There is a substantial Chinese Samoan community centred in Apia. Most of the Europeans and Asians residing in the country are involved in UN development projects, business investment or volunteer aid organisations, such as the Peace Corps.

TYPICAL APIAN

Samoans are tradition-oriented and follow closely the social hierarchies, customs and courtesies established long before the arrival of Europeans. They are outwardly friendly and responsive people. The social system can produce as much pressure as it does wellbeing. Beneath the light-heartedness, a strict and demanding code of behaviour is upheld with expectations that can stifle individuality and creativity.

DEFINING EXPERIENCE

Spending a lazy morning exploring the Flea Market and Maketi Fou (main market) and snacking on *palusami* (coconut cream wrapped in taro leaves), visiting the churches along the city's waterfront, then snorkelling the afternoon away at Palolo Deep National Marine Reserve.

PETER HENDRIE

TOP BRASS – THE SAMOAN POLICE BAND BELTS OUT A MARCHING TUNE.

STRENGTHS

- Palolo Deep National Marine Reserve
- The Madonna-topped Catholic cathedral
- Madd Gallery
- Friendly people
- Samoan buses, with names such as 'Don't Tell Mum'
- The Polynesian feast cooked in an *umu* (above-ground oven)
- Samoan *fiafia* (dance performances)
- Aggie Grey's Hotel
- Tomb of the Tu'imaleali'ifano dynasty

WEAKNESSES

- Year-round high humidity
- Cyclones
- Deforestation
- Traffic congestion due to lack of town planning
- Stray dogs

GOLD STAR

The pace of life – it's so laid-back it's only a heartbeat away from being a nice little snooze.

STARRING ROLE IN...

- *A Chief in Two Worlds* (1992)
- *Island of Lost Souls* (1993)
- *Where We Once Belonged* by Sia Figiel
- *Leaves of the Banyan Tree* by Albert Wendt

See Apia from the Mt Vaea Scenic Reserve, where you'll find the beautifully restored home of Robert Louis Stevenson and rainforest trails.

Eat a breakfast of Samoan pancakes (like small doughnuts) washed down with a cup of addictive *koko Samoa* (locally grown cocoa served hot and black with lots of sugar) at the Maketi Fou or the foodstalls behind the Flea Market.

Drink Independent Samoa's excellent locally brewed lager, Vailima.

Do go snorkelling in Palolo Deep to experience the sudden drop from the shallow reef into a deep blue hole flanked by walls of coral and densely populated by colourful species of fish.

Watch a spectacular *fiafia* (dance show) at Aggie Grey's Hotel.

buy locally made *siapo* (decorated bark cloth), kava bowls and coconut jewellery at the Flea Market.

After dark head to Y-Not – overlooking the harbour it's the most fun place in town.

SNORKELLING IS THIS WAY AT PALOLO DEEP NATIONAL MARINE RESERVE.

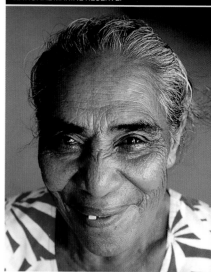

THE WELCOMING SMILE OF AN OLDER APIAN.

CHURCH'S OUT AND THE KIDS ARE RUNNING WILD.

STARING PAST STEEPLES AT THE MOUNTAINS FLANKING AREQUIPA.

Arequipa

NICKNAME THE WHITE CITY **DATE OF BIRTH** 1540; REFOUNDED BY THE SPANISH AT THE SITE OF A PRE-INCAN SETTLEMENT **ADDRESS** PERU (MAP 3, C10) **HEIGHT** 2325M **POPULATION** 865,000 **LONELY PLANET RANKING** 140

Arequipa is a one-of-a-kind example of South American life – the lanes, museums, churches and rich culture of the town and its resilient people are resplendent after nearly 500 years of volcanic earthquakes and tumultuous politics.

ANATOMY

At over 2km above sea level, Arequipa nestles in a fertile valley under the perfect cone-shaped volcano of El Misti (5822m). The Río Chili flows around the northern boundary of the town. The city centre is easily navigable as it is based on a colonial checkerboard pattern around Plaza de Armas. Addresses, however, can be confusing, as streets change names every few blocks. Walk, cycle or catch minibuses, buses and taxis to get around the city.

PEOPLE

About half of Arequipa's population is Indian (*indígenas* is an appropriate term; *indios* is insulting). The majority of the rest of the population is mestizo, and there are also white, black and Asian minorities. As is clear from the many religious buildings and churches, Christianity is the dominant religion and a significant part of daily life. Though the Peruvian constitution allows complete religious freedom, its citizens remain almost exclusively Christian, with about 90% identifying themselves as Roman Catholic.

TYPICAL AREQUIPAN

The Arequipans are rugged and proud people, fond of intellectual debate, especially about their fervent political beliefs, which find voice through regular demonstrations in the main plaza. In fact, their stubborn intellectual independence from Lima is so strong that at one time they even designed their own passport and flag.

DEFINING EXPERIENCE

Spending the morning exploring the Museo Santuarios Andinos, the home of Juanita, 'the ice princess' and numerous other ice mummies, artefacts and curiosities, then savouring a leisurely lunch of the spicy *rocoto relleno*

TAXIS PATIENTLY AWAITING THEIR TURN IN THE PLAZA DE ARMAS.

THE BLESSEDLY TRANQUIL EXTERIOR OF THE MONASTERIO DE SANTA CATALINA.

ALL OUT OF ICE CREAM, A VENDOR LUGS HER PORTABLE MARKET BACK TO HOME BASE.

(hot peppers stuffed with vegetables, meat and rice) at one of the balcony restaurants overlooking Plaza de Armas.

STRENGTHS

- Alpaca knitwear
- *Criollo* cuisine (spicy local fare)
- Ice mummies
- Gateway to El Misti
- Dazzling *sillar* (a light-coloured volcanic rock) stonework
- The nearby Cañón del Colca and its condor residents
- River running the Rio Chili
- La Catedral

WEAKNESSES

- Petty theft and illegitimate tour rip-offs
- Volcanoes
- Sparse midweek nightlife
- Animal cruelty (bullfights and cockfights)

GOLD STAR

Tradition – Arequipa is a preserve of the uniquely eclectic Peruvian culture; so much more than a transit stop to the mountains, it has carved its own niche in the South American psyche.

STARRING ROLE IN...

- *Parelisa* (1999)
- *Path to Arequipa* by Mark Jacobi

See the astonishing views of Arequipa and El Misti flanked by its two siblings, Chachani (6075m) and Pichu Pichu (5571m) from the mirador (observation tower) in the suburb of Yanahuara.

Eat *chupede camarones* (prawn soup) or *chancho al horno* (suckling pig) at the lively Sol de Mayo.

Drink *chicha* (fermented maize beer) at the tourist mecca Déjà Vu.

Do go on a guided tour of La Catedral, which dominates Plaza de Armas.

Watch the bullfights, which are not as bloodthirsty as their Spanish counterparts (the Peruvian way is to pit two bulls against each other for the favour of a female, usually culminating in one making a sensible exit).

Buy a high-quality alpaca sweater from Patio del Ekeko.

After dark hit the town for all-night dancing in a sizzling nightclub.

Ashgabat

NICKNAME THE CITY OF LOVE (THE MEANING OF ASHGABAT IN ARABIC) **DATE OF BIRTH** 1881; AS A RUSSIAN FORT **ADDRESS** TURKMENISTAN (MAP 8, G3) **HEIGHT** 226M **POPULATION** 650,000 **LONELY PLANET RANKING** 200

Ashgabat is a city-sized monument to Turkmenistan's former leader, the megalomaniac Saparmyrat Niyazov, self-declared 'Turkmenbashi', leader of the Turkmen. Part Las Vegas, part Stalingrad, this desert oasis is enjoying a new political era, but in its sprawling boulevards and wedding-cake architecture it retains no end of quirkiness.

ANATOMY

The old Russian town was wiped off the face of the earth in a 1948 earthquake and the rebuilt city is entirely a product of Niyazov's dictatorship. The city's main thoroughfares are dotted with recently added white-marble residential buildings that seem permanently empty. These are broken up by fantastically elaborate palaces and monuments, including those of the stunningly weird suburb of Berzengi.

PEOPLE

The population is a mix of Russians left behind after the end of the Soviet Union and native Turkmen. Ashgabat is by far the most Russian city in Turkmenistan.

TYPICAL ASHGABATI CITIZEN

Ashgabat dwellers exhibit the spontaneous hospitality and innate generosity characteristic of Turkmen nomadic traditions. After enduring years of eccentric autocracy during the reign of Turkmenbashi, Ashgabatis are resilient and resourceful. But under the new outward-looking regime they are optimistic and enjoying new opportunities – pensions and maternity benefits, the lifting of internet restrictions. Still, they are not so naive to believe that democracy is just around the corner.

DAZZLING JEWELLERY ON DISPLAY AT THE SUNDAY BAZAAR.

DEFINING EXPERIENCE

Standing beneath the Arch of Neutrality with a golden revolving Turkmenbashi overhead and the fantastically Orwellian ensemble of marble buildings around Independence Sq.

STRENGTHS

◢ Irrigated greenery contrasting with the surrounding desert sparseness
◢ Friendly locals
◢ Extremely safe at all times
◢ The best restaurants and hotels in the country
◢ Almost no tourists

WEAKNESSES

◢ Restricted freedom of the press
◢ The 'companionship' of your official guide at all times
◢ Occasional dust storms – you're in the middle of a desert, you know
◢ Bugged hotel rooms

GOLD STAR

Tolkuchka Bazaar, a few kilometres outside the city in the nearby desert, is one of the most colourful and fascinating markets on earth, where you can buy anything from carpets to camels.

STARRING ROLE IN...

◢ There's no modern movie industry here, but Ashgabat is crying out to be used in a Bond movie of the future.
◢ *Unknown Sands: Journeys Around the World's Most Isolated Country* by John W Kropf

See spectacular views of Ashgabat, endless desert vistas and an 80m-high artificial waterfall from the Turkmenbashi Cableway on Kopet Dag.

Eat at expat favourite the Iranian Truck Stop for a real culinary treat.

Drink national beers Zip and Berk, both of which go down very well in the heat of the late desert afternoon.

Do some riding in the rugged countryside around the city on iconic Akhal-Teke horses.

Watch a traditional Turkmen opera at the spanking new National Theatre.

Buy stunning Turkmen carpets at Tolkuchka Bazaar for a fraction of their price at home.

After dark check out the British Pub, which hosts local rock bands.

RELIGIOUS REFLECTIONS – THE MIRROR IMAGE OF A MOSQUE.

LARGER THAN LIFE – PRESIDENT NIYAZOV.

TWO VILLAGE CHILDREN JUSTIFIABLY PROUD OF THEIR RIGHTEOUS OUTFITS, ON THE OUTSKIRTS OF ASHGABAT.

THIS ART DECO APOTHECARY RETAINS ITS COLONIAL ITALIAN BEAUTY.

Asmara

DATE OF BIRTH 12TH CENTURY; ENCOURAGED BY THE PLENTIFUL SUPPLIES OF WATER, SHEPHERDS FROM THE AKELE GUZAY REGION FOUNDED FOUR VILLAGES ON THE HILL THAT IS NOW THE SITE OF AN ORTHODOX CHURCH **ADDRESS** ERITREA (MAP 3, B8) **HEIGHT** 2355M **POPULATION** 650,000 **LONELY PLANET RANKING** 117

Like a film set from an early Italian movie, old espresso machines churn out macchiatos, Cinquecento taxis putt-putt about and all over town you can see Art Deco architecture – Asmara is one of the safest, cleanest and most enchanting capital cities on the continent.

ANATOMY

Built according to a strict urban plan, Asmara is divided into four main areas: the administrative centre, the colonial residential quarter, the native quarter and the outbuildings. Liberation Ave, lined with majestic palms, striking architecture and busy cafés, is flanked by September 1 Sq at the eastern end and the Governor's Palace in the west. The old Italian residential quarter with its Art Deco villas is south of Liberation Ave. Central Asmara is small enough to walk everywhere, but even the locals have trouble keeping up with the changing street names.

PEOPLE

Asmarinos are a mix of nine ethnic groups, each with its own language and customs. The Tigrinya make up the majority; this is the language you'll hear widely spoken, although Arabic, English and Amharic are also prevalent. On a Sunday the clashing sound of cathedral bells and the Muslim call to prayer provide aural evidence of the communities' ability to coexist, notwithstanding all government efforts to the contrary.

TYPICAL ASMARINO

Cosmopolitan, dignified and welcoming are words often used to describe Asmarinos. Presentation is everything and it's not uncommon to see a well-groomed man walking out of his tin-roofed shack sporting a suit, leather jacket and gold galore. Locals love to dance, and the traditional style is unique, with lots of variations on shaking body parts, but if you give it a go, you'll win a lot of friends. With a small city, and such social people, Asmarinos can't walk more than a block without running into somebody they know. Cycling is popular, but bikes seem to spend more time lined up outside the cafés than on the streets.

RELIGIOUS FESTIVITIES GIVE THIS YOUNG PRIEST SOMETHING TO THINK ABOUT.

CHRISTIAN, MUSLIM AND ORTHODOX FAITHS LIVE SIDE BY SIDE IN ASMARA.

EDUCATION EQUALS OPPORTUNITY FOR THESE YOUNG GIRLS.

Asmara

DEFINING EXPERIENCE

Watching the world go by and enjoying a cappuccino in one of the many 1930s Italian-style cafés, then taking a *gari* (horse-drawn cart) tour of Asmara's fascinating architecture before joining in the sunset *passeggiata* (promenade; when the whole town takes a turn around the streets) to catch up with friends and generally take things easy.

STRENGTHS

- Sublime architecture – from Art Deco to cubist, expressionist, functionalist, futurist, rationalist and neoclassical styles
- *Mies* (local honey wine)
- Blue skies eight months of the year
- Excellent coffee and pizza and a lively café culture
- Medeber market
- Endless dinner/lunch invitations to strangers' homes
- *Injera* (spongy bread)

WEAKNESSES

- Asmara gin
- Lack of water
- No cheap flights and a lack of tourist infrastructure
- Not a great diversity of food

GOLD STAR

The Cultural Assets Rehabilitation Programme (CARP) – set up in 1996 to record the city's architecture and to educate children, businesspeople and developers to look after their urban heritage.

STARRING ROLE IN...

- *Towards Asmara* by Thomas Keneally
- *Ciao Asmara* by Justin Hill

See the locals strolling the boulevards during the sunset *passeggiata*.

Eat *injera* and *tibs zil zil* (sizzling lamb) in the Milano Restaurant.

Drink an espresso from a vintage Italian coffee machine at one of the many outdoor cafés.

Do take the Eritrean State Railway steam train down the escarpment from Asmara to the Red Sea at Massawa.

Watch a film in the beautifully restored Art Deco Cinema Impero.

Buy a tailor-made leather jacket.

After dark do the *iskista* (a dance with a lot of shaking of body parts).

113

Aswan

DATE OF BIRTH 300 BC; ELEPHANTINE ISLAND (ADJACENT TO ASWAN) WAS THE ORIGINAL SETTLEMENT AND A NATURAL FORTRESS
ADDRESS EGYPT (MAP 8, A5) **HEIGHT** 112M **SIZE** 679 SQ KM
POPULATION 265,000 **LONELY PLANET RANKING** 177

Once the gateway to Africa and a crossroads for the ancient caravan routes, Aswan is a mellow winter resort boasting sun-filled days, jostling markets and sweeping views of the desert on the most picturesque part of the Nile.

ANATOMY

The Nile flows down from the dams and around the giant granite boulders and palm-studded islands that protrude from the waters at the edge of Aswan. There are only three main avenues, and most of the city runs parallel to the Nile, making it easy to navigate. The train station, at the northern end of town, is only three blocks east of the river and the Corniche el-Nil, and is fronted by Aswan's market street, where the souqs (markets) overflow with colourful, tempting and aromatic wares. Running parallel to this is Sharia Abtal at-Tahrir, where you'll find the youth hostel and a few hotels. Across the river on Elephantine Island, modern Nubian culture thrives. Hire a bike or a taxi to get around.

PEOPLE

Beside the Egyptians, there are a handful of separate indigenous groups with ancient roots in Aswan. The city is finely threaded with Nubian culture. The traditional lands of Nubia, home to the tall, dark-skinned Nubian people, were drowned with the building of the High Dam in the 1970s to provide a water supply for the region. Despite this, Egyptians and Nubians live relatively harmonious, if independent, lives.

TYPICAL ASWANIAN

Aswanians distinguish themselves from the rest of Egypt by being particularly laid-back and pleasant. They love their souqs and their slice of the Nile and enjoy nothing more than watching the water move by after a long day of working numerous jobs to support their large families. Their laughter lubricates the wheels of social exchange and transactions are done with a smile. While religion cushions life's blows, in Aswan jokes and wisecracks are its parlance.

MANY EGYPTIAN FABRICS ARE STILL MADE THE TRADITIONAL WAY WITH A LOOM.

GRACEFUL FELUCCAS, EGYPT'S TRADITIONAL SAILBOATS, RIDE THE SOUTHERLY BREEZE UP THE NILE.

GRAIN AND SPICE SELLERS AT THE SOUQ READY TO WRAP UP THE DAY.

NUBIAN DANCERS PERFORMING IN STYLE.

DEFINING EXPERIENCE

Spending the morning in the narrow alleyway souqs, tasting life as it has been for many centuries, before sailing gently across the Nile on a felucca to the cliffs of Elephantine Island and visiting the Nubian villages for henna tattoos, Nubian music and a sunset 'tea' buffet overlooking the river and the desert beyond.

STRENGTHS

- Sunset on the desert
- The Nile
- Nubian culture
- Elephantine Island
- The tombs of the Nobles
- Nubia Museum
- Feluccas
- Souqs
- History-packed streets

WEAKNESSES

- Expensive tours
- Lecherous souq tattooists
- Unbearable summer heat (June to August)
- Safflower sold as saffron

GOLD STAR

Feluccas – you haven't seen Aswan, or Egypt for that matter, until you've seen it from a felucca on the Nile.

STARRING ROLE IN...

- *Death on the Nile* by Agatha Christie
- *Elephantine: The Ancient Town* by the German Archaeological Mission

See the sun set over the desert from the peaceful Ferial Gardens.

Eat *daoud basha* (meatballs in tomato sauce) as the Nile slides slowly past the Aswan Moon Restaurant.

Drink delicious fruit cocktails and take in the views at Emy Restaurant.

Do visit the breathtaking history, art and culture of the Nubia Museum.

Watch the *tahtib* on a winter's eve by the Aswan folkloric dance troupe.

Buy the best henna in Egypt in Aswan's colourful souqs.

After dark take a boat ride to Philae (Agilkia Island) to experience the sound and light show and wander through the temple at night.

Athens

DATE OF BIRTH 1400 BC; FOUNDED BY THE MYCENAEANS
ADDRESS GREECE (MAP 5, R9) **HEIGHT** 107M **SIZE** 428 SQ KM
POPULATION 3.8 MILLION **LONELY PLANET RANKING** 038

Ancient and modern, with equal measures of grunge and grace, Athens is a mix of history and edginess. Iconic monuments mingle with first-rate museums, cafes and alfresco dining.

ANATOMY

The city is bounded on three sides by Mt Parnitha, Mt Pendeli and Mt Hymettos. Within Athens there are eight hills, of which the Acropolis and Lykavittos are the most prominent. The city's boundary on the southern side is the Saronic Gulf. The metro system makes getting around the centre of Athens relatively painless. There's also an extensive bus and trolleybus network.

PEOPLE

A large proportion of Athens's residents today are relative newcomers to the city, who migrated here from other parts of Greece or from Greek communities around the world. Greece, which lost much of its population to mass migration, is now attracting large numbers of migrants, both legal and illegal, including many Albanians and refugees from the Balkans, the former Soviet Union, Bangladesh, Pakistan, Iran and Iraq.

TYPICAL ATHENIAN

Athenians are affable, warm and welcoming. The pace of life in Athens can be fast (the public service aside) but people still take time out for endless coffees. The younger generations of Athenians are highly literate, with a large number studying abroad. A high proportion speak English and are in tune with world trends, fashion and music. Almost all of the Greek population belong to the Greek Orthodox Church.

DEFINING EXPERIENCE

Emerging from a hectic dance club at 5am then heading to the central meat market, where the tavernas turn out huge pots and trays of tasty, traditional home-style dishes, 24 hours a day.

SCOTT BARBOUR / GETTY IMAGES

FATHER AND SON FROLIC ON FILOPAPPOU HILL OVERLOOKING THE ACROPOLIS.

STRENGTHS

- The Acropolis standing sentinel over Athens
- The many city streets and squares fringed with orange trees
- National Archaeological Museum
- Refreshing your lungs in the delightfully shady National Gardens
- Shopping for antiques in Antiqua
- The bohemian Exarhia district – home to cheap tavernas, cafés, *rembetika* clubs and small live-music venues
- *Loukoumades* (Greek doughnuts) served with honey and walnuts
- Dining on the terrace at Pil Poul, with views of the Acropolis
- Seeing Euripides performed in the Odeon of Herodes Atticus
- Balconies bulging with geraniums

WEAKNESSES

- *Nefos* (smog) and traffic
- Concrete
- Greek bureaucracy and economy
- Summer heat

GOLD STAR

The Acropolis – time, war, pilfering, earthquakes and pollution have taken their toll on the sacred hill, yet it stands defiant over Athens.

STARRING ROLE IN...

- *Anthismeni Amigdhalia* (Almond Trees in Bloom, 1959)
- *Landscape in the Mist* (1988)
- *The Last Temptation* by Nikos Kazantzakis

See dusk settle on the symbol of the glory of ancient Greece, the Parthenon (Virgin's Chamber), which stands on the highest point of the Acropolis.

Eat Athen's best, fresh *tiropites* (cheese pastries) at Ariston.

Drink a homemade brew from one of the many on offer at Brettos, a small bar with a refreshingly old-fashioned feel.

Do get lost among the little whitewashed cube houses in Anafiotika before ascending to explore the Acropolis.

Watch a film at the outdoor cinema in the Zappeio Gardens, where you can get a wine and gourmet snack-pack to add to your viewing pleasure.

Buy a pair of traditional Jesus sandals from septuagenarian sandal-maker Stavros Melissinos' store in the market district of Monastiraki.

After dark enjoy the heady cocktail of the hedonistic Greek spirit and relaxed drinking laws that make Athens one of the liveliest European cities.

EVZONES, A HISTORIC ARMY UNIT, CHANGE THE GUARD AT THE PARLIAMENT BUILDING.

SEEN FROM THE ACROPOLIS, THE CRADLE OF CIVILISATION NURTURES AN URBAN JUNGLE.

KAISARIANI MONASTERY HAS STOOD ON THE NORTH SIDE OF MT HYMETTUS SINCE THE 11TH CENTURY.

WARMING UP AT LION ROCK AND PIHA BEACH.

Auckland

NICKNAME CITY OF SAILS; TAMAKI MAKAURAU (IN MAORI)
DATE OF BIRTH 1840; WHEN THE SETTLEMENT WAS MADE NEW
ZEALAND'S CAPITAL (IT INDECISIVELY LOST THIS STATUS TO
WELLINGTON IN 1865), BUT MAORI SETTLEMENT DATES BACK AT LEAST
800 YEARS **ADDRESS** NEW ZEALAND (MAP 10, N8) **HEIGHT** 26M
SIZE 502 SQ KM **POPULATION** 1.4 MILLION **LONELY PLANET RANKING** 068

With beaches in its backyard and an international gateway to Polynesia, Asia and, if you must, Australia – this is a truly relaxed world city.

ANATOMY

The commercial main street is Queen St, stretching from QEII Sq near
the waterfront to the hip wining and dining precinct around
Karangahape Rd (known as K Rd to most Aucklanders). Get on the bus
for posh Ponsonby Rd to the city's west, another hot spot for eating and
shopping. A ferry ride across the harbour is Devonport, which is *the*
Sunday afternoon spot with B&Bs, galleries and beaches. Public transport
consists of buses, trains and ferries.

PEOPLE

Home to almost a third of the Kiwi population, Auckland has a huge cross-
section of people from its traditional Maori communities to more recent Asian
arrivals. Indeed, Auckland now has the world's largest concentration of
Polynesians, which gives the city a unique cultural make-up.

TYPICAL AUCKLANDER

Aucklanders certainly are a diverse lot, migrating from Indonesia to
Invercargill. 'Jafas', as Aucklanders are called by other Kiwis, have a
reputation for being smugly cosmopolitan, with the migration from New
Zealand's regions to the big smoke triggered by work or cultural life. The
longstanding rivalry with Wellington is shrugged off by many
Aucklanders who are too busy enjoying their better weather and beaches
to care for the windy city to the south.

DEFINING EXPERIENCE

Brunching on K Rd before a harbour sail, catcing a ferry over to Devonport
to fossick among the art galleries, cycling up to Takapuna Beach for a well-
deserved laze, having a relaxed dinner in one of Ponsonby's more exclusive
eateries, and gearing up for a night of clubbing along Queen St.

CHILLING OUT AT THE MINUS 5 DEGREES BAR, PRINCES WHARF.

TACKING ACROSS WAITEMATA HARBOUR.

STRENGTHS
- Harbourside views
- Volcanic hills pocked with *pa* (fortified villages)
- K Rd dining
- Beaches
- Maori culture
- Ponsonby
- Rugby
- Multicultural population of Polynesian and Asian peoples
- Latte bowls
- Stardome Observatory
- Hauraki Gulf Islands

WEAKNESSES
- Buses suffering from privatisation
- Weather
- Rush-hour traffic
- Tough walking on hilly streets
- Howick Historical Village
- Sinking of the *Rainbow Warrior*

GOLD STAR
Yachting – they scored the America's Cup in 1995 and 2000, and the city's yachties are keen to show you why.

STARRING ROLE IN...
- *The Navigator: A Medieval Odyssey* (1988)
- *Whale Rider* (2002)
- *Once Were Warriors* (1994)
- *Shortland Street* (since 1992)
- *An Angel at My Table* (1990)

See the view from Sky Tower.

Eat late-night kumara chips from the White Lady bus on Shortland St.

Drink a glass of excellent white wine from the Marlborough region, such as Cloudy Bay.

Do the Two Volcanoes walk, taking in Mt Victoria and a great panorama.

Watch a cultural performance at Auckland Museum.

Buy Polynesian hip-hop bootlegs or other crafts from Otara Markets.

After dark head for a big night out at the bars and clubs along K Rd.

THE EXHILARATING LEAP FROM SKY TOWER.

125

Austin

NICKNAME LIVE MUSIC CAPITAL OF THE WORLD **DATE OF BIRTH** 1842; WHEN IT BEGAN LIFE AS THE VILLAGE OF WATERLOO **ADDRESS** USA (MAP 1, L9) **HEIGHT** 178M **SIZE** 651 SQ KM **POPULATION** 820,000 (CITY); 1.8 MILLION (METRO AREA) **LONELY PLANET RANKING** 169

Skip the bighorn of Houston and the Ala-ho-hum: Texas is all about its weird and wonderful capital, which hosts innovative IT, live music that's more than just alt-country, a burgeoning film industry and the best Tex-Mex you can gobble down in the state.

ANATOMY

Downtown Austin is laid out in an easily navigable grid, with Congress Ave running from the city's south, across the Colorado River and continuing to the Texas State Capitol. Parallel to Congress, Guadalupe St becomes the Drag, a student mecca for cheap eats and music stores. East 6th St – also running alongside Congress – is known as the Strip and boasts an array of clubs, bars and nightspots. The Warehouse District to the southwest of Congress is another entertainment district, catering for an older hootenanny, often with gay and lesbian nights. The city's public bus network is a solid system of inexpensive neighbourhood, express and downtown routes.

PEOPLE

Austin is relatively cosmopolitan by Texan standards with almost two-thirds of the population identifying as Caucasian. Hispanic and Latin Americans make up around a third, with Spanish spoken amid the predominant English. African Americans, Native Americans and Asians also make up the diverse background of the capital.

TYPICAL AUSTINITE

After being bucked from the dot-bronco, Austinite digital cowboys have had to take a breather, but the city is still the shining star of teched-up Texas. GPS is the new cowboy hat (though the city has never been into uniforms – there's an unspoken 'no-suits' policy). Almost 50,000 residents attend UT (as University of Texas is better known), making for a massive student population to keep the music live and the art cutting edge. Yep, Austinites prize their strangeness,

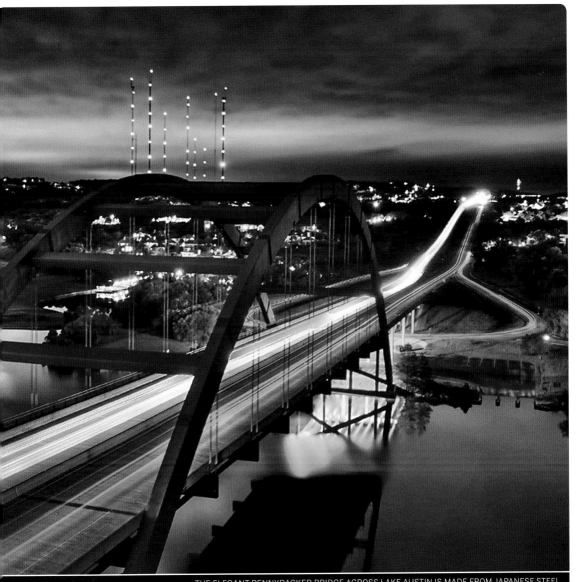
THE ELEGANT PENNYBACKER BRIDGE ACROSS LAKE AUSTIN IS MADE FROM JAPANESE STEEL.

TIME TO SAY YOUR PRAYERS AT SIMPSON UNITED METHODIST CHURCH.

even going so far as to stage protests to 'Keep Austin Weird', and see themselves as very different from their oil-rich, cowpoke Texan neighbours. 'I don't live in Texas', local troubadour Jerry Jeff Walker once said, 'I live in Austin'.

DEFINING EXPERIENCE

Grabbing a barbecue breakfast – a spicy start to any day – then working it off with Frisbee golf through Zilker Park, attending a seminar on film at UT, then hoeing-down at a hootenanny, sinking a few margaritas in a honky tonk on 6th St, and being spooked by the 1.5 million-strong bat colony under Congress Ave Bridge.

STRENGTHS

- ◢ South by Southwest (SXSW)
- ◢ Zilker Park and Barton Springs Pool
- ◢ McKinney Falls State Park
- ◢ UT
- ◢ Colorado River
- ◢ Texas State Capitol

- ◢ Bikes Not Bombs (free bikes for visitors)
- ◢ Pennybacker Bridge
- ◢ Frisbee golf courses
- ◢ Texas State Capitol
- ◢ Free Silver 'Dillo (short for armadillo) buses
- ◢ Moonlight Towers

WEAKNESSES

- ◢ Good ol' boys
- ◢ Boiling heat
- ◢ Dull chain hotels lining I-35

PROVE YOU AIN'T NO CHICKEN BY ENTERING THE 'WHERE WILL THE POOP LAND' COMPETITION AT GINNY'S.

GOLD STAR

Live music – every other bar has tunes to get your foot tapping and your boot scooting.

STARRING ROLE IN...

- ▲ *Armadillos and Old Lace* by Kinky Friedman
- ▲ *Slacker* (1991)
- ▲ *Dazed and Confused* (1993)
- ▲ *Spy Kids* (2001)
- ▲ *Secondhand Lions* (2003)
- ▲ *Miss Congeniality* (2000)
- ▲ *Office Space* (1999)
- ▲ *Sin City* (2005)

See the eerie view from the 9m-tall UT Tower.

Eat a dripping taco al *pastor* (pork and pineapple) washed down with a margarita or 12 at Guero's Taco Bar.

Drink a few Buds at the Shady Grove on Thursday evening with Austin's local bands rocking the stage.

Do a warm-up lap on the Town Lake Trail, a 10-mile loop that takes in the Stevie Ray Vaughan statue.

Watch (and maybe get dragged onto the floor yourself) for Texas dancehall at Broken Spoke.

Buy a 'Keep Austin Weird' bumper sticker from any cigar store.

After dark check out the best retro country (and the cheap brews) at Ginny's Little Longhorn Saloon, a genuine honky tonk.

129

SHOP TILL YOU DROP IN THE BEAUTIFUL DISTRICT AROUND FOUNTAIN SQ.

STEPHANE VICTOR

Baku

DATE OF BIRTH BRONZE AGE; THERE IS EVIDENCE OF HABITATION SINCE THIS TIME, ALTHOUGH THE FIRST HISTORICAL REFERENCE TO BAKU WAS ONLY MADE IN THE 9TH CENTURY **ADDRESS** AZERBAIJAN (MAP 8, E2) **HEIGHT** 1M **SIZE** 86,600 SQ KM **POPULATION** 2.1 MILLION **LONELY PLANET RANKING** 182

The ancient walled city at Baku's heart is a magnificently preserved collection of mosques and imposing Moorish architecture, while just outside the city fascinating relics of Zoroastrianism will astound anyone with an interest in religion.

ANATOMY

Baku curls majestically around the Bay of Baku, an inlet from the oil-rich Caspian Sea, from which the scent of black gold wafts through the city. The very heart of the town is the Içəri Şəhər, the old Muslim walled city, which contains several beautiful mosques and the famous Maiden's Tower. The modern city is congregated around the Içəri Şəhər and provides a stark contrast in its mercurial modernity. There is a range of public transport, including a metro, buses and trolleybuses.

PEOPLE

While Azerbaijan is a multicultural nation, the vast majority of Baku's population are ethnic Azeris. There are also small groups of Russians, Tatars, Lezgins, Kurds and Armenians. Azerbaijan is a Shiite Muslim nation, though Sunni Muslims and Russian Orthodox Christians comprise a significant proportion of the population. Fiercely proud of the young republic of Azerbaijan, many of the most educated people in the city nevertheless speak Russian rather than Azeri at home – a not uncommon contradiction in the post-Soviet world.

TYPICAL BAKUNIAN

Cosmopolitan and bilingual, Bakunians are well known for their sly business instincts, and the city's economic boom can be attributed as much to the character of the city's natives as it can to the oil wealth beneath the Caspian. That said, most Bakunians you meet are exceptionally laid-back, hospitable and talkative people who love nothing more than to engage in drawn-out debates and discussions.

DOM SOVIET, BAKU'S GOVERNMENT HOUSE, WAS DESIGNED BY MICHAEL USEYNOV.

CHRISTOPHER HERWIG / GETTY IMAGES

Whatever you do here, you'll come away feeling like you've got some new friends to visit on your return.

DEFINING EXPERIENCE

Leaving bustling downtown Baku with its busy oil men, glass-and-steel tower blocks and fast food, and slipping into another world entirely by wandering into the Içəri Şəhər, seeing the carpet sellers and fruit stalls, watching families going about their daily lives in the narrow backstreets and hearing the call to prayer at the grand mosques contained within the city's ancient walls.

STRENGTHS

◢ Cool breeze from the sea, which keeps the city pleasant even during the stifling summer months
◢ The friendly *çayxanə* (traditional teahouse) society will convert even ardent espresso-fans to the delights of tea
◢ You'll see very few tourists but plenty of Western businesspeople
◢ The food is delicious and markets overflow with fresh fruit and vegetables

WEAKNESSES

◢ The smell of oil from the Caspian
◢ Corrupt officials always on the lookout for some extra earnings
◢ The dismal political situation

GOLD STAR

The fascinating world of the Içəri Şəhər.

STARRING ROLE IN...

◢ *The World Is Not Enough* (1999)

See the majestic view from the top of the mysterious Maiden's Tower.

Eat fresh and delicious *lulə* (kebab) at any restaurant in town.

Drink tea over a game of *nard* (backgammon) in a Bakunian *çayxanə*.

Do explore the fascinating Palace of the Shirvan Shahs in the Içəri Şəhər.

Watch out when discussing politics – the war with Armenia remains a taboo subject.

Buy carpets galore at the open-air market in the Içəri Şəhər.

After dark enjoy a display of live music and belly dancing in any smart restaurant.

Bamako

DATE OF BIRTH 1700S; WHEN THE NIARÉ CLAN ARRIVED IN THE REGION AND NAMED THE TOWN 'CROCODILE RIVER' (BAMA-KO IN BAMBARA) AFTER THE NUMEROUS CROCODILES THEY SAW IN THE NIGER **ADDRESS** MALI (MAP 6, C7) **HEIGHT** 340M **POPULATION** 1.9 MILLION **LONELY PLANET RANKING** 195

Bamako is a riot of sound and colour: women in flamboyant clothing with towers of tomatoes on their heads; men selling plastic combs, toys and bottles; table football games; the scorching sun; and a rousing soundtrack of Bambara music.

ANATOMY

Sitting on the northern bank of the River Niger, Bamako city centre is a triangle formed by Ave Modibo Keita, Blvd du Peuple and the train tracks. At the heart of the city off Rue Baba Diarra is the train station. The main road out of town is Route de Ségou. You reach this by heading south from Ave Modibo Keita to Square Lumumba then taking Pont des Martyrs. Catch one of Bamako's yellow taxis or a green *dourounis* (van).

PEOPLE

The majority of Malians are Muslim, but animist beliefs are common. The main tribal groups are Bambara, Malinke and Soninke.

TYPICAL BAMAKO CITIZEN

Mali is one of the world's poorest nations. Two-thirds of Mali's population struggle below the poverty line, and infant mortality is very high. The civil war in the Côte d'Ivoire, Mali's biggest trading partner, caused the country massive problems. Despite all of this, Bamako is a harmonious place. The government is stable and popular and committed to stamping out corruption, and the media is relatively free. Women are revered, although genital mutilation and polygamy are still practised. Bamako's citizens are proud of Mali's history. They are warm, friendly and as loud as their clothing. And in such a musical city it's no surprise that they like to party.

DEFINING EXPERIENCE

Wandering through the markets, spying the dead-animal potions at the

THE BCEAO TOWER OF BAMAKO CASTS ITS REFLECTION FROM THE NORTHERN BANK OF THE RIVER NIGER.

THE PEOPLE OF BAMAKO REMAIN PROUD AND NOBLE DESPITE THE PRESSURES OF POVERTY.

SHARING GOOD TIMES IN THE SHADE.

MARKET EXTRAVAGANZAS ARE AN EXPERIENCE WORTH ENJOYING.

Fetish Market before buying henna decorations at the Marché de Médina and heading to Djembe for a drink and a dance to the sound of *griots* (poets, musicians and historical storytellers).

STRENGTHS

- The library and concerts at the Centre Culturel Français
- *Kora* (traditional 12-string instrument)
- Grand Marché
- Woodcarvings at the Maison des Artisans
- Artisans' work at the Institut National des Arts
- Fetish Market
- *Bogolan* (hand-painted mud cloth)
- Marché de Médina
- Musée National
- The streets at prayer time, full of genuflecting people
- Bold, colourful clothing
- The Niger River
- Table football

WEAKNESS

- Muggings around the train station, riverbanks and near the Maison des Jeunes de Bamako

GOLD STAR

Live music – Bamako certainly has rhythm.

STARRING ROLE IN...

- *Bamako Sigi-Kan* (2002)
- *Je chanterai pour toi* (2002)
- *Yeleen* (1987)

See the stunning views from Point de Vue Touristique above Bamako.

Eat cakes with real coffee at the Pâtisserie le Royaume des Gourmands.

Drink at old favourite Byblos and watch male expats chatting up high-heeled hookers.

Do take drumming or dancing lessons at the Carrefour des Jeunes.

Watch the vibrant dealings of the Grand Marché, whose stalls are crammed with dried fish, extravagant fabrics and potions.

Buy fabulous woodcarvings and jewellery from the Maison des Artisans.

After dark dance under the stars and catch a kora performance by Toumani Diabaté.

Bangkok

NAME BANGKOK OR *KRUNG THEP MAHANAKHON AMON RATTANAKOSIN MAHINTHARA AYUTHAYA MAHADILOK PHOP NOPPHARAT RATCHATHANI BURIROM UDOMRATCHANIWET MAHASATHAN AMON PIMAN AWATAN SATHIT SAKKATHATTIYA WITSANUKAM PRASIT* (TRANSLATION: THE CITY OF ANGELS, THE GREAT CITY, THE ETERNAL JEWEL CITY, THE IMPREGNABLE CITY OF GOD INDRA, THE GRAND CAPITAL OF THE WORLD ENDOWED WITH NINE PRECIOUS GEMS, THE HAPPY CITY, ABOUNDING IN AN ENORMOUS ROYAL PALACE THAT RESEMBLES THE HEAVENLY ABODE WHERE REIGNS THE REINCARNATED GOD, A CITY GIVEN BY INDRA AND BUILT BY VISHNUKARN) **NICKNAME** VENICE OF THE EAST **DATE OF BIRTH** MID-16TH CENTURY; FOUNDED AS A TRADING POST **ADDRESS** THAILAND (MAP 9, E7) **HEIGHT** 2M **SIZE** 1569 SQ KM **POPULATION** 8.3 MILLION (CITY); 14.6 MILLION (METRO AREA) **LONELY PLANET RANKING** 008

It's a city of contrasts: glass and steel buildings shaped like cartoon robots standing next to glittering temple spires; wreaths of jasmine flowers dangling from the rear-view mirrors of buses and taxis; shaven-headed, orange-robed monks walking barefoot along the street beneath a bank of giant Sony screens blasting MTV Asia.

ANATOMY

Bangkok is located in the basin of the Chao Phraya River. The land is crisscrossed with canals and rivers. The sky is littered with high-rises in the form of shopping malls and major hotel chains but the side streets (*sois*) harbour canals and traditional Thai buildings and, perhaps, even a few teak houses. The Skytrain is an efficient and air-conditioned mode of transportation that circumnavigates the city. A túk-túk (motorised rickshaw) will take you wherever you want to go.

PEOPLE

The population is mostly Thai, although there are many Chinese immigrants and an increasing number of Indians.

TYPICAL BANGKOKIAN

About one in every 10 Thais is said to be from Bangkok. Patriotic taxi drivers will welcome you and wax lyrical about their city, with a polite smile on their face. They are down-to-earth and remarkably calm, despite the bureaucracy and traffic congestion.

GOLDEN BUDDHAS AT WAT SUTHAT TEMPLE, ONE OF BANGKOK'S LARGEST.

DEFINING EXPERIENCE

Heralding the day with a bit of t'ai chi in Lumphini Park and, if you can manage to move after a gruelling massage at the Wat Pho school of massage, taking high tea in the Author's Lounge at the Mandarin Oriental, alongside the ghosts of Joseph Conrad and Graham Greene.

STRENGTHS

- You can buy anything for a (very cheap) price, anything
- Markets around every corner
- Five-star hotels for a song
- Open 24 hours
- Beautiful fabrics
- Gilt stupas in the centre of the madness

WEAKNESSES

- Pollution – you may as well smoke a packet a day
- *Faràng* (Westerners) with beer guts, wearing silk shirts and with sweaty arms around young Thai boys
- Traffic congestion despite an organised Skytrain network
- Black-as-tar river (don't ask why the river taxis have covered windows)

GOLD STAR

Ayuthaya Historical Park – a Unesco World Heritage Site, Ayuthaya's historic temples are scattered throughout this once magnificent city.

STARRING ROLE IN...

- *Bangkok Hilton* (1989)
- *Nang Nak* (1998)
- *The Shutter* (2004)
- *A Siamese Fairy Tale* by Somerset Maugham

See the dizzying mobile-phone floor at MBK shopping centre.

Eat a bag of green mango wedges coated in sugar, lime juice and chilli – not for a weak stomach.

Drink Singha Beer while people-watching on Khao San Rd.

Do have a heavy-duty one-hour massage on the sprawling king-sized beds at the Wat Pho school of massage.

Watch river life and longboats cruise languidly by from a riverside café.

Buy a protective amulet from the amulet market near the Grand Palace or the funkiest clothing for your pooch at the Chatuchak weekend market.

After dark wander around Patpong and take in a show.

JUVENILE WATER PISTOL COMMANDOS WREAK HAVOC AT THE SONGKHRAN 'WATER-SPLASHING FESTIVAL' TO CELEBRATE NEW YEAR.

IBERIAN HAM IS AN ESSENTIAL PART OF THE SPANISH PLATE.

Barcelona

DATE OF BIRTH 3RD CENTURY BC; WHEN ROMANS ESTABLISHED BARCINO **ADDRESS** SPAIN (MAP 5, G5) **HEIGHT** 93M **SIZE** 487 SQ KM **POPULATION** 1.7 MILLION **LONELY PLANET RANKING** 004

The city of Gaudí and Miró captivates with its proud Catalan identity, roaring nightlife, fabulous cuisine, sunny weather, sandy beaches and sheer style – Barcelona is addictive.

ANATOMY

The tree-lined boulevard La Rambla is Barcelona's main thoroughfare, leading from the port up to Plaça de Catalunya where you'll find buses and taxis. East of La Rambla is the Barri Gòtic with its medieval winding streets and Catedral. Over the road El Raval, the more run-down part of the old quarter, is being gentrified. North, L'Eixample is home to most of the city's Modernista architecture. To the southwest stands the 173m hill of Montjuïc. Along the coast are Port Vell, the working-class district of La Barceloneta and Port Olímpic.

PEOPLE

Bilingual Barcelona (Catalan and Castilian Spanish) has become a multicultural city, with around one fifth of the population coming from as far afield as Ecuador, Morocco and Pakistan. The city is not as Catalan as the region and many residents come from other parts of Spain.

TYPICAL BARCELONIN

Barcelonins who live in the city generally inhabit apartments – a lack of space means a lack of houses. All dream of an apartment with a *terrassa* (terrace). Barcelonins are known for being serious and hard-working but party just as hard as other Spaniards. *Tapear* (tapas-bar-hopping) is popular but with rising prices, dinner parties are gaining ground. People take pride in their appearance and follow fashion. Football is almost a religion and most people support FC Barcelona. Remember that Barcelonins live in Catalonia, not Spain.

DEFINING EXPERIENCE

Breathing in the morning air on La Barceloneta beach before strolling into El Born for a coffee, then heading up to L'Eixample for Gaudí architecture at La Pedrera and a spot of shopping.

THE FANTASTIC ENTRANCE TO GAUDÍ'S SURREAL PARC GÜELL.

A DANCER AT BARCELONA'S FLAMENCO FESTIVAL.

DON'T WOBBLE – HUMAN TOWERS AT THE CATALAN FESTA DE LA MERCÈ.

STRENGTHS

- *Arròs negre* (rice in black cuttlefish ink)
- Late-night partying
- Festes de la Mercè, the city's main festival
- Proximity to the Pyrenees for skiing and hiking
- Romanesque and Gothic churches
- Modernista architecture
- FC Barcelona football and basketball teams
- Urban planning and sustainability initiatives
- Bans on smoking and bullfighting
- Museu Picasso
- La Sagrada Familia and Parc Güell
- La Pedrera
- Museu Marítim

WEAKNESSES

- Expensive real estate
- Suppression of Catalan interests within Spain
- The economy
- Els Boixos Nois (The Mad Boys), local football hooligans
- Noise pollution

GOLD STAR

Modernista architecture adorns the city.

STARRING ROLE IN...

- *El Gran Gato* (2003)
- *L'Auberge Espagnol* (The Spanish Apartment, 2002)
- *Todo Sobre Mi Madre* (All About My Mother, 1999)
- *Vicky Cristina Barcelona* (2008)

See Gaudí's huge architectural confection, La Sagrada Familia, unfinished and yet awe-inspiring.

Eat *melindros* (soft sugar-coated biscuits) dipped into *cacaolat* (thick hot chocolate) at Salvador Dalí's favourite dairy bar, Granja Dulcinea.

Drink cocktails at the 1933 Art Deco Boadas whose founder served Hemingway in Havana.

Do learn about Picasso's early works at the fascinating Museu Picasso.

Watch men offering women roses and women giving men books on Día de Sant Jordi, the feast of Catalonia's patron saint.

Buy affordable Spanish fashion at Mango or Zara in L'Eixample.

After dark bump and grind in Port Olímpic for your pick of the clubs.

Bath

DATE OF BIRTH 800 BC; REPUTEDLY FOUNDED BY KING BLADUD, A TROJAN REFUGEE AND FATHER OF KING LEAR **ADDRESS** ENGLAND (MAP 4, F8) **HEIGHT** 181M **SIZE** 29 SQ KM **POPULATION** 90,000 **LONELY PLANET RANKING** 119

When sunlight brightens the honey-coloured stone, and people out for a stroll fill the streets and line the river, stylish and lively Bath, England's first spa resort, reveals its charm.

ANATOMY

Bath is nestled at the bottom of the Avon Valley in the southern Cotswolds and is famed for its seven hills, with buildings climbing the steep streets. The River Avon, tamed by a series of weirs, runs through the town centre. The town's most obvious landmark is the abbey, across from the Roman Baths and Pump Room. Walk, cycle or catch a bus.

PEOPLE

The typical Bath resident is healthy, comes from a white ethnic background, has an average age of about 40, and is of the Christian faith, although around 20% of the population register no religion. The city has small populations of other ethnic groups, including Asians and blacks.

TYPICAL BATH CITIZEN

Citizens of Bath are much like their fellow countrymen – they drink tea, form orderly queues while awaiting service and enjoy a pint at the pub.

DEFINING EXPERIENCE

Strolling through the historic baths and enjoying luxurious spa treatments at Thermae Bath Spa, tasting the waters from the fountain before tea and scones in the elegant Pump Room, then visiting the Roman Baths Museum, wandering through the 500-year-old abbey, strolling through the riverside Parade Gardens and taking a boat tour at Poulteney Weir, before getting an architectural, gossip and trivia overview on a free walking tour of the city, viewing the crowning glory of Georgian Bath (Royal Crescent and The Circus), and travelling through four centuries of fashion at the Costume Museum.

STRENGTHS

- ◢ The thermal baths, which have hosted kings and queens
- ◢ Exquisite mosaics

PULTENEY BRIDGE IS A GREAT VANTAGE POINT FOR VIEWING THIS WEIR ON THE RIVER AVON.

- Georgian splendour and original limestone buildings
- Wide parades
- The wonderful fan vaulting of Bath Abbey's nave
- The majestic sweep of Royal Crescent and the Circus
- Shopping
- Bath International Music Festival
- Atmospheric restaurants and bars
- Hidden pockets of Georgiana found up steep streets
- The self-guided Jane Austen Bath Walk
- Carved mythical beasts in the choir stalls of the abbey
- The carnivalesque chaos of Walcot Nation Day
- Bath Fringe Festival

WEAKNESSES
- Florence-style tourist congestion
- Traffic
- Trying to read stone-carved street signs

GOLD STAR
Bath's star attraction, the Roman Baths, and their stunning mosaics.

STARRING ROLE IN...
- *Three Tenors Concert* (2003)
- *Vanity Fair* (2003)
- *Persuasion* by Jane Austen (film 1994)
- *House of Eliot* (1991–94)
- *The Music Lovers* (1969)
- *Northanger Abbey* by Jane Austen
- *Pickwick Papers* by Charles Dickens

See angels climbing up and down (head first!) a stone ladder on the exterior west façade of Bath Abbey.

Eat cream tea or a traditional English meal at Sally Lunn's, founded by the Huguenot refugee in 1680.

Drink a Gem ale, brewed in the city by Bath Ales.

Do taste the waters in the elegant Pump Room.

Watch the cinematic rendering of a Jane Austen classic for a view into the grand times of Georgian Bath.

Buy some luxurious pampering at Thermae Bath Spa, bohemian treasures on Walcot St or secondhand books from the covered Guildhall Market.

After dark take a 'ghost walk' of Bath, departing from the reputedly haunted Garricks Head pub.

THE SANDSTONE TERRACE OF BATH'S ROYAL CRESCENT GLOWS GOLD IN ENGLAND'S OCCASIONAL SUNSHINE.

Beijing

NICKNAME THE NORTHERN CAPITAL **DATE OF BIRTH** 500,000 YEARS AGO; WHEN THE SOUTHERN AREA OF BEIJING WAS INHABITED BY 'PEKING MAN'; THE CITY'S MODERN HISTORY DATES FROM 1045 BC **ADDRESS** CHINA (MAP 9, G2) **HEIGHT** 52M **SIZE** 750 SQ KM **POPULATION** 19.6 MILLION **LONELY PLANET RANKING** 063

The sheer size and scale of the capital of the world's most-populous nation is awe-inspiring, and if you look hard enough between the six-lane highways and skyscrapers you'll find fascinating Chinese imperial history dwarfed by everything around it.

ANATOMY

At the heart of the massive conurbation lies Tiananmen Sq and beyond it the vast imperial palace within the Forbidden City. The city's most controversial new building is the National Centre for the Performing Arts (dubbed 'the egg' by locals), just behind the Great Hall of the People and a stone's throw from the Forbidden City. The city is served by a first-rate metro system and an extensive bus network, but many visitors will find that the only way to truly get around is by cab.

PEOPLE

Like a magnet, Beijing attracts Chinese seeking their fortunes from all over the country, although the vast majority of the population is made up of Han Chinese speaking *beijinghua* – a dialect of the national standard dialect (Mandarin) unique to the capital. There's a big expat community centred on Sanlitun, which is a major nightlife draw and the one truly 24-hour area of town.

TYPICAL BEIJINGER

Beijingers know they live in the cultural, political and psychological centre of China. Unlike their mercurial Hong Kong and Shanghai cousins (whom they dismiss as calculating and stingy respectively), Beijingers are not showy and prefer understatement (as suggested by the city's skyline compared to those of China's two other pre-eminent economic centres). They are also extremely generous and will argue with ferocity over who gets to pay the bill in restaurants.

ANDREW J LOFTERTON / GETTY IMAGES

RECLINING UNDER A RED CANOPY, A RICKSHAW DRIVER TAKES A WELL-DESERVED NAP IN NANYAN HUTONG DISTRICT.

DEFINING EXPERIENCE

Thundering down one of the city's vast main avenues in a cab and suddenly turning into a side street where, between building sites and vast new structures, you'll be deposited at a medieval lamasery (monastery), standing quite oblivious to the modernity around it.

STRENGTHS

- ◢ Superb food on every corner
- ◢ Epic imperial grandeur
- ◢ The *hutong* (side streets where traditional housing and ways of life continue as ever) give the city a human face
- ◢ Fantastic optimism and dynamism

WEAKNESSES

- ◢ Smog
- ◢ The city's sheer size and unmanageability
- ◢ Enormous building works everywhere
- ◢ The endless erosion of the *hutong* and the advance of concrete and asphalt

GOLD STAR

Coming across a genuine Beijing duck restaurant in a run-down *hutong*, and having a delicious meal without gawping tour groups present.

STARRING ROLE IN...

- ◢ *The Last Emperor* (1987)
- ◢ *Farewell My Concubine* (1993)
- ◢ *The Gate of Heavenly Peace* (1995)
- ◢ *Beijing Bicycle* (2001)

See the astonishing imperial apartments and temples within the Forbidden City.

Eat Beijing duck with plum sauce, knocked back by a Yanjing beer.

Drink green tea at a traditional teahouse.

Do make the effort to get out of town to a remote stretch of the Great Wall.

Watch Beijing Opera for an unforgettably Chinese night out.

Buy your Mao Zedong watches at the not-very-Communist gift shop outside his mausoleum.

After dark head out for a midnight boat ride on magical Houhai Lake.

HIGH TEA – A DRAMATIC DEMONSTRATION OF THE ART OF TEA POURING IN LAO SHE TEAHOUSE.

CHARMING SILK LANTERNS SWAY IN THE LIGHT BREEZE AT THE PANJIAYUAN MARKET.

PENNANT-WIELDING PATRIOTS FLY THE NATIONAL FLAG IN TIANANMEN SQ.

A HEADSTRONG MAN MAKES HIS WAY THROUGH THE BEACH MARKET.

Beira

NICKNAME THE HEART **DATE OF BIRTH** 1891; FOUNDED AS THE HEADQUARTERS OF THE PORTUGUESE COMPANHIA DE MOZAMBIQUE ON THE SITE OF AN OLD MUSLIM SETTLEMENT
ADDRESS MOZAMBIQUE (MAP 7, E6) **HEIGHT** 10M **POPULATION** 436,000
LONELY PLANET RANKING 198

The ultimate coastal chill-out zone, Beira's laid-back blend of sandy beaches, outdoor nightlife, live music and dilapidated colonial heritage bestows a subtle and authentic flavour on the city.

ANATOMY

One of Southern Africa's oldest cities, Beira is a major port and rail terminus at the mouth of the River Pungwe. The city spreads along the coast from the port to the famous lighthouse overlooking Macuti Beach. Navigation is difficult through its maze of streets, mostly built in a Mediterranean style with colonial buildings and plazas. The architecture is prettiest near the pulsating Praça (main square) where you find banks, shops and other facilities. Catch buses or *chapas* (minibuses) to get around.

PEOPLE

Ships passing through the port ensure there is always a steady flow of different nationalities in addition to Mozambique's usual array of African, Arabic, Portuguese and Chinese ethnic communities. Portuguese is the official language and Bantu and Swahili are also spoken.

TYPICAL BEIRAN

Beira emerged from two decades of civil war only to be hit by floods in 2000 and again in 2001. Remarkably the people remain sanguine and are inspiringly strong. The city is now experiencing rapid economic development. As a result the people are confident, positive, friendly and laid-back, and will often welcome the chance to practise their English.

DEFINING EXPERIENCE

Losing yourself among the labyrinthine streets, stumbling unexpectedly into Largo do Município, playing beach volleyball under the searing sun before cooling off with a swim in the shadow of the *Macut* shipwreck on Macuti Beach, gorging on a different prawn curry every night of the

FRESH PRODUCE AT BEIRA'S CITY MARKETPLACE.

ARIADNE VAN ZANDBERGEN / GETTY IMAGES

week, getting blown away by the live percussion acts, and listening to locals telling you what life was like during the civil war.

STRENGTHS

⊿ Best facilities for many kilometres
⊿ Casa Infante de Sagres
⊿ Tropical climate
⊿ Culturally diverse
⊿ Gaudy 1930s-inspired Art Deco
⊿ The shipwrecks
⊿ Farol do Macuti, the lighthouse
⊿ Inspiring locals

WEAKNESSES

⊿ AIDS
⊿ Malaria
⊿ No street signs
⊿ Water pollution
⊿ Floods and cyclones
⊿ Poverty

GOLD STAR

Beaches – dazzling hot sand, broad-leaved palm trees and spectacular shipwrecks make Beira's beaches sing like sirens.

STARRING ROLE IN...

⊿ *Carlos Cardosa – Telling the Truth in Mozambique* by Paul Fauvet and Marcello Mosse
⊿ *The Veranda under the Frangipani* by Mia Couto

See the desolate shipwrecks off Macuti Beach at dusk.

Eat rice and chicken on your favourite stretch of beach.

Drink a cup of coffee at the old-world sidewalk Café Riviera and watch the passing scene.

Do check out, but don't purchase, the contraband on sale in the market at Tchungamoyo (literally, 'brave heart').

Watch an all-comers-welcome rugby match played on the sand in front of Clube Náutico on Saturdays.

Buy a locally made drum and a Makonde woodcarving.

After dark enjoy the ever-changing music, art and entertainment program at Art Bar Café.

Beirut

NICKNAME THE PEARL; PARIS OF THE MIDDLE EAST **DATE OF BIRTH** STONE AGE; THE EARLIEST TRACES OF HUMANS DATE FROM THIS TIME, WHEN BEIRUT WAS TWO ISLANDS IN THE DELTA OF THE BEIRUT RIVER **ADDRESS** LEBANON (MAP 8, C2) **HEIGHT** 34M **POPULATION** 1.8 MILLION (CITY) 2.6 MILLION (METRO AREA) **LONELY PLANET RANKING** 136

In Beirut beautiful architecture exists alongside concrete eyesores, traditional houses in jasmine-scented gardens are dwarfed by modern buildings, and swanky new cars vie with vendor carts.

ANATOMY

Bound north to south by the Mediterranean Sea, the west of Beirut is very hilly, flattening out to the east. The Hamra district in West Beirut is one of the city's hubs, where you'll find major banks and hotels. North of Hamra is Ras Beirut, filled with coffee bars and restaurants. The Corniche is the area where Beirutis come to promenade. On the hill to the southeast is the prosperous Achrafiye; here many older buildings are still intact. Most people use service taxis to get around.

PEOPLE

Beirut boasts significant Christian and Muslim communities. Ethnic groups comprise Arabs, Palestinians, Kurds and Armenians, and Arabic, French, English and Armenian are spoken.

TYPICAL BEIRUTI

After 15 years of living in a battle zone, the typical Beiruti tries to forget a troubled past by eating well, dancing and enjoying life, imbuing Beirut with a buzz absent from every other city in the region. It's rare to see any interaction between people that doesn't begin with profuse greetings, enquiries into the other's health and myriad niceties. As an *ajnabi* (foreigner), if you make the effort to come up with the right expression at the appropriate moment, you'll be warmly regarded for it.

DEFINING EXPERIENCE

Exploring the remains of the civil war along the city's former Green Line, seeing 6000 years of history at the National Museum before watching dusk descend over the Mediterranean at a seafront café.

NAFTALI HILGER / GETTY IMAGES

TAKING THE PLUNGE – DIVERS LEAP OFF BEIRUT'S CORNICHE.

STRENGTHS

◢ The Corniche
◢ The National Museum
◢ A city reborn at the Beirut Central District
◢ Ottoman houses
◢ American University of Beirut Museum
◢ Genuine hospitality
◢ Pigeon Rocks
◢ Seafront cafés
◢ Vibrant arts scene
◢ St George Cathedral
◢ Religious and social diversity

WEAKNESSES

◢ The political situation is often tumultuous and tense – stay informed
◢ Land mines outside of Beirut – avoid off-road and unmarked areas
◢ Oppressive summers
◢ Wild traffic, potholes and unlicensed taxis
◢ Lack of street numbers and conflicting street names

GOLD STAR

Optimism – a city well on the mend, visitors to Beirut can see a phoenixlike transformation in progress.

STARRING ROLE IN...

◢ *The Hills of Adonis* by Colin Thubron
◢ *A House of Many Mansions* by Kamal Salibi
◢ *Pity the Nation* by Robert Fisk

See modern Lebanese plays in Arabic, French and occasionally English at the Al-Madina Theatre.

Eat a fusion of Eastern and Western cuisines in Casablanca (Rue Ain al-Mraisse), set in one of the few intact Ottoman houses on the Corniche.

Drink your coffee short, strong and at every available opportunity, as the locals do.

Do peruse the traditional Palestinian embroidery at Al-Badia; the shop has garments handmade by refugee women who benefit from the proceeds.

Watch horse racing of a Sunday at the Hippodrome, one of the only places in the Middle East where you can legally place a bet.

Buy melt-in-your-mouth baklava and other pastries from Amal al-Bohsali.

After dark be part of Beirut's social mosaic; stroll along the Corniche.

PUTTING ON THE FINISHING TOUCHES AT THE CRYSTAL NIGHTCLUB.

HEAVENLY RAYS SHOW OFF THE SPLENDOUR OF THE GRAND MOSQUE.

BUY A MEATY SNACK AT BEDO IN BOURJ HAMMOUD, A BEIRUTI INSTITUTION.

GLASSY WATERS REFLECT THE TECHNOLOGICAL MARVEL OF THE RIVER LAGAN WEIR.

Belfast

DATE OF BIRTH 1611; WHEN CHICHESTER'S COLONY OF ENGLISH AND SCOTTISH SETTLED HERE, THOUGH THERE WAS A NORMAN CASTLE BUILT IN 1177; CELTIC OCCUPATION DATES BACK TO THE IRON AGE **ADDRESS** NORTHERN IRELAND (MAP 4, E6) **HEIGHT** 67M **SIZE** 115 SQ KM **POPULATION** 277,000 (CITY); 645,000 (METRO AREA) **LONELY PLANET RANKING** 163

Belfast has earned its stripes; after years of violence and stagnation, there's a palpable positive energy, plus interesting industrial architecture and a slew of glorious drinking holes.

ANATOMY

Belfast's compact city centre, a child of the Industrial Revolution, curls around the undulating west bank of the River Lagan, with the steep slopes of Black Mountain and Cave Hill beyond. The city's former shipbuilding yards – the birthplace of RMS Titanic – stretch along the east side of the river. The area is undergoing a £1 billion regeneration project known as Titanic Quarter, which plans to transform the long-derelict docklands. Buses and trains do the job, and chartered black cabs – the people's taxis – ply the main roads of sectarian West Belfast.

PEOPLE

Historically, Belfast's only ethnic divisions were those between Catholics and Protestants. Today there is greater equality between the two groups, and sectarian tensions are often linked to issues of class. As in other large Irish cities, there are now significant migrant communities, mainly from China, the Philippines, Africa, the Middle East and Pakistan. This influx of new cultures, as well as a large student population, has contributed to the decreasing importance of religion. But the transition isn't an easy one, with ongoing violence towards ethnic minorities, especially those living in poorer Protestant neighbourhoods.

TYPICAL BELFASTIAN

Belfastians surprise visitors with their infectious confidence and gregariousness. Like their Dublin neighbours they take their social lives seriously but, more than anywhere in Ireland, really do dress up for a night out. They remain vitally interested in politics, but are more likely to talk about their favourite DJ or the next sun holiday to Portugal than casually discuss the peace process. They are masters at taking the piss but don't take

A PICTURE OF IRISHNESS – YOUNG BELFAST BOYS LOOK THE PART.

it personally; they're also known for asking any new-found acquaintances to a party on pub closing.

DEFINING EXPERIENCE

Hitting Topshop for some gear, fixing up the fake tan then off to Spring & Airbrake for that new alt-country band and a wee pint before going to BT1, hanging out in the unisex toilets because it's where the action is, then heading home for a few hours' sleep and a fry-up, grabbing the steamer and heading away to the coast – the East Strand at Portrush is pumping.

STRENGTHS

- ◢ Amazing Victorian architecture: City Hall and the Grand Opera House
- ◢ The Titanic Quarter
- ◢ Beautiful Botanical Gardens
- ◢ Views of the encircling mountains
- ◢ Queen's University
- ◢ Ulster Museum
- ◢ Compact but still resolutely urban centre
- ◢ Friendly to visitors
- ◢ Lagan Towpath
- ◢ Burgeoning restaurant scene
- ◢ City Hall
- ◢ Belfast Art College
- ◢ Resilience

WEAKNESSES

- ◢ July
- ◢ Undeserved grim reputation
- ◢ The marriage of old-school sectarianism and millennial xenophobia
- ◢ *Spides* (the Belfastian term for local male hoodlums)

A REPUBLICAN MEMORIAL MURAL ON FALLS RD HONOURS THE DEAD.

GOLD STAR

Black, black sense of humour: Belfastians love to laugh, and the humour tends towards the surreal and sarcastic.

STARRING ROLE IN...

◢ *Divorcing Jack* (1998)
◢ *The Most Fertile Man In Ireland* (1999)
◢ *The Mighty Celt* (2005)
◢ *This Human Season* by Louise Dean

See Samson and Goliath, the giant yellow cranes of the Harland & Wolff shipyards, from a boat on the River Lagan.

Eat posh – perhaps local game cooked up by Michael Deane in his eponymous Michelin-starred restaurant.

Drink a hot whiskey with cloves and lemon while ensconced in a snug in the high-Victorian camp of the Crown Liquor Saloon.

Do the Falls and Shankills Rds by people's taxi and take in the murals.

Watch a big-name act play the Ulster Hall or an up-and-coming one at the Limelight.

Buy yourself a treat from the ultra-hip Lisburn Rd (from Eglantine Ave out to Balmoral Ave) – a long strip of red-brick and mock-Tudor facades.

After dark hear harder and heavier beats at Shine, a venerable club night at the Queen's Students' Union.

Belgrade

NICKNAME WHITE CITY **DATE OF BIRTH** 2300 YEARS AGO; SINCE THEN BELGRADE HAS BEEN DESTROYED AND REBUILT 40 TIMES **ADDRESS** SERBIA AND MONTENEGRO (MAP 5, P4) **HEIGHT** 132M **SIZE** 360 SQ KM **POPULATION** 1.8 MILLION **LONELY PLANET RANKING** 143

With its underground nightlife scene and enchanting above-ground Stari Grad (Old Town), unpretentious Belgrade is a dishevelled teenager compared with its slick European cousins, but it's fast reinventing itself.

ANATOMY

Terazije is the heart of modern Belgrade. Knez Mihailova, Belgrade's lively pedestrian boulevard, runs northwest through Stari Grad from Terazije to the Kalemegdan Citadel, which lords over the Sava and Danube Rivers estuary. Buses and an underground metro train network will get you around town.

PEOPLE

The city is a rich tapestry of ethnicities. Over half the population is Serb, there is a significant Albanian community, plus small Montenegrin, Hungarian, Croatian, Romano and Magyar groups. The official tongue is Serbian.

TYPICAL BELGRADER

Belgraders are a proud, forthright and strong-willed bunch with a melancholic core. Tourists are only now returning to Belgrade and foreign visitors are warmly greeted. In fact, it is not uncommon for Belgraders to offer to show you round their city, and treat a newcomer to family-oriented hospitality, which revolves around eating, football and partying. Hopelessly romantic, Belgraders love to fall in love and then overdramatise it all.

DEFINING EXPERIENCE

Checking out the Kalemegdan Citadel before wandering along vibrant Knez Mihailova, a café-lined pedestrianised boulevard, and chatting with a bunch of university types who are likely to invite you to a poetry reading coupled with plenty of *pivo* (beer).

A GREAT WAY TO SEE BELGRADE IS FROM A RIVERBOAT ON THE DANUBE.

LIFE'S FULL OF LAUGHTER FOR THESE ROMA CHILDREN.

STRENGTHS

- World-class nightlife
- A living history
- Go-anywhere bus and train network
- Grandiose old buildings
- Deli central: melt-in-your-mouth *kajmak* (a salted cream turned to cheese) and delectable grilled meats (*pljeskavica* and *ražnjići*)
- Multilingual population
- Outstanding museums
- Polite and gregarious young people
- A smorgasbord of fun-filled festivals, from summer jazz to film festivals
- Religious celebrations held in honour of the city saint and protector, Spasovdan

WEAKNESSES

- A lingering postwar sadness
- US-wannabe gangsters
- Daytime traffic congestion
- Next to no vegetarian options (they will ask what sickness you're suffering from)

GOLD STAR

The city boasts the kind of effortlessly cool nightlife that promoters the world over can only dream of recreating. Belgraders are happy to dance all night and go straight to work the next day.

STARRING ROLE IN...

- *The Wounds* (1998)
- *Cabaret Balkan* (1998)
- *Loving Glances* (2003)
- *Underground* (1995)
- *Black Lamb & Grey Falcon* by

THE HUSTLE AND BUSTLE OF BELGRADE'S INFAMOUS NIGHTLIFE SCENE.

Rebecca West
▲ *Balkan Blues: Writing out of Yugoslavia* edited by Joanna Labon

See Belgrade's ancient Kalemegdan Citadel.

Eat the famed *burek*, a greasy pie made with *sir* (cheese), *meso* (meat), *krompiruša* (potato) or occasionally *pečurke* (mushrooms), at one of the alfresco cafés along Trg Republike.

Drink an apéritif at hip watering hole Kafana Pavle Korčagin.

Do saunter along Knez Mihailova, a treasure-trove of historical buildings with great people-watching.

Watch summer musical, theatrical and cabaret performances at Skadarska – Belgrade's answer to Paris' Montmarte.

Buy something lacy to perk up your table life; or hand-knitted woollens from the vendors in Kalemegdan Park.

After dark dance hands-in-the-air style to Belgrade's very own 'turbo folk' at one of the city's many night-owl haunts, such as Andergraund or Plastic.

Belize City

DATE OF BIRTH 1779: WHEN 'BELIZE TOWN' BECAME THE BRITISH HEADQUARTERS IN BELIZE **ADDRESS** BELIZE (MAP 2, H5) **HEIGHT** 5M **SIZE:** 2 SQ KM **POPULATION** 70,000 **LONELY PLANET RANKING** 183

Belize City's ramshackle streets are alive with colourful characters representing every facet of the city's ethnic variety, especially the Creoles whose culture has always been rooted here.

ANATOMY

Haulover Creek, bisecting the city, separates the commercial area (focused on Albert St) from the slightly more genteel Fort George district to the northeast. The Swing Bridge – hub of the city – crosses Haulover Creek to link Albert St with Queen St. North up the coast from the Fort George district are the Newtown Barracks and Kings Park neighbourhoods. West of Albert St is the Southside, the poorest quarter. There is a bus network, but walking is often your best option.

PEOPLE

Belize City enjoys a fabulous ethnic diversity. Creoles – descendants of British loggers and colonists and African slaves – form a quarter of the population. Racially mixed and proud of it, Creoles speak a unique version of English, the country's official language. Over the last couple of decades, mestizos (of mixed Spanish and indigenous descent) have become Belize's largest ethnic group. The rest is a mix of the Maya, the Garifuna, 'East Indians' (from the Indian subcontinent), Chinese, Arabs, North Americans and Europeans.

TYPICAL BELIZEAN

Because of the mix of ethnicities and cultures in Belize, its people are very open, tolerant and accepting of others. Poverty is still widespread and crime is almost a way of life for some. You can admire lovely, large, breezy, two-storey, old-Caribbean-style wooden houses in parts of Belize City, but most Belizeans live in smaller dwellings, and new houses are often cinder-block boxes, while old ones may be composed of rotting wood. Labour – whether washing dirty hotel sheets, cutting sugar cane or packing bananas – is poorly paid, and prices are high in comparison. It is estimated that one-third of the population lives below the poverty line.

ANTHONY PLUMMER / GETTY IMAGES

HEALTHY ALTERNATIVE – A MAN OFFERING BANANAS AND MELONS TO PASSERS-BY IN DOWNTOWN BELIZE.

DEFINING EXPERIENCE

Visiting the centre of activity in Belize City, the Swing Bridge, enjoying the traditional Belizean dish of rice and beans, then taking in the colonial architecture and cooling sea breezes of the Fort George district.

STRENGTHS

- Multiculturalism and tolerance
- Image Factory art gallery
- Crooked Tree Wildlife Sanctuary
- Lovingly cooked Creole-style fish
- Calypso music and the street vibe
- Relaxed atmosphere

WEAKNESSES

- Low wages and poor housing
- All-too-frequent shootings around the Southside district
- Influx of cruise-ship tourists
- Divide between rich and poor

GOLD STAR

The atmosphere and street life, more than anything, are what make Belize City worth exploring.

STARRING ROLE IN...

- *The Dogs of War* (1980)
- *Mosquito Coast* (1986)
- *Heart of Darkness* (1993)

See the heart and soul of Belize City life, the Swing Bridge, which is crossed by just about everyone here just about every day.

Eat rice-and-bean Belizean standards at Dit's, a local favourite.

Drink a 'seaweed shake' sold by a street vendor – a blend of condensed milk, spices and extract of the seaweed *Eucheuma isoforme*, which grows underwater as a tangle of yellow branches.

Do encounter howler monkeys at the Community Baboon Sanctuary.

Watch Belize's amazing wildlife at the Belize Zoo.

Buy exquisite carvings made from the strikingly streaked wood zericote at the National Handicraft Center.

After dark catch a concert of traditional Belizean music at the 600-seat Bliss Centre for the Performing Arts.

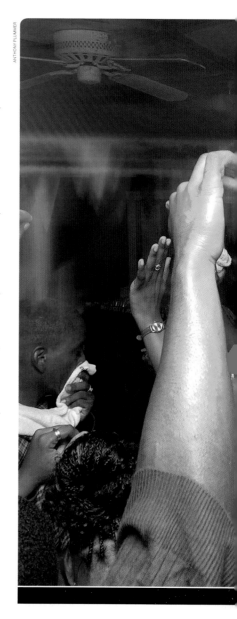

FRIDAY NIGHT LIGHTS – CLUBBING IN BELIZE IS A HIGH POINT.

BERLIN'S CATHEDRAL, THE BERLINER DOM, HAS HAD AN EVENTFUL 600-YEAR HISTORY.

Berlin

NICKNAME EUROPE'S BIGGEST BUILDING SITE **DATE OF BIRTH** 1307; TRADING POSTS BERLIN AND CÖLLN JOINED TO FORM A CITY **ADDRESS** GERMANY (MAP 4, M9) **HEIGHT** 55M **SIZE** 892 SQ KM **POPULATION** 3.5 MILLION (CITY); 6 MILLION (METRO AREA) **LONELY PLANET RANKING** 018

Berlin is evolving, adapting, throwing up surprises and questioning its identity; while filled with history, she is determined to move ever forward.

ANATOMY

Apart from rivers and lakes, the city lacks distinctive geographical features – you're more likely to use buildings as a way of orienting yourself. Some of the city's rare hills were actually made from WWII rubble. Berlin's spread-out nature means you'll be relying on its U-bahns, S-bahns, buses and trams.

PEOPLE

Berliners enjoy a reputation for being liberal and well educated and the city itself is a patchwork of people from almost 200 countries. The most obvious immigrant group is the Turkish community. English is widely spoken, although less so among people of the former East, who will have learnt Russian as a second language.

TYPICAL BERLINER

Polite, friendly and fond of dry, sharp humour, Berliners are hard to shock. They live in high-ceilinged, airy apartments full of art and Ikea, make weekend brunches an essential experience and always seem to know where the 'scene' is and what's happening culturally.

DEFINING EXPERIENCE

Losing yourself in any of the city's blockbuster galleries and museums, keeping up with the locals by attending one of the 1500 cultural events that are crammed into Berlin's calendar, and reminding yourself that Potsdamer Platz was once 'No Man's Land'.

STRENGTHS

- History around every corner
- Willingness to make modern architectural statements
- Entrepreneurial spirit of young Berliners

URBANITES RELAX ON A SUNNY AFTERNOON IN HALENSEE PARK.

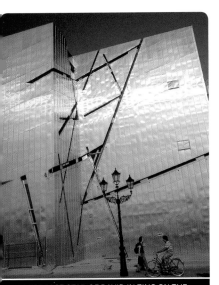

AN ABSTRACT STAR OF DAVID IN ZINC ON THE JEWISH MUSEUM BY DANIEL LIBESKIND.

THE BERLIN OPERA HOUSE IS A HIGHLIGHT OF UNTER DEN LINDEN IN MITTE.

◢ Imaginative protests
◢ Coffee and cake as a ritual
◢ Efficient public transport
◢ Citywide love of new ideas
◢ Vital contemporary arts scene
◢ Late-night kebabs
◢ Tiergarten (zoo)
◢ Schloss Charlottenburg
◢ Parades

WEAKNESSES
◢ 'The wall in the mind'
◢ Mullet hangovers
◢ Dog poo on the streets of Friedrichshain
◢ Confusing transport maps
◢ Needing to take public transport between attractions
◢ Racial tensions
◢ Techno doof doof when you're trying to sleep
◢ Weather

GOLD STAR
Nightlife – Berlin is determined to remain one of the coolest clubbing spots and her citizens throw themselves into the fray with abandon.

STARRING ROLE IN...
◢ *Die Fetten Jahre sind vorbei* (The Edukators, 2004)
◢ *Good Bye Lenin!* (2003)
◢ *Der Himmel über Berlin* (Wings of Desire, 1987)
◢ *Lola rennt* (Run Lola Run, 1997)
◢ *Herr Lehmann* (Berlin Blues, 2003)
◢ *Berlin: Sinfonie einer Großstadt* (Symphony of a City, 1927)

See what all the fuss is about at the domed Reichstag.

Eat Vietnamese food cheek by jowl with locals at Monsieur Vuong.

Drink while checking out the other patrons at Cookies.

Do a tour of the cutting-edge galleries in the former East Berlin.

Watch the most exciting developments in the cinematic world at the Berlin Film Festival.

Buy a GDR-era souvenir at Flohmarkt am Arkonaplatz.

After dark graffiti-bedecked Tacheles can still throw up night-time surprises for arty partiers.

Bern

NICKNAME BEAR (DUKE BERTHOLD V OF ZÄHRINGEN ALLEGEDLY NAMED THE CITY AFTER AN ANIMAL HE KILLED WHILE HUNTING; THE BEAR HAS BEEN BERN'S HERALDIC ANIMAL FOR SEVEN CENTURIES) **DATE OF BIRTH** 1191; WHEN IT WAS FOUNDED AS A MILITARY POST; BERN BECAME CAPITAL WHEN THE SWISS CONFEDERATION CAME TO LIFE IN 1848 **ADDRESS** SWITZERLAND (MAP 5, K2) **HEIGHT** 509M **SIZE** 52 SQ KM **POPULATION** 128,000 (CITY); 660,000 (METRO AREA) **LONELY PLANET RANKING** 112

Bern is a charmingly quaint city despite its status as the capital of Switzerland; it boasts a medieval heart, a 15th-century town hall and a thriving alternative arts scene.

ANATOMY

The compact town is contained within a sharp U-shaped bend, limiting some streets to pedestrian and public transport access. The main train station is at the mouth of the U and within easy reach of the main sights, and a loan of city bikes is free.

PEOPLE

The majority of Bern's friendly residents speak Swiss German as a first language, while others speak French. Bernese German incorporates several words from Matteänglisch, a secret language that few people now speak, which was used in the former workers' quarter of Matte.

TYPICAL BERNESE

The typical Bern resident is modest, well-groomed, bilingual in French and German, predominantly Protestant and lives a quiet life in the pleasant Swiss capital. The Bernese enjoy the arts and regularly go to Bern's numerous cinemas to watch films in their original language.

DEFINING EXPERIENCE

Climbing the tower of Bern's Gothic Münster (cathedral) for fantastic views, joining a tour of the Bundeshäuser (Houses of Parliament), viewing the Paul Klee exhibition at the Kunstmuseum and watching the twirling figurines before the chiming of the Zeitglockenturm, an elaborate medieval clock tower with moving puppets.

QUIRKY STREET DECORATIONS, BERNESE-STYLE.

STRENGTHS

- ◢ Bern's Unesco World Heritage–listed medieval city centre
- ◢ Summer rafting on the River Aare
- ◢ Marking time at the Zeitglockenturm
- ◢ The ornate Bundeshäuser
- ◢ The Bern Onion Market
- ◢ Kunstmuseum's collection, including Picasso and Paul Klee
- ◢ Swimming in the open-air, riverside Marzili pools
- ◢ The Art Deco Hotel Belle Epoque
- ◢ Reitschule's alternative scene
- ◢ Toblerone chocolate

WEAKNESSES

- ◢ An abundance of local rules and regulations

GOLD STAR

Stupendously vertiginous views of the medieval town, River Aare and Berner Alps from the lofty spire of Bern's Gothic 15th-century Münster.

STARRING ROLE IN...

- ◢ *On Her Majesty's Secret Service* (1969)
- ◢ Ferdinand Hodler's artwork

See a bird's-eye view of Bern from the Münster's spire.

Eat fondue with *rösti* (fried potatoes).

Drink Bärner Müntschi (Bern's kiss) beer or Apenzeller Alpenbitter (Alpine bitters), a liquor made from the essences of 67 flowers and roots.

Do look into someone's eyes when you chink glasses.

Watch twirling figurines mark time's passing on the Zeitglockenturm.

Buy a Swiss army knife.

After dark head to the Reitschule and its vibrant alternative arts scene.

CHRIS CLOSE / GETTY IMAGES

THE SOCIAL WHIRL IN CENTRAL BERN ON A SPRING EVENING.

FAIRYTALE BEAUTY – THE CHURCH OF SANTA MARIA OVERLOOKS LAKE BLED WITH THE JULIAN ALPS IN THE BACKGROUND.

Bled

DATE OF BIRTH EARLY IRON AGE; BLED WAS THE SITE OF A HALLSTATT SETTLEMENT **ADDRESS** SLOVENIA (MAP 5, N3) **HEIGHT** 501M **POPULATION** 10,900 **LONELY PLANET RANKING** 090

With its emerald-green lake, islet with picture-postcard church, medieval castle clinging to a rocky cliff and some of the highest peaks of the Julian Alps and the Karavanke Mountains as a backdrop, Bled is simply magical.

ANATOMY

Surrounded by mountains, Bled's focus is its idyllic 2km-long lake, its beauty enhanced by a tiny island with a red-and-white-spired belfry rising above the trees. The built-up area to the northeast is the largest of the settlements located around the lake and contains most of the hotels. Bled's main road, Ljubljanska cesta, runs eastward from here. Bled is served by a bus station and two train stations.

PEOPLE

Slovenes are polyglots, and virtually everyone in the resort town of Bled speaks some English, German and/or Italian.

TYPICAL BLED CITIZEN

For centuries Bled was a mecca for pilgrims, and since the 19th century it has attracted hordes of tourists and health devotees – you're far more likely to encounter visitors than locals. There's nothing fuddy-duddy about Bled, but given that it is a spa town renowned for its curative waters, many of its visitors are, well, older. If you're lucky enough to find a real local, chances are they'll love a good polka and regular schnapps pick-me-ups. They will also be filled with pride at the achievements of the many world-class ski champions the mountains have produced. It is obvious, from the ship-shape state of the city, that its residents are eager to preserve its history.

DEFINING EXPERIENCE

Rising early to explore the lake at its most breathtaking before embarking on a romantic gondola trip to the island to wish for what you most desire on the wishing bell, then enjoying a lunch of good home-cooked food and local wine at a countryside inn.

WITH GONDOLA RIDES INCLUDED, WEDDINGS ON PICTURESQUE BLED ISLAND ARE INCREASINGLY POPULAR.

STRENGTHS

- The country's best golf course, and one of Europe's most beautiful
- Bled's precipitous medieval castle
- Hikes galore
- Ice skating on the lake in winter
- Trips on the Old Timer vintage steam train
- Crystal-clear warm water
- Hot-air ballooning over the town
- The Okarina Folk Festival of folk and world music
- Summertime concerts at the castle, Festival Hall and the parish church
- Excellent bread, especially the braided loaves at Christmas
- Clean air and mountain light
- Polka dancing
- A plethora of outdoor activities
- Panoramic flights in Cessna 172s
- Charming towns such as Radovljica – an easy day trip away

WEAKNESSES

- The congestion at the top of Slovenia's highest peak, Triglav
- Droves of tourists in midsummer
- Leaving

GOLD STAR

The spectacular Vintgar Gorge, just west and north of Bled, is a peaceful bit of beauty hidden by steep canyons. A wooden walkway built in 1893 hugs the rock walls of the gorge for 1600m along the Radovna River, crisscrossing the raging torrent four times over rapids, waterfalls and pools before reaching the 13m-high Šum Waterfall.

BLED CASTLE HAS MORE THAN 1000 YEARS OF HISTORY AND A VIEW TO DIE FOR.

STARRING ROLE IN...

◢ The poetry of France Prešeren

See the stunning view from the summit of Velika Osojnica – over the lake, island and dramatic castle, with the peaks of the Karavanke in the background.

Eat Bled's culinary speciality, *kremna rezina* (cream cake), a layer of vanilla custard topped with whipped cream and sandwiched neatly between two layers of flaky pastry.

Drink Zlatorog, Slovenia's best *pivo* (beer), at the friendly Pub Bled, the town's late-night venue of choice.

Do the polka – it only takes three minutes to learn.

Watch the clouds roll by as you twirl around the lake or head to the castle in a horse-drawn carriage.

Buy a traditional beehive panel illustrated with folk motifs.

Do ring the wishing bell in the 15th-century belfry of Bled island's baroque church to ask a favour.

After dark try your luck at the gaming tables of Casino Bled.

Bogotá

DATE OF BIRTH PRE-COLUMBIAN; INHABITED BY ONE OF THE MOST ADVANCED PRE-COLUMBIAN INDIAN GROUPS, THE MUISCA
ADDRESS COLOMBIA (MAP 2, O10) **HEIGHT** 2645M **SIZE** 25 SQ KM
POPULATION 7.4 MILLION (CITY); 10.1 MILLION (METRO AREA)
LONELY PLANET RANKING 155

Bogotá is a city of futuristic architecture, a vibrant and diverse cultural and intellectual life, splendid colonial churches and brilliant museums.

ANATOMY

Bogotá is bordered to the east by a mountain range topped by the two peaks of Monserrate and Guadalupe. Bogotá's northern sector consists mainly of upmarket residential districts, while the city's southern part is a vast spread of undistinguished lower-income suburbs, culminating in the vast shanty towns on the southernmost outskirts. The urban bus service TransMilenio is efficient and fast.

PEOPLE

About three-quarters of the population is of mixed blood, composed mainly of mestizos (of mixed Spanish and indigenous heritage) and mulattos (with one black and one white parent). There are also small groups of *zambos* (of African-Indian blood) and Indians. Spanish is the official language.

TYPICAL BOGOTANO

Bogotanos are courteous, polite and hospitable. Everyday life is remarkably open and public, and much family life takes place outside the home: in front of the house, in the street, in a bar or at the market. As a result Colombians may seem indiscreet about their behaviour in public places. Someone in a bar may discuss personal problems at a volume that allows all the patrons to follow the conversation. A driver may urinate on the tyre of his bus after he has stopped for a break on the road. Couples hug and kiss passionately in parks and in the street.

DEFINING EXPERIENECE

Strolling around La Candelaria, Bogotá's historic quarter, and stopping off for a *santafereño* (hot chocolate served with cheese and local bread) at Pastelería Florida, then exploring the Museo del Oro (Gold Museum), before conducting a crawl around the pubs and discos of Zona Rosa.

JOHN COLETTI / GETTY IMAGES

OLD AND NEW – BOGOTÁ CONFOUNDS EXPECTATIONS.

Museo del Oro

STRENGTHS

- ◢ Friendliness of the locals
- ◢ Museo del Oro
- ◢ Donación Botero
- ◢ Festival Iberoamericano de Teatro de Bogotá – one of the best theatre festivals in Latin America
- ◢ Colonial churches such as the Iglesia Museo de Santa Clara
- ◢ The nightlife
- ◢ Amazing variety of fruits, some of which are endemic to the country
- ◢ Futuristic architecture
- ◢ El Señor Caído (the Fallen Christ) statue
- ◢ Intellectual life

WEAKNESSES

- ◢ Guerrillas
- ◢ Cocaine thugs
- ◢ Vast shantytowns
- ◢ Street urchins

GOLD STAR

The view of the city from the top of Cerro de Monserrate – on a clear day spot Los Nevados, the volcanic range in the Cordillera Central, 135km away, noted for the symmetrical cone of the Nevado del Tolima.

STARRING ROLE IN...

- ◢ *Maria Full of Grace* (2004)
- ◢ *El Rey* (The King, 2004)
- ◢ *One Hundred Years of Solitude* by Gabriel García Márquez

See more than 34,000 gold pieces from all the major pre-Hispanic cultures in Colombia at the gold museum, Museo del Oro.

Eat the Bogotano speciality *ajiaco* (soup made with chicken and potato) at Restaurante La Pola.

Drink the excellent *tinto* (a small cup of black coffee) – the number one drink in Bogotá – first thing in the morning.

Do go to Galería Café Libro, a popular *salsoteca* (salsa nightclub) always packed with salsa fans.

Watch a local theatre production at the inspiring Teatro de la Candelaria.

Buy emeralds at a *joyería* (jewellery shop) in the city centre.

After dark head to Gótica, a large nightclub offering different musical ambiences on different levels, including salsa, techno and trance.

POMP AND CEREMONY ACCOMPANY THE CHANGING OF THE GUARD AT PLAZA DE BOLÍVAR.

SIZE MATTERS – BRATISLAVA CASTLE WAS A KEY POINT BETWEEN THE ALPS AND THE CARPATHIANS.

Bratislava

NICKNAME: BEAUTY ON THE DANUBE **DATE OF BIRTH:** 1919 AND
AGAIN IN 1993; BRATISLAVA WAS THEN NAMED THE CAPITAL OF
THE NEWLY INDEPENDENT SLOVAK REPUBLIC (SEPARATED FROM
CZECHOSLOVAKIA, NOW THE CZECH REPUBLIC) **ADDRESS:** SLOVAKIA
(MAP 5, O2) **HEIGHT:** 153M **SIZE:** 367 SQ KM **POPULATION:** 462,000
LONELY PLANET RANKING: 110

A vibrant, pulsing city encapsulating the best of urban Slovakia, Bratislava's vibrant core lies beneath the capital's plain exterior – here you can immerse yourself in the country's finest museums, choose from an ever-increasing array of international cuisine and party till dawn in some of Eastern Europe's most progressive bars and clubs.

ANATOMY

The Staré Město (Old Town), which sits on the north bank of the Danube, holds the city's historical heart and its life. A compact strip of cafés, restaurants and nightclubs fills this pedestrianised 500-sq-metre area. On a clear day from the castle hill, you can see Hungary and Austria, while the new town spreads northeastwards to the bland, high-rise suburbs beyond. South, across the Danube via the striking hypermodern Nový most (New Bridge), is the model socialist suburb of Petržalka, home to some 117,000 Bratislavans. Squeezed between the castle and the old town is what is left of the old Jewish quarter, pulled down to accommodate the bridge. There is an extensive public transport system of trams, buses and trolleybuses.

PEOPLE

Having once been joined to the Czech Republic, Bratislava shares much of its history and people with that country. The persecution of Jewish Slovaks during WWII is silently expressed in every rebuilt stone – Nový most was built over the bulldozed remains of the city's old Jewish quarter. The slow rise of tourism and the influence of communism have kept this city fairly monoculturally Slovak, though international music, films and languages are now served up alongside old Slovak favourites.

PEOPLE-WATCHING ON HLAVNÉ NÁMESTIE, A CENTRAL SQUARE, CAN YIELD SURPRISES.

TYPICAL BRATISLAVAN

Bratislavans are young, energetic Slovaks who work and play hard, enjoying the increasing buzz of their country's capital. They are business-minded and straightforward – a Bratislavan knows what he or she wants, that's why they are there. They are exceedingly polite, especially on public transport. They make a definite distinction between those who take their country seriously and those who don't. A troubled history only reinforces their sense of national identity and pride.

DEFINING EXPERIENCE

Taking an afternoon stroll through the old town to the Bratislava castle (stopping off at the excellent Museum of Jewish Culture on the way), enjoying a glass of wine and a meal at Hradná Vináreň before joining a film club for a night of well-trodden classics, and then dancing at Hlbočina till dawn.

STRENGTHS

- The old town
- Magnificent views
- Devin Castle's ruins
- Easy access to Hungary and Austria
- Great clubs
- Danubiana Meulensteen
- The river cruise
- Pedestrian-friendly streets
- Slovak National Gallery
- The public transport system
- The Bratislava Lyre (festival)
- September jazz days

DEVÍN CASTLE, NOW A RUIN, GUARDED THE APPROACH TO THE DANUBE RIVER.

WEAKNESSES

- ◢ Communist-era architecture
- ◢ Strict driving rules
- ◢ Pickpockets
- ◢ Sky-high suburban sprawl

GOLD STAR

Superb museums – the Museum of Folk Music, the Museum of Clocks, the Decorative Arts Museum and the Museum of Jewish Culture, to name just a few.

STARRING ROLE IN...

- ◢ *The Year of the Frog* by Martin M Simecka

See the *Watcher*, the *Frenchman* and the *Photographer* – Bratislava's quirky and very photogenic bronze statues.

Eat Hradná Vináreň's *bryndzové halušky* (potato dumpling dish) at the candlelit tables overlooking the old town.

Drink crisp Slovak beer while soaking up the jazzy atmosphere of the underground Nu Spirit.

Do escape the summer heat by hiring a rowing boat at Zlaté piesky (Golden Sands) lake resort.

Watch the live summer performances at the Museum of Folk Music.

Buy Slovakian folk handicrafts and souvenirs at Uľuv.

After dark take in an opera that rivals anything in Europe at the lush Slovak National Theatre.

Bridgetown

NICKNAME LITTLE ENGLAND **DATE OF BIRTH** 1628; FOUNDED BY THE BRITISH – PURPORTEDLY THE ONLY EVIDENCE OF PREVIOUS INDIGENOUS OCCUPATION WAS A SIMPLE BRIDGE (THAT PUT THE 'BRIDGE' IN BRIDGETOWN) SPANNING THE CONSTITUTION RIVER **ADDRESS** BARBADOS (MAP 3, E2) **HEIGHT** 55M **POPULATION** 101,000 **LONELY PLANET RANKING** 156

Amid the white-sand and turquoise-water tropical idyll, Barbados' only city is a modern and colonial architectural mishmash with side streets sprinkled with rum shops and chattel houses.

ANATOMY

Bridgetown is a busy commercial city set on Carlisle Bay, developed around an inlet known as the Careenage. True to the island's British heritage, there are obelisks, Gothic Parliament buildings and an Anglican cathedral. Broad and Swan Sts are thick with vendors. The city is easily covered on foot and taxis can be hailed on the street.

PEOPLE

Bajan culture displays trappings of British life, such as cricket, polo and horse racing, yet on closer examination, Barbados is deeply rooted in Afro-Caribbean tradition. The typical Bridgetown citizen's roots are African, with the rest made up of a mix of English, Scottish and East Indian cultures. Religions observed are Protestantism (the majority), Roman Catholicism and others. Just under a fifth of people are atheists.

TYPICAL BRIDGETOWN CITIZEN

Like other Caribbean cultures, Bridgetown's citizens are conservative but the bond with London has made Barbados more open-minded than its neighbours. Special events are carried out with pomp and ceremony, and older ladies are fond of donning prim little hats. For all its surface 'Britishness', family life, food, music and dress have more in common with the Windward Islands than West London.

DEFINING EXPERIENCE

Snorkelling the coral-encrusted tug *Berwyn* in Carlisle Bay and lazing on Pebbles Beach followed by an afternoon trip of spiritual healing, calypso-cocktail style, at the Malibu beachfront distillery.

SALTY SCRUB – HORSES ARE WASHED IN THE SEA OFF BRIDGETOWN'S BEACH.

STRENGTHS

- ◢ Congaline Carnival
- ◢ Rum!
- ◢ Paynes Bay Beach
- ◢ Barbados Museum
- ◢ Crop-Over Festival
- ◢ Flying-fish sandwiches
- ◢ Calypso rhythms
- ◢ Harry Bayley Observatory
- ◢ Workin' up (dancing)
- ◢ St Michael's Cathedral

WEAKNESSES

- ◢ Sparse accommodation
- ◢ A somewhat macho culture
- ◢ Densely populated beaches
- ◢ Berthing 'super cruise ships'
- ◢ The well-oiled pre-fab tourist machine
- ◢ Ship pollution

GOLD STAR

'British' Bridgetown is West Indian to the core – with calypso rhythms and its own quirky characteristics, it has enough local flavour to feel 'exotic' yet has enough of the familiar to feel comfortable.

STARRING ROLE IN...

- ◢ *The Castle of My Skin* by George Lamming
- ◢ *Treasures of Barbados* by Henry Fraser
- ◢ *Island in the Sun* (1957)

See engaging displays on all aspects of Bajan history, with exhibits on early indigenous inhabitants, slavery, emancipation, military history and plantation-house furniture at the excellent Barbados Museum.

Eat local specialities flying fish and coconut prawn (shrimp) at the Rusty Pelican – the 2nd-floor balcony affords a pleasant view over the Careenage.

Drink with the locals at Bridgetown's many rollicking rum shops along Baxter Rd, just north of the centre.

Do tussle with the crowds on the pristine white sands of Pebbles Beach on Carlisle Bay.

Watch world-class cricket at Kensington Oval, Fontabelle.

Buy pottery, leather, wood and fabric handicrafts at Pelican Craft Village.

After dark view the night sky from the Harry Bayley Observatory.

CARIBBEAN FRUIT FOR SALE ON BRIDGETOWN'S STREETS.

LOCALS RENDEZVOUS BENEATH THE CLASSICAL COLUMNS OF LA BOURSE.

Brussels

DATE OF BIRTH AD 695; WITH A SETTLEMENT CALLED BRUOCSELLA, ALTHOUGH NEOLITHIC SETTLERS WERE THERE FROM AROUND 2250 BC **ADDRESS** BELGIUM (MAP 4, H9) **HEIGHT** 100M **SIZE** 161 SQ KM **POPULATION** 1.1 MILLION (CITY); 1.8 MILLION (METRO AREA) **LONELY PLANET RANKING** 093

Purveyor of gourmet treats such as mussels, beer and chocolate, capital of Europe, and showcase for cobbled streets and extravagant architecture, Brussels is more than a Eurocrat conference room.

ANATOMY

The Ring, a large motorway, encircles the city while a polygon of busy boulevards called the Petit (Small) Ring hugs the old centre. Central Brussels is made up of the Lower Town and the Upper Town. The former is Brussels' medieval heart, crisscrossed with cobbled streets anchored in the Grand Place. The Upper Town is the old aristocratic quarter, lined with wide boulevards. The EU area, towered over by the European Parliament and other high-rises, is to the east. The metro contains a chapel, bars and artworks, as well as trains.

PEOPLE

Bilingual Brussels is in Flemish-speaking Flanders, yet the majority of the population speaks French. The city is home to Europeans, Arabs and Africans, mostly from the former Belgian colony of the Congo. Around three-quarters of Belgians are Catholic.

TYPICAL BRUSSELS CITIZEN

Belgians dislike rules but can be pedantic. They insist on efficiency yet seem unable to finish building projects on time. Nervous about change, they embrace technology. They are staunchly enamoured of the monarchy. Belgians come across as severe but have a cheeky sense of humour, evidenced by their treatment of the symbol of Brussels, Mannekin Pis, a statue of a naked boy that they dress up.

DEFINING EXPERIENCE

Spending your pennies on Avenue Louise, then exploring Ixelles' Art Nouveau streets before doing a circuit of the Musée Horta and relaxing with a beer in an old Brussels pub.

TRADITIONAL BELGIAN FOLK MUSICIANS IN FRONT OF ST-JACQUES-SUR-COUDENBERG CHURCH.

LIGHTS COME ON AS EVENING FALLS ON ST GORIK'S SQ AND WORKERS WIND DOWN WITH AN APERITIF.

THE TOWER OF BRUSSELS'S TOWN HALL.

STRENGTHS

- Free museums on the first Wednesday of the month
- Grand Place
- Centre Belge de la Bande Dessinée (Belgian Comic Strip Centre)
- Cathédrale des Sts Michel et Gudule
- Godiva and Neuhaus chocolates
- Belgian beer, waffles and *moules et frites* (mussels and chips)
- Window boxes crammed with geraniums
- Gothic Hôtel de Ville
- Musée Bruxellois de la Gueuze (the old Cantillon Brewery)
- Parc de Bruxelles
- Musées Royaux des Beaux-Arts de Belgique
- Art Nouveau Ixelles
- Traditional pubs

WEAKNESSES

- Expensive restaurants around Grand Place
- Ineffectiveness of pedestrian crossings
- Disappointing contemporary architecture
- Canine emissions

GOLD STAR

Beer – Belgium produces between 500 and 800 brews.

STARRING ROLE IN...

- *Meisje* (2002)
- *La vie sexuelle des Belges* (The Sexual Life of the Belgians, 1994)
- *Plenty* (1985)
- *Far West* (1973)
- *The good beer guide to Belgium & Holland* by Tim Webb

See the captivating façades of the Hôtel de Ville (town hall) and the guildhalls on the Grand Place.

Eat *moules et frites* at local favourite, Aux Armes de Bruxelles.

Drink a 3L magnum of Duvel at Beer Mania (perhaps not by yourself).

Do admire fascinating zoological exhibits while pondering Belgium's actions in the Congo at the Musée Royal de l'Afrique Centrale.

Watch the carpet of 800,000 begonias being laid in the Grand Place in August.

Buy slabs of delectable chocolate in Neuhaus and forget that diet.

After dark head to Music Village to hear Belgian blues singers and young European talent.

Bucharest

DATE OF BIRTH 70 BC; GETO-DACIAN TRIBES INHABITED THE
REGION THAT IS NOW MODERN-DAY BUCHAREST
ADDRESS ROMANIA (MAP 5, S4) **HEIGHT** 92M **SIZE** 228 SQ KM
POPULATION 1.9 MILLION **LONELY PLANET RANKING** 141

Emerging from a tumultuous and sometimes tragic past, Bucharest is blossoming into one of Eastern Europe's most cosmopolitan cities, where a flourishing music scene and lively nightlife complement the rich historical feel of the city.

ANATOMY

Despite two devastating earthquakes and allied bombings in WWII, much of Bucharest's rich and chequered history is preserved in the blend of neoclassical architecture, Romanian Orthodox churches, Parisian-style parks and the stony-faced buildings of the Communist era, including the monstrous Palace of Parliament. The main attractions cluster in the heart of the city and are easily accessible via Bucharest's transit system – one of the largest in Central and Eastern Europe – which includes buses, trolleybuses, trams and the underground urban railway, the Metro.

PEOPLE

The capital's population mirrors that of the nation, with a majority of Romanian citizens. The remaining population is made up of Hungarians, Roma (formerly known as Gypsies), Germans and Ukrainians. The official language is Romanian and the vast majority of the citizens follow the Eastern (Romanian) Orthodox religion.

TYPICAL BUCHAREST CITIZEN

With a low unemployment rate most locals work and, as Bucharest is the least expensive city in Europe, the citizens of the post-Communist capital are also voracious consumers. They love to show-pony the latest-model cars in the streets of the capital, and take great pride in their personal appearance – shopping is an increasingly popular pastime. Etiquette is important, and affectionate public embraces are common. They are both a traditional and dynamic population, with a resilience and optimism born of hard-won freedom.

RICHARD I'ANSON / GETTY IMAGES

PATRIARCHAL CATHEDRAL IS THE CENTREPIECE OF THE ROMANIAN ORTHODOX FAITH.

ENJOY A SPOT OF SHOPPING AT THE TRADITIONAL CITY MARKETS.

DEFINING EXPERIENCE

Breathing in the morning air atop the Triumphal Arch, then catching a train to the monastery by Snagov Lake to see the supposed tomb of Dracula before heading back into town to dine with expats on the terrace of the decadent Athénée Palace Hilton, and ending the evening with some sexy dance moves at Cuban club Salsa 2.

STRENGTHS

- ◢ Live music
- ◢ Ice skating on lakes in winter
- ◢ Greenery of the urban parklands
- ◢ Mainstream and art-house cinemas
- ◢ History round every corner
- ◢ Variety of pubs, clubs and cafés
- ◢ Friendly locals
- ◢ Sailing across Herăstrău Lake in summer
- ◢ Selection of tasty, hearty local and international cuisine
- ◢ Local beer and wine
- ◢ Museum of the Romanian Peasant
- ◢ Stavropoleos Church
- ◢ Patriarchal Cathedral
- ◢ Triumphal Arch

WEAKNESSES

- ◢ Stray dogs
- ◢ Daredevil drivers and the worst potholes in Romania
- ◢ State buses for long-distance travelling
- ◢ Poorly signposted train stations
- ◢ Flirty taxi drivers (ladies: take the back seat)
- ◢ Crowded transit system during peak hour

MUSIC TAKES ON A LIFE OF ITS OWN IN BUCHAREST'S LIVE MUSIC VENUES.

GOLD STAR

After-dark music scene – whether it's checking out live rock, getting into the traditional sounds, dancing to your favourite '70s tunes, toe-tapping at a jazz bar or a more refined experience with the George Enescu Philharmonic Orchestra, there is something for all tastes in Bucharest. Plugging into the local scene is easy – advertisements posted around the city promote clubs and hot DJs.

STARRING ROLE IN...

- ◢ *Philanthropy* (2002)
- ◢ *The Wild Dogs* (2002)
- ◢ *Children Underground* (2000)

See the crystal chandelier in the decadent Palace of Parliament that weighs 2.5 tonnes.

Eat exquisite French/Thai fusion at Balthazar, the best and hippest restaurant in the city.

Drink Guinness at the Dubliner as you swap stories with other travellers.

Do head into the residential areas of Bucharest to see the old-style Bucharest housing – before the apartment blocks of Ceauşescu's era.

Watch some fine jazz acts at the intimate Green Hours 22 Jazz Club.

Buy a bottle of the famous anti-ageing magic potion – Gerovital face cream – (allegedly used by Elizabeth Taylor and JFK) available at pharmacies.

After dark soak up the flavour of Romania's cultural scene with a ballet performance at the Opera House.

205

Budapest

NICKNAME PARIS OF EASTERN EUROPE **DATE OF BIRTH** 1873; WHEN HILLY, RESIDENTIAL BUDA AND HISTORIC ÓBUDA ON THE WESTERN BANK OF THE DANUBE RIVER MERGED WITH FLAT, INDUSTRIAL PEST ON THE EAST TO FORM WHAT WAS AT FIRST CALLED PEST-BUDA **ADDRESS** HUNGARY (MAP 5, P2) **HEIGHT** 139M **SIZE** 525 SQ KM **POPULATION** 1.7 MILLION (CITY); 3.2 MILLION (METRO AREA) **LONELY PLANET RANKING** 033

Beautiful Budapest has a complex history, amazing architecture and a rich cultural heritage.

ANATOMY

Budapest is a sprawling city. Two ring roads – Nagykörút (the big one) and the semicircular Kiskörút (the little ring road) – link three of the bridges across the Danube and essentially define central Pest. It is divided into 23 *kerület* (districts), which usually have traditional names such as Lipótváros (Leopold Town) in district XIII or Víziváros (Watertown) in district I. The Roman numeral appearing before each street address signifies the district. Budapest has an ageing but safe, inexpensive and efficient public-transport system.

PEOPLE

With just under two million inhabitants, Budapest is home to one-fifth of the national population. Most are Magyars, an Asiatic people who do not speak an Indo-European language and make up the vast majority of Hungary's 10 million people. Life expectancy is low by European standards: about 69 years for men and 77 for women.

TYPICAL BUDAPESTER

Well educated and reserved, Budapesters are very polite, shake hands profusely on greeting, love a drink and are comfortable with public displays of affection. In summer, going topless is almost the norm for women in parks. Citizens of all ages love to overindulge their dogs.

DEFINING EXPERIENCE

Taking in the views at Castle Hill, exploring the Old Town on foot or in a horse-drawn carriage, bathing at the cathedral-like Gellért Baths, visiting the Royal Palace and, finally, dining at Menza, whose parody of Communist style (a *menza* was a state-run canteen) gives insight as to what much of '70s Budapest looked like – well into the '90s.

MARTIN MOOS / GETTY IMAGES

THE OPULENT INTERIOR OF THE NEO-RENAISSANCE OPERA HOUSE, DESIGNED IN 1884.

STRENGTHS

◢ Hungarian State Opera
◢ Thermal baths
◢ *Kertek* (outdoor 'garden clubs')
◢ The Basilica of St Stephen
◢ Aquincum Museum
◢ Buda Castle Labyrinth
◢ The bridges of Budapest
◢ Wonderfully restored Great Market Hall
◢ Hungarian National Museum
◢ House of Hungarian Photographers
◢ Applied Arts Museum

WEAKNESSES

◢ Margaret Island after dark
◢ 'Accidentally' inflated restaurant bills and other scams
◢ Hailing cabs
◢ Polluting waste created by the Soviet military
◢ Scapegoating of Hungarian Roma (formerly known as Gypsies)

GOLD STAR

The view from Fisherman's Bastion on Castle Hill.

STARRING ROLE IN...

◢ *A Life in Suitcases* (2005)
◢ *Underworld* (2003)
◢ *Napoleon* (2002)
◢ *Spy Game* (2001)
◢ *Werckmeister Harmonies* (2000)
◢ *Evita* (1996)

See the two icons of Hungarian nationhood: the crown of St Stephen in the Parliament building and the saint-king's remains in the Basilica of St Stephen.

Eat excellent goose-liver dishes at the elegant Kisbuda Gyöngye.

Drink coffee at Gerbeaud, the most famous of Budapest's cafés, bar none.

Do have a soak at any of the city's celebrated thermal baths, especially the Gellért, Rudas or Széchenyi.

Watch and listen to opera in incredibly rich surrounds at the beautiful neo-Renaissance Hungarian State Opera House.

Buy hot salami, paprika, a bottle of boutique Hungarian wine and some colourful folk embroidery.

After dark head to a *táncház* (dance house) to hear Hungarian music.

DRESSED TO IMPRESS IN TRADITIONAL HUNGARIAN EMBROIDERY.

UNDER VAJDAHUNYAD CASTLE, SPEED SKATERS WHIZZ AROUND THE LAKE AT SZÉCHENYI PARK.

THE CLASSICAL OPULENCE OF THE GELLÉRT THERMAL BATHS, AN OTHERWORLDLY OASIS IN THE HEART OF THE METROPOLIS.

ARGENTINIAN SOCCER MATCHES ARE NO PLACE FOR THE FAINT-HEARTED – THESE ARE THE COLOURS OF LOCAL TEAM BOCA JUNIORS.

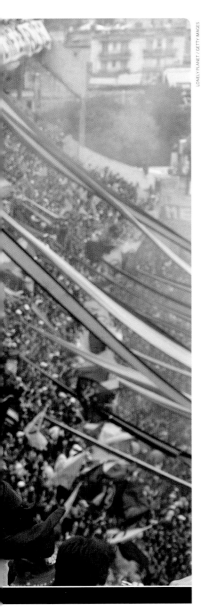

Buenos Aires

NICKNAME PARIS OF THE SOUTH **DATE OF BIRTH** 1536; FOUNDED AS SANTA MARÍA DEL BUEN AIRE (ST MARY OF THE GOOD AIR) BY SPANISH SAILOR PEDRO DE MENDOZA **ADDRESS** ARGENTINA (MAP 3, E14) **HEIGHT** 27M **SIZE** 200 SQ KM **POPULATION** 3 MILLION (CITY); 12.8 MILLION (METRO AREA) **LONELY PLANET RANKING** 016

One of the world's most seductive, sophisticated and cool cities, Buenos Aires is the pounding cultural and economic heart of Argentina.

ANATOMY

The city sits beside the Atlantic on the edge of a fertile pampas by the River Plate. It is Argentina's richest city with one of the highest skyscraper counts anywhere. Each of its 47 *barrios* (neighbourhoods) has its own idiosyncrasies. Parkland, boulevards and graceful historic architecture lend the city a European edge. The rail network services the suburbs, while the Subte (Underground) is South America's oldest subway and an efficient way to get around. Buses ply the streets.

PEOPLE

Greater Buenos Aires holds two-fifths of Argentina's population; most are descended from Spanish and Italian immigrants. The German, British, Jewish, Eastern European and Middle Eastern communities, known collectively as *turcos*. Mestizos (of mixed Native Indian and European heritage) are a growing minority, making up a quarter of the population. The Spanish spoken is rhythmically closer to Italian.

TYPICAL PORTEÑO

Locals call themselves *porteños* (port people) and have a reputation outside Buenos Aires for being arrogant know-it-alls. They are proud of their city and sing its praises at length. Whatever the occasion they are always meticulously turned out. They work hard and play harder, and exude a seductive charisma through their uniquely lyrical language.

DEFINING EXPERIENCE

Feeling the world change as you traverse different neighbourhoods, mingling with the elite around the Cementerio de la Recoleta, taking a cheeky siesta in one of Palermo's parks, catching your breath on the riverside patio at club Mint, wandering 'home' via Plaza Serrano as the sun rises, amazed at how good the *porteños* still manage to look.

COLOURFUL AND HOT – AND THAT'S JUST OUTSIDE THE WALLS!

ARGENTINE FLAGS FLUTTER BENEATH THE IMPASSIVE PIRAMIDE DE MAYO MONUMENT.

EUROPEAN SOUNDS IN SOUTH AMERICA.

STRENGTHS

- Plaza de Mayo
- Buenos Aires International Tango Festival
- Safe neighbourhoods
- Neighbourhood diversity
- Unpredictable
- Beautiful people
- Cementerio de la Recoleta
- Succulent beef steaks
- Friendly locals
- Parks
- Botanical Gardens
- Theatre

WEAKNESSES

- Air pollution
- Crowded streets
- A few dodgy neighbourhoods
- Flooding
- Unemployment

GOLD STAR

Nightlife – the *boliches* (discos) are the heart of the city's world-famous nightlife. Dress hot, dance cool and arrive well after 2am.

STARRING ROLE IN...

- *Evita* (1996)
- *Motorcycle Diaries* (2004)
- *Labyrinths* by Jorge Luis Borges

See Buenos Aires' hip-shakin' young things at Cocoliche, an electronic-music paradise based in a glamorous old mansion.

Eat *flan casera* (homemade flan) at Munich Recoleta, where legendary poet Jorge Luis Borges was once a regular.

Drink maté at the trendy Nucha café.

Do hire a bicycle one weekend and check out the city's parks, including the Reserva Ecológica Costanera Sur.

Watch majestic mayhem unfold at a Boca Juniors versus River Plate *fútbol* (football) match.

Buy outrageous sexy and crazy fashion from the weird and wonderful collection at Objeto.

After dark funk it up to some wicked hip-hop beats at Club 69.

Bukhara

DATE OF BIRTH AD 900; WHEN IT WAS THE CAPITAL OF THE SAMANID STATE AND CENTRAL ASIA'S RELIGIOUS AND CULTURAL HEART **ADDRESS** UZBEKISTAN (MAP 8, H2) **HEIGHT** 230M **POPULATION** 263,000 **LONELY PLANET RANKING** 146

Central Asia's holiest city and a place uniquely preserved from pre-Russian Turkistan, Bukhara is a sprawl of truly fascinating Islamic architecture.

ANATOMY

The *shakhristan* (old town) lies at the centre of sprawling modern Bukhara and its streets and squares probably haven't changed much in two centuries. The very centre of the city is the Lyabi-Hauz, a square with a pool in the middle of it (Lyabi-Hauz means 'around the pool' in Tajik) where people congregate for tea and conversation. Buses and taxis service the city.

PEOPLE

Bukhara is primarily Uzbek, but also has significant numbers of Tajiks and other Central Asian ethnic communities.

TYPICAL BUKHARAN

The pride the locals take in their city is hard to overstate. After years of neglect by the Soviet government, for whom the city represented Islam in all its counter-revolutionary glory, Bukhara's recovery since independence in the early 1990s has been quite amazing. A restoration program has made the city a highlight of Central Asia. Bukharans are conservative but generally very hospitable and kindly people who are always happy to see visitors in their ancient city.

DEFINING EXPERIENCE

Drinking tea by the Lyabi-Hauz and having a quiet chat in the shade as you watch the city bustle go on about you.

STRENGTHS

◢ Fascinating architecture
◢ The sheer scale and awe-inspiring devotion of the mosques and *medressas* (Islamic academies)
◢ Extremely open and welcoming attitude to tourists

BACK TO SCHOOL IN BUKHARA.

SHAPING UP – UZBEKISTAN IS A COUNTRY RICH IN SPORTING ACHIEVEMENT.

PETER TURNLEY / CORBIS

WEAKNESSES

⊿ Pushy children selling souvenirs and begging
⊿ The extreme heat and dust in summer
⊿ The good restaurants in the old town are block-booked by tour
groups for months throughout the summer

GOLD STAR

The Char Minar, the gatehouse of a long-gone Bukhara *medressa* – this is one of the most perfect buildings anywhere in the world, surely?

STARRING ROLE IN...

⊿ Bukhara has yet to grace the silver screen in any major way, although when a city is as superbly preserved as this, it can only be a matter of time.

See the Ark, the royal town-within-a-town, for an insight into how the all-powerful emirs of Bukhara lived.

Eat delicious and cheap *laghman* (noodles) and *samsas* (samosas) at the alfresco teahouses around the old town.

Drink tea in the blissful quiet of a summer afternoon by the Lyabi-Hauz.

Do climb the astonishing Kalon Minaret for an amazing view – Genghis Khan was so impressed that he didn't destroy it.

Watch puppetry at the amateur theatre by the Lyabi-Hauz.

Buy jewellery, silk, carpets and trinkets from one of the fabulous bazaars.

After dark you'll be limited to a belly-dancing show or some beers in one of the few bars of the *shakhristan*.

PATTERNS THAT MATTER AT THE TENTMAKERS' SOUQ IN CAIRO.

Cairo

NICKNAME THE CITY OF A THOUSAND MINARETS **DATE OF BIRTH** AD 150; THE ROMAN BABYLON FORT WAS THE FIRST SETTLEMENT ON THE LOCATION OF MODERN CAIRO **ADDRESS** EGYPT (MAP 9,A3) **HEIGHT** 116M **SIZE** 214 SQ KM **POPULATION** 9.1 MILLION (CITY); 19.4 MILLION (METRO AREA) **LONELY PLANET RANKING** 194

Cairo dominates Egypt with one of the world's highest population densities. Its minarets dominate the skyline and ancient obelisks and extraordinary works of art greet you in the most unlikely places.

ANATOMY

Cairo is relatively easy to navigate. Islamic Cairo is the medieval centre of the city. Heading east, Downtown ends at Midan Ataba and the old but still kicking medieval heart of the city known as Islamic Cairo takes over. Bordering Downtown to the west is the Nile River, which is obstructed by two sizable islands. The more central of these, connected directly to Downtown by three bridges, is Gezira, home to the Cairo Tower and the Opera House complex. The west bank of the Nile is less historical and much more residential. Giza stretches some 20km west on either side of the long, straight road that ends at the foot of the pyramids. The metro is startlingly efficient, but the masses still use minibuses.

PEOPLE

More than a quarter of Egyptians live in Cairo, Africa's largest city. The majority of its population is Egyptian, with a small number of Bedouins, Nubians from Sudan and an almost negligible number of Greeks, Armenians, Italians and French. While Muslim is the official religion, around 10% of Cairenes are Coptic Christian.

TYPICAL CAIRENE

The people of Cairo are both curious and generous. They'll gladly help you across the maddening roads with cars that never stop for anything and at the same time ask you a million questions about where you're from and even offer to show you some ancient treasures that are hidden to tourists.

DEFINING EXPERIENCE

Smoking a *sheesha* (a tobacco water pipe, often flavoured with honey or

RUSH HOUR ON CAIRO'S SUBWAY – A MODERN SYSTEM SERVING AN ANCIENT CITY.

apple) surrounded by dusty gilt mirrors, tourists, travellers and locals alike at the renowned El Fishawi café in the Khan el-Khalili souq (market).

STRENGTHS

- Khan el-Khalili
- Pyramids and Sphinx at your doorstep
- The Egyptian Museum
- King Tutankhamun's relics
- The land of a million guides

WEAKNESSES

- Guides – they'll take you anywhere, as long as you visit a papyrus 'museum', jewellery shop, camel rental etc
- Cars that sink into the melting bitumen
- The heat in June
- Tourist police who, for a little baksheesh (tip), know where everything is
- Tourists falling out of tour buses at the Egyptian Museum wearing short shorts

GOLD STAR

The pyramids and the Sphinx – both larger and smaller than you could ever imagine, respectively.

STARRING ROLE IN...

- *Death on the Nile* (1978)
- *Gallipoli* (1981)
- *Malcolm X* (1992)
- *The Spy Who Loved Me* (1977)
- *The Ten Commandments* (1956)
- *The Purple Rose of Cairo* (1985)
- *The Cairo Trilogy: Palace Walk, Palace of Desire, Sugar Street* by

A LONE FIGURE POLISHES THE TILES IN THE BEAUTIFUL INTERIOR OF THE MAUSOLEUM OF BARQUQ.

Naguib Mahfouz
▲ *The Map of Love* by Ahdaf Soueif
▲ *Under the Same Sky – Rooftops in Cairo* by photographer Randa Shaath
▲ *Messages from Tahrir: Signs from Egypt's Revolution* by Karima Khalil
▲ *Irhal* Remy Essam's 2011 protest song that became the anthem of the revolution

---

See the pyramids during the heat of the day – you'll be guaranteed that there will be few tourists around and you can sit within the depths of Cheops listening only to the sound of your own beating heart.

Eat a great spread of felafel, salads, *fuul* (seasoned chickpeas), bread, tahini and omelettes at Akher Sa'a.

Drink *karkadeh* (hibiscus tea) – found everywhere.

Do get a Coptic cross tattooed on your wrist in the Coptic Christian quarter.

Watch feluccas sail down the Nile.

Buy pure jasmine oil in a hand-blown glass bottle from one of the many stalls in the Khan.

After dark check out the light-and-sound show at the pyramids after a spectacular sunset.

Cape Town

NICKNAME THE MOTHER CITY **DATE OF BIRTH** 1652; WHEN THE
DUTCH PULLED UP AT THE BASE OF TABLE MOUNTAIN AND
ESTABLISHED SOUTH AFRICA'S FIRST EUROPEAN SETTLEMENT
ADDRESS SOUTH AFRICA (MAP 7, A9) **HEIGHT** 17M **SIZE** 300 SQ KM
POPULATION 3.5 MILLION **LONELY PLANET RANKING** 009

**Even transient visitors can't help but devote
a few million brain cells to storing images of Cape
Town's grandeur, from its striking Table Mountain
backdrop to its glorious beaches and strange and
wonderful wildlife.**

ANATOMY
A major part of Cape Town's allure is the 1073m-high mountain slap-bang
in the centre of the 'City Bowl': Table Mountain and its attendant peaks
– Devil's Peak and Lion's Head – are Cape Town's most enduring image. If
you drive (or ride a bus) 70km south, you'll find the fabled Cape of Good
Hope. While Cape Town has a good rail and bus network, taxis, although
pricey, are well worth considering late at night.

PEOPLE
Of Cape Town's population, more than half are coloured: blacks account for
about a third of the total and whites and other groups comprise the
balance. In the Cape Town area three of South Africa's 11 official languages
are prominent: Afrikaans (spoken by many whites and coloureds), English
(spoken by nearly everyone) and Xhosa (spoken mainly by blacks).

TYPICAL CAPETONIAN
There is no such thing as a 'typical' Capetonian – the city's range of
cultures and ethnicities put paid to that. However, since the fall of
apartheid, all citizens, regardless of background, generally share a
political optimism. While Cape Town is reasonably safe, citizens living
in the townships on the Cape Flats endure a neighbourhood rife with
crime and poverty.

DEFINING EXPERIENCE
Hiking Table Mountain then making the exhilarating abseil down (lazy
bones could ride the cable car) before taking in a glorious Cape Town
sunset and South African wine or few on a harbour cruise of Table Bay.

FRANS LEMMENS / GETTY IMAGES

THE REGION AROUND CAPE TOWN PRODUCES WORLD-CLASS WINES OF ASTONISHING VALUE.

STRENGTHS

◢ Robben Island
◢ The Bo-Kaap
◢ Lively music and cultural scene
◢ Cape of Good Hope Nature Reserve
◢ District Six Museum
◢ Houses of Parliament
◢ Rust-en-Vreugd
◢ Kirstenbosch Botanical Gardens
◢ South African National Gallery

WEAKNESSES

◢ Rampant crime and poverty on the Cape Flats
◢ The wealthy indifference
◢ The black/white/coloured divide and mutual distrust

GOLD STAR

Hospitality – Cape Town's mix of trendy hostelries match those in any other cosmopolitan city, and, for all of the city's contradictions, you'll find Capetonians likable, (generally) open-minded and relaxed.

STARRING ROLE IN...

◢ *Long Walk to Freedom* by Nelson Mandela
◢ *In My Country* (2004)
◢ *Lord of War* (2005)
◢ *The Last Face* (2005)
◢ *Refuge* by Andrew Brown

See Unesco World Heritage Site Robben Island, used as a prison from the early days of the VOC (Dutch East India Company) right up until the first years of majority rule.

Eat at one of Madame Zingara's crowd-pleasing establishments.

Drink potent straw rum as you rock the kasbah Cape Town–style at Fez on Hout St – roundly toasted as the city's hippest bar.

Do forgo the cable car and hike up Table Mountain for an unforgettable view, taking the time to sniff over 1400 species of flowering plants.

Watch any one of Cape Town's three teams in the national soccer league.

Buy a colourful, highly patterned 'Madiba' shirt from Greenmarket Sq – as popularised by Nelson Mandela.

After dark pick up your own *djembe* drum and fold into the mesmerising rhythm of the drum circle at the Drum Café.

ADMIRING CAPE TOWN'S BEAUTIFUL HARBOUR FROM THE DECK OF A CATAMARAN.

SOUTH AFRICA'S FUTURE GENERATIONS HAVE HOPE.

AN AFTER-DARK AMBIENCE IN THE STYLISH METROPOLE HOTEL ON LONG ST.

THE URBAN JUMBLE OF CARACAS FLOWS ALONG THE CONTOURS OF THIS NARROW, FORESTED VALLEY.

Caracas

DATE OF BIRTH 1560; WHEN EXPLORER FRANCISCO FAJARDO
FOUNDED A SETTLEMENT, WHICH HE CALLED SAN FRANCISCO
ADDRESS VENEZUELA (MAP 3, D3) **HEIGHT** 1042M **SIZE** 78 SQ KM
POPULATION 5.9 MILLION (CITY); 6.5 MILLION (METRO AREA)
LONELY PLANET RANKING 148

The capital of Venezuela is a huge, vibrant, energetic South American city, bringing together the tremendously wealthy and the desperately poor.

ANATOMY

Caracas sprawls for 20km along a long and narrow coastal valley, bordered to the north by the verdant and refreshingly unpopulated Parque Nacional El Ávila. To the south it's a different story, with modern suburbs and precarious shantytowns invading the steep hillsides. The city's pride and joy, the metro, is fast, easy, well organised, clean and cheap. Caracas' bus system isn't bad either, covering all suburbs within the metropolitan area as well as major neighbouring localities.

PEOPLE

Three-quarters of the population is a blend of European, Indian and African ancestry, or any two of the three. The rest are whites, blacks and Indians. Spanish is the official language.

TYPICAL CARAQUEÑO

An estimated three-quarters of *caraqueño* families live below the poverty line. It's common for haphazardly built barrios (shantytowns) to sit directly alongside opulent hillside mansions. Despite this, everyday life is remarkably open and public and often takes place outside the home. People may dance to the tune of the car stereo in the street or drink a leisurely beer together on the sidewalk curb. Personal affairs are discussed loudly and without embarrassment. Of central importance to *caraqueños* is the family, and especially the mother figure. Young *caraqueños* almost always live with their families until they are married.

DEFINING EXPERIENCE

Strolling around the green haven of Parque del Este, before heading to the gastronomic hub of Las Mercedes, then chilling out at the centuries-old coffee hacienda at La Estancia and finishing the day at one of the city's hedonistic nightclubs with the cream of suave, young *caraqueños*.

A STREET SCENE IN DOWNTOWN CARACAS.

SLAM DUNK! THE COMPETITION HEATS UP ON THIS FRIENDLY GAME OF BASKETBALL.

THE MAJORITY OF VENEZUELANS ARE CATHOLIC.

STRENGTHS

- ◢ The *teleférico* (cable car) to the summit of El Ávila
- ◢ Nightlife of Las Mercedes, El Rosal, Altamira and La Castellana
- ◢ Winding streets of El Hatillo
- ◢ Museo de Arte Contemporáneo and Museo de Arte Colonial
- ◢ Cuisine scene of Las Mercedes, Altamira, Los Palos Grandes and La Candelaria
- ◢ Tomb of national treasure Simón Bolívar in the Panteón Nacional
- ◢ The steep, wooded slopes of Parque Nacional El Ávila
- ◢ Mosaics and murals gracing the streets

WEAKNESSES

- ◢ Barrios, petty crime and poverty
- ◢ Bulldozing the past
- ◢ Traffic jams and pollution
- ◢ Political instability

GOLD STAR

The bright lights of Caracas' stylish nightlife – there are myriad opportunities for clubbers, bar-hoppers and live salsa aficionados to mingle with the city's famously die-hard party crowd.

STARRING ROLE IN...

- ◢ *Shoot to Kill* (1991)
- ◢ *Sicario* (1995)
- ◢ *Little Thieves, Big Thieves* (1998)
- ◢ *Huelepega* (1999)

See the Asemblea Nacional (National Assembly) with its domes, neo-classical pediments and portraits of elites in its Salón Elíptico.

Eat at one of the *tascas* (Spanish-style bar-restaurants) dotted around town, most heavily concentrated in La Candelaria.

Drink excellent espresso at Gran Café – an open-air café right in the thick of a street market, alive with sharp-eyed urchins and haggling.

Do take a trip to the summit of El Ávila on the *teleférico*.

Watch Venezuelan *béisbol* (baseball) madness at a Leones de Caracas game at Estadio Universitario.

Buy hammocks, papier-mâché devil masks or stuffed piranhas at the biggest craft shop of them all at Hannsi in El Hatillo.

After dark head to the hedonistic clubs of Caracas and bear testament to the *caraqueños'* religious devotion to having a good time.

Carcassonne

DATE OF BIRTH 3500 BC; WHEN THE FIRST NEOLITHIC
SETTLEMENTS APPEARED **ADDRESS** FRANCE (MAP 5, G4)
HEIGHT 130M **POPULATION** 49,000 **LONELY PLANET RANKING** 130

One of the largest and best preserved walled towns in the world, Carcassonne enfolds centuries of history within the defensive ramparts of La Cité.

ANATOMY

The River Aude separates the Ville Basse (Lower Town) from La Cité, located on a hill 500m southeast and surrounded by two concentric walls. Pedestrianised rue Georges Clemenceau leads from the train station and Canal du Midi southwards through the heart of the lower town. You can catch buses around town.

PEOPLE

The inhabitants of Carcassonne live mostly in the Ville Basse and surrounding suburbs, with only a small percentage living in La Cité itself. The majority are Roman Catholic and some speak Catalan rather than French. In recent years the population has been greatly boosted by British migrants.

TYPICAL CARCASSONNAIS

Carcassonne's residents go about their daily lives seemingly oblivious to the hordes of tourists and the cacophony of buskers, tour guides and souvenir vendors. While celebrating their proud Cathar history at every chance, they certainly don't adopt the austere lifestyle of their predecessors, preferring to cultivate a convivial café culture and a predilection for local wine and *cassoulet* (a piping hot dish blending white beans, juicy pork cubes, sausage and – in the most popular local variant – duck).

DEFINING EXPERIENCE

Walking around the city (along 3km of defensive ramparts), visiting Porte Narbonnaise, Basilique St-Nazaire and Château Comtal, dining on *cassoulet* at L'Écu d'Or, followed by a twilight walk outside the now-illuminated castle walls, for a different perspective.

LET IT GO – THE POPULARITY OF ACCORDION MUSIC DECLINED DRAMATICALLY IN FRANCE IN THE 1960S.

THE FAIRY-TALE WALLS OF THE MEDIEVAL OLD CITY GLOW MAGICALLY AT NIGHT.

STRENGTHS

⊿ Your first glimpse of La Cité's witches-hat turrets as you approach
⊿ World Heritage listing
⊿ Basilique St-Nazaire
⊿ 12th-century Château Comtal
⊿ Musée Lapidaire
⊿ Massive bastion of Porte Narbonnaise
⊿ Embrasement de la Cité (Setting La Cité Ablaze) – Bastille Day celebrations
⊿ *Cassoulet*

WEAKNESSES

⊿ Hellishly crowded with tourists (over two million) in high summer
⊿ An oversupply of kitsch souvenir shops
⊿ Cheesy/tacky private museums
⊿ Can be expensive
⊿ Variable quality of Château Comtal guided tour

GOLD STAR

La Cité itself, dramatically illuminated at night and enclosed within its two rampart walls punctuated by 52 towers, is simply breathtaking.

STARRING ROLE IN...

⊿ *Robin Hood: Prince of Thieves* (1991)

See graceful Gothic transept arms and superb 13th- and 14th-century windows at Basilique St-Nazaire.

Eat *cassoulet* at Au Bon Pasteur, where simple decor belies the sophistication of the cooking.

Drink your favourite coffee from the huge selection available at La Cité des Arômes.

Do take in the view of La Cité from the Pont Neuf or Pont Vieux, straddling the River Aude.

Watch birds of prey dive and swoop in falconry demonstrations at Les Aigles de La Cité (The Eagles of La Cité), 800m south of the city walls.

Buy kitsch souvenirs, or better yet, some of the region's wines.

After dark most tourists have left La Cité, so enjoy a quiet post-dinner stroll and experience the city anew under floodlights.

Cardiff

DATE OF BIRTH AD 75; WHEN THE CITY BEGAN AS A ROMAN FORT – IT WAS ONLY MADE A CITY IN 1905 AND A CAPITAL IN 1955 **ADDRESS** WALES (MAP 4, E8) **HEIGHT** 62M **SIZE** 120 SQ KM **POPULATION** 346,000 **LONELY PLANET RANKING** 171

Stunning scenery, historic, battle-scarred castles, a menu of outdoor activities, and gleaming bars and shops make the modern yet traditional capital of Wales a compelling place to visit.

ANATOMY

Central Cardiff's main landmarks are Cardiff Castle and the Millennium Stadium, by the River Taff. High St, St Mary St, Queen St, Bridge St and Charles St are a shopper's paradise, while the Civic Centre north of the castle houses government buildings. The harbour area to the south, once the world's top coal port, is now a redeveloped commercial centre called Cardiff Bay. The bus and train stations are near the stadium.

PEOPLE

Only one-fifth of Wales' population now speak Welsh and just over one-fifth of people come from England. Young people are migrating from the country to the city. Butetown is Cardiff's most multicultural area.

TYPICAL CARDIFF CITIZEN

Welsh people are very proud of their national identity. They are supportive of the National Assembly, despite its limited powers, and are keen to maintain their flagging language (Welsh is taught in schools). Cardiff residents work long hours and are relatively affluent. They enjoy sport and are passionate about rugby. They are friendly and good fun, and confident and positive about Wales future.

DEFINING EXPERIENCE

Sipping a shot of caffeine with the papers at Coffee#1, before wandering over to Bute Park to sunbathe near the ruins of Blackfriars Priory, then heading to Cardiff Central Market to refuel and Queen St for some retail therapy.

TURN BACK TIME – AN OLD-FASHIONED SHOP AT THE ST FAGAN'S NATIONAL MUSEUM OF WALES IN CARDIFF.

CHOICES, CHOICES – DIFFICULT DECISIONS AT CARDIFF MARKET'S SECONDHAND RECORD STORE.

STRENGTHS

- National pride
- Cardiff Festival (July/August)
- Winning the Six Nations Rugby Championship in 2012
- Millennium Stadium
- National Museum & Gallery of Wales
- Cardiff Bay
- Cardiff Castle
- Caerphilly Castle
- Castell Coch
- Roman fortress at Carleon
- Brecon Beacons National Park
- Artes Mundi Prize (Arts of the World)
- St Fagans: National History Museum
- National Assembly
- Rugby – Cardiff Blues and the Welsh team
- Cycling the Lôn Las Cymru trail
- St David's Hotel & Spa
- Surfing off the Gower Peninsula
- Welsh rarebit
- Welsh cheese, eg Caerphilly and Celtic Blue
- The Great British Cheese Festival
- Cardiff University
- Llandaff Cathedral
- Bute Park
- Techniquest
- EU financial aid
- Lower prices than in the rest of the UK
- Royal National Eisteddfod

WEAKNESSES

- Inclement weather
- Political apathy
- Rural economic problems
- Dwindling number of Welsh speakers

SNOW ADDS SPARKLE TO CARDIFF CASTLE AND BUTE PARK.

GOLD STAR

Castles – Wales is famous for them and Cardiff doesn't let the side down.

STARRING ROLE IN...

- ◢ *Human Traffic* (1999)
- ◢ *Twin Town* (1997)
- ◢ *Doctor Who* (2005–)
- ◢ *Dat's Love* by Leonora Brito

See Cardiff Castle complete with Great Hall and minstrel's gallery, as well as a Norman keep.

Eat exceptional Welsh cakes hot off the griddle at the Riverside Market.

Drink the local Brains SA (meaning Special Ale, Same Again or Skull Attack depending on how many you've had), brewed by the same family concern since 1882.

Do visit the National Museum Wales for impressionist art, volcanic eruptions and the world's largest turtle.

Watch international football and rugby matches at the Millennium Stadium or do a tour and check out the players' tunnel.

Buy lovespoons, dragons and souvenir T-shirts at Castle Welsh Crafts or explore the trendy shops of High St Arcade.

After dark check out the latest local bands at Clwb Ifor Bach.

FEBRUARY IS COSTUME TIME AT CARTAGENA'S CARNAVAL.

Cartagena

NICKNAME LA CIUDAD HEROICA (THE HEROIC CITY), ACCORDING TO SIMÓN BOLÍVAR **DATE OF BIRTH** 1533: WHEN IT WAS THE SECOND SPANISH CITY TO BE FOUNDED ON THE COLOMBIAN COAST **ADDRESS** COLOMBIA (MAP 2, O7) **HEIGHT** 5M **POPULATION** 1.2 MILLION **LONELY PLANET RANKING** 073

Cartagena de Indias is legendary both for its history and its beauty: it has been immortalised on countless canvases, glorified in hundreds of books and photographed a zillion times – and, as Colombia's most fascinating city and a World Heritage Site, it deserves every one of these tributes.

ANATOMY

The heart of Cartagena is the old town, facing the sea to the west and almost entirely separated by water from the mainland to the east. The old town's walled sections are separated by a channel, the Caño de San Anastasio. This was later filled up to make way for the construction of the wedge-shaped modern district, La Matuna. South of the old town is the L-shaped peninsula occupied by the trendy seaside resorts. Walk around town, or catch the large green-and-white buses.

PEOPLE

The majority of *cartageneros* are mestizos with Spanish background, with the rest of the population made up of Afro-Colombians. The more European your background, the higher your social status is, the greater your wealth and more stable your livelihood.

TYPICAL CARTAGENERO

Cartageneros drink eternal coffees but their true love is rum. The local passions are family, *fútbol* (football) and going out to rumba, in that order. They're isolated from the difficulties of most of the country, but never forget they are Colombians. They're relaxed and friendly to strangers, in good Caribbean fashion, but always put their family first. They *always* know they live in the most beautiful city in Colombia.

DEFINING EXPERIENCE

Having a breakfast coffee with bread, a relaxing stroll around the streets, a big lunch then stopping for a *tintico* (short black coffee), dining on a good

FORMERLY A PRISON, THE 23 VAULTS OF LAS BÓVEDAS NOW HOST A LINE-UP OF LOCAL ARTS AND CRAFTS.

SELLING COCADA, A SWEET MADE OF PANELA (CANE SUGAR) AND COCONUT OR PEANUTS.

COLONIAL CHARM ON THE STREETS OF THE WALLED CITY.

seafood meal at a *cantina* (bar) in El Centro, then heading off to Bocagrande for rum and rumba until dawn.

STRENGTHS
- *Chivas* (colourful local buses)
- Beautiful remnants of colonial history – Las Murallas (the thick walls built to protect the old town)
- Perfect Caribbean climate all year round
- Music – rumba, *vallenato, paseo…*
- Dancing, partying and rum
- Glamour and Colombian fashion

WEAKNESSES
- Street moneychangers
- Fraudulent boat captains
- Violent social history
- Machismo

GOLD STAR
Having the most stubborn military saviour – Blas de Lezo, who had lost a leg, an eye and an arm in various battles, but with only 2500 troops defended the city against 25,000 British troops in the 1741 Battle of Cartagena de Indias.

STARRING ROLE IN...
- *The Mission* (1986)
- *Love in the Time of Cholera* by Gabriel García Márquez

See films at the International Film Festival in March/April.

Eat sweets made from coconut, milk, tamarind and local fruits at el Portal de Los Dulces.

Drink good Colombian coffee in any café.

Do take yourself on a tour of the old city, particularly the walled town.

Watch the Reinado Nacional de Belleza (Colombia's national beauty pageant) on 11 November.

Buy emeralds at Las Bóvedas.

After dark try for a table at Restaurant 8-18 then dance the night away at Café Havana.

Cayenne

DATE OF BIRTH 1643: WHEN IT WAS FOUNDED BY THE FRENCH, WHO SET UP A FORT ON THE HIGHEST HILL **ADDRESS** FRENCH GUIANA (MAP 3, G4) **HEIGHT** 6M **POPULATION** 57,000 **LONELY PLANET RANKING** 189

French colonial buildings, flowered balconies, vibrant markets, Creole and Guianese cuisine and a multicultural population make Cayenne one of South America's most charming capitals.

ANATOMY

Place des Palmistes in the northwest of Cayenne is the beating heart of the city, filled with cafés, outdoor foodstalls and beckoning palm trees. Place Léopold Héder (aka Place Grenoble), to the west of Place des Palmistes, is one of the oldest parts of Cayenne. The city itself sits at the western end of a small hilly peninsula between the Mahury and Cayenne Rivers. There are limited buses; taxis may be more reliable.

PEOPLE

Cayenne is a melting pot of French people, Brazilians, Haitians, American Indians, Vietnamese and Chinese people. The Boni are the only endemic tribe of Surinamese Maroons (descendants of escaped African slaves), although members of the Aucaner (Djuka) and Paramaccaner tribes live in French Guiana. There are also two Hmong groups who originally hailed from Laos. Most of French Guiana is Catholic.

TYPICAL CAYENNE CITIZEN

French Guiana is the smallest of the Guianas. It is an overseas department of France and therefore part of the EU. Significant wads of euros from its mother country mean the people of Cayenne enjoy a good lifestyle and an infrastructure comparable to rural France. Some people advocate greater freedom from France, but most appreciate the cash injections too much to support this. Guianese people are warm, friendly and proud of their ethnic mix. Not surprisingly, they also love their food.

DEFINING EXPERIENCE

Pottering around the varied stalls at the market, before tanning on Plage Montjoly then returning to town for some irresistible crêpes from the night-time foodstalls on Place des Palmistes.

PHILIPPE MICHEL / GETTY IMAGES

WATCHING OVER CAYENNE FROM THE FORT.

STRENGTHS

◢ Plage Montjoly – Cayenne's best beach and home to spawning leatherback turtles in summer
◢ Musée Départemental
◢ Musée des Cultures Guyanaises
◢ Carnaval (February and March)
◢ The lively market
◢ French colonial architecture
◢ Ecotourism
◢ Office Culturel de la Région Guyane
◢ Virgin rainforest in French Guiana's interior
◢ Wildlife, such as tapirs, jaguars, poison-arrow frogs and caymans
◢ Good roads
◢ Centre Spatial Guyanais (Guianese Space Centre) – launch site for the European Space Agency's Ariane rockets an hour away

WEAKNESSES

◢ Hunters of leatherback turtles
◢ Brutal penal system until 1953
◢ Shady characters after dark in the Village Chinois (Chinatown) area

GOLD STAR

French-Latin-Caribbean vibe.

STARRING ROLE IN...

◢ *Papillon* by Henri Charrière (film 1973)

See what's left of 17th-century Fort Cépérou and check out the views of the town and river.

Eat delectable pastries and sandwiches Parisian-style, at Le Café Crème.

Drink at Harry's Bar, a congenial bar offering 50 brands of whisky and multiple beers.

Do visit Montsinéry (45km west of Cayenne) and spot caymans, jaguars, tapirs and toucans at the Réserve Animalière Macourienne.

Watch the city go mad for live music and parades at carnaval.

Buy tropical fruits and sizzling Vietnamese soup at Cayenne's main market.

After dark listen to the tinkling of the ivories or try your luck with a pool cue at the piano bar at La Case Café Show.

BEST FRIENDS FOREVER – TWO GIRLS ENJOYING LIFE BY THE FISH MARKET.

FRENCH IS THE INTERNATIONAL LANGUAGE OF SNACKS.

ON TOUR – A BAND HITS THE ROAD FOR A GIG.

UMBRELLAS SHIELD SHAN NOVICES FROM THE SUN DURING POY SANG LONG, THEIR INITIATION AT WAT KU TAO TEMPLE.

RELIGIOUS IMAGES/UIG / GETTY IMAGES

Chiang Mai

NAME NOPBURI SI NAKHON PING CHIANG MAI (SHORTENED TO CHIANG MAI) **NICKNAME** ROSE OF THE NORTH **DATE OF BIRTH** 1296; WHEN THAI KING MENGRAI TOOK OVER A MON SETTLEMENT TO FOUND CHIANG MAI **ADDRESS** THAILAND (MAP 9, E6) **HEIGHT** 314M **SIZE** 4506 SQ KM **POPULATION** 174,000 **LONELY PLANET RANKING** 071

Chiang Mai is a small cosmopolitan metropolis with a striking mountain backdrop, over 300 temples, a quaint historical aura and its Thai culture firmly ingrained.

ANATOMY

Chiang Mai is surrounded by mountains and forests. The old city is surrounded by a moat and parts of the old city walls, which surround most of the city's important temples. Today the city is far larger than its ancient walls suggest and has especially expanded towards the Ping River in the east, the location of the Night Bazaar. Chiang Mai is easy to navigate once you've mastered the system of streets. Get around by flagging down one of the many red *songthaew* (a converted pick-up truck) or by túk-túk (motorised rickshaws).

PEOPLE

Only a small portion of Chiang Mai's population live within the city. The majority are locals by birth, and speak a Thai dialect. People from China, Laos and Myanmar have long traded in Chiang Mai, thanks to its location along the northern region of Southeast Asia. Its Karen, Lahu, Hmong, Lisu, Lua, Akha, Mien and Palong cultures also enliven its heritage.

TYPICAL CHIANG MAIAN

Individual lifestyles in Chiang Mai vary tremendously according to family background and income. A Chiang Maian may work as a cleaner for a higher-income family, may be a civil servant, or studying at university. High value is placed on education and there are private and international schools for the foreign and local elite. Thai men are expected to shave their heads and don monastic robes at least once in their lives.

DEFINING EXPERIENCE

Watching a puddle of sweat form at your feet as you perform a death-defying yoga pose in the early dawn from a 1st-floor room overlooking the moat and the early traders.

247

SPIRITUAL HIGH – THERE ARE MORE THAN 300 TEMPLES IN CHIANG MAI.

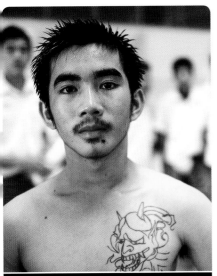

SWEAT AND STEELY RESOLVE ON THE FACE OF A JUNIOR KICKBOXER AT A SPORTS CARNIVAL.

UNDERWEAR SUSPENDED AT WOROROT MARKET FORMS A CHEEKY HANGING MOBILE.

STRENGTHS

◢ Easy to navigate
◢ Hundreds of sacred wáts (temples)
◢ Starting point for hill-tribe treks
◢ *Mai pen rai* (take it easy) attitude
◢ Plenty of great food for vegetarians

WEAKNESSES

◢ Seedy bars lined with girls, girls, girls, some wearing numbers
◢ Staged hill-tribe treks
◢ Too much to see, not enough time
◢ Traffic police blocking every corner, adding to the congestion

GOLD STAR

It is said that there are more than 300 temples within the walls of the old city. The wáts are breezy and meditative and a reminder of the region's culture beyond the bazaars and go-go bars.

STARRING ROLE IN...

◢ *Rambo 3* (1988)
◢ *Operation Dumbo Drop* (1995)
◢ *Smoking Poppy* by Graham Joyce
◢ *Fast Eddie's Lucky 7 A Gogo* by David Young
◢ *The Teachers of Mad Dog Swamp* by Khammaan Khonkhai

See gold leaf artisans at work at the jungle wat, Ko Tao.

Eat freshly made *tom sam* (green papaya salad) from one of the many street stalls; *kaeo soy* (like laksa but different) in the Muslim quarter; or *kao lam* (sticky rice, coconut milk and fried mung beans wrapped into a bamboo pole and roasted over coals) at the Tha Pei Gate market.

Drink long iced coffee from Aroon Rai made with a dark brew and sweetened condensed milk and a bucket of ice, or pull up a stool at a mobile cocktail van and slam back a tequila sunrise.

Do rent a scooter and take in the nearby villages of Bo Sang and San Kamphaeng and get lost on roads with signs only in Thai.

Watch a night of *muay thai* boxing at the Kawila Boxing Stadium – the highlight is the mounting frenzy of the bookmakers and gamblers alike as the main event draws near.

Buy all manner of products and enjoy a good dose of provincial culture at the Sunday Walking Street market.

After dark wander around the south side of the moat and sample great street cuisine or fried grasshoppers, whatever floats your boat.

Chicago

NICKNAME THE WINDY CITY; HOG BUTCHER FOR THE WORLD; SECOND CITY **DATE OF BIRTH** 1779; WHEN JEAN BAPTISTE POINTE DU SABLE ESTABLISHED A TRADING POST ON THE NORTH BANK OF THE CHICAGO RIVER **ADDRESS** USA (MAP 1, O4) **HEIGHT** 251M **SIZE** 588 SQ KM **POPULATION** 2.8 MILLION (CITY); 9.8 MILLION (METRO AREA) **LONELY PLANET RANKING** 034

Though it ranks third in size behind Los Angeles and New York, the Windy City is a vast, vibrant metropolis where running shoes and a good train map are a must if you even *hope* to make a dent in the city's attractions.

ANATOMY

The Windy City sprawls along the western side of Lake Michigan, with towering buildings constructed on swampy land forming an artificial landmark. The Loop is the city's historic heart, sitting on a small peninsula where the Chicago River meets the lake. The city and suburbs fan out across the prairie in all directions.

PEOPLE

Chicago's 'diversity index' – a percentage likelihood that two randomly chosen people in an area will be of different races – is 74%, a full 25% higher than the USA as a whole. Blacks outnumber whites in Chicago, with Latinos running a close third. Chicago has the largest Catholic archdiocese in the country, and a sizable Jewish population as well.

TYPICAL CHICAGOAN

The quintessential Midwesternness of the natives – cheerful, hard-working and a little conservative – acts as a steadying anchor for the city's more adventurous impulses. Despite the high diversity, integrated neighbourhoods are rare in Chicago: blacks tend to live in the city's south and west sides, Latinos in Pilsen and many areas on the North Side, and Asians in Chinatown and along Argyle St in Uptown.

DEFINING EXPERIENCE

Starting a high-speed day with breakfast at the Original Pancake House in Bellevue Plaza, followed by a cab ride down to the Art Institute, then to the Berghoff for lunch, followed by window-shopping on Michigan Ave, dining on deep-dish pizza at Giordano's, then sunset drinks way up on the 96th floor of the John Hancock Center's Signature Lounge.

LONELY PLANET / GETTY IMAGES

BASEBALL FANS KEEP A CLOSE EYE ON THE GAME DURING THE PLAYOFFS AT WRIGLEY FIELD.

STRENGTHS

⊿ Lake Michigan
⊿ Chicago Blues Festival
⊿ Navy Pier Ferris Wheel
⊿ St Patrick's Day – yes, they really do dye the river green
⊿ Storefront churches
⊿ Frank Lloyd Wright's Prairie School–style houses

WEAKNESSES

⊿ Freezing winter weather: icy pavements and salty roads
⊿ Rats
⊿ Corruption in city politics
⊿ The cost of motel and hotel rooms

GOLD STAR

The Art Institute of Chicago is as impressive a museum as can be found anywhere. Turn any corner and you find yet another breathtaking piece of art, from medieval armour to Mondrian abstracts. So this is where it ended up! On the shores of Lake Michigan, the institute has a wondrous collection of impressionist paintings as well as 20th-century modernism.

STARRING ROLE IN...

⊿ *The Adventures of Augie March* by Saul Bellow
⊿ *Blues Brothers* (1980)
⊿ *Ferris Bueller's Day Off* (1986)
⊿ *Chicago* (2003)

See Steppenwolf Theater, the legendary ensemble group that helped put Chicago theatre on the map.

Eat on Division St in Ukrainian Village, the hipster's dining paradise that includes several of the best brunch places in town – Smoke Daddy Rhythm & Bar-B-Que or Mirai.

Drink from the hundreds of beers on offer at Quencher's.

Do check out Second City, a must-see club (John Belushi, Bill Murray, Dan Aykroyd and Elaine May got their start here) where performers give sharp and biting commentaries on life, politics and love.

Watch the beaches in smelt season, when the tiny fish swarming into Chicago harbours to spawn are met by amateur anglers, nets and deep-fat fryers.

Buy clothes, accessories, anything on Milwaukee Ave (Wicker Park), where the funkier cousin to Damen Ave features blocks and blocks of hip stores.

After dark check out the dance scene – Chicago was one of the hotbeds of house in the early '80s, and the audiences have aged with the music.

THE SMURFIT-STONE SKYSCRAPER STANDS 177M TALL.

A COMMUTER TRAIN NEAR GRANT PARK HEADS TO THE OTHER SIDE OF THE TRACKS.

SCENE FOR MANY A MOVIE CAR-CHASE – CHICAGO'S ELEVATED TRAIN TRACKS.

THE VIEW FROM SUMNER CAPTURES THE NATURAL BEAUTY OF THE CITY AGAINST THE BACKDROP OF SOUTHERN ALPS.

Christchurch

NICKNAME THE GARDEN CITY **DATE OF BIRTH** 16TH CENTURY; WHEN THE MAORI ARRIVED; IN 1850 EUROPEANS SETTLED HERE **HEIGHT** 10M **SIZE** 452 SQ KM **ADDRESS** NEW ZEALAND (MAP 10, M9) **POPULATION** 363,000 **LONELY PLANET RANKING** 105

New Zealand's second-largest city is rising again following the devastating earthquakes of 2010 and 2011 with a robust combination of spirit, determination and innovation. New cafe, bar and restaurant scenes are popping up in fringe neighbourhoods, and the city's calendar of festivals reminds us that there's still plenty to celebrate.

ANATOMY

Welcome to a 'doughnut' city in transition. At the time of writing, Christchurch's CBD was still closed for post-earthquake demolition and construction. The city's bruised heart is surrounded by a halo of suburbs: leafy and prosperous to the west, and sprawling and grittier to the east. Hagley Park is a green haven, and the city is bordered to the south by the Port Hills, to the east by the Pacific, and to the north and west by farmland.

PEOPLE

Mostly of solid Anglo-Celtic stock, but Christchurchians are increasingly from elsewhere. Maori make up 7% of the population, followed by Pacific Island and Asian communities. A significant number of families left after the earthquakes, replaced by a younger population of single people working on the city's rebuild.

TYPICAL CHRISTCHURCHIAN

The typical Christchurchian is a passionate supporter of their seismically-challenged city, evident in their unwavering support of the provincial rugby team, and an ongoing rivalry with bigger, bolder Auckland. Civic and regional pride has been magnified since the earthquakes, and as the city's rebuild continues, there's a growing distrust of the input and influence of New Zealand's government politicians in Wellington.

DEFINING EXPERIENCE

After breakfast at the Addington Coffee Co-op, wander back to the city via leafy South Hagley Park. Stop for punting on the Avon River at the Antigua Boat Sheds, before exploring the Canterbury Museum. In the evening, meet the locals over pub food and craft beers at Pomeroy's Old Brewery Inn.

STRENGTHS

◢ The innovation and energy of the post-earthquake rebuild
◢ The city's unique opportunity to rethink urban form and design
◢ The resilience and pragmatism of the city's population
◢ The shipping/shopping containers of the RE:Start Mall
◢ The creative spirit of the Gap Filler Charitable Trust
◢ Blooming natural beauty at the Ellerslie Flower Show in March
◢ Walking and mountain biking the trails on the Port Hills
◢ Sumner Beach
◢ The Botanical Gardens and Hagley Park
◢ The Avon River, twisting and turning through the city
◢ The Tannery and The Brewery developments in Woolston
◢ The bohemian music and arts scene of Lyttelton
◢ The Antarctica exhibits in the Canterbury Museum

WEAKNESSES

◢ Smog in winter
◢ Post-earthquake road detours
◢ The painstaking demolition and rebuild of the city's CBD
◢ The loss and damage of so much of Christchurch's heritage architecture

GOLD STAR

The spirit and fortitude of the people of Christchurch. In the most challenging of circumstances, they have remained proud and supportive of their southern city.

STARRING ROLE IN...

◢ *Heavenly Creatures* (1993)
◢ *When a City Falls* (2011)
◢ *The Colour* by Rose Tremain

See the ongoing efforts of the city's rebuild on a bus tour through the cordoned-off CBD.

Eat sustainable and artisan produce at the Christchurch Farmers Market.

Drink at the CBD Bar for homegrown Cassels beers and views of the Red Zone cordon.

Do hire a bike to explore lovely Hagley Park.

Watch the sun set behind the Southern Alps, from atop the Port Hills.

Buy designs and crafts from local artists at Hapa in the Re:START mall.

After dark try the bars and restaurants along Victoria St.

LOCAL RUGBY TEAMS IN A RUCK – CHRISTCHURCH HAS APPROACHED RECENT DISASTERS IN A SIMILARLY COMBATIVE STYLE.

Christiansted

DATE OF BIRTH 1733: CHRISTIANSTED SERVED BRIEFLY AS THE CAPITAL OF THE DANISH WEST INDIES **ADDRESS** US VIRGIN ISLANDS (MAP 2, S2) **HEIGHT** 5M **SIZE** 1572 SQ KM **POPULATION** 3000 **LONELY PLANET RANKING** 159

Christiansted is beautiful, historical, easy to travel around and, best of all, totally Caribbean in look and feel.

ANATOMY

Pressed between hills and a shallow, reef-protected harbour, Christiansted, on the island of St Croix, is a traveller's delight. For decades, its greatest appeal lay in its six-block historic district, but in recent years, Christiansted has evolved into a vibrant entertainment district. With its historical significance, cleanliness, walkability and array of dining and nightlife opportunities, Christiansted embodies almost everything many travellers hope for in a West Indies town – you can kick back at a waterfront brewpub or in a courtyard restaurant and make friends with the West Indians at the next table. You can walk around town and catch buses to get around the island, or hire a car to be your own tour guide.

PEOPLE

The majority of Christiansted residents are of African descent, with a number of expats from the US mainland – often young whites who run hotels, inns and sports operations. Don't forget to add a smattering of immigrants from Puerto Rico, the Leeward Islands and the Dominican Republic, and even the odd Danish plantation family or French land-holder. English is the official language.

TYPICAL CHRISTIANSTED CITIZEN

Cruzans, as the residents of Christiansted and the rest of St Croix call themselves, consider their home island the 'stepchild' of the US Virgin Islands. The origins of the image are rooted in St Croix' isolated location, and Christiansted residents show an independence and self-motivation that comes from this separation. They're proud of their wealth and comfortable status, and always ready for a party as soon as you crank up the music. People from Christiansted know how to eat well, party well and live well – get in there with them!

CHRISTIANSTED HAS PRESERVED ITS 18TH-CENTURY DANISH-STYLE BUILDINGS.

DEFINING EXPERIENCE

After a coffee on a Saturday, head to Market Sq for fresh fruit, take a leisurely walk along the Kings Wharf boardwalk, enjoy some duty-free shopping in Gallows Bay, then dine on seafood overlooking the harbour and dance the night away at a full-moon party.

STRENGTHS

◣ Historic yellow buildings and their stories
◣ Vibrant music scene and steel-drum bands
◣ The St Patrick's Day Parade
◣ Cruise ships and the yacht-charter industry
◣ One of the highest standards of living in the Caribbean
◣ Danish street signs
◣ Maps that still show the names and boundaries of old plantations

WEAKNESSES

◣ Hurricanes
◣ Perpetually exorbitant 'tourist' prices for everything
◣ Swanky resorts and the armada of cruise ships

GOLD STAR

For tourism achievement – the successful blending of centuries of colonial history with natural beauty to make a genuinely relaxed and attractive tourist destination.

STARRING ROLE IN...

◣ *Treasure Island* by Robert Lewis Stevenson
◣ *Sunfon Calypso* by Julian Putley
◣ *Don't Stop the Carnival* by Herman Wouk

See 'Jump Up' – a carnival-like evening (held four times a year) filled with steel bands, dancing, local arts and crafts, island food, and fun.

Eat West Indian dishes heaped on plates at Harvey's, a classic tropical cafe.

Drink local Cruzan Estate Diamond Rum.

Do a late-night turtle-watch during the nesting and hatching seasons, sponsored by the St Croix Environmental Association.

Watch the waves lapping the deserted beaches of nearby Buck Island.

Buy a bracelet with a 'Cruzan hook' from the Caribbean Bracelet Company.

After dark check out the gin mills that line the Kings Wharf boardwalk; there's always live music at one of them.

MEDICAL MEMOIR – THIS APOTHECARY MUSEUM WAS ONCE A WORKING PHARMACY.

CALMING COPENHAGEN REGULARLY TOPS QUALITY OF LIFE SURVEYS.

Copenhagen

NICKNAME WONDERFUL, WONDERFUL COPENHAGEN
DATE OF BIRTH 1167; BISHOP ABSALON CONSTRUCTED A FORTRESS
ON SLOTSHOLMEN **ADDRESS** DENMARK (MAP 4, L7) **HEIGHT** 9M
SIZE 88.3 SQ KM **POPULATION** 552,000 (CITY); 1.9 MILLION (METRO
AREA) **LONELY PLANET RANKING** 120

Copenhagen is one of the few places left where the term 'fairy tale' can be used freely – from its most enduring literary legacy to its most recent royal romance. The old and the new combine to form an attractive, civilised, ergonomic and punctual confection.

ANATOMY

Copenhagen sits on the east coast of Denmark's largest island, Zealand (Sjælland). It is separated from Sweden by the Øresund and is largely low-rise, with few skyscrapers. Most of the city's obvious attractions are found near the main square of Rådhuspladsen and the islands of Slotsholmen and Christianshavn. Public transport can involve buses, boats or the automated (and driverless) metro system.

PEOPLE

The vast majority of Copenhageners seem to come from the same stock, ie the Teutonic ancestry so common to Scandinavia. However, there is also a substantial population of foreign nationals in Copenhagen, home to half of Denmark's immigrants.

TYPICAL COPENHAGENER

The clichéd local will have Jensen, Nielsen or Hansen for a surname, be tall, prepared to join a queue and fond of biting, irony-laden humour. They will have strongly held opinions on where to dine and what to dine on, and will give the impression that little else is of great importance. That and what you should sit on when you eat – beautiful chairs are a citywide obsession.

DEFINING EXPERIENCE

Thinking about your next feed, while taking advantage of even a hint of a sunny day by sitting outside at a café where the owners have thoughtfully provided blankets for their patrons, riding a bicycle across beautiful

THE AMALIENBORG PALACE IS THE WINTER HOME OF THE DANISH ROYAL FAMILY.

bridges such as Knippelsbro to funky Islands Brygge and taking a dip at the canalside public baths.

STRENGTHS

- Culinary revolution and New Nordic pioneer Noma
- Imaginative *smørrebrod* (buttered bread) toppings at Ida Davidsen
- Timely and tidy public transport
- Christianshavn
- Royal Palaces
- Statens Museum for Kunst
- Tivoli

- Local beers
- Islands Brygge Havnebadet (harbour bathing)
- Good-looking gene pool
- Modern architecture
- An easy-going monarchy
- Cycle chic
- Bakeries
- Herring

WEAKNESSES

- Licensing laws
- Taciturn locals
- Daredevil cyclists

- Stubborn refusal to do things that aren't 'the Danish style'
- Long, cold, dark winters

GOLD STAR

Design – Copenhagen is always bang on the money when it comes to marrying form with function. Thanks to architects such as Jan Gehl, the city has become a model for smooth and equitable urban design, where cyclists, cars and pedestrians co-exist relatively harmoniously.

A SERIOUS FIGURE TRUDGES BENEATH THE FRIVOLOUS SIGN FOR THE TIVOLI AMUSEMENT PARK ON HC ANDERSENS BLVD.

STARRING ROLE IN...

◢ *Miss Smilla's Feeling for Snow* by Peter Høeg
◢ *Smilla's Sense of Snow* (1977)
◢ *The Idiots* (1998)
◢ *Open Hearts* (2003)
◢ *Reconstruction* (2003)

See the citywide panorama from atop glorious Vor Frelsers Kirke in Christianshavn.

Eat at one of the city's 10 Michelin-starred restaurants.

Drink Carlsberg beer in Carlsberg's microbrewery.

Do a long, lazy stroll down Strøget – the world's longest pedestrian mall.

Watch a Dogme 95 film at the Danish Filmhuset.

Buy a stunning piece of silver from the Georg Jensen flagship store.

After dark watch the fireworks display at Tivoli.

WITH REVERENTIAL POISE AN INDIAN WOMAN HOLDS OUT AN OFFERING AT THE INTI RAYMI FESTIVAL, PLAZA DE ARMAS.

Cuzco

NICKNAME NAVEL OF THE EARTH **DATE OF BIRTH** 12TH CENTURY; WHEN THE INCAS SETTLED IN THE AREA **ADDRESS** PERU (MAP 3, C9) **HEIGHT** 3225M **POPULATION** 350,000 **LONELY PLANET RANKING** 058

At the heart of the once-mighty Inca Empire, the magnetic city of Cuzco lies in exceptionally beautiful Andean surroundings.

ANATOMY

The heart of the city is Plaza de Armas, while nearby Avenida El Sol is the main business thoroughfare. Just a few blocks north or east of the plaza are twisting, cobbled streets little changed for centuries. The pedestrianised street between Plaza del Tricentenario and Huaynapata gives great views over Plaza de Armas. The central street leading from the northwestern side of the plaza is named Procuradores (tax-collectors' street). Local buses are slow, cheap and crowded.

PEOPLE

As with the rest of Peru, about half of Cuzco's population is Indian. A large portion of the other half is mestizo (mixed European and Indian descent) or white (Spanish descent), with the remaining black, Asian or of other backgrounds. Spanish, Quechua and Aymara are spoken.

TYPICAL CUZQUEÑO

The *cuzqueños* are politically passionate, warm and hospitable, crazy for *fútbol* (football), unshakably patriotic but highly critical of their political leaders, energetic, never short of a smile, curious, very talkative, entrepreneurial and hard-working people. Cuzco is essentially a bicultural society, with one part containing the mainly white and mestizo middle and upper classes, and the other containing mainly the poor Indian *campesinos* (peasants or country people), many of whom live in poverty.

DEFINING EXPERIENCE

Starting the day at El Buen Pastor, which has a great selection of breads, cakes and wonderful hot chocolate, then exploring the Inca walls of the city, relaxing in the afternoon by cruising the area surrounding Plaza San Blas – Cuzco's artisan quarter, packed with the workshops and showrooms of local craftspeople.

A SONG AND DANCE – TRADITIONAL PERUVIAN MUSICIANS.

LOCALS IN TRADITIONAL DRESS MAKE THEIR WAY DOWN A COBBLED STREET.

DANCERS SPIN UP A STORM AT THE VIRGIN OF CARMEN DAY PROCESSION.

STRENGTHS
▲ The continent's archaeological capital and oldest continuously inhabited city with massive Inca-built walls
▲ The craft workshops of San Blas
▲ Centuries of colonial treasures in Cuzco's cathedral
▲ Proximity to Machu Picchu
▲ Inti Raymi (Festival of the Sun)
▲ Fantastic Peruvian food
▲ Bird life

WEAKNESSES
▲ Treatment of animals
▲ Legacy of the disappeared
▲ Altitude sickness
▲ Strikes

GOLD STAR
Soaking up the amazing history and culture of this magnetic city, whether it be exploring the colonial and religious splendours built on the hefty stone foundations of the Incas or marvelling at the many fascinating and accessible archaeological sites.

STARRING ROLE IN...
▲ *It Happened in Huayanay* (1981)
▲ *You Only Live Once* (1992)
▲ *The Dancer Upstairs* (2002)
▲ *The Green House* by Mario Vargas Llosa

See the views of Cuzco Valley from the Pukapukara archaeological site.

Eat the Andean speciality tamales (boiled corn dumplings filled with cheese or meat and wrapped in a banana leaf) at a *quinta* (country house), such as Quinta Zárate, with its shady garden and good views.

Drink a pisco sour at Los Perros, one of Cuzco's best drinking dens with a funky, laid-back couch bar and a top-notch music collection.

Do explore Plaza de Armas – surrounded by colonial arcades, it's fronted by a large flight of stairs and flanked by the cathedral and the churches of Jesús María and El Triunfo.

Watch a live folklore show at Centro Qosqo de Arte Nativo.

Buy beautiful locally made items from a tremendous variety of woollens, textiles, pottery, jewellery and art at Centro Artesanal Cuzco.

After dark head to Ukuku's for good, sweaty dance fun.

269

Dakar

DATE OF BIRTH 1857; THE FRENCH ESTABLISHED DAKAR AT THE SITE OF A FISHING VILLAGE, AND IN 1895 IT BECAME FRENCH WEST AFRICA'S ADMINISTRATIVE CENTRE **ADDRESS** SENEGAL (MAP 6, A7) **HEIGHT** 40M **SIZE** 547 SQ KM **POPULATION** 2.5 MILLION **LONELY PLANET RANKING** 109

Relentless and complex, Dakar is a giant termite nest, tough on the outside and teeming with life on the inside.

ANATOMY
A massive square called Place de l'Indépendance (usually simply called the 'Place') is the city's heart. From here, major streets stem outwards, including Av Léopold Senghor (which passes the Palais Présidentiel) and Av Pompidou, the main street, which leads west to Marché Sandaga. From here, Av du Président Lamine Guéye goes north to the Gare Routière Pompiers and the autoroute, leading inland. The train station is 3km north of Place de l'Indépendance.

PEOPLE
The vast majority of Senegal's population is Muslim, including the Wolof and Mandinka. (The Fula, or Peul, and the Diola are animists by tradition, while many of the Sérèr are Catholics.) French is the official language and Wolof the principal African tongue. The Fula speak Pulaar (or Fula), while the Sérèr speak Sérèr. Arabic expressions are also widely used.

TYPICAL DAKAR CITIZEN
Like many African tribes, Senegal's main indigenous group, the Wolof, has a highly stratified society. At the top are traditional noble and warrior families, followed by the farmers, traders and persons of caste – blacksmiths, leather workers, woodworkers, weavers and *griots*. *Griots* are the lowest of the castes but are highly respected, as they are in charge of passing on the oral traditions. Many descendants of former slaves still work as tenant farmers for the masters of old. Few people would make a big decision without consulting their town's *marabout* (holy man), thought to link Senegalese Islam's disciples and Allah.

DEFINING EXPERIENCE
Quaffing tasty pastries at one of the pâtisseries du jour and bargaining at Marché Kermel before hightailing it to the floodlit landmark minaret of the Grande Mosquée.

THE STRIKING MOSQUE AT PLAGE D'OUAKAM IS SET AGAINST THE STUNNING BACKDROP OF THE ATLANTIC OCEAN.

STRENGTHS

- A glimpse of the African urban future
- Palais Présidentiel
- Marché Kermel
- Delicious *poisson yassa* (fish grilled with onions, lemon and mustard)
- Dakar's IFAN Museum
- Grande Mosquée
- Senegalese beer (especially Gazelle and Flag)
- Saying 'non merci!' three times (effective in staving off hustlers)
- Joggers running barefoot along urban thoroughfares

WEAKNESSES

- Muggings, scams and petty theft
- The sickeningly wealthy and sickeningly impoverished
- Aggressive street sellers
- Pickpockets (broad daylight is no deterrent)

GOLD STAR

The IFAN Museum is one of the best museums in West Africa. The imaginative displays show masks and traditional dress from the whole region and provide an excellent overview of styles. You can also see beautiful fabrics and carvings, drums and tools.

STARRING ROLE IN...

- *Touki Bouki* (1973)
- *West Africa: An Introduction to Its History* by Michael Crowde
- *Topics of West African History* by Adu Boahen

See an impressive collection of masks, statues, musical instruments and agricultural implements from all over West Africa at the IFAN Museum.

Eat Senegalese *yassa poulet* (grilled chicken marinated in an onion and lemon sauce).

Drink at the glitzy party parlours in Les Almadies..

Do visit the fishing village of Soumbédioune, west of the city centre, especially at dusk to witness pirogues beach themselves.

Watch traditional Senegalese wrestling matches (*les luttes* in French) at or near the Stade Iba Mar Diop.

Buy beautiful West African fabrics at Marché Sandaga.

After dark hit Club Thiossane, a hot, crowded place in La Médina owned by international music star Youssou N'Dour (who might grace the stage).

LOCAL SALT COLLECTORS PRACTISE THEIR TRADE AT LAC ROSE.

Dar es Salaam

NICKNAME DAR **DATE OF BIRTH** AD 1866; WHEN THE ARAB SULTAN
OF ZANZIBAR SAW THE POTENTIAL OF DAR AS A DEEP-WATER PORT
ADDRESS TANZANIA (MAP 7, G3) **HEIGHT** 14M **SIZE** 165 SQ KM
POPULATION 3.1 MILLION **LONELY PLANET RANKING** 144

**A total escape from the big-city hustle, a week
in 'Dar' is chilling out on the coast Robinson
Crusoe–style with the crystal-green waters,
palm-fringed white beaches and coral reefs that
frame Tanzania's unofficial capital.**

ANATOMY

Dar's city centre, with most of the cheaper hotels and restaurants, is
spread out around the harbour. The green and pleasant area around
Shaaban Robert St holds foodstalls and hole-in-the-wall cafés, and
hotels line Libya St. Suburbs spread out west and north, and a ferry
connects the centre with the tranquil southern beaches outside the
village of Kigamboni. To the north are resorts and white-sand tropical
beaches. Dar's city centre is fairly compact, and if you can stand the
relentless heat, you should have no problems getting around on foot.
Otherwise, catch city buses, *dalla-dallas* (pick-up or minibus) or taxis,
which are everywhere.

PEOPLE

Almost the entire local population is native African (over 100 tribes),
while the remainder is made up of Asians, Europeans and Arabs.
Kiswahili (Swahili) is the language of Dar es Salaam, though some
English is spoken due to the huge influx of expatriates attracted to Dar's
beaches. A vibrant Asian population spices up the city and its food,
while a Middle Eastern influence is still present. Around two-fifths are
Christian, with another two-fifths Muslim and the rest following
indigenous beliefs.

TYPICAL DARIEN

Dariens are open, warm and unfailingly generous. They are predominantly
married and very family-oriented. They are as hospitable as they are
conservative and might just as easily take you on a hand-held guided tour
through the dusty streets as look askance at your piercings and tattoos.
Regardless, the word 'welcome' is on every Darien's lips.

THE LIFE OF A FISHERMAN IS NOT ALL HARD WORK AND NO PLAY.

DEFINING EXPERIENCE

Sipping spiced tea over breakfast then heading to the stunning Kim Beach to alternate swimming and strolling along the white sand before checking out the thriving local hip-hop scene at the latest off-the-beaten-track venue.

STRENGTHS

◢ Beaches second to none
◢ Safaris
◢ Cheap hotels
◢ The National Museum of Tanzania
◢ Shaaban Robert St
◢ International flights
◢ Global cuisine
◢ Chilled-out atmosphere

WEAKNESSES

◢ Relentless heat
◢ Horrendously late trains
◢ The *bhangi* (marijuana) scam
◢ Muggers

GOLD STAR

Beaches – Dar is blessed with glorious lost-in-a-tropical-paradise beaches just a few kilometres from the city centre.

STARRING ROLE IN...

◢ *Zanzibar* by Giles Foden
◢ *Uharu Street* by MG Vassanji
◢ *Dar es Salaam by Night* by Ben Mtobwa

See the art exhibitions, witchcraft and ritual items from all over the country at the attractive National Museum of Tanzania.

Eat the famous *mishkaki* (grilled meat) with the locals at Chef's Pride.

Drink a liquid lunch in the fun beachfront bar at Coco Beach.

Do take a 'day-in-the-life' tour with the Kigamboni Community Centre.

Watch *ngoma* (drumming and dancing) performances at the Village Museum.

Buy jewellery, sculptures, candles, stationery and other items crafted by disabled artists from recycled materials at the Wonder Workshop.

After dark make a beeline for the Mbalamwezi Beach Club, a popular beach bar right on the sand.

HE SELLS SEA SHELLS BY THE SEASHORE.

A REMNANT OF ISLAMIC DESIGN.

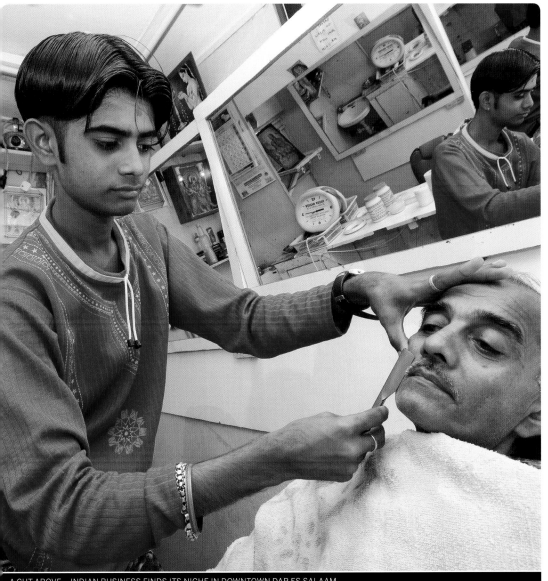

A CUT ABOVE – INDIAN BUSINESS FINDS ITS NICHE IN DOWNTOWN DAR ES SALAAM.

THE DEVOUT FIND A PLACE FOR PRAYERS AT THE RED MOSQUE.

Delhi

DATE OF BIRTH 500 BC; HISTORICAL EVIDENCE INDICATES SETTLEMENT AT ABOUT THIS TIME; THE BRITISH MADE DELHI THE CAPITAL IN 1911 **ADDRESS** INDIA (MAP 9, B4) **HEIGHT** 218M **SIZE** 1483 SQ KM **POPULATION** 12.8 MILLION (CITY); 17 MILLION (METRO) **LONELY PLANET RANKING** 060

Don't let your first impressions of Delhi stick like a sacred cow in a traffic jam: get behind the madcap façade and find the inner peace of a city rich with culture and human diversity, deep with history and addictive to epicureans.

ANATOMY

In Old Delhi there's the main Inter State Bus Terminal (ISBT), and to the south, the New Delhi train station. Near the station is Paharganj, packed with cheap accommodation and acting as a buffer zone between the old and new cities. New Delhi can be broken into the business and residential areas around Connaught P1 (the city's core) and the government areas around Rajpath to the south. Running south from Connaught P1 is Janpath, which has the tourist office, hotels and a shopping strip. Take your choice of buses, auto-rickshaws, motorised rickshaws or taxis.

PEOPLE

Due to Delhi's extreme cultural diversity, few city residents can lay claim to being 'real' Delhi-wallahs. Most of the population comprises Hindu-Punjabi families originally from Lahore, with a constant influx of new residents. The main languages spoken are Hindi, English and Punjabi. After the Partition (1947), the largely Muslim city became mostly Hindu.

TYPICAL DELHI-WALLAH

Shrewd, wily and resourceful, the typical citizen is generally tolerant of religion and the lack of personal space. Arranged marriages are still the norm, though in Delhi more residents marry for love than ever before. Delhi-wallahs share a fondness for great food, good cricket and a big shindig, with some sort of festival to be found round every corner.

DEFINING EXPERIENCE

Rambling around Old Delhi's historic Red Fort and Jama Masjid before diving into the old city's rambunctious bazaars and recuperating later on in the serene surrounds of Humayun's Tomb.

279

A TRICYCLE MADE FOR THREE – SOMETIMES PEDAL POWER IS THE QUICKEST WAY AROUND TOWN.

A YOUNG BOY OPTS FOR A WINDOW SEAT ON A TRAIN LEAVING OLD DELHI STATION.

PRACTITIONERS OF YOGA RELAX AND CONTORT AT A MORNING CLASS IN LODI GARDENS.

STRENGTHS
◢ Chandni Chowk bazaar
◢ The Red Fort
◢ *Dilli-ka-Chaat* (Delhi street food) – cheap, delicious cuisine
◢ Hazrat Nizam-ud-din Dargah
◢ Behemoth bazaars
◢ Jama Masjid
◢ Coronation Durbar site
◢ Raj Ghat
◢ Shalimar Bagh

WEAKNESSES
◢ Scams, touts and crooked taxi-wallahs
◢ Extreme traffic congestion and pollution
◢ Stench
◢ Unscrupulous travel agents
◢ Poverty

GOLD STAR
Delhi's beguiling charm – lose yourself while unwinding the secrets of the city's Mughal past in the labyrinthine streets of Old Delhi before emerging into the wide open spaces of imperial New Delhi with its generous leafy avenues.

STARRING ROLE IN...
◢ *Monsoon Wedding* (2001)
◢ *The Guru* (2002)
◢ *American Daylight* (2004)

See India's largest mosque, the awe-inspiring Jama Masjid, the final architectural extravagance of Shah Jahan.

Eat fat, syrupy *jalebis* (fried, sweet 'squiggles') at Jalebiwala, near the Sisganj Gurdwara.

Drink brutally good Bloody Marys at the Imperial Hotel, as you unwind from haggling hard at the nearby Janpath Market.

Do chill out from the vicissitudes of Delhi life in the pleasant grounds of Humayun's Tomb, a superb example of early Mughal architecture.

Watch Bollywood blockbusters at the Imperial Cinema.

Buy eye-popping handicrafts, *agarbathi* (incense), spices and tea from Chandni Chowk, Old Delhi's famous shopping street of bazaars.

After dark catch the Dances of India at the Parsi Anjuman Hall; regional performances include Tamil, Kathakali and Manipuri.

Dhaka

NICKNAME CITY OF MOSQUES **DATE OF BIRTH** AD 4; AS A SMALL
BUDDHIST TOWN **ADDRESS** BANGLADESH (MAP 9, C5) **HEIGHT** 8M
SIZE 414 SQ KM **POPULATION** 12.8 MILLION **LONELY PLANET RANKING** 100

Colourful and chaotic at a glance, Dhaka throbs with the raw (and infectious) energy of a spirited capital juggling civic deterioration, modern development and the realities of daily life as one the world's densest cities.

ANATOMY

Situated amid a maze of rivers and canals, Dhaka is both a city of relics and a melting pot of architectural styles. The frenzied – and yet curiously effective – network of bus services, trains and rickshaws will get you around town to see the main attractions. These sites are clustered in the three major sections of the city: Old Dhaka, a labyrinth of narrow streets lined with Moghul-era structures, including the premier attraction – the Lalbagh Fort on the Buriganga River; Central Dhaka, which retains the whitewashed colonial buildings of its former role as the British part of the city and is now home to the celebrated National Assembly building designed by American architect Louis Kahn; and suburban Dhaka, where the best restaurants in town are to be found.

PEOPLE

The nationality of Dhaka's citizens is almost 100% Bengali (Bengal being the regional entity that was split into West Bengal and East Pakistan at the time of Indian/Pakistani independence in 1947). The nation's official language is Bangla (also known as Bengali) and while just under a fifth of the population is Hindu, the vast majority is Muslim.

TYPICAL DHAKA CITIZEN

Most citizens are working-class Islamic men and women who navigate their way through the gridlock of rickshaws to spend long hours in factories, on the river or in the fields. On the way home they may stop at one of the dilapidated floating restaurants on the river's edge for a quick bite. Despite their industry, they are also prepared to strike, and demonstrations are common in the capital. While high unemployment is a problem throughout Bangladesh, in the capital there is a growing middle class. This stratum is made up of young, educated Bangladeshis – often found in hip cafés – or families from the well-to-do inner suburbs.

MONSOON MONET – BOATMEN PICK A PATH THROUGH LUSH WATER HYACINTHS ON BURIGANGA RIVER DURING THE WET SEASON.

DEFINING EXPERIENCE

Riding into town for a leisurely hot breakfast at Café Mango, followed by bird-watching in the Botanical Gardens, wandering along the riverbanks to see the Lalbagh Fort and the Pink Palace, and then heading to Gulshan Ave for an indulgent meal.

STRENGTHS

- ◢ The romantic Old Dhaka region
- ◢ Bazaars and handicrafts
- ◢ Good variety of great local, Asian and European restaurants
- ◢ *Shankharis* (Hindu artisans)
- ◢ Diversity of Eastern and Western-influenced architecture
- ◢ Botanical Gardens and the National Museum
- ◢ Asian Art Biennale – a month-long cultural event

WEAKNESSES

- ◢ Heat and humidity during the summer months; floods
- ◢ Poverty
- ◢ Overpopulation, leading to frequent traffic jams and air pollution
- ◢ Pickpockets
- ◢ Hard to get a beer (aside from expat bars, alcohol is banned)

GOLD STAR

Its many faces – the Eastern and Western influences of the city's past are richly woven into the challenging realities of today, giving modern-day Dhaka a uniqueness that surmounts the apparent clutter of the city.

STARRING ROLE IN...

- ◢ *Tale of the Darkest Night* (2001)
- ◢ *The Shadow Lines* by Amitav Ghosh

See the activity on the Buriganga River as people bathe, rest, fish and cook.

Eat Mexican at El Toro, the only Mexican restaurant in Bangladesh, and surely the best on the Indian subcontinent.

Drink alcohol with a newly befriended expat in one of the few legal drinking establishments in Dhaka.

Do a walking tour around the historic Hindu artisan hub of Hindu St.

Watch the moving gallery on Dhaka's streets as the rickshaws pass displaying the bright and varied artwork on their back panels.

Buy a personalised piece of rickshaw art.

After dark try to get into an international club.

AN ELDERLY RICKSHAW WALLAH CROUCHES BY HIS VEHICLE TO WAIT FOR HIS NEXT CUSTOMER.

RICKSHAW GRIDLOCK ON A CITY STREET DURING A PUBLIC TRANSPORT STRIKE.

CHILDREN IMPROVISE A CRICKET PITCH IN AN ALLEYWAY OF OLD DHAKA.

FIFTY YEARS AGO THERE WAS ONLY DESERT AND A SMALL TRADING POST HERE.

Dubai

NICKNAME DO BUY **DATE OF BIRTH** 5000 BC; WHEN TRADE IN THE AREA BEGAN **ADDRESS** UNITED ARAB EMIRATES (MAP 8, F6) **HEIGHT** 5M **SIZE** 35 SQ KM **POPULATION** 2.3 MILLION **LONELY PLANET RANKING** 115

With a slightly surreal mix of dazzling consumerism and Arabian culture with an Islamic influence, Dubai has a cosmopolitan and easy-going charm that makes it the best introduction to the Middle East.

ANATOMY

Dubai is really two towns split by the Dubai Creek (Khor Dubai), an inlet of the Gulf. North of the creek lies Deira, an older city centred on creekside Baniyas Rd, while the south has the glittering new office buildings of Bur Dubai clustered along Sheikh Zayed Rd (also known as Trade Centre Rd) and crowned by Burj Khalifa, the world's tallest man-made structure. There's little public transport in the city, so to negotiate Dubai you'll pay out a small fortune for taxis.

PEOPLE

The majority of Dubai's residents are expats (many drawn from Asia and the Philippines), who were born in other countries and have chosen to make the city their home. UAE nationals (or Emiratis) are a minority. While the official language is Arabic, you can expect to hear English, Persian, Hindi and Tagalog spoken throughout the city.

TYPICAL DUBAI CITIZEN

Emiratis like to shop and Dubai is certainly the fashionista capital, with more Porsches than you're ever likely to see in a showroom, but the city is anything but superficial. The call to prayer is probably the only thing that will get people off their mobiles, but Muslims are very devout in the city. Every neighbourhood has its own mosque and Ramadan is a month that stops DJs spinning in town. Even partying expats respect the Muslim customs and restrict their drinking to a select group of hotels.

DEFINING EXPERIENCE

Window shopping at Deira City Centre, sailing in for a closer view of the iconic glass sail of Burj al-Arab, sniffing the richness of Deira Spice Souq, catching a dhow to Deira, and finally relaxing with a *sheesha* (tobacco water pipe often flavoured with honey or apple) in a courtyard café.

NOT YOUR AVERAGE FAMILY CAR – DUBAI'S WEALTH IS VERY VISIBLE.

STRIKINGLY BEAUTIFUL JUMEIRAH MOSQUE IS AN EXQUISITE EXAMPLE OF ARABIAN ARCHITECTURE.

FACELIFT – DUBAI IS A CITY UNDER PERMANENT CONSTRUCTION.

STRENGTHS

- ◢ Burj Khalifa
- ◢ Burj al-Arab
- ◢ Dubai Museum
- ◢ Jumeirah Mosque
- ◢ Deira Gold and Spice Souqs
- ◢ Dhows
- ◢ Sheikh Saeed al-Maktoum House
- ◢ Meydan Racecourse
- ◢ Wild Wadi Waterpark
- ◢ Jumeirah Beach Park

WEAKNESSES

- ◢ Living and working conditions of labourers
- ◢ Beachfront resorts
- ◢ Searing summer heat

GOLD STAR

Wacky construction projects – whether it's the world's largest indoor ski slope, biggest mall or reclaiming islands in the shape of the globe, there's always design challenges being dreamed up in Dubai.

STARRING ROLE IN...

- ◢ *Code 46* (2003)
- ◢ *Dubai Tales* by Mohammad al-Murr
- ◢ *Don't They Know It's Friday?* by Jeremy Williams

See the world's tallest building, the Burj Khalifa – at 828m, a ground-breaking feat of architecture and engineering.

Eat fish so fresh it's still flapping at the Fish Market, where you select the city's best seafood and pay by weight.

Drink nothing but water as you hit the mellow sheesha cafes to sample local life and play a game of backgammon.

Do take a dhow cruise to see how spice, gold and perfume are still delivered to the souqs (markets).

Watch the Bedouin dance *ayyalah* – a celebration of the tribe's courage, strength and unity – performed at the Heritage Village.

Buy spices at a souq, but only after haggling to save five dirhams.

After dark head to the candlelit Rooftop Bar for panoramic views – it's one of Dubai's most sublime spots.

Dublin

NICKNAME DUB **DATE OF BIRTH** 6TH CENTURY; ESTABLISHED AS
A MONASTIC SETTLEMENT **ADDRESS** IRELAND (MAP 4, E7)
HEIGHT 47M **SIZE** 921 SQ KM **POPULATION** 528,000 (CITY);1.8
MILLION (METRO AREA) **LONELY PLANET RANKING** 028

Dublin may not be a particularly pretty city, but for poetry, pubs, sporting life and garrulous sociability, you can't do better.

ANATOMY

Dublin sprawls around Dublin Bay with the River Liffey dividing the city. North of the river, busy O'Connell St leads to Parnell Sq and, to the west, revitalised Smithfield. On the south side lie the increasingly tedious Temple Bar and the stately houses and elegant parks of Georgian Dublin. The DART train line links the seaside suburbs, and the LUAS light-rail system connects the south to the centre.

PEOPLE

Traditionally, a Dubliner hails from between the canals, but it's now hard to put your finger on the city's physical or social boundaries. Expats returning home and migrants from the rest of Ireland are joined by significant numbers of Nigerians, Chinese, Romanians and Bosnians. A long way from the Gaeltacht (Irish-speaking region), Dubliners may speak a smattering of Irish, but are more famous for their own particularly colourful take on the English language.

TYPICAL DUBLINER

Dublin is one of Europe's most expensive cities, but with over half the population under 30, there's a youthful exuberance and open, optimistic spirit evident. Dubliners pride themselves on their irreverent humour, razor wit and keenness to debate. Although still overwhelmingly Roman Catholic, they tend to be relatively liberal; they're also fabulously self-deprecating and have a strong aversion to pretence of any kind. The rest of Ireland – pejoratively known as bogmen or *culchies* in the local vernacular – may not see this easy-going side, and tend to think that Dubliners are overly smug.

DEFINING EXPERIENCE

Skipping the fry-up because you can't be arsed with the weekend crowds

TAIL-LIGHTS BLAZE A BUSY TRAIL THROUGH DAME ST.

ALL HAIRSTYLES ARE WELCOME AT THE MARKET BAR.

at your local café, instead scoffing a bun and a cup of tea in Bewley's, then heading off to an international rugby test at Lansdowne Rd (Aviva Stadium), seeing Ireland getting the lard beaten out of them, and then going to Ba Mizu for pints and a plate of stew, though not getting too bladdered because you've got tickets to see a gig at Whelan's.

STRENGTHS

◢ Cracking nightlife, every night of the week
◢ Well-preserved Georgian streetscapes
◢ The restaurant scene, including great Modern Irish food
◢ St Stephen's Green
◢ Proud literary heritage
◢ Kilmainham Gaol
◢ The banter
◢ Trinity College
◢ The Liffey's bridges
◢ Sports-obsessed culture
◢ Fitzwilliam Sq
◢ Irish Museum of Modern Art, both the collections and the site

WEAKNESSES

◢ City-centre traffic, especially on the quays
◢ Crass, soulless 'theme' bars
◢ Overpriced pints
◢ Urban planning, or lack of it
◢ The rain

GOLD STAR

Pub culture – despite the onslaught of gastropubs and chains, Dublin is still the best place for a pint in the world.

THE HA'PENNY BRIDGE GRACEFULLY ARCHES OVER THE LIFFEY.

STARRING ROLE IN...

- *Veronica Guerin* (2003)
- *Intermission* (2003)
- *The General* (1997)
- *Circle of Friends* (1995)
- *Into the West* (1992)
- *The Commitments* (1991)
- *My Left Foot* (1989)
- *The Dead* (1988)
- *Ulysses* by James Joyce
- *Paddy Clarke Ha Ha Ha* by Roddy Doyle
- *Cowboys and Indians* by Joseph O'Connor

See panoramic views of the city through the bottom of a pint glass at the Gravity Bar – part of the Guinness Storehouse.

Eat the national edible icon, Irish stew, a slow-simmered one-pot wonder of lamb, potatoes, onions, parsley and thyme (note, no carrots).

Drink the porter at Grogan's on South William St.

Do everything in your power to get a ticket to the All-Ireland Hurling Finals at Croke Park in September.

Watch a play at the Abbey Theatre during the Dublin Theatre Festival.

Buy a luxe Lainey Keogh sweater from Brown Thomas on Grafton St.

After dark take advantage of the late licence and the mood lighting upstairs at Hogan's.

THE CHURCH OF ST SAVIOUR'S STEEPLE TOWERS OVER THE PLAZA THAT ALSO, COINCIDENTALLY, BEARS HIS NAME.

RICHARD I'ANSON / GETTY IMAGES

Dubrovnik

NICKNAME THE CITY; THE PEARL OF THE ADRIATIC
DATE OF BIRTH 7TH CENTURY; WHEN THE RESIDENTS OF THE ROMAN
CITY OF EPIDAURUM (SITE OF PRESENT-DAY CAVTAT) FLED TO THE
ROCKY ISLET (WHICH THEY DUBBED LAUS), LOCATED AROUND THE
SOUTHERN WALLS OF PRESENT-DAY DUBROVNIK **ADDRESS** CROATIA
(MAP 5, O5) **HEIGHT** 49M **SIZE** 143 SQ KM **POPULATION** 47,000
LONELY PLANET RANKING 059

The lure of the magical walled city of Dubrovnik, adorned with fine Renaissance carvings and marble-paved streets, has given a boost to the entire region, creating a 'Dubrovnik Riviera' that is welcoming to residents and visitors alike.

ANATOMY

The city extends about 6km from the mouth of the Rijeka River in the west to the cape of Sveti Jakov in the east and includes the promontory of Lapad, a leafy residential suburb popular with tourists thanks to its rocky beaches, hostel and hotels. The old walled town lies southeast of Lapad at the foot of Srd Hill, halfway between Gruž Harbour and Sveti Jakov. The entire old town is closed to cars and is divided nearly in half by the wide street of Placa, also referred to as Stradun. Pile Gate is the western entrance to the old town and the eastern gate is Ploče. The city boundaries also include the Elafiti Islands (Šipan, Lopud, Koločep, Olipa, Tajan and Jakljan). Walking or cycling is the best way to get around; public transport in Dubrovnik is pretty well limited to buses and taxis.

PEOPLE

Since the 1991–95 war Dubrovnik's population has been almost exclusively Croat and almost exclusively Catholic, with small minority groups of Serbs, Slovenians, Italians, Czechs and Muslims.

TYPICAL DUBROVNIK CITIZEN

Dubrovnik's residents are generally relaxed and cheerful; their Mediterranean character is evident in everything from their second language (likely to be Italian) to the casual office hours that allow people to enjoy the long hours of sunlight on a beach or in an outdoor café. They are proud of their city and its cultural heritage and generally have strong and passionate views on the 'Homeland' or 'Patriotic' war.

LOOKING OVER ROOFTOPS FROM THE CITY WALLS REVEALS AN ORANGE THEME.

A SOLITARY PRIEST WENDS HIS WAY PAST THE ARCH OF THE FRANCISCAN MONASTERY.

A BELLY-DANCER CREATES AN ARCH OF HER OWN AT THE TROUBADOUR CAFÉ AND BAR.

DEFINING EXPERIENCE

Strolling along the walls of the fortified city, taking in the patchwork of honey-coloured roofs, before making your way down the town's pedestrian promenade, Placa, where you'll be overwhelmed by the heady rush of cultural, religious and historic landmarks – not to mention some fantastic cafés.

STRENGTHS

- Dubrovnik's Summer Festival – the most prestigious in Croatia
- The visible results of a dedicated reconstruction effort since the bombs of 1991
- Fortified town walls and gleaming marble streets
- Proximity to the quiet Elafiti Islands and the beaches of Cavtat
- Vibrant street life

WEAKNESSES

- Located in a zone that is both geologically and politically seismic
- The scramble of private-accommodation owners at the bus station eager for the tourist dollar

GOLD STAR

The wide marble street, Placa, lined with businesses, cafés, churches and palaces, encourages the fusion of commerce, pleasure and faith into a vibrant community life.

STARRING ROLE IN...

- *Casanova* (2005)
- *The Ragusa Theme* by Ann Quinton
- *The Road to Dalmatia* by Christopher Dilke

See the restored roofs of Dubrovnik from a walk around its walls.

Eat the local mussels at Kamenice, a convivial hang-out on one of Dubrovnik's more scenic squares.

Drink a strongly brewed espresso at the inviting Café Festival, while watching the crowds ambling down Placa.

Do take the kids to the aquarium where they can 'ooh' and 'aah' at the electric rays, conger eels, scorpion fish and seahorses.

Watch Shakespeare on the Lovrjenac fort terrace during the Summer Festival.

Buy local products at the city's colourful market.

After dark head to the city's hippest bar, Troubadour, for Marko's jazz stylings.

Edinburgh

NICKNAME ATHENS OF THE NORTH; AULD REEKIE (OLD SMOKY)
DATE OF BIRTH 900 BC; THERE ARE SIGNS OF HUMAN HABITATION
AT CASTLE ROCK AND ARTHUR'S SEAT FROM THIS TIME
ADDRESS SCOTLAND (MAP 4, F5) **HEIGHT** 134M **SIZE** 260 SQ KM
POPULATION 495,000 **LONELY PLANET RANKING 021**

Since the reinstatement of the Scottish Parliament in 1999, Edinburgh has been booming with rising property prices, new building projects, and wealthy inhabitants – in financial and cultural terms.

ANATOMY

Edinburgh is hilly and green, with Castle Rock the most prominent hill and Holyrood Park (home to Arthur's Seat) the largest green space. The only river, the water of Leith, runs along the northwestern border of New Town. New Town's Georgian terraces and squares are separated from the Old Town, to the south, by the valley of Princes St Gardens. Old Town is a delightful maze of medieval alleys trickling off the Royal Mile, which climbs from the Palace of Holyroodhouse up to Edinburgh Castle. Bus services are to be joined by a limited and much-delayed tram line.

PEOPLE

Edinburgh is Scotland's most cosmopolitan and middle-class city. Many Irish and English people have settled here and there are smaller ethnic communities, including Indians, Pakistanis, Bangladeshis, Italians, Poles, Chinese and Spanish. During the Edinburgh Festival the city's population swells to twice its size.

TYPICAL EDINBURGHER

Years of living on top of each other in densely packed tenements is often the reason given for Edinburghers' interest in each other's business. That said, locals are unlikely to start chatting to strangers. Although Leith (Edinburgh's port) became part of the city in 1920, its inhabitants are Leithers. A typical young professional probably spends his/her salary earned in financial services paying off a large mortgage on a tenement flat in the Southside; what's left goes on eating out.

SUNSET OVER EDINBURGH FROM CALTON HILL WITH THE DUGALD STEWART MONUMENT TO THE LEFT.

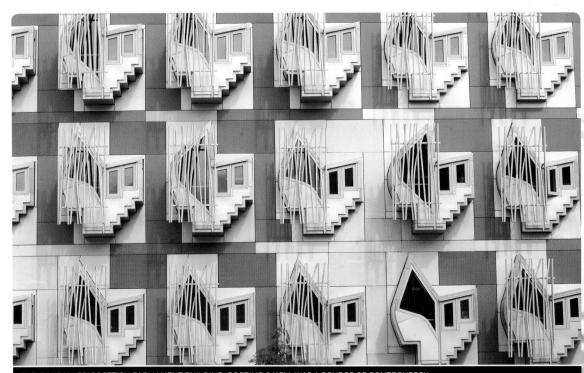

ENRIC MIRALLES' SCOTTISH PARLIAMENT BUILDING, COSTING £415M, WAS A SOURCE OF CONTROVERSY.

DEFINING EXPERIENCE

Sip a latte in Grassmarket before strolling the Royal Mile to Holyrood Park and climbing Arthur's Seat, followed by shopping in Harvey Nichols and a dish of oysters on ice at the Café Royal Oyster Bar.

STRENGTHS

- Museum of Scotland
- Cycling on Union Canal towpath
- Elegant Georgian terraces
- Arthur's Seat
- Scottish Enlightenment
- Scottish Parliament Building
- Princes St Gardens
- Victorian tenements to the south
- Modern Scottish cuisine
- The cleaning of sooty buildings
- The Edinburgh Festival Fringe
- The Military Tattoo
- Royal Mile
- Hogmanay – Scottish New Year's celebrations
- Clubbing in Cowgate

WEAKNESSES

- Soaring house prices
- Dearth of parking spaces
- Traffic jams

GOLD STAR

The Edinburgh Festival Fringe.

STARRING ROLE IN...

- *Trainspotting* (1996)
- *The Prime of Miss Jean Brodie* (1969)
- *Complicity* by Ian Banks
- Ian Rankin's Inspector Rebus series

THE ROYAL MILE, AS SEEN THROUGH THE LEGS OF A DEFIANT KILT-WEARER.

See Edinburgh Castle on its perfectly defensible perch, Castle Rock.

Eat chargrilled Aberdeen Angus fillet steak at the Tower, and peer over at the castle.

Drink one or two of the 100 malts on offer at Victorian Bennet's Bar.

Do walk up Arthur's Seat for an unbeatable view of the city.

Watch obscure plays with an audience of one at the Edinburgh Festival Fringe.

Buy exquisite, contemporary jewellery from Scottish jeweller Annie Smith.

After dark enjoy a night of theatre cabaret at the unusual Bongo Club.

THE BLUE-TONED MAJESTY OF IMAM SQ.

Esfahan

NICKNAME HALF THE WORLD (FROM THE PERSIAN RHYME, 'ESFAHAN NESF-E JAHAN': LITERALLY 'ESFAHAN IS HALF THE WORLD') **DATE OF BIRTH** 1587: WHEN SHAH ABBAS I CAME TO POWER AND HE SET OUT TO MAKE ESFAHAN A GREAT CITY **ADDRESS** IRAN (MAP 8, F3) **HEIGHT** 1773M **POPULATION** 1.6 MILLION **LONELY PLANET RANKING** 082

Iran's masterpiece, Esfahan is a stunning, colourful architectural gem, the centre of Persian arts and culture, brought to prominence by Shah Abbas the Great, set amid the desert of the central Iranian plateau.

ANATOMY

Chahar Bagh, 5km long, is the north–south artery through the centre of town. The Zayandeh River, crisscrossed by a series of historic arched bridges, runs roughly east–west. Northeast of the river are the expansive Imam Sq and the Bazar-e Bozorg (Grand Bazaar), while to the south lies the Armenian neighbourhood of Jolfa and the high-rises of the new town. Taxis and minibuses ply the main thoroughfares of the city, and if your haggling skills are good you could negotiate a private taxi.

PEOPLE

The population of Esfahan is as diverse as anywhere else in Iran. Besides Persians there are Azaris, occasionally visiting Bakhtiyari nomads, an Armenian Christian community, Zoroastrians (the first monotheists of Persia)and Afghan refugees, plus small Jewish and Baha communities.

TYPICAL ESFAHANI

Esfahanis are proud of their home and its status as the capital of Persian arts and culture. The typical Esfahani is likely to be articulate, educated and urbane, and as welcoming as Iranians elsewhere. They will be conscious of their Muslim faith, and tend to be family oriented, living at home until – and even after – they are married. An appreciation of art will be matched by a passion for football. Young people predominate – the majority of the Iranian population is younger than 30 years of age.

DEFINING EXPERIENCE

Wandering around the domed expanse of the Bazaar-e Bozorg, taking tea and smoking a *qalyan* (water pipe) at the outdoor tables of the Qeysarieh Tea Shop looking onto Imam Sq, poring over the exhibits at the Decorative

DANCE CLASS IN ESFAHAN IS AN ALL-MALE AFFAIR.

KEEPING THE FAITH, A MULLAH CLUTCHES A GOLD-EMBOSSED VOLUME OF THE HOLY KORAN.

Arts Museum of Iran, venturing to the Ateshkadeh-ye Esfahan to see the fire ceremonies of the Zoroastrians, strolling along the Zayandeh River and sipping tea in a teahouse under the bridges, musing on the frescoes and gardens of the Chehel Sotun Palace.

STRENGTHS
- The grandeur of Imam Sq
- Calligraphy, tile making, metalwork, glassware
- Carpets – where better to buy a Persian carpet?
- Haggling in the bazaar
- Teahouses and *qalyan*
- Armenian cathedrals
- Architectural greatness – palaces, mosques, grand squares

WEAKNESSES
- Touts around Imam Sq and the hard sell in the bazaar
- Scams involving impostor 'police'
- Pollution and hectic traffic
- Taxi drivers

GOLD STAR
Colour scheme – the symphony of royal blue, sunflower yellow and emerald tiles set atop the voluptuous domes and pointed arches of Imam Sq, all beneath a peerless, cloudless Persian blue sky.

STARRING ROLE IN...
- *The Road to Oxiana* by Robert Byron
- *Travels in Persia* by Sir John Chardin
- *The Siege of Isfahan* by Jean-Christopher Rufin
- *Portrait Photographs from Isfahan: Faces in Transition* by Parisa Damandan

See the view over Imam Sq from the elevated terrace of Ali Qapu Palace.

Eat *dolme bademjan* (stuffed eggplants) with rice, or *gaz* (nougat with pistachio and other chopped nuts).

Drink *chay* (tea) while holding a sugar lump between your teeth.

Do spend time absorbing the frescoes of Chehel Sotun Palace, including the depiction of a man kissing the foot of a half-naked maiden.

Watch craftsmen hammering copper pots, painting miniatures or enamelling copperware in the bazaar.

Buy a carpet or craftwork in the Grand Bazaar, but prepare to haggle.

After dark loiter over a *qalyan* in one of the teahouses.

LOOK OUT – ONE OF THE MANAR JOMBAN (SHAKING MINARETS), BUILT IN THE SAFAVIDS PERIOD.

Essaouira

NICKNAME WINDY CITY **DATE OF BIRTH** LATE 1500s; WHEN IT WAS FOUNDED BY THE PORTUGUESE **ADDRESS** MOROCCO (MAP 6, C2) **HEIGHT** 7M **POPULATION** 70,000 **LONELY PLANET RANKING** 184

Deemed a Unesco World Heritage Site, this picture-perfect town is an elegant marriage of Arabic and Mediterranean architecture. Bustling spice markets and winding whitewashed streets filled with artisan workshops combine a European sensibility with careful attention to Moroccan heritage.

ANATOMY

Essaouira has a marvellous setting between the Atlantic Ocean, a dune forest and river-mouth wetlands, and all attractions are within walking distance. The medina (old city), enclosed by walls with five main gates, is the main attraction. The walled town is pretty compact, split into the *mellah* (the old Jewish quarter), medina and kasbah, all laid out on a surprisingly simple grid system. The main thoroughfare, Ave de l'Istiqlal, merging into Ave Mohammed Zerktouni, runs from Bab Doukkala in the northeast to the main square, Place Moulay Hassan, in the southwest. Beyond the square is the historic port, fish market and bastion of Skala du Port, where there are panoramic views of the harbour, sweeping beaches to the east, and the offshore islands, Îles Purpuraires. The bus stations and taxis are 1km northeast of town.

PEOPLE

The official language is Arabic, but both French and Berber are spoken. As in the rest of Morocco, almost all of Essaouira's population is Muslim, with small groups of Christians and Jews.

TYPICAL ESSAOUIRA CITIZEN

The Moroccan people's love of the theatrical is most prominent in Essaouira, where you'll find a musician on every corner (some of them only just knee high...). Bodily contact plays an important role in communication: handshakes are a crucial icebreaker and affectionate public greetings are an art form. The people are also big on community. Family loyalty and responsibility extends to everyone in the neighbourhood: beggars are always offered money and a displaced woman always has a place to sleep.

MUSIC EMANATES JOYOUSLY FROM THE STREETS OF ESSAOUIRA.

DEFINING EXPERIENCE

Getting lost in the labyrinth of narrow whitewashed lanes and discovering tranquil squares, spice markets and artisans in tiny workshops, then watching the sun set behind the picturesque stone ramparts of the historic port and sating your appetite at the sizzling seafood stalls lining the harbour.

STRENGTHS

- Recently classified as a World Heritage Site by Unesco
- Pedestrian-only (apart from donkeys and bicycles) medina
- World-class surfing destination
- Endless sandy beaches
- All attractions are within walking distance
- Labyrinthine backstreets filled with artisan workshops and markets
- Thriving local and international music and arts scene
- Fresh seafood

WEAKNESSES

- Hordes of day-trippers because of its proximity to Marrakesh
- Relentless, strong coastal wind
- Lack of environmental awareness

GOLD STAR

Seemingly more Mykonos than Morocco, Mediterranean Essaouira has something for everyone – it is both a windsurfing mecca and a cultural hub for music and international and local art.

STARRING ROLE IN...

- *Kingdom of Heaven* (2004)
- *Alexander* (2005)

See the Gnaoua and World Music Festival, Essaouira's four-day musical extravaganza.

Eat freshly caught seafood sizzling on outdoor grills down in the port.

Drink mint tea in Place Moulay Hassan.

Do a camel-riding excursion through the sand dunes or break your first sweat in a classic *hammam* (bathhouse).

Watch the sun set over the Atlantic from the historic 18th-century clifftop ramparts and turrets of Skala de la Ville.

Buy a painting by a local up-and-coming artist, or a beautiful raffia work.

After dark chill out at the laid-back bar on the lamp-lit roof terrace of Taros.

GET SOME SPICE IN YOUR LIFE AT THE MEDINA MARKETS.

MUSLIM WOMEN IN A BLUE DOORWAY – TYPICAL OF BLUE-AND-WHITE ESSAOUIRA.

SEAGULLS WATCH FROM THE UNESCO-LISTED CITY WALLS AS A FISHERMAN REPAIRS HIS NETS.

COBALT BLUE IS THE TRADITIONAL COLOUR OF CERAMICS MADE IN FEZ.

Fez

NICKNAME ATHENS OF AFRICA **DATE OF BIRTH** AD 789: FOUNDED BY IDRIS I **ADDRESS** MOROCCO (MAP 6, E2) **HEIGHT** 378M **SIZE** 16 SQ KM **POPULATION** 1 MILLION **LONELY PLANET RANKING** 067

As the first Islamic city in Morocco, Fez is the centre of Morocco's cultural and religious life and its calls to prayer five times a day serve as a strident reminder of this fact.

ANATOMY

Fez is a hotchpotch of twisting streets that are so narrow you can barely raise a decent yawn and stretch. Even smaller alleys venture off the main paths and people brush against people, overloaded donkeys, household goods and bags of wheat at every turn. The medina of Fez el-Bali (Old Fez), which is separated from modern Fez (the Ville Nouvelle) by the ancient walls, is where the city's mosques, shops, crafts, spices, and souq (market) are located along some 9000 streets. It is closed to motorised vehicles, so strap up your donkey.

PEOPLE

The majority of Fassis are Sunni Muslims of Arab, Berber or mixed Arab-Berber lineage. The Arab culture was established when Arabs invaded Morocco in the 7th and 11th centuries. While Arabic is the official language, Berber dialects are widely spoken and French is also seen as the language of business, government and diplomacy. In (much) earlier times, Fez was the scientific and religious centre of Morocco, where Muslims and Christians from Europe came to study.

TYPICAL FASSIS

The young Fassis have cast aside the trappings of their parents' lives, adopting fashions and lifestyles more readily identified with the West. However, many remain without work, and the smart, clean Ville Nouvelle disguises the sad lot of the poorer people living on the periphery. Fez' million or so inhabitants are straining the city to the utmost, and the old city, some experts have warned, is slowly falling apart. Fez continues to act as a barometer of popular sentiment – Morocco's independence movement was born here, and when there are strikes or protests, they are always at their most vociferous in Fez.

WORKERS AT A LEATHER TANNERY KNEAD ANIMAL SKINS.

FEZ-WEARING FASSIS STRAIN FOR A GLIMPSE OF THE KING ALONG A CITY STREET.

DEFINING EXPERIENCE

Walking through one of the medina's seven ancient gateways, then exploring its labyrinthine streets and crumbling grandeur before pulling up a goat-leather stool and tucking into a traditional tagine.

STRENGTHS

- Luxurious *hammams* (bathhouses)
- *Zellij* mosaics (hand-cut tiles arranged in geometric and/or abstract patterns)
- Ancient doorways and walls
- Islamic architecture

WEAKNESSES

- The overwhelming smell from the tanneries – sniffing mint might settle the nerves
- The plundering of ancient private homes for their doors and windows for exportation

GOLD STAR

The annual Festival of World Sacred Music, which celebrates all manner of music: Sufi, Sephardic, Zulu, Pakistani *ghazal* chants, Renaissance, baroque Christian, and American gospel songs.

STARRING ROLE IN...

- *The Mummy* (1999)
- *The Amazing Race 3* (2002)
- *Aziz and Itto: A Moroccan Wedding* (1991)
- *The Jewel of the Nile* (1985)
- *Kundun* (1997)
- *The Last Temptation of Christ* (1988)
- *This Blinding Absence of Light* by Tahar Ben Jelloun

See the Bab Bou Jeloud (Blue Gate) of Old Fez.

Eat traditional tagines, *pigeon bastila* (a large pigeon pie) and mounds of hand-blended couscous.

Drink bladder-bursting amounts of *atay* (mint tea).

Do take a panoramic tour of the city in a taxi.

Watch the day unfurl from a café in Old Fez.

Buy a traditional Moroccan carpet in the medina.

After dark be serenaded in the courtyard of La Maison Bleue before eating a sumptuous feast of local fare under superb cedar ceilings.

SLOW FOOD – SNACK-SIZED SNAILS FOR SALE IN THE MARKET.

Florence

DATE OF BIRTH 30 BC; JULIUS CAESAR NAMED HIS GARRISON TOWN ON THE ARNO FLORENTIA **ADDRESS** ITALY (MAP 5, L4) **HEIGHT** 38M **SIZE** 3514 SQ KM **POPULATION** 375,000 **LONELY PLANET RANKING** 027

Star of the Renaissance, Florence is an aesthetic feast of world-famous paintings and sculpture, stunning churches and palaces, and beautiful people.

ANATOMY

Florence's city centre is relatively compact. The river Arno flows through the town, with the striking dome of Florence's Duomo (cathedral) and the *centro storico* (historic centre) on the northern side. The famous Ponte Vecchio crosses the river directly south of the cathedral and not far from the main square, Piazza della Signoria, and the Uffizi. On the other side of the Arno is the Oltrarno area, which is quieter and far less touristy. Walking or catching a bus is the best way to get around.

PEOPLE

The population comprises Italians originating from Florence and other parts of Italy and migrants from Asia, Africa (Tunisia and Senegal) or the Balkans. Makeshift settlements on the edge of the city house immigrants from Albania and Kosovo. The majority of Florentines are Catholic, while Muslims, Protestants and Buddhists make up the rest.

TYPICAL FLORENTINE

Most Florentines are unfairly good-looking and known for taking care of their appearance. They are polite and friendly, although they can sometimes appear standoffish – with the constant invasion of tourists, this is perhaps forgivable. They tend to be conservative, and modern architectural proposals cause massive controversy. They like it if visitors attempt to speak Italian, and may even award lower prices in return. Smoking is forbidden in many bars and restaurants, but a Florentine who wants to smoke will light up anyway.

DEFINING EXPERIENCE

Craning your neck admiring the ceiling of the Duomo, before ambling through the historic centre, strolling over the Ponte Vecchio and enjoying a gelato in Piazza Pitti.

THE BASILICA DI SANTA MARIA DEL FIORE LIGHTS UP THE NIGHT WITH ITS BEAUTY.

STRENGTHS

- Art everywhere you turn
- Restoration of medieval centre
- *Bistecca alla fiorentina* (Florentine steak) with Chianti or Brunello wine
- Cosimo de' Medici
- Duomo
- Uffizi
- Michelangelo's *David*
- Campanile
- Ponte Vecchio and Palazzo Vecchio
- Haggling at San Lorenzo market
- Boboli Gardens
- Fine-arts faculty at the Università degli Studi di Firenze
- Skiing the Abetone pistes north of Pistoia

WEAKNESSES

- Air pollution
- Constant restoration means things are often closed
- Crowds
- Snooty sales assistants
- Smelly streets and traffic
- Street prostitution
- Pigeons and rats

GOLD STAR

The Renaissance – it was born in Florence.

STARRING ROLE IN...

- *Hannibal* (2001)
- *La Vita è Bella* (Life is Beautiful, 2001)
- *Tea with Mussolini* (1999)
- *A Room with a View* (1986)

See Botticelli's *Birth of Venus,* Leonardo da Vinci's *Annunciation* and other artistic marvels at the Uffizi (book in advance to beat the crowds).

Eat devilishly good chocolate confections on the terrace of Caffè Rivoire and savour the view of the Palazzo Vecchio.

Drink a glass of Chianti Classico with the locals on Piazza Santo Spirito.

Do cross the Ponte Vecchio and mosey through the the the Oltrarno.

Watch 27-a-side football matches at the Gioco del Calcio Storico.

Buy a Pucci bikini and guarantee future beach cred.

After dark head to the moonlit outdoor dance area of Central Park.

PALE IMITATION – MICHELANGELO WAS A FLORENTINE.

PIAZZA SANTA CROCE HOSTS A FLORENTINE FOOTBALL MATCH, A 16TH-CENTURY GAME.

WHEN THE SUN GOES DOWN, TAKE A STROLL TO ADMIRE THE BUILDINGS AND OTHER STROLLERS.

LINING UP FOR WATERFRONT VIEWS – HOUSES ON THE HARBOUR AND RIVERSIDE ARE IN HIGH DEMAND.

Galway

NICKNAME CITY OF TRIBES **DATE OF BIRTH** 1124; WHEN THE CASTLE OF BUN GAILLMHE WAS BUILT FOR THE KING OF CONNACHT **ADDRESS** IRELAND (MAP 4, D6) **HEIGHT** 21M **SIZE** 50 SQ KM **POPULATION** 76,000 **LONELY PLANET RANKING** 080

Galway city is a rare confluence of elements: it's arty, romantic, youthful, eccentric and historic.

ANATOMY

Galway's tightly packed historic town centre lies on both sides of the fast-flowing River Corrib, and its curved, cobbled streets run down to the busy harbour. High St is closed to traffic most of the time, so often swarms with a festive crowd. The uninspiring Eyre Sq and the bus and train stations, as well as most of the main shopping areas, are on the river's eastern bank. To the southeast of Wolfe Tone Bridge is the historic, but now totally redeveloped, district of Claddagh; to the west is the faded beach resort of Salthill.

PEOPLE

Galway is one of Europe's most rapidly growing cities, with migrants from Eastern Europe, Asia and Sub-Saharan Africa mixing with a predominantly Irish Catholic community. Most notable, though, is the large percentage of students and a general skew towards those under 45. Although it's known as the gateway to the Gaeltacht (the Irish-speaking region), Galway has not had a solely Irish-speaking population since the 1930s.

TYPICAL GALWEGIAN

Galway has long been seen by the rest of Ireland, and beyond, as an essentially Celtic place. While Galwegians today are mostly young, and often progressive or even alternative in their outlook, it remains a city where historic cultural traditions are embraced and sustained. A local may be a musician, artist, thespian or intellectual, or combine an artistic pursuit with a boomtown professional life in IT or biotech. Galwegians have a high regard for a night out, and join the large number of students and, in the summer, tourists, in the pubs, restaurants and the streets.

DEFINING EXPERIENCE

Up early selling your hand-printed clothes at the Saturday markets, picking up some organic olives and brown bread after you've packed up your stall (it was a bit damp after all), grabbing a coffee at Griffin's, then taking your

QUAINT SHOPS ON QUAY STREET IN GALWAY.

FLESHING OUT A THOUGHT – AN INTROSPECTIVE LOCAL DAWDLES PAST A BUTCHER'S MOSAIC.

ST NICHOLAS COLLEGIATE CHURCH ON THE RIVER CORRIB

bodhrán (traditional Celtic drum) to Taaffe's for a session and fitting in a few pints before a comedy act at the King's Head.

STRENGTHS

- Galway Arts Festival and Galway Film Fleadh
- Lynch's Castle
- Traditional Irish music pubs
- Taibhdhearc na Gaillimhe (Irish-language theatre)
- Salthill Golf Course
- Collegiate Church of St Nicholas of Myra
- Seafood
- The wild beauty of the surrounding landscape
- Street life in summer
- Cute painted houses

WEAKNESSES

- The rise of the super-pub
- Prodigious rainfall
- Petty crime
- Race Week crowds

GOLD STAR

Laid-back cool – Galway comfortably incorporates traditional and alternative lifestyles.

STARRING ROLE IN...

- *City of the Tribes* by Walter Macken
- *The Guards* by Ken Bruen
- *Belios* by Órfhlaith Foyle

See Galway Bay from the beach at Salthill, after eating your fill at the Oyster Festival.

Eat Cratloe Hills Gold, Irish ham and wild salmon, from Sheridans Cheesemongers.

Drink locally made Johnny Jump Up cider at Neáchtains.

Do check out the Hall of the Red Earl for a sense of Galway life some 900 years ago.

Watch buskers on Shop or Quay Sts.

Buy *Anna Livia Plurabelle* by James Joyce at Charlie Byrne's Bookshop.

After dark catch a *céilidh* session at Tig Cóilí.

Georgetown

DATE OF BIRTH 1786; WHEN IT WAS FOUNDED BY BRITISH EAST INDIA COMPANY TRADER CAPTAIN FRANCIS LIGHT **ADDRESS** MALAYSIA (MAP 9, E9) **HEIGHT** 3.9M **POPULATION** 300,000 (CITY); 1.2 MILLION (METRO AREA) **LONELY PLANET RANKING** 180

Georgetown, capital of Pulau Penang, is an easy-going, colourful, good-time port city full of crumbling old shop houses, trishaws and ancient trades, such as carpentry, seal-making and prostitution.

ANATOMY

The old colonial district centres on Fort Cornwallis. Lebuh Pantai is the main street of the 'city', a financial district crammed with banks and stately buildings that once housed the colonial administration. You'll find many of Georgetown's popular cheap hotels along Lebuh Chulia in Chinatown, packed in among travel agencies, budget-priced restaurants and internet cafés. At the northern end of Lebuh Chulia, Jalan Penang is a main thoroughfare and a popular shopping street. It's a compact city; most places can easily be reached on foot or by trishaw.

PEOPLE

People of Chinese origin account for almost two-thirds of Georgetown's population, while Malays, Thais, Indians and Europeans comprise the rest. Languages spoken are English, Chinese, Malay and Tamil. Georgetown is home to a lively mix of Buddhists, Taoists, Muslims, Christians and Hindus.

TYPICAL GEORGETOWN CITIZEN

Georgetown has a long tradition of attracting adventurers, artists, intellectuals, scoundrels and dissidents, making for a spirited town ethos. From a fisher to a street hawker, the typical Georgetown resident is good-humoured and open-minded, embracing the long, colourful legacy of the 'melting pot of Asia' (perhaps better realised as a hot and spicy curry laksa) their city enjoys.

DEFINING EXPERIENCE

Sitting down to a fine tiffin lunch at Sarkies Corner in the grand Eastern & Oriental Hotel, before riding a trishaw around the colonial heart of Georgetown and stepping back in time at the Cheong Fatt Tze Mansion.

MONKEY BUSINESS – A BOY HANGS OUT IN PENANG.

STRENGTHS

- World Heritage–listed colonial district
- Penang Museum
- Eastern & Oriental Hotel
- Cheong Fatt Tze Mansion
- Fort Cornwallis
- Kek Lok Si Temple
- Snake Temple
- Little India
- Hawker stalls
- Khoo Kongsi clanhouse
- Affordable international-standard golf courses
- Temple of the Reclining Buddha

WEAKNESSES

- Pickpocketing, scams and petty crime
- Polluted beaches
- Attacks and muggings in dimly lit (and not a whole lotta) Love Lane

GOLD STAR

Old-school Chinese flavour – in its older neighbourhoods you could be forgiven for thinking that Georgetown's clock stopped 50 years ago.

STARRING ROLE IN...

- *Indochine* (1992)
- *Anna and the King* (1999)
- *The Touch* (2002)

See awesome views from the pagoda at the Kek Lok Si Temple.

Eat cheap Chinese noodles, satay and *popiah* (rice-paper rolls) courtesy of the many vendors in Chinatown's popular outdoor hawker centre, Hsiang Yang Fast Food.

Drink an Eastern & Oriental Sling at Farquhar's Bar, an upmarket British pub inside the E&O Hotel.

Do take in the sights, sounds and exotic scents of Georgetown's Little India.

Watch local girls throw oranges into the sea from the esplanade on Chap Goh Meh, the 15th day of the New Year celebrations.

Buy Penang pewter (a more affordable version of the better-known Selangor pewter, though of equal quality) from stores along Jalan Penang.

After dark go gigging Georgetown-style at Rock World as local Chinese bands hit the stage each weekend.

A YOUNG BASKETBALLER PEERS FROM THE BALCONY ON WASHING DAY.

LOCKED BICYCLES REST AGAINST THE COLUMNS OF AN ARCADE IN THE CENTRE OF TOWN.

LEAPING FOR JOY – SCOTTISH DANCERS AT A HIGHLAND GAMES IN GLASGOW.

Glasgow

NICKNAME GLESCA; RED CLYDESIDE **DATE OF BIRTH** 6TH CENTURY; WHEN GLASGOW GREW UP AROUND THE CATHEDRAL FOUNDED BY ST MUNGO **ADDRESS** SCOTLAND (MAP 4, F5) **HEIGHT** 8M **SIZE** 198 SQ KM **POPULATION** 635,000 (CITY); 2.8 MILLION (METRO AREA) **LONELY PLANET RANKING** 106

Scotland's largest city is the original rough diamond, with a fair share of economic pressure to create dazzling live music, a 24-carat bar scene and the hardest dialect to decipher in English.

ANATOMY

Rambling Glasgow has sights scattered throughout it, though the city centre on the north side of the Clyde River has two train stations that link even the most distant quarters of the city via the UK's second-largest metropolitan train network. The main centre is George Sq, though Sauchiehall St (running along the ridge of the northern part of the city) is a popular pedestrian mall with shops and pubs. Parallel to the river, Argyle St is another important shopping strip, along with its tributary, Buchanan St. The aptly named Merchant City is the commercial district in the city's centre, while the university is near Kelvingrove Park to the northwest, in the area deceptively known as the West End. Pollok Country Park and the Burrell Collection are in the South Side, southwest of the centre.

PEOPLE

Glasgow's population is overwhelmingly Caucasian, with a small group of Asians and Afro-Caribbeans. While English is theoretically the lingua franca, you could get confused by the slang and thick accents of Glaswegians.

TYPICAL GLASWEGIAN

Glaswegians are a tough, hard-working lot who love a pint and speak their own language, which they've cheerfully made impenetrable to visitors. There's a rough humour to it with a Glaswegian Kiss being a head butt and a lexicon that includes *wanner*, *stiffen* and *mollocate* for getting beaten up. Folk from Edinburgh refer to Glaswegians as *weegies* or *soap dodgers* – a dig at the city's working-class roots. Glaswegians are known for their fierce support of unions and the Labour Party, with huge protests against the poll tax in the 1990s, some of which ended in that other choice piece of Glaswegian patois, a *stoush*.

ARCHITECT NORMAN FOSTER'S SCOTTISH EXHIBITION AND CONVENTION CENTRE IS NICKNAMED 'THE ARMADILLO'.

SEAFARING CITY – THE CLYDE ARC AND FINNIESTON CRANE FACE EACH OTHER

THE RED KILTS OF THE SCOTS GUARDS.

DEFINING EXPERIENCE

Brunching in the West End's finest cafés, strolling and browsing the Barras flea market, picnicking in Kelvingrove Park, sampling the best of the pubs along Sauchiehall St, and then rocking out to the next Franz Ferdinand at the Barrowlands.

STRENGTHS

◢ Live-music scene
◢ Merchant City
◢ Willow Tea Rooms
◢ St Mungo's Museum of Religious Life & Art
◢ Hunterian Art Gallery
◢ Burrell Collection
◢ Tenement House
◢ Mitchell Library

WEAKNESSES

◢ Economic depression
◢ Unique dialect
◢ Neds (Non-Educated Delinquents)

GOLD STAR

Art – from Charles Rennie Mackintosh to Franz Ferdinand there's no doubt Glasgow has made a huge impact on the arts.

STARRING ROLE IN...

◢ *Young Adam* (2003)
◢ *Shallow Grave* (1994)
◢ *The Borrowers* (1997)

See the architectural canniness of Mackintosh House and get the rest of the Hunterian Art Gallery into the bargain.

Eat seasonal Scottish organic produce in the Victorian-era Buttery.

Drink at the Horse Shoe, a legendary city pub dating from the late 19th century, and largely unchanged, with the longest continuous bar in the UK.

Do stroll the grounds and woodland trails of Pollok Country Park and imagine you're the monarch of the glen.

Watch Glasgow's next big things at King Tut's Wah Wah Hut, where Oasis notoriously played their debut.

Buy everything you could imagine on Glasgow's 'Style Mile'.

After dark hang under the Arches, which attracts visiting DJs.

Granada

DATE OF BIRTH 1238; WHEN IT WAS FOUNDED BY IBN AHMAR, A PRINCE OF THE ARAB NASRID TRIBE **ADDRESS** SPAIN (MAP 5, D7) **HEIGHT** 680M **POPULATION** 258,000 **LONELY PLANET RANKING** 197

If there were a beauty contest lining up all the towns and cities of Spain, Granada would surely be declared the fairest of them all – it's a heart-stealer!

ANATOMY

Encapsulating Spanish allure, with atmospheric streets and masterful architectural feats, Granada is closer to Morocco's Tangier than Spain's capital of Madrid. The two major central streets, Gran Vía de Colón and Calle Reyes Católicos, meet at Plaza Isabel La Católica. From here, Calle Reyes Católicos runs southwest to Puerta Real, an important intersection, and northeast to Plaza Nueva. The street Cuesta de Gomérez leads northeast up from Plaza Nueva towards the Alhambra on its hilltop. The Albayzín, Granada's old Muslim quarter, rambles over another hill rising north of Plaza Nueva, separated from the Alhambra hill by the valley of the Río Darro. Below the southern side of the Alhambra is the old Jewish district, Realejo. The bus station (northwest) and train station (west) are out of the centre but linked to it by buses.

PEOPLE

Granada boasts a buzzing Spanish and international student population. Spanish is the language of choice but many tourism operators dabble in English.

TYPICAL GRANADINO

Granadinos are a gregarious, close-knit bunch, deeply rooted in their families and communities, and age-old traditions such as religious festivals, fairs and flamenco music. Like their fellow Andalucians, the people of Granada have a great capacity for enjoying themselves and give little emphasis to timetables and schedules.

DEFINING EXPERIENCE

Witnessing the Moorish splendour of the 11th-century Alhambra, the famed fortress and palace complex, and exploring the city's mystical old quarter where Gypsy-style music floats through the labyrinthine streets and households gather for late-afternoon feastings.

RENAUD VISAGE / PHOTOLIBRARY

SUNSHINE AND THE BEAUTIFUL SETTING OF THE PALACIO DE CAMARES IN THE ALHAMBRA ARE CONDUCIVE TO DAYDREAMING.

STRENGTHS

- Old-world atmosphere
- Compact and made for walking
- Interesting past: history buffs rejoice!
- University-town vibe
- The Alhambra's Palacio Nazaríes (Nasrid Palace), dubbed the best Islamic building in Europe
- Festivals and events including classical music extravaganzas
- Hiking and skiing aplenty in Sierra Nevada National Park

WEAKNESSES

- Stifling summer heat
- Tourist hordes, queues and accommodation headaches
- Downtown noise
- Bag snatchers who loiter at some tourist sights

GOLD STAR

Experiencing a taste of North Africa at Calle Calderería's many Arab-style cafés and Albayzín teahouses.

STARRING ROLE IN...

- *Doctor Zhivago* (1965)
- *Tales of the Alhambra* by Washington Irving
- *Driving over Lemons: An Optimist in Andalucia* by Chris Stewart
- *Moorish Spain* by Richard Fletcher
- *Andalucia* by Michael Jacobs
- *The Assassination of Federico García Lorca* by Ian Gibson

See Capilla Real, Granada's outstanding ode to late-Gothic splendour, mid-morning to soak up the atmosphere minus the tourist masses.

Eat in the narrow streets of Albayzín at El Agua where first-rate views of the Alhambra are guaranteed.

Drink *cava* (sparkling wine) at one of the tapas bars along on Calle de Elvira.

Do get lost while exploring the Darro Valley and the bohemian Albayzín.

Watch flamenco at Peña de la Platería, a genuine aficionados' club in an Albayzín warren.

Buy some *taracea* (marquetry; tiny pieces of bone and hardwood arranged in geometric patterns), used on boxes, tables, chess sets and frames – the best pieces have shell, silver or mother-of-pearl inlays.

After dark dance the night away with the oh-so-groovy student set at Granada 10, which opens at midnight.

ONE OF MANY PROCESSIONS IN HOLY WEEK.

LUMINOUS ALHAMBRA'S PALACIO NAZARIES HAS ENCHANTED VISITORS FOR GENERATIONS.

THE SLOPES OF THE SIERRA NEVADA OFFER SKIING IN WINTER.

THE SHIPPING TRADE SHAPED HAMBURG AND ITS WATERWAYS.

Hamburg

NICKNAME GATEWAY TO THE WORLD; CAPITAL OF LUST
DATE OF BIRTH AD 9: A MOATED FORTRESS CALLED HAMMABURG
WAS CONSTRUCTED IN WHAT IS TODAY THE CITY CENTRE
ADDRESS GERMANY (MAP 4, L8) **HEIGHT** 22M **SIZE** 755 SQ KM
POPULATION 1.8 MILLION **LONELY PLANET RANKING** 078

The entertainment capital of Germany, beautiful and historic Hamburg is both economically and culturally prosperous, with strong industry, an impressive music scene and a colourful and diverse local culture.

ANATOMY

Hamburg is shaped by water, with a wonderful harbour at its centre, three rivers and canals running through it, a number of lakes and around 2500 bridges. Most attractions cluster around the bustling core, with several vast green spaces to break up the intensity of the busy port. The Alsterfleet canal splits the centre into the Old Town, which is full of churches and Renaissance-style arcades, and the New Town, which contains the baroque church of St Michaeliskirche. The inner suburbs house popular entertainment districts, including the seedy Reeperbahn. There's a network of ferries, trains and buses.

PEOPLE

Hamburg's citizens are mostly German, with European immigrants comprising 15% of the population. Most locals are either Lutheran or Hindu. There are small groups of Jews and Muslims. German and its dialects are the main languages, though English is widely spoken.

TYPICAL HAMBURGER

The city's population comprises more millionaires than any other German city; the majority of Hamburgers live comfortably. They are proud of their city and love to shop and eat out. Most are political with concerns ranging from social democracy to the environment.

DEFINING EXPERIENCE

Strolling through the rowdy Fischmarkt munching a bratwurst (grilled sausage), balancing a beer and browsing for tulips as vendors hawk their wares, toe-tapping along to the locals joining in on the choruses of German pop tunes cranked out by bands at the market.

SIGHTSEEING THE SLOW WAY.

CHILEHAUS, FRITZ HÖGER'S EXPRESSIONIST TRIUMPH, MERCHANT DISTRICT.

BRAVE THE CHILL FOR THE CHRISTMAS FAIR.

STRENGTHS

◢ Drinking holes around virtually every corner
◢ Excellent and free tourist maps
◢ Cruises around the port
◢ Great music scene
◢ Historic buildings, bridges and churches
◢ The 'Art Mile' (string of art galleries and museums)
◢ Great café culture
◢ Flat city (good for cycling)
◢ German beer
◢ International cuisine
◢ Diverse character of the city
◢ Hamburger Dom festival

WEAKNESSES

◢ Junkies
◢ High cost of living
◢ Confusing train timetables

GOLD STAR

Entertainment central – whether you are up for clubbing, bar-hopping, a night of live music or a refined night at the theatre there are heaps of options...and it seems as though you are never more than a five-minute walk from a bar or pub in Hamburg.

STARRING ROLE IN...

◢ *Mirador* (1978)
◢ *Tomorrow Never Dies* (1997)
◢ *Bella Marta* (Mostly Martha, 2002)

See the saucy exhibits at the Erotic Art Museum, which showcases a collection of erotic art from the 16th century to the modern day.

Eat classic French fare at Café Paris, an elegant yet relaxed brasserie housed within a spectacularly tiled 1882 butchers' hall and adjoining art-deco salon.

Drink (weather permitting) at Strandperle, the mother of Hamburg's much-loved beach bars.

Do check out the animated collection of bars, sex clubs, restaurants and pubs in the 'sin centre' of St Pauli.

Watch a cutting-edge adaptation of Goethe's Faust at Thalia Theater.

Buy a bratwurst and a beer at the boisterous Fischmarkt.

After dark pay tribute at the famous basement of the Kaiserkeller – one of the local live venues gigged by the Beatles in the '60s.

Hanoi

DATE OF BIRTH 1010; WHEN IT WAS TRANSFERRED FROM THE MOUNTAINS TO ITS PRESENT LOCATION **ADDRESS** VIETNAM (MAP 9, F6) **HEIGHT** 16M **SIZE** 2146 SQ KM **POPULATION** 6.5 MILLION **LONELY PLANET RANKING** 023

Hanoi's beguiling boulevards, *belle époque* architecture and peaceful parks and pagodas are enough to recommend it, but there's also the bonus of a vibrant, optimistic population and fantastic food.

ANATOMY

Hanoi sprawls along the Red River (Song Hong), which is spanned by three bridges. The city is divided into seven central districts *(quan)*, surrounded by outlying neighbourhoods called *hyyen*. Peaceful Hoan Kiem Lake lies between the maze of the Old Quarter in the north, and the elegant Ba Dinh district (French Quarter) to the south. Go west for the monument-strewn former Imperial City, or north to West Lake. Here two wheels *are* better than four: motorbike, bicycle and *cyclo* (pedicab) beat the buses every time.

PEOPLE

Ethnic Vietnamese *(kihn)* dominate Hanoi, though there are a small number of ethnic minorities from around Vietnam. Second languages reflect a historical chronology: those under 30 (almost three-quarters of the population) speak English, the middle-aged may have a smattering of Russian and German and the elderly are often fluent in French.

TYPICAL HANOI CITIZEN

Hanoi residents are known for their reserve and strength of character, coupled with energy and resourcefulness. After a history of colonisation, war and Communist rule, they tend to be suspicious both of authority and of outsiders but are also hospitable. Family values abound – beneath the nonchalant cool-kid-on-motorbike pop-culture persona there's usually a strong sense of Confucian responsibility and discipline. The younger generation are well educated and optimistic about the future.

DEFINING EXPERIENCE

Having your shoes shined at 5am, watching merchants setting up their stalls, then off to the flower market to buy blooms and some plastic baskets, followed by *pho* (beef noodle soup) for breakfast with ground pork and mushrooms at the little place next to the Binh Minh Hotel.

A SHOULDER TO LEAN ON – SCHOOLCHILDREN STICK TIGHTLY TOGETHER.

HUC BRIDGE CROSSES HOAN KIEM LAKE TO CONNECT WITH JADE ISLAND.

TIME OUT FOR A BOWL OF PHO, VIETNAM'S STAPLE SOUP.

SHORT BACK AND SIDES FOR A YOUNG CUSTOMER AT A STREET SALON.

STRENGTHS

- Youthful energy
- Long Bien Bridge
- Temple of Literature
- Communist monuments – drab and spectacular in turn
- City lights reflecting on Hoan Kiem Lake
- Mung dumplings with sweet ginger sauce in winter
- Hotel Metropole and other French colonial architecture
- Tree-lined boulevards
- *Ga tan* (stewed chicken with herbs, dates and grilled baguettes)
- One Pillar Pagoda
- Coffee – strong and sweet
- Tight-knit sense of community

WEAKNESSES

- Traffic
- Bureaucracy
- Censorship
- Over-the-top architectural styles of the newly wealthy
- Overcrowding
- Government surveillance

GOLD STAR

The 36 streets of the Old Quarter combine hundreds of years of history with intriguing shopping and an insight into Hanoi's heart.

STARRING ROLE IN...

- *Les Filles du botaniste chinois* (2005)
- *The Quiet American* (2002)
- *Daughter from Danang* (2002)
- *Marché à Hanoi* (1903)

See the t'ai chi practice at Hoan Kiem Lake at dawn.

Eat fried squid with dill, tofu with tomatoes and grilled chicken at a *bia hoi* (beer tavern) in the old town – maybe Quan Bia Minh on Dien Liet.

Drink *xeo* (rice wine) and hang with the Minsk motorcycle club.

Do play a game of badminton in Lenin Park.

Watch out for the giant 200kg turtle inhabiting Hoan Kiem Lake.

Buy bolts of silk or order bespoke shirts along Pho Hang Gai.

After dark catch a Vietnamese pop star performing at the Hanoi Opera House then go for a motorbike ride around West Lake.

RESTORATION NATION – VINTAGE AMERICAN CARS AND THE CRUMBLING BUILDINGS ALONG THE MALECON BOTH NEED TENDER LOVING CARE.

Havana

DATE OF BIRTH 1514: WHEN THE PORT OF SAN CRISTÓBAL DE LA HAVANA WAS FOUNDED BY DIEGO VELÁZQUEZ
ADDRESS CUBA (MAP 2, K2) **HEIGHT** 24M **SIZE** 740 SQ KM
POPULATION 2.1 MILLION **LONELY PLANET RANKING** 035

The jewel of the Caribbean, Havana's faded colonial grandeur, magnificent Malecón (waterfront promenade) and charming old town make it a hit.

ANATOMY

The city faces the Straits of Florida (a big temptation for many) with its vast seafront, the famed Malecón. The centre of the city is divided up into La Habana Vieja (Old Havana), a Unesco World Heritage Site despite the crumbling colonial buildings, and Centro Habana, the modern city to the west. Train is the best way to get around.

PEOPLE

Havana is almost entirely populated by Cubans, with a small diplomatic community. The majority of citizens are of Spanish descent, with the rest of mixed race or African descent, and some Chinese. Almost half are Catholic; a small minority are Protestant or Santería (many Catholics also practice Santería). Spanish is the official language.

TYPICAL HABANERO

Definitely a highlight of the trip, the Habaneros are great fun. Forget any preconceptions you might have of life under a totalitarian government – Habaneros carry on regardless, with an almost bloody-minded determination to be as happy and unfazed by the problems of everyday life as possible.

DEFINING EXPERIENCE

Knocking back an ice-cold *mojito* (a cocktail of rum, lime, sugar, mint and soda water) at almost any bar in the old town, as locals stare down at you from their dilapidated balconies (a hobby among Habaneros, particularly the elderly).

STRENGTHS

⊿ Extraordinarily friendly and fun-loving locals
⊿ Festival Internacional de Jazz

ON THE STREETS OF THE OLD TOWN, A GLAMOROUS HABANERA PAUSES FOR A PUFF.

- Mind-blowing buildings and bright colours everywhere
- Few better places to drink rum-based cocktails and listen to live music

WEAKNESSES

- The food can be extremely unexciting after a few days
- The appalling human-rights record
- Beach resorts that keep Cubans apart from foreigners

GOLD STAR

La Habana Vieja – the best-preserved colonial Spanish complex in the Americas – is a joy to walk round. True, much of it has been sanitised far more than is proper, but stray into the backstreets from the revamped roads and you'll be mesmerised by the sultry Caribbean charm of Havana once more.

STARRING ROLE IN...

- *Fresa y Chocolate* (1994)
- *The Buena Vista Social Club* (1999)
- *Before Night Falls* (2000)

See the Capitolio Nacional, former seat of the Cuban government and one of the highlights of Havana's rich architectural heritage.

Eat ice cream at the famous Coppelia Ice Cream parlour for the true Habanero experience.

Drink plenty of delicious mojitos and Cuba Libre cocktails at the fabulous neoclassical Inglaterra Hotel in Parque Central.

Do not forget that there's more to Havana than the old town – explore the further-flung parts and don't miss the Playas del Este.

Watch the monthly display of hundreds of singers and musicians performing in Plaza de la Catedral.

Buy from an endless array of books and posters from the unofficial stands on Plaza Vieja.

After dark head to a nightspot or cabaret club in La Habana Vieja.

Heidelberg

DATE OF BIRTH AD 765; WHEN SETTLERS CAME TO THE AREA
ADDRESS GERMANY (MAP 5, L1) **HEIGHT** 110M **POPULATION** 147,000
LONELY PLANET RANKING 099

Germany's oldest university city oozes dreamy charm with pretty 18th-century buildings, an alluring semi-ruined castle and a general air of intelligentsia – Goethe was enchanted, as you will be too.

ANATOMY

The main feature of Heidelberg is the Neckar River, spanned by the Alte-Brücke at the eastern end and the Theodor-Heuss-Brücke towards the west. South of the river lies the evocative Altstadt (old town), whose main street, the pedestrianised Hauptstrasse, known as the Royal Mile, runs from Bismarckplatz (the old town's epicentre) through the Markt to Karlstor. Dominating the city from a hill to the southeast is the fairy-tale Schloss (castle). Public transport consists of buses and trams.

PEOPLE

Heidelberg is a student town, with one in five residents reportedly there for learning. The city receives 3.3 million visitors every year, the majority of whom come from the USA and Japan, with the UK and other European countries also contributing. There are two US military communities southwest of the Altstadt. Less than a fifth of Heidelberg's inhabitants are not German nationals.

TYPICAL HEIDELBERG CITIZEN

Heidelberg is one of Germany's great centres of intellectual study, so the fact that its inhabitants are largely well educated and cultured will hardly come as a surprise. Concerts, which are held outdoors in summer, are well attended, and foreign films are popular. Well accustomed to receiving visitors, people are very friendly and most speak some English.

DEFINING EXPERIENCE

Taking the funicular up to the Schloss and admiring the city from up high, then descending to town, hiring a bicycle and exploring the surrounding countryside before retiring to the Altstadt for a refreshing litre of beer and a good book.

A WOMAN TEARS PAST THE ALTE-BRÜCKE.

STRENGTHS

- Neckar River
- Schloss
- Ruprecht-Karl-Universität (Heidelberg university)
- Alte-Brücke
- Heiliggeistkirche
- 19th-century romantics such as Goethe
- Architectural unity (due to a total rebuild in the 18th century after invading French troops under Louis XIV devastated the city)
- Philosophising on Philosophonweg
- Cosy pubs
- Good beer
- Heidelberger Herbst, the massive autumn festival
- Christmas market
- Authentic charm
- Mild winters

WEAKNESSES

- Expensive and elusive accommodation
- Dull modern part of the city to the west (well, it can't all be gorgeous)
- Dearth of cheap eating options
- Students?

GOLD STAR

Intellectual charm: Heidelberg is the thinking person's crumpet.

STARRING ROLE IN...

- *A Tramp Abroad* by Mark Twain
- *Heidelberg: Sunset* by William Turner

See the crumbling magic of the Schloss, one of Germany's best Gothic-Renaissance castles, and survey the town in a regal manner.

Eat 'student kisses' (chocolate-covered wafers) at Café Knösel.

Drink dangerously addictive microbrewed beer in the convivial bar, Vetters im Schöneck.

Do a summer German-language course at Heidelberg University and waft around the town enjoying your part in the city's academic tradition.

Watch kaleidoscopic snap, crackle and pops at Schlossbeleuchtung, the triannual fireworks festival.

Buy a ticket for a castle-spotting boat trip through the Neckar Valley.

After dark join the crooners in Germany's oldest jazz club, Cave 54, where Louis Armstrong once played.

A STYLISED GIRAFFE PEERS INQUISITIVELY AT A MODERN BUILDING BY THE HAUPTBAHNHOF.

A PARADE'S BRASH BRASS SECTION RINGS OUT AT THE MARKETPLACE BY THE TOWN HALL.

MARK TWAIN WAS AN ADMIRER OF HEIDELBERG CASTLE'S PICTURESQUE RUINS.

POHJOISESPLANADI ST SEPARATES THE SEA FROM HELSINKI.

Helsinki

NICKNAME DAUGHTER OF THE BALTIC; WHITE CITY OF THE NORTH
DATE OF BIRTH 1550; WHEN IT WAS FOUNDED BY SWEDISH KING
GUSTAV VASA **ADDRESS** FINLAND (MAP 4, Q3) **HEIGHT** 46M
SIZE 686 SQ KM **POPULATION** 602,000 (CITY); 1.4 MILLION (METRO
AREA) **LONELY PLANET RANKING** 064

Progressively high-tech Helsinki is a fascinating combination of Swedish and Russian influences, an intimate city that is fast becoming one of Europe's hottest destinations, with a strong cultural vein and a nightlife that's the envy of northern Europe.

ANATOMY

Helsinki is built on a peninsula, with links by bridge and ferry to nearby islands. The city centre is built around the main harbour, Eteläsatama. The *kauppatori* (market square) – also known as the fish market – is on the waterfront between the ferry terminals. Further inland, but still within walking distance, are the bus and train stations. The Meilahti area, northwest of the centre, gives you access to the museum island of Seurasaari.

PEOPLE

Most people from Helsinki speak Finnish as their mother tongue, though there's a sizable population of Swedish-speaking Swedish-Finns. Many Finns look very Scandinavian, with blonde hair and blue eyes. Recent immigrants include people from the Baltic States and the former USSR.

TYPICAL HELSINKI CITIZEN

The average Helsinki resident is well educated and reserved yet warm and friendly to visitors, surfs the net, loves reading and drinks around nine cups of coffee per day. They relish outdoor pursuits, and flee the city for summer cottages around the lakes in July. They possess tremendous resilience and love their saunas.

DEFINING EXPERIENCE

Strolling around the 19th-century Senate Sq and taking in the scene from the steps of the blue-domed Tuomiokirkko (Lutheran Cathedral), poking around the harbour-side *kauppatori* (square) in search of salmon

MODESTLY DRAPED LADIES SAVOUR THE THERAPEUTIC HEAT OF A CITY SAUNA.

chowder, ferrying to the historic fortress island of Suomenlinna, listening to gospel at the rock-hewn Temppeliaukion Kirkko and partaking in the social ritual of relaxing in a Finnish-style sauna – hitting each other on the back with a bundle of birch twigs to get the circulation going, then rolling around in the snow or jumping in the cold lake before running back to the sauna – then drinking coffee and eating salty food.

STRENGTHS

- The underground Itäkeskus swimming hall, carved from rock
- Multilingual 'Helsinki Helpers' (in the summertime)
- Saunas – anywhere, anytime
- Fascinating museums such as Kiasma and the Ateneum
- Go-karting
- Diverse architecture
- Easy cycling on flat paths and free city bikes
- Helsinki's proximity to Tallinn, the capital of Estonia
- Rambling around the ruins of the fortress on Suomenlinna Island
- Coffee at the Kauppahalli (market hall)

WEAKNESSES

- Waiting for a taxi in rush hour
- Parking, or attempting to

GOLD STAR

Ferrying out to explore the fortress at Suomenlinna Island and discovering Finland's heritage at the Seurasaari Open-Air Museum.

ART-LOVERS ENJOY A QUIET CUPPA IN THE AUSTERE ENVIRONS OF THE MUSEUM OF CONTEMPORARY ART.

STARRING ROLE IN...

- *The Man Without a Past* (2002)
- *Kites over Helsinki* (2001)
- *Spy Games* (1999)
- *Night on Earth* (1991)
- *Helsinki Napoli – All Night Long* (1987)
- *Born American* (1986)
- *Billion Dollar Brain* (1967)

See the city from a different perspective by taking a ferry around its outlying islands.

Eat sautéed reindeer and Baltic herring.

Drink on the one-of-a-kind Spårakoff – a historic tram that has been converted into a pub.

Do a lap of Kaivopuisto Park on rollerblades or a bike, or a lap of a go-kart track.

Watch and listen to gospel and classical concerts at the underground Temppeliaukion Kirkko.

Buy traditional Sámi handicrafts such as a *kuksa* (cup) and woven wall hangings, Moomintroll souvenirs, a Savoy vase designed by Alvar Aalto, woven pine baskets and birdhouses.

After dark bar-hop around central Helsinki's many terraces, bars and clubs.

Hiroshima

DATE OF BIRTH 1589; WHEN FEUDAL LORD MORI TERUMOTO NAMED THE TOWN AND ESTABLISHED A CASTLE **ADDRESS** JAPAN (MAP 9, K2) **HEIGHT** 4M **SIZE** 742 SQ KM **POPULATION** 1.2 MILLION (CITY); 2 MILLION (METRO AREA) **LONELY PLANET RANKING** 133

An example of the true Japanese experience and much more than a reminder of one of the modern world's darkest hours, Hiroshima's cherry-blossom-lined streets, local artisans and entertainment venues embrace a city sparkling with hope and tradition.

ANATOMY

Hiroshima (meaning 'broad island') is built on a series of sandy islands on the delta of Ota-gawa river. JR Hiroshima Station is east of the city centre and, although there are a number of hotels around the station, the central area, with its very lively entertainment district, is much more interesting. Hiroshima's main east–west avenue is Heiwa-Ōdōri (Peace Blvd). Parallel to it runs the busiest road (with the main tram lines from the station), Aioi-dōri. Just south of this is the busy Hon-dōri shopping arcade. There is an extensive tram system.

PEOPLE

People from Hiroshima have an average age around 40 and are mainly Japanese. A small city for a Japanese metropolis, Hiroshima affords its constituents an element of Japanese traditional rural charm.

TYPICAL HIROSHIMAN

Like most Japanese people, Hiroshimans are hard-working and obstinately polite. Their dedication to etiquette can be daunting to the uninitiated, but they are also warmly hospitable. Though their city's name is tied to the horrors of 6 August 1945, when it was the victim of the world's first atomic attack, it is by no means their whole story. The people of Hiroshima hold steadfastly to their traditions all the more for this experience and look optimistically forward.

DEFINING EXPERIENCE

Relishing a lunch of *kaki-ryōri* (oyster cuisine) at Kaki-tei before touring the town in a streetcar to take in the heroic collection of tributes and memorials, most notably Peace Memorial Park.

FAST TIMES AT MORNING PRAYERS, MIYAJIMA.

TRADITIONALLY DRESSED WOMEN MULL OVER HOW BLUE THE DAY IS.

HUNDREDS OF PAPER CRANES ON DISPLAY.

A MOMENT OF CONTEMPLATION – PAPER
LANTERNS REPRESENT SOULS OF THE FALLEN.

STRENGTHS

- Hijiyama Park, noted for its cherry blossoms
- City Manga Library
- The small nearby island of Miyajima, a Unesco World Heritage Site
- Atomic Bomb Dome
- Asa Zoo
- Mazda Museum
- DJ scene
- Hiroshima-jō (also known as Carp Castle)
- Hiroshima Museum of Art
- Japanese baseball

WEAKNESSES

- Omnipresent history
- Expensive accommodation
- Very cold winters
- Westernisation

GOLD STAR

Hope – Hiroshima is a hopeful and optimistic beacon to the rest of the world and a living argument against war and the use of nuclear weapons.

STARRING ROLE IN...

- *Shockwave : Countdown to Hiroshima* by Stephen Walker
- *Hiroshima* by John Hershey
- *Hiroshima Mon Amour* (1959)

See the Flame of Peace, which will only be extinguished once the last nuclear weapon on earth has been destroyed.

Eat *Hiroshima-yaki*, a local version of *okonomiyaki* (egg-based savoury pancakes), from one of the mini-restaurants at Okonomi-mura.

Drink sake at one of the 10 sake breweries in Saijō, a short train ride east of Hiroshima.

Do visit the popular Mazda Museum and see the world's longest assembly line – 7km.

Watch the memorial service held in Peace Memorial Park on 6 August, where thousands of paper lanterns for the souls of the dead are floated down the Ota-gawa.

Buy unique *ukiyo-e* (wood-block prints) from local artisans.

After dark check out the latest local DJ playing everything from hard techno to reggae at the cool and cosy Commune.

COLOURFULLY CLAD SCHOOL CHILDREN FORM A DISORDERLY LINE BEFORE CLASS.

Ho Chi Minh City

NICKNAME HCMC; ALSO KNOWN AS SAIGON, BUT CAREFUL HOW YOU USE THIS – IT'S BEST TO STICK TO HO CHI MINH CITY WHEN DEALING WITH GOVERNMENT OFFICIALS **DATE OF BIRTH** 6TH CENTURY; WHEN THE FUNANESE CONSTRUCTED A CANAL SYSTEM THAT MOST LIKELY EXTENDED TO THE SITE OF PRESENT-DAY HO CHI MINH CITY **ADDRESS** VIETNAM (MAP 9, F8) **HEIGHT** 9M **SIZE** 2356 SQ KM **POPULATION** 7.4 MILLION **LONELY PLANET RANKING** 041

Crazy-making and seductive, HCMC (formerly known as Saigon) beats with a palpable energy, day and night.

ANATOMY

HCMC is not so much a city as a small province, with rural regions making up the majority of the land area. HCMC is divided into 16 urban districts (*quan*, derived from the French *quartier*) and five rural districts (*huyen*). District 1 (once Saigon) is the downtown area and the location of most of the city's sights, while District 5 spans the huge Chinese neighbourhood called Cholon (Big Market). The city's neoclassical and international-style buildings and pavement kiosks selling rolls and croissants give neighbourhoods such as District 3 a vaguely French atmosphere. Travelling HCMC's chaotic streets is not for the faint-hearted. Metered taxis, *cyclos* (pedicabs) and *xe oms* (motorbike taxis) are the common forms of transport.

PEOPLE

HCMC has the largest ethnic Chinese community in Vietnam, mostly found in Cholon. While most fled in 1975, a small community of Indians remains; Vietnam's other minorities (Khmers, Chams and Hill Tribes) tend to live in other regions of the country.

TYPICAL HO CHI MINH CITY CITIZEN

At first sight, HCMC may seem to be populated with a million bandana-bedecked women bandits on the verge of a giant traffic accident. And the pattern in the streets reflects an organised chaos in a city that attracts people from all over the country hoping to better their fortunes. A young office worker manoeuvres her Honda Future through rush-hour traffic, long hair flowing, high heels working the brake pedal. The sweating Chinese businessman chats on his mobile phone, cursing his necktie in the heat. A desperate beggar suddenly grabs your arm – a reminder that this is still a developing city.

MAN OF STEEL – STREET PERFORMERS BEND METAL AROUND A STRONGMAN'S NECK.

DEFINING EXPERIENCE

Strolling through the crisscross streets of historic District 1, wrangling a *cyclo* into Cholon, sniffing around local markets and browsing the sumptuous shops around Dong Khoi, before journeying further afield to the Cao Dai Great Temple and Cu Chi Tunnels.

STRENGTHS

▲ The bustling, dynamic and spirited atmosphere
▲ *Cyclo* drivers who give you an insight into their city
▲ Proximity to the Mekong Delta
▲ Smiling, friendly residents
▲ Bustling, intriguing Cholon

WEAKNESSES

▲ Pickpockets
▲ *Cyclo* drivers who overcharge and taxi drivers on commission
▲ Confusingly named streets
▲ Traffic
▲ Pollution

GOLD STAR

Silk boutiques – more diverse, less traditional and cheaper than those in Hanoi.

STARRING ROLE IN...

▲ *The Quiet American* (2002)
▲ *Indochine* (1992)

See the War Remnants Museum for a graphic depiction of the impact of US military action from the point of view of 'the other side'.

Eat traditional banh xeo (rice-flour pancakes stuffed with bean sprouts, prawns and pork), especially at swoon-worthy restaurant Banh Xeo 46A.

Drink cocktails while taking in the city view and cool breezes at the Rex Hotel's rooftop garden bar.

Do take a cyclo trip through the city before the municipal government phases them out.

Watch hordes of young people checking each other out in the Dong Khoi area every weekend.

Buy a carved seal featuring your name in Vietnamese.

After dark join HCMC's fashion-conscious, alternative crowd at Q Bar near the Municipal Theatre.

Hobart

DATE OF BIRTH 1803; WHEN EUROPEAN COLONIALISTS ARRIVED, BUT THE AREA HAD PREVIOUSLY BEEN INHABITED BY THE SEMINOMADIC ABORIGINAL MOUHENEENNER TRIBE **ADDRESS** AUSTRALIA (MAP 10, H9) **HEIGHT** 54M **SIZE** 1360 SQ KM **POPULATION** 212,000 **LONELY PLANET RANKING** 091

Small but perfectly formed Hobart pulses with the energy of a city on the up, proud of its well-preserved historic buildings and beautiful natural setting.

ANATOMY

Hobart has an enviable location, perched at the mouth of the Derwent River in the shadow of the imposing 1270m-high Mt Wellington. The easily navigated city centre is arranged on a grid pattern around the Elizabeth St mall, west of which awaits retail temptation. Most of the tourist attractions are on the picturesque waterfront and Battery Point. Following the river south you meet Sandy Bay, home to the university and Wrest Point casino. Towards the north of the centre lies the Domain area, which includes the Botanical Gardens. Cars, buses, boats and bicycles nip through the city.

PEOPLE

The majority of Hobart's inhabitants are of European (especially British) descent. Around 2% of Hobart's population is of Aboriginal descent – a legacy of the massacres that occurred in Tasmania.

TYPICAL HOBART CITIZEN

Hobart is Australia's second-oldest city, which makes its inhabitants some of the oldest Australians in terms of generations. Their home is also the country's southernmost capital and is in one of Australia's most picturesque settings – no wonder they like where they live and are keen to conserve their environment. The setting also encourages an active life, and cycling, walking and watersports are particularly popular. They are cultured and appreciate art-house and international films as well as the Tasmanian Symphony Orchestra, whose home is in Hobart.

DEFINING EXPERIENCE

Wandering through the myriad stalls of the fantastic Salamanca Market, pottering and purchasing, people-watching and enjoying the street performers, before picking up some cheap but tasty fish and chips from a barge on the dock.

HOBART'S WORKING HARBOUR IS FRINGED BY GREEN HILLS.

THE FIRST SUNBEAMS OF THE DAY TOUCH HOUSES AT THE FOOT OF MT WELLINGTON.

STRENGTHS

- Museum of Old & New Art (MONA)
- Well-preserved colonial buildings
- Natural beauty
- Compact size
- The Georgian warehouses of Salamanca Place
- Salamanca Arts Centre
- Salamanca Market
- Mt Wellington
- Sailing activities including the Royal Hobart Regatta and Sydney to Hobart Yacht Race
- Fish and chip barges
- Tasmanian Museum and Art Gallery
- Battery Point
- Royal Tasmanian Botanical Gardens, housing the largest collection of mature conifers in the southern hemisphere
- Excellent locally produced food and wine
- Moorilla Estate Vineyard and cellar doors on the city's doorstep
- Cheap car rental (lower rates than on mainland Australia)
- Tasmanian Gothic literature
- The Taste Festival
- Henry Jones Art Hotel
- Surfing at Clifton Beach

WEAKNESSES

- Relatively expensive if good accommodation
- Aesthetically challenged Federation Concert Hall
- Aboriginal massacres by the colonialists

BIT.FALL BY JULIUS POPP, DEEP IN MONA'S SANDSTONE CAVERNS.

GOLD STAR

Australian colonial architecture: there are more than 90 buildings classified by the National Trust in Hobart.

STARRING ROLE IN...

- ◢ *The English Passengers* by Matthew Kneale
- ◢ *The Tilted Cross* by Hal Porter
- ◢ *The Fatal Shore* by Robert Hughes

See the flotilla of sails at the climax of the New Year Sydney to Hobart Yacht Race.

Eat a Vietnamese salad or an all-day breakfast while watching your washing spin at the Machine Laundry Café.

Drink a free sample or two while on a tour of Australia's oldest brewery, Cascade.

Do be amazed and entertained at the astounding $75-million Museum of Old & New Art (MONA).

Watch the city and southwest wilderness from the cosy comfort of a seaplane.

Buy a piece of Tasmanian art or something made of Tasmanian wood.

After dark preen and pose with the in-crowd at fashionable waterfront bistro-wine bar, T-42°.

365

Hoi An

DATE OF BIRTH 200 BC; THE LATE–IRON AGE SA HUYNH CIVILISATION ARE THOUGHT TO HAVE BEEN THE FIRST INHABITANTS OF HOI AN **ADDRESS** VIETNAM (MAP 9, G7) **HEIGHT** 12M **SIZE** 60 SQ KM **POPULATION** 131,000 **LONELY PLANET RANKING** 123

Wander through Vietnam's past – with its traditional architecture and distinctive cuisine, Hoi An envelops you in a sense of history that oozes charm and culture from every corner.

ANATOMY

Hoi An is a living museum linked to the sea by the shallow Thu Bon River. Moss-covered pagodas and the pedestrian-friendly Old Town make many a visitor feel that they have been transported back centuries. Hoi An's brick-coloured *am* and *duong* (Yin and Yang) roof tiles, meticulously restored temples, and unique bridges can be explored on a day's walking tour, a bicycle ride or by boat.

PEOPLE

Hoi An's sea port has a rich history as a vibrant international trading centre and was the site of southern Vietnam's first Chinese settlement. Today, around 1300 of Hoi An's population are ethnic Chinese. Relations between them and the ethnic Vietnamese have always been harmonious, with the Chinese here even speaking Vietnamese among themselves.

TYPICAL HOI ANIAN

Hoi Anians are entrepreneurial, with an almost aggressively competitive edge. They are traditional and family-oriented and many a restaurant or internet café will be run by immediate and extended family. They are commonly devout in their everyday life. They are used to visitors and welcome them into their temples, pagodas and even their homes (occasionally for a fee). They are a solid community who gather together in times of trouble and joy.

DEFINING EXPERIENCE

Walking through Hoi An's pedestrian-friendly town centre to choose the silk for a new (and astonishingly cheap) tailored outfit, then crossing the sparse beauty of the Japanese Covered Bridge to take in a gallery or two before donning the finished clothes to walk along lantern-lit streets to

AN AGE-OLD SCENE AT HOI AN'S FISH MARKET.

the monthly Hoi An Legendary Night (Hoi An Full Moon Festival) where hot 'white rose' (steamed prawns wrapped in rice paper) are eaten amid the sound and colour of traditional song, dance and games.

STRENGTHS
- Traditional Vietnam at its best
- Historical buildings
- Temples and pagodas
- Pedestrian-friendly streets
- Cheap tailors
- Local artisans
- Boat rides along the river
- Waterside eateries
- Thirty kilometres of pristine, palm-lined beach

WEAKNESSES
- Unsafe swimming for six months of the year (November to March)
- Occasional late-night bag snatching
- Complicated ticketing systems to tourist attractions
- Fake antiques
- Quiet nightlife

GOLD STAR
Architectural history – Hoi An serves as a museum piece of Vietnamese history and more than 800 structures of historical significance have been officially identified here. It is recognised as a Unesco World Heritage Site.

STARRING ROLE IN...
- *The Quiet American* (2002)

See the clear streams that run between the monuments of My Son.

Eat cao lau at the Ba La Well restaurant located conveniently by the well from which water is used to make genuine cao lau.

Drink fine wine in the lovingly restored tea warehouse at Tam Tam Café.

Do a cooking course at the Red Bridge – buy from the market, take your groceries home on a river cruise, cook up local dishes and eat the results.

Watch a traditional music concert in the historic Hoi An Old Town.

Buy local art and craft at the fair-trade gift shop, Reaching Out.

After dark eat fresh seafood from the bright line of kiosks leading to the moonlit beach.

WHAT A CORACLE LOSES IN STABILITY, IT GAINS IN MANOEUVRABILITY

FLAVOURS OF DISTINCTION – THE MEMORABLE EXPERIENCE OF DINING IN HOI AN.

BUY ALL THE PAPER LANTERNS YOU'LL EVER NEED AT THIS SHOP IN HOI AN.

THE FUTURISTIC SKYLINE OF HONG KONG BY NIGHT.

Hong Kong

NICKNAME THE CITY OF LIGHTS **DATE OF BIRTH** 206 BC; WHEN THE
EASTERN HAN DYNASTY RULED **ADDRESS** CHINA (MAP 9, G5) **HEIGHT** 33M
SIZE 1100 SQ KM **POPULATION** 7.1 MILLION **LONELY PLANET RANKING** 012

Hong Kong is a noisy, vibrant fusion of West and East, packed with businesspeople, markets, temples, futuristic buildings, double-decker trams and boats crisscrossing the harbour – it is unlike anywhere else on earth.

ANATOMY

Four main areas make up Hong Kong. To the south lies Hong Kong Island containing most major businesses and government offices and many top-end hotels and restaurants, all overlooked by Victoria Peak. Over the harbour to the north bustles the Kowloon Peninsula, where you'll find even more people and tempting shopping opportunities. The New Territories, which spreads from Kowloon towards mainland China, and the 234 outlying islands, complete the puzzle. Public transport is cheap, fast and generally efficient. Take your pick of buses and trains.

PEOPLE

The majority of Hong Kong's population is ethnic Chinese, but only just over half of Hong Kong Chinese were born in the territory. The three largest foreign groups are Filipinos, Indonesians and Canadians, then Americans. Australians and Britons make up the smallest portion. The largest religious groups in Hong Kong are Buddhists and Christians.

TYPICAL HONG KONG CITIZEN

Beneath the consumerist veneer of Hong Kong, Chinese beliefs and traditions remain. Top concerns are appeasing spirits and predicting the future. Memories of economic oppression and hunger mean the pursuit of wealth also scores highly. People used to have a reputation for rudeness but etiquette is important. Hong Kong society is highly educated, with a literacy rate of about 93%. Popular pastimes include dining together, betting on horses and watching sport.

DEFINING EXPERIENCE

Riding the Star Ferry to Tsim Sha Tsui for a stroll before heading to Kowloon Park for some t'ai chi, soaking up the buzz of Nathan Rd, then refuelling with afternoon tea at the Peninsula Hong Kong hotel.

WORDSMITHS IN WANCHAI DWARFED BY THEIR NEON CREATION IN THE CITY OF LIGHTS.

A WINDOW CATCHES THE REFLECTION OF A TAXI IN A SWIRL OF MOVEMENT AND ELECTRIC LIGHT.

A YOUNG DINER HELPS HERSELF AT FOOK YING HOT POT RESTAURANT.

STRENGTHS

- ◢ Victoria Peak
- ◢ Star Ferry
- ◢ Hong Kong trams
- ◢ Temple St night market
- ◢ Tian Tan Buddha statue
- ◢ Shopping in Central and Causeway Bay
- ◢ Beaches and hiking on Lamma
- ◢ More than 600 temples
- ◢ Noodle restaurants
- ◢ Karaoke bars, happy hours and Canto-pop
- ◢ Low crime rate
- ◢ Hong Kong Museum of History
- ◢ Rugby Sevens

WEAKNESSES

- ◢ Noise, water and air pollution
- ◢ Crowds
- ◢ Overexcited air-conditioning
- ◢ Expensive beer

GOLD STAR

Business.

STARRING ROLE IN...

- ◢ *Tomb Raider 2* (2003)
- ◢ *Rush Hour* (1998)
- ◢ *Double Impact* (1991)
- ◢ *Year of the Dragon* (1985)
- ◢ *The Man with the Golden Gun* (1974)

See the jaw-dropping view from the summit of Victoria Peak and enjoy the gravity-challenging ride there on the Peak Tram.

Eat dim sum delights at the noisy, authentic Maxim's Palace.

Drink bubbly at the Grand Hyatt Champagne Bar.

Do take a nocturnal lantern-festooned Star Ferry from Tsim Sha Tsui to Central and enjoy the cityscape by night.

Watch thousands make the pilgrimage to the Tian Tan Buddha statue on Buddha's Birthday in May.

Buy a custom-made suit from Sam's Tailor or try your luck on Nathan Rd.

After dark check out Hong Kong's live-music scene – it's thriving.

Innsbruck

NICKNAME OLYMPIC TOWN **DATE OF BIRTH** 1180; WHEN THE SMALL
MARKET SETTLEMENT ON THE NORTH BANK OF THE INN RIVER
EXPANDED TO THE SOUTH BANK **ADDRESS** AUSTRIA (MAP 5, M2)
HEIGHT 582M **POPULATION** 120,000 **LONELY PLANET RANKING** 075

**Innsbruck is an 800-year-old snow bunnies'
paradise: laden with art treasures and stunning
Gothic and baroque buildings, it's set against a
postcard-perfect Alpine backdrop.**

ANATOMY

In the valley of the Inn River, Innsbruck is wedged between the northern
chain of the Alps and the Tuxer Vorberge (Tuxer Mountains) to the south.
Mountain transport facilities radiate from the city and provide walking
and skiing opportunities, particularly to the south and west. The town
centre is compact, with the Hauptbahnhof (main train station) just a
10-minute walk from the pedestrian-only Altstadt (old town). The main
street in the Altstadt, Herzog-Friedrich-Strasse, links with Maria-Theresien-
Strasse. Getting around by foot is easy, but there also are buses and trams.

PEOPLE

Austrians are predominantly of Germanic origin, and there are also
Slovene, Croat and Turkish minorities. The official language is German
with Turkish, Slovenian, Croatian and English also spoken.

TYPICAL INNSBRUCK CITIZEN

Quietly confident, the typical Innsbruck citizen is friendly, intelligent and,
like all Austrians, has a dollop of good-natured grumpiness thrown in.
Hosting the Winter Olympics in 1964 and 1976, the people of Innsbruck are
sporty, cosmopolitan and proud of their city, the largest in the European
Alps. In summertime, locals swap their skis for hiking boots and mountain
bikes to enjoy Innsbruck's spectacular surrounds. Almost one-sixth of the
population of Innsbruck are university students.

DEFINING EXPERIENCE

Wandering the quaint cobblestone alleyways and baroque buildings of the
Altstadt, then exploring the gardens and museum collections of Schloss
Ambras, and topping it off by viewing the enchanting Goldenes Dachl
(Golden Roof) against the Nordkette Mountains.

HOUSES ALONG MARIA THERESIEN STRASSE BASK IN THE STARK AFTERNOON LIGHT AND MOUNTAINS LOOM IN THE BACKGROUND.

OLD MEETS NEW IN THE TOWN CENTRE, WHERE STATELY 19TH-CENTURY HOUSES ARE REFLECTED IN THE WINDOWS OF A MODERN BUILDING.

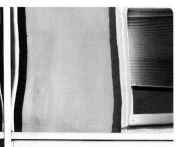

STRENGTHS

- Goldenes Dachl
- Snow!
- 25 nearby village resorts
- The new Bergisel Ski Jump
- Gothic and baroque architecture
- Rafting and canyoning
- Alpine air and flowers
- Medieval houses
- Sightseeing Trolley Tour
- Nordkettenbahn Cableway
- Pastries, cakes and strudel

WEAKNESSES

- Meat-and-dumpling-heavy meals
- Complicated Austrian etiquette
- (Some) old-school attitudes and prejudices

GOLD STAR

The Olympia SkiWorld Innsbruck – with 75 ski-lifts across nine ski fields, Innsbruck caters to everyone, from the daredevil seeking out the black runs to wannabe boarders who don't know goofy from natural.

STARRING ROLE IN...

- *Die Freiheit des Adlers* (2002)
- *As In Heaven* (2003)
- *Crazy Canucks* (2004)
- *Overnight to Innsbruck* by Denyse Woods

See the magnificent Goldenes Dachl, constructed for Emperor Maximilian I as his box seat for tournaments in the square below.

Eat a tasty Wiener schnitzel at Goldener Adler, Innsbruck's 600-year old restaurant popular for both its history and Austrian and Tyrolean cuisine.

Drink top-notch Alpine cocktails at the Hofgarten Café as you numb your ski-aches to the latest beats spun by local DJs.

Do brave the Nordkettenbahn Cableway all the way to the 2334m-high Hafelekar Top Terminal where you'll enjoy jaw-dropping views of the Zillertal, Stubai and Ötztal Alps.

Watch home-grown opera, ballet, drama and comedy at Landestheater.

Buy glittering trinkets at the Swarovski shop on Herzog-Friedrich-Strasse.

After dark get piste (guffaw*!*) with other adrenalin junkies at Jimmy's.

BE PREPARED TO BARGAIN IN ISTANBUL'S GRAND BAZAAR.

Istanbul

DATE OF BIRTH 657 BC; WHEN BYZAS, SON OF THE GOD POSEIDON, ESTABLISHED THE CITY **ADDRESS** TURKEY (MAP 5, U6) **HEIGHT** 114M **SIZE** 1991 SQ KM **POPULATION** 14 MILLION **LONELY PLANET RANKING** 010

The masterpiece of the Byzantine and Ottoman Empires in its former incarnations as Byzantium and Constantinople, this is a rambunctious, energetic and bewitching city.

ANATOMY

Straddling two continents, Istanbul is separated into European and Asian districts by the Bosphorus. The heart of Old Istanbul is at Sultanahmet and the Bazaar district on the European side. Across the Golden Horn is the former diplomatic quarter of Beyoğlu, now a swish shopping district. Buses connect all corners of the city, but the best way to cross the city is on the ferries that ply the Bosphorus strait.

PEOPLE

Istanbul is largely Turkish, but the fabric of the city and its citizens is interwoven with diverse influences. There are small Greek, Armenian and Jewish communities, as well as Russian and Georgian traders. Many Istanbul families can trace their origins to the years of the Ottoman Empire, but many villagers from Anatolia have also arrived in recent years, seeking the opportunities that the thriving metropolis provides.

TYPICAL ISTANBULLU

Istanbullus are gregarious and talkative and admirably relaxed for citizens of such an enormous city. They love a cup of *çay* (tea) and an opportunity to discuss the matters of the day. Istanbul residents are increasingly proud of the history and legacy of their great city. They are uniformly football mad and love green spaces in which to conduct elaborate and lengthy picnics. Family plays an integral role in everyday life, and many Istanbullus holiday in ancestral villages in Anatolia.

DEFINING EXPERIENCE

Contemplating the mighty domes of Aya Sofya and the Blue Mosque, getting lost in the arcades of the Grand Bazaar, going underground at the Basilica Cistern beneath the heart of Sultanahmet, window-shopping on cosmopolitan İstiklal Caddesi, chilling out with a *nargile* (water pipe), catching a ferry to Ortaköy and having a drink on the waterfront.

CARTING HIS GOODS ACROSS TOWN THROUGH THE HISTORIC DISTRICT OF SAMATYA.

STRENGTHS

- Vibrant arts, music and fashion
- History around every corner
- Bosphorus cruises
- Gregarious Turks
- Privately endowed contemporary art museums, including ARTER and the SALT cultural centres
- Eating baklava and *lokum* (Turkish delight)
- Commuting on ferries
- *Meyhanes* (taverns) on Nevizade Sokak
- Topkapı Palace
- Carpets, textiles and Turkish handicrafts
- Architecture – from Byzantine to ultramodern
- Old books and maps at Sahaflar Çarşısı
- The Balık Pazarı (Fish Market) at Beyoğlu
- Wrought-iron balconies and cobbled streets
- Sea views

WEAKNESSES

- Carpet-shop touts
- Traffic
- Smokers everywhere
- Old neighbourhoods being lost
- Wooden houses, dripping with character, falling into disrepair

GOLD STAR

The interaction of air, water, land and architecture – to appreciate this, climb the Galata Tower at twilight to watch the sun set across two continents and silhouette the voluptuous skyline of Old Istanbul.

FOOD FOR BODY AND SOUL – A MOTHER BREAKS TO FEED HER CHILD OUTSIDE NEW MOSQUE, EMINÖNÜ.

STARRING ROLE IN...

- ◢ *From Russia with Love* (1974)
- ◢ *Topkapi* (1964)
- ◢ *Hamam* (1996)
- ◢ *Distant* (2003)
- ◢ *The Black Book* and *Istanbul: A Memoir* by Orhan Pamuk
- ◢ *The Birds Are Also Gone* by Yashar Kemal
- ◢ *Portrait of a Turkish Family* by Irfan Orga
- ◢ *The Turkish Embassy Letters* by Lady Mary Wortley Montagu

- ◢ *Istanbul the Imperial City* by John Freely

See the treasures of the Ottoman sultans at the Topkapı Palace.

Eat a fish sandwich from the vendors on the boats at Eminönü.

Drink rakı (aniseed spirit) accompanied by meze (selection of hot and cold starters).

Do surrender to the steam in an Ottoman-era hamam (bathhouse).

Watch commuters at Eminönü in the late afternoon.

Buy carpets or traditional craftwork in the Grand Bazaar – prepare to haggle.

After dark head across to Beyoğlu to the bars around İstiklal Caddesi.

Jaipur

NICKNAME THE PINK CITY **DATE OF BIRTH** 1727; WHEN JAI SINGH DECIDED TO MOVE HIS CAPITAL FROM AMBER
ADDRESS INDIA (MAP 9, A5) **HEIGHT** 390M **POPULATION** 3.3 MILLION
LONELY PLANET RANKING 092

Acid-bright colours punctuate the streets: crouched porters group by the station in red shirts and turbans, billowing saris catch the eye like butterflies and shopfronts glitter with fierce fabrics.

ANATOMY

The walled Old City is in the northeast of Jaipur, while the new parts spread to the south and west. The main tourist attractions are in the Old City and taxis and auto-rickshaws are the best way to get around.

PEOPLE

Jaipur's population is predominantly Hindu, with a sizable Muslim minority. There are small communities of Jains, Sikhs and Christians. Tribal (Adivasi) groups were the first inhabitants of this region, and today they form about 12% of the population – the national average is around 8%. The main languages are Hindi and Rajasthani.

TYPICAL JAIPURIAN

Heirs to a rich intellectual heritage, Jaipurians, Hindu and Muslim men alike have bright Rajput turbans and swashbuckling moustaches while the women wear colourful saris. Jaipurians go about their business among streets jam-packed with cars, cows, rickshaws, snuffling pigs, motorcycles and death-defying pedestrians. Street children beg outside huge jewellery shops and palatial hotels.

DEFINING EXPERIENCE

Taking a trip out to Amber Fort to see the elephants and architecture, lunching at Copper Chimney in the middle of the day and exploring the City Palace, then wandering through town to look at the *havelis*, taking in a little shopping – textiles, carpets, handicrafts or jewellery – before eating on MI Rd and catching a Hindi film at Raj Mandir Cinema, with its shell-pink interior.

NOBORU KOMINE

THE STATELY WIND PALACE LOOKS DOWN OVER A BUSTLE OF ACTIVITY IN BADI CHAUPLE SQ.

STRENGTHS

- Gangaur (Harvest) festival
- Jantar Mantar, Jaipur's remarkable observatory
- Hawa Mahal (Palace of the Winds)
- Old City
- Maharaja Sawni Mansingh II Museum
- Rajasthan Astrological Council & Research Institute
- Modern Art Gallery
- Nahargarh (Tiger Fort)
- Amber Fort
- *Havelis* (ornately decorated traditional residences)

WEAKNESSES

- The hassle
- The pressure to buy
- Gem scams
- Traffic jams
- Overzealous rickshaw-wallahs and hotel touts

GOLD STAR

The Old City, which is partially encircled by a crenellated wall, is notable for its town planning: avenues divide the Pink City into neat rectangles, each of which specialises in certain crafts. At dusk the sunset-shaded buildings have a magical glow.

STARRING ROLE IN...

- *A Princess Remembers* by Gaytari Devi and Santha Rama Rau
- *Jaipur: The Last Destination* by Aman and Samar Singh Jodha

See a film at Raj Mandir Cinema, the world's only meringue-shaped film house.

Eat lal maas (mutton in a thick spicy gravy) at Copper Chimney, a classy place with the requisite waiter army and a big rollicking horse mural.

Drink at the Polo Bar in the Rambagh Palace Hotel with its arched, scalloped windows overlooking perfect lawns.

Do make the trip out to the magnificent delicate-pink, fort-palace of Amber, a beautiful, ethereal example of Rajput architecture.

Watch a polo match at the polo ground next to the Rambagh Palace.

Buy precious and semiprecious stones – gold, silver and fine, highly glazed enamel work known as *meenakari*, a Jaipur speciality.

After dark head for the DJ bar Hightz in Mansingh Hotel; however, you might find a Hammond organ as entertainment rather than the promised DJ.

A SNAKE CHARMER HYPNOTISES A COBRA AT THE GATES OF THE CITY PALACE.

A MOTHER FINISHES HER DAUGHTER'S FACE PAINT AHEAD OF THE GANGAUR FESTIVAL.

PREENING PALACE GUARDS FLAUNT COLOURFUL UNIFORMS IN FRONT OF THE LEGENDARY PEACOCK DOOR OF THE CITY PALACE.

TIME FOR SOME MALE BONDING (NO LADIES ALLOWED) AT A LOCAL TEAHOUSE.

Jeddah

NICKNAME JIDDAH **DATE OF BIRTH** AD 646; THE CALIPH UTHMAN
OFFICIALLY ESTABLISHED JEDDAH AS THE GATEWAY TO MECCA
ADDRESS SAUDI ARABIA (MAP 8, B6) **HEIGHT** 6M **SIZE** 560 SQ KM
POPULATION 3.7 MILLION **LONELY PLANET RANKING** 166

A microcosm of the Islamic world and the pulse of modern Saudi Arabia, Jeddah has all the vibrancy of a liberal, fast-moving, modern commercial capital, with the added charm of century-old alleyway souqs (markets), the waterfront corniche and the gateway to the holy Islamic cities of Mecca and Medina.

ANATOMY

Jeddah's heart is its Al-Balad district, with enchanting buildings made of coral overlooking the narrow lanes of the souqs. King Abdul Aziz St is its main north–south thoroughfare and has a host of restaurants, banks and shops. The city has bloated to 1000 times its original size; the bulk of the sprawl is north of Al-Balad, and Medina Rd is the main street running north from the centre, flanked to the west by Al-Andalus St – all reached by a network of buses and taxis. The waterfront corniche (Al-Kournaish Rd) runs the length of Jeddah's coastline from Jeddah Islamic Port (in the southern part of town) to the city's northern outskirts.

PEOPLE

Although no official census exists in the kingdom, it would be safe to say that Jeddah's citizens are both typically and atypically Saudi. The city reflects the largely urbanised Saudi Arabia – Jeddah boasts residents from all over the world, including a large expatriate business population. Although Islam prevails, expatriates quietly retain Christian and other beliefs. Jeddah is on the path to Mecca for thousands of haj pilgrims.

TYPICAL JEDDAHN

Cosmopolitan, modern and as swift as the traffic, Jeddahns are a sleeker, more progressive version of their Saudi counterparts. They work hard and speak a multitude of languages. Typical Saudi wariness is relaxed here – Jeddahns have been opening their city to pilgrims for centuries. Jeddahns hold dear the Islamic traditions of dress, strict gender roles and prayer, but young Saudis, who gently push the boundaries of the kingdom's traditions, push a little harder here.

A WOMAN AND CHILD ENJOY QUALITY TIME AT THE BEACH IN THE SHADOW OF A MINARET.

ENOUGH DATES TO FILL A CALENDAR.

THE TRADITIONAL ARABIAN FAÇADE OF
SHORBATLY HOUSE.

DEFINING EXPERIENCE

Soaking up Arabia at its best at the enchanting Souq al-Alawi during the haj season, as wonderful old houses tower above and pilgrims from across the sea and desert follow the calls to prayer, which fill the lanes at sunset, as they have done for more than a millennia.

STRENGTHS

- ◢ Souqs (markets)
- ◢ Comparatively relaxed *mutawwa* (religious police)
- ◢ Diving and windsurfing
- ◢ Casual private resorts
- ◢ Heritage architecture
- ◢ Hotels for every budget

WEAKNESSES

- ◢ Reckless driving
- ◢ Lack of trees
- ◢ Dilapidated buildings
- ◢ Ordinary beaches
- ◢ Limited freedoms for women

GOLD STAR

The haj pilgrimage – Jeddah has been the historical gateway for pilgrims travelling to the holy Islamic cities of Mecca and Medina for almost 15 centuries.

STARRING ROLE IN...

- ◢ *Seven Pillars of Wisdom* by TE Lawrence
- ◢ *Eight Months on Ghazzah Street* by Hilary Mantel
- ◢ *Exit Only* by Liam Bracken

See the delightfully restored Naseef House, standing in the centre of the Al-Alawi souq.

Eat from the delicious seafood buffet at Al-Bouhaira Restaurant.

Drink coffee at a traditional coffee house.

Do dive in the Red Sea, at the relaxed Al-Nakheel Beach Resort.

Watch a classic flick in the makeshift cinema at the Italian Cultural Centre.

Buy dates, nuts and nibbles at the famous Khayyam Al-Rabie Est, an Aladdin's cave for the sweet-toothed.

After dark stroll along Jeddah's corniche and catch a Red Sea breeze amid the eclectic collection of sculptures, which includes a Henry Moore.

Jerusalem

NICKNAME J-TOWN **DATE OF BIRTH** AROUND 2000 BC; ORIGINALLY A SMALL JEBUSITE SETTLEMENT, JERUSALEM OCCUPIED THE SLOPES OF MT MORIAH, WHERE, ACCORDING TO THE OLD TESTAMENT, ABRAHAM OFFERED HIS SON ISAAC AS A SACRIFICE; IN 997 BC, KING DAVID CAPTURED THE CITY AND MADE IT HIS CAPITAL **ADDRESS** ISRAEL AND THE PALESTINIAN TERRITORIES (MAP 8, B3) **HEIGHT** 557M **SIZE** 122 SQ KM **POPULATION** 780,000 **LONELY PLANET RANKING** 019

Jerusalem's place in the hearts and minds of so many people endows it with a charged atmosphere unlike any other city.

ANATOMY

Built on a series of hills, Jerusalem is on the watershed, the edge of the narrow fertile strip that clings to the Eastern Mediterranean. To the west there are green hills, spotted with villages. To the east, the brown desert hills are only rarely blessed with rain, which covers them in a ghostly sprinkling of bright green. There are two city centres, one Palestinian and one Israeli, both fairly compact and about 1.2km from each other. Jerusalem is laced with a very good network of city bus routes.

PEOPLE

Officially, Jews make up two thirds of the population and Arabs one third, but these figures are skewed by the inclusion of outlying Jewish settlements. The Jewish population comes from almost every corner of the earth, and ranges from long-bearded ultra-orthodox men in their traditional 17th-century Polish gabardine, to secular Moroccans partying in the latest American fashions. Hebrew and Arabic are the dominant languages, but many people speak English, especially in West Jerusalem.

TYPICAL JERUSALEMITE

Jerusalemites are both rude and hospitable. They'll keep you waiting 10 minutes before serving you at a counter, then invite you home to dinner. They will gladly get involved in an argument with you about anything, but usually about politics, religion, or why a good-looking girl/guy like you isn't married yet. Living on a holy mountain, they look down, literally and figuratively, on the sweaty plains-dwellers.

SPENCER PLATT / GETTY IMAGES

TANNED TEENS HANG OUT IN WEST JERUSALEM.

DEFINING EXPERIENCE

Sharing coffee and stories with an old man at the Damascus Gate, watching the sunset ignite the Dome of the Rock from the Mount of Olives, making a do-it-yourself felafel on Ben Yehuda St, before beer and live Russian music at the Pargod Theatre.

STRENGTHS

- An architectural patchwork of cultures and historical periods
- Hilltop views
- Local hospitality
- Sabbath quiet
- Mild and dry weather
- A centre of traditional Jewish learning
- The Mount of Olives
- Home to many idealists

WEAKNESSES

- Bombings (sometimes)
- Violent demonstrations (sometimes)
- Tension (always)
- Crazy drivers
- Too much machismo
- Home to many idealists

GOLD STAR

There's no substitute for standing where *those feet* actually trod.

STARRING ROLE IN...

- The Bible
- *Jerusalem* by Larry Collins and Dominique Lapierre
- *Kadosh* (1999)
- *Rana's Wedding* (2004)

See the hills of Judea from the road to Jericho.

Eat eat the Mahane Yehuda Market – it's crammed with cafes and food stalls.

Drink sweet cardamom coffee.

Do the ramparts walk on the walls of the old city.

Watch the best of Israeli cinema at Cinematheque.

Buy quality arts and crafts from the city's local artisans at the Bezalel craft fair, held every Friday near the Bezalel Art School.

After dark sample Hebrew blues or trilingual rap at Mike's Place.

THE SPICE IS RIGHT – A STALL OWNER MIXES SPICES AT A MARKET IN WEST JERUSALEM.

THE CHURCH OF MARY MAGDALENE SITS ABOVE A VALLEY OF WHITE RESIDENTIAL BUILDINGS.

IN THE KAPPAROT RITUAL OF YOM KIPPUR, A PERSON'S SINS ARE TRANSFERRED TO A LIVE CHICKEN THAT IS THEN SLAUGHTERERD.

THE SUN IS SHINING AND THE WEATHER IS SWEET AT A POOL PARTY IN JOHANNESBURG.

Johannesburg

NICKNAME JO'BURG; JOZI **DATE OF BIRTH** 1886; FOUNDED WHEN GOLD WAS DISCOVERED IN THE TRANSVAAL **ADDRESS** SOUTH AFRICA (MAP 7, D8) **HEIGHT** 1665M **SIZE** 2500 SQ KM **POPULATION** 5.7 MILLION **LONELY PLANET RANKING** 167

The huge beating heart of the Rainbow Nation, Johannesburg is a cosmopolitan African city, at once untamed and sophisticated, hazardous and welcoming, now shedding its shameful past and embracing the richness and lessons of its history.

ANATOMY

Johannesburg is built on an inland plateau, with river systems and reserves breaking up the cityscape. Unfolding from the office-block jungle of the city centre, the main sights in this expansive city spread across the cultural and social hub of Newtown, past the ring of black neighbourhoods and out into the wealthy white suburbs of the north and the black township of Soweto in the southwest. While the African flavour of Jo'burg is virtually absent in the northern suburbs, it crowds the streets of the city centre with street stalls and vendors. Johannesburg is best navigated by car, though there are buses, minibus taxis and a sometimes dangerous train system.

PEOPLE

The population of Johannesburg is mostly black African with one-fifth white and the remainder comprising other nationalities. While South Africa has 11 official languages, the most common here are Afrikaans, English, Zulu and Sesotho. The religious demographics of Johannesburg are similarly diverse; half the population belongs to mainstream Christian churches, with the rest being atheist, members of African Independent churches, or Muslim, Jewish or Hindu.

TYPICAL JOHANNESBURGER

In a city still economically segregated, the typical Johannesburger can range from the unspeakably poor to the grossly affluent. They love music and the entertainment scene and tend to live it up in ethnically distinct areas. They love to drink, watch sport and relax in the great outdoors. Though acutely aware of their infamous history, they disarm visitors with their open and friendly manner.

CELEBRATING MARRIAGE THE TRADITIONAL WAY IN SOWETO'S FAMOUS REGIONAL MUNDI CHURCH.

KEEPING THE PEACE AT THE POPULAR COLOR BAR.

JO'BURG'S MINIBUSES ARE A POPULAR WAY OF GETTING AROUND THE CITY.

DEFINING EXPERIENCE

Sifting through crafts at Rosebank Rooftop Market, then soaking up the hospitality of Soweto with a buffet meal and African brews at Wandie's Place before manning the *braai* (barbecue) pitch-side while watching international test cricket at the Wanderers Stadium.

STRENGTHS

◢ Many free art galleries
◢ Ethnic diversity
◢ World-class theatre
◢ International sporting events
◢ Apartheid Museum
◢ Botanical Gardens

WEAKNESSES

◢ Carjacking and dangerous neighbourhoods
◢ High unemployment
◢ Wearing a camera round your neck signals 'Mug me'
◢ AIDS epidemic

GOLD STAR

The high life – cigar lounges, stylish restaurants, world-class theatre productions and excellent shopping are all part of the fun of high living in one of the cheapest major cities in the world.

STARRING ROLE IN...

◢ *Cry, the Beloved Country* (1995)
◢ *Cry Freedom* (1987)
◢ *Long Walk to Freedom* by Nelson Mandela

See the Cradle of Humankind site – 50km out of the city centre – where human ancestor fossils up to 3.5 million years old have been excavated.

Eat African-Asian fusion at Gramadoela's – join Hillary Clinton and Denzel Washington on the list of diners at this classic restaurant.

Drink a pint on the terrace of the Guildhall Bar & Restaurant.

Do – if you can afford it – spend a night at the luxurious Saxon hotel, where Nelson Mandela put the final touches to his autobiography.

Watch rugby at the hallowed Ellis Park with the fanatical fans.

Buy traditional medicine at the Faraday Market.

After dark Jo'burg is an excellent place to see live music; Newtown and Braamfontein are the best places to kick off an evening.

Kabul

DATE OF BIRTH 1772; WHEN IT WAS MADE THE CAPITAL OF AFGHANISTAN, THOUGH THERE HAS BEEN HUMAN HABITATION SINCE PREHISTORIC TIMES **ADDRESS** AFGHANISTAN (MAP 8, J4) **HEIGHT** 1827M **SIZE** 250 SQ KM **POPULATION** 3 MILLION **LONELY PLANET RANKING** 118

A precious preserve of thriving Afghan culture, Kabul is one of the world's ancient cities and continues to sparkle through tumultuous change.

ANATOMY

Kabul sits on a plain ringed by the mountains of the Hindu Kush. The Koh-e Sher Darwaza mountains run south, topped by the old city walls, then veer east to the royal citadel of Bala Hissar. The Kabul River divides the capital. To the north is the rich Shahr-e Naw area, centred on its park and Pashtunistan Sq.

PEOPLE

Afghanistan's spot at the crossroads of Asia has produced a jigsaw of nationalities. The largest ethnic groups are the Pashtun, Tajik and Hazara, but over a dozen smaller nationalities live in Afghanistan, from the Uzbek Baluchi and blue-eyed Nuristanis, to nomadic Kuchi and Kyrgyz. The majority of the population is Sunni Muslim; 15% follow Shiite Islam. Sufism has always been a part of Afghan Islam.

TYPICAL KABULI

Through many manmade disasters, tragedies and rebuilding, the people of Kabul have maintained their hospitality. However, travellers that have returned since in recent years have noted that these experiences have hardened local people. Though encouraged by modern changes, many Kabulis remain fearful.

DEFINING EXPERIENCE

Brunching on a chicken kebab from a vendor on Cinema Zainab Rd while strolling through the park on your way to the Afghan Handicrafts Centre.

A 12-YEAR-OLD GIRL CARES FOR HER TWO-YEAR-OLD COUSIN IN AN ABANDONED, WAR-RAVAGED BUILDING.

MEN DO THE SHOPPING IN KABUL'S BIRD MARKET.

DESPITE LIBERATION FROM THE TALIBAN, RIGHTS AND EDUCATION FOR WOMEN REMAIN ELUSIVE.

A BOY SELLS FLOWERS AS SMOKE FROM GRILLED MEATS FILLS THE AIR.

STRENGTHS
- Chicken St Markets
- Darulaman Palace
- Mausoleum of Abdur Rahman Khan
- OMAR Land Mine Museum
- The fortress of Bala Hissar
- Musical instrument makers

WEAKNESSES
- Sparse nightlife and restricted drinking
- Few streetlights
- Strong presence of foreign armies
- Land mines

GOLD STAR
Preservation of Afghan culture – Kabul has retained an ancient culture, rising above the awful reputation given to the Afghani people by the Taliban.

STARRING ROLE IN...
- *Kandahar* (2001)
- *Osama* (2003)
- *Little Game* by Timor Shah

See the bird markets and musical instrument makers in the old city for a taste of traditional Afghan life.

Eat *Qabli pulao* (pilaf of rice and fried vegetables with almonds, raisins and grated carrot) from street vendors.

Drink a glass of sweet, spiced chai.

Do suck black tea through a sugar cube as you overlook the city from the beautiful terraces of Babur's Gardens.

Watch the concerts of Afghan music and poetry on Saturdays at the Foundation for Culture & Civil Society.

Buy a genuine Afghan rug from the Carpet Bazaar.

After dark on Thursday is kebab night at the Mustafa Hotel, which includes a rooftop barbecue.

Kairouan

NICKNAME LITTLE CAIRO **DATE OF BIRTH** AD 670; WHEN ARAB CONQUEROR UQBA IBN NAFI ESTABLISHED MILITARY POSTS ACROSS NORTH AFRICA AND SET UP A TEMPORARY ENCAMPMENT AT WHAT LATER BECAME KAIROUAN **ADDRESS** TUNISIA (MAP 6, H1) **HEIGHT** 60M **POPULATION** 118,000 **LONELY PLANET RANKING** 168

Tunisia's spiritual heart, ancient Kairouan is serene, magnetic, lively and proud: this ancient beauty of exquisite arches, columns and stonework enthrals the mind and eyeballs.

ANATOMY

Easy to navigate by foot, the old walled holy city of Kairouan encloses crumbling, whitewashed, blue- and green-edged houses, some hung with birdcages and many marked by the hand of Fatima. Away from the main souvenir drag, it's lovely to wander through the narrow cobblestone streets and big doorways of the medina (old quarter).

PEOPLE

Almost all Kairouans are Arab-Berber, with the remainder European and Jewish nationals. Islam is the dominant religion, with Kairouan historically known as 'the City of 100 Mosques'.

TYPICAL KAIROUAN

In an ancient city revered as one of Islam's holiest of holiest it shouldn't be surprising that Kairouans are a traditional people, home to a civilisation that was closed to outsiders for many years. Men get about in red-felt hats and many local women are wrapped in the traditional Berber cream shawls, their faces marked with traditional tattoos.

DEFINING EXPERIENCE

Coveting carpets woven by artisans in the medina, then picnicking with a feast of *makhroud* (honey-soaked pastry stuffed with dates) by the Aghlabid Basins' 9th-century reservoirs, and admiring the breathtaking pillars and columns of the Roman and Byzantine buildings and Great Mosque by twilight.

THE OLD WALLED CITY OF KAIROUAN IS A FINE EXAMPLE OF EARLY ISLAMIC ARCHITECTURE.

STRENGTHS

- The Great Mosque and its ancient minaret (said to be the oldest in the world)
- Mosque of the Three Doors
- Carpet museum
- Zaouia of Sidi Abid el-Ghariani
- Medina
- Mosque of the Barber – Zaouia of Sidi Sahab
- *Makhroud*

WEAKNESS

- Poor treatment of animals

GOLD STAR

Koran kudos – many Muslims, particularly Sunni Muslims, consider Kairouan to be Islam's fourth-holiest city (after Mecca, Medina and Jerusalem).

STARRING ROLE IN...

- *Raiders of the Lost Ark* (1984)
- *The Great Mosque of Kairouan* by Paul Sebag
- *Sleepless Nights* by Ali Duaji
- *Pillar of Salt* by Albert Memmi
- *Will to Live* by Abu el-Kacem el-Chabbi

See the Mosque of the Three Doors, famous for the rare intertwined floral and Arabic inscriptions carved in its façade.

Eat local delicacies at the Restaurant Sabra, a friendly popular local eatery with a piercingly loud bird in a cage.

Drink espresso shots in school chairs in the delightful tree-shaded café of Hôtel Sabra.

Do brave Kairouan's side streets and get among the animated locals going about their daily lives.

Watch the fascinating flux of faithful pouring out of afternoon prayer at the Great Mosque on Friday afternoon.

Buy exquisite hand-knotted pile Alloucha carpets, Kairouan's local speciality, from one of the hundreds of shops in the medina's souq (market).

After dark hightail it out of the city walls to get a view from the outside as the sun sets over this mind-bogglingly ancient holy city.

BRINGING HOME THE DAILY BREAD.

A MOSQUE IS READY TO WELCOME THE FAITHFUL.

WHITE-WASHED BUILDINGS SPRAWL LIKE MODERN ART UPON THE CANVAS OF KAIROUAN, ISLAM'S FOURTH HOLIEST CITY.

THE CHAOTIC BUSTLE OF LIFE IS PLAYED OUT DAILY ON THE RED STREETS OF KAMPALA.

Kampala

DATE OF BIRTH 1894; DECLARED BRITISH PROTECTORATE, THOUGH LOCAL TRIBES HAVE INHABITED THE AREA SINCE PREHISTORIC TIMES
ADDRESS UGANDA (MAP 7, E1) **HEIGHT** 1312M
POPULATION 1.5 MILLION **LONELY PLANET RANKING** 154

In 1907 a pioneering tourist named Winston Churchill dubbed Uganda the 'Pearl of Africa' and 100 years on, though much has transpired, it's still Africa's best-kept secret and Kampala is by far the jewel in its crown.

ANATOMY

Like Rome, Kampala is said to be built on seven hills. Nakasero Hill, encompassing the city centre, is where much of the action is. Between Nakasero and the lower part of the city is Kampala's main thoroughfare, Kampala Rd (which turns into Jinja Rd to the east and Bombo Rd to the west). Here you'll find banks, the main post office, shops and a few hotels and restaurants. Below this are a hotchpotch of shops, markets, budget hotels and eateries. Minibuses and taxis are the best way to get around.

PEOPLE

Uganda has a kaleidoscopic range of tribes and Kampala displays this wonderfully. The most prominent is the Buganda, with substantial representation from the Lango, Acholi and Teso people. There are also the Karamojong from the northeast of Uganda and Pygmies from the forests in the west. The church is a guiding light and often interwoven with traditional beliefs. There is also a small minority of Muslims, which once included Idi Amin, who converted to Islam to win financial support from Arab states in the 1970s.

TYPICAL KAMPALAN

Kampalans are educated, informed and globally aware. Their home remains one of the continent's great centres of learning. They love to engage visitors in conversations about Africa and the world beyond. Ethnically and culturally diverse, they take pride in their cosmopolitan lifestyle.

DEFINING EXPERIENCE

Whiling away the afternoon at art gallery-cafe-bar MishMash, then planning a gorilla-spotting and white-water rafting adventure in the surrounding area.

ON THE ROAD – AVENUES OF RED DIRT LEAD TO KAMPALA.

A CHILD IN KAMPALA READS A LETTER FROM HIS CHILDFUND SPONSOR.

BEAUTIFUL AFRICAN PRODUCE, ON SALE DOOR TO DOOR.

STRENGTHS
◢ Uganda Museum
◢ The contemporary art scene
◢ National parks
◢ Speed-boating and white-water rafting
◢ Entebbe Botanic Gardens
◢ Lake Victoria
◢ Local gorillas
◢ Owino Market
◢ Ethiopian restaurants
◢ Uganda Wildlife Education Centre
◢ Kibuli Mosque

WEAKNESSES
◢ Security searches
◢ Limited shopping
◢ A bloody history
◢ Thrill-seeking tourists

GOLD STAR
Survival – after Uganda's many troubled years of war and political turmoil, Kampala has carefully forged its own unique culture and remains strongly linked to world politics.

STARRING ROLE IN...
◢ *The Last King of Scotland* (2005)
◢ *ABC Africa* (2001)

See traditional dance and music at the Ndere Centre.

Eat the house vegetarian masala or a *tilapia* (fish) curry at Haandi.

Drink a beer in the relaxed, local atmosphere of the Iguana Bar.

Do visit the Kasubi Tombs, reed and bark-cloth buildings trumpeted as Africa's largest thatched mausoleum.

Watch the chimps frolic at Ngamba Island Chimpanzee Sanctuary on Ngamba Island in Lake Victoria.

Buy bargain secondhand clothes at the vibrant Owino Market.

After dark the Speke Hotel has a popular terrace bar out the front and is always packed with people.

Kathmandu

NICKNAME THE DOORWAY TO THE HIMALAYA **DATE OF BIRTH** AD 723; FOUNDED BY KING GUN KAMDEV **ADDRESS** NEPAL (MAP 8, C5) **HEIGHT** 1338M **SIZE** 395 SQ KM **POPULATION** 1 MILLION **LONELY PLANET RANKING** 013

This amazing city seems, in places, unchanged since the Middle Ages; at other times it is just another developing-world capital rushing into a modern era of concrete and traffic pollution.

ANATOMY

The high, fertile Kathmandu Valley, surrounded by terraced hills, is the cultural and political heart of Nepal. Most of the interesting things to see in Kathmandu are clustered in the old part of town from Kantipath (the main north–south road) west towards the Vishnumati River. There are taxis (cheap) and buses (crowded).

PEOPLE

Kathmandu's population is fairly homogeneous, but Tibetans and other Nepali ethnic groups contribute to its populace. The valley was a meeting place of Mongoloid peoples from the Tibetan plateau (Buddhist) and a large influx of Indo-Aryan people (Hindu) from the south.

TYPICAL KATHMANDU CITIZEN

Although these days there is more money around, most of it has remained in the pockets of the upper class. Kathmandu has one of the highest inflation rates in Asia, so the cost of living can really take it out of the average pay packet. And while the city's literacy and health have improved over the last 20 years, they're still under par. Despite all this, people retain a good-humoured self-respect and integrity.

DEFINING EXPERIENCE

Strolling around the medieval-like old town and exploring Hanuman Dhoka (Old Royal Palace) before lunching at Babar Mahal Revisited, chilling out in the late afternoon in a rooftop garden and then choosing from the many Thamel restaurants for dinner.

BUSINESS IS BLOOMING AT A FLOWER STALL ON THE BUSY JUNCTION OF ASAN TOLE.

STRENGTHS
- Thamel
- Pashupatinath
- Swayambhunath
- Hanuman Dhoka
- Bodhnath
- Garden of Dreams
- Durbar Sq
- The flight in and out with awe-inspiring views of the Himalaya

WEAKNESSES
- Pollution
- The political situation
- The poverty
- The failings of autocracy

GOLD STAR
Within the city itself are four Unesco World Heritage Sites: Durbar Sq, Swayambhunath, Bodhnath and Pashupatinath.

STARRING ROLE IN...
- *The Tutor of History* by Manjushree Thapa
- *Forget Kathmandu: An Elegy for Democracy* by Manjushree Thapa
- *Escape from Kathmandu* by Kim Stanley Robinson
- *The Window of the House Opposite* by Govinda Bahadur Malla
- *The Guru of Love* by Samrat Upadhyay
- *Arresting God in Kathmandu* by Samrat Upadhyay

See Mt Everest and the Himalaya on a one-hour mountain flight.

Eat very good Thai food or Himalayan perch at Yin Yang Restaurant in Thamel.

Drink at New Orleans Café – a very mellow vibe.

Do wander from Pashupatinath temple, the Hindu funeral site on the banks of the Bagmati River, across the fields to Bodhnath, the Buddhist stupa.

Watch the devotees climb the steps and circle the stupa in prayer at Swayambhunath.

Buy clothes, cushions and bags from Maheela, part of the Women's Foundation (50% of monies go back to the producers).

After dark have a drink and listen to some music at Jatra in Thamel.

THE ALL-SEEING EYES OF BUDDHISM DECORATE A STUPA.

COLOUR FOR SALE – TRADITIONAL TIKKA BRIGHTENS UP AN OPEN-AIR MARKET.

GOING STRAIGHT TO THE SOURCE – MEN CONGREGATE AROUND NEWSPAPER VENDORS TO CATCH THE LATEST NEWS.

A FLASH OF VIVID COLOUR AMID THE SWIRLING DUST.

Khartoum

DATE OF BIRTH 1821; ESTABLISHED AS AN EGYPTIAN ARMY CAMP
ADDRESS SUDAN (MAP 8, A7) **HEIGHT** 390M **POPULATION** 5 MILLION
LONELY PLANET RANKING 174

Where the azure and pale waters of the Blue and White Niles meet lies Sudan's modern capital – Khartoum is a haven of hospitable people, tree-lined boulevards and souqs (markets) lining the banks of the legendary river.

ANATOMY

The two Niles converge in the centre of Khartoum, splitting the capital into three main wedges: Khartoum, Bahri (Khartoum North) and Omdurman. Omdurman is Khartoum's most traditional suburb and home to the largest souq in the country. Buses, minibuses and shared taxis cover most points in the city and it is a short ride from the airport to central Khartoum and UN Sq, south of which are countless informal joints serving up Sudanese classics.

PEOPLE

As much of Sudan's population, including around two million nomads, live in rural areas, the residents of Khartoum form an urban minority. More than 100 languages are spoken around the country, but Arabic is the official language and the mother tongue of Khartoum, and Islam is the predominant religion, in keeping with much of northern Sudan. English, widely used here, is by no means universal.

TYPICAL KHARTOUMAN

For Khartouman read hospitality. Khartoumans will pay for everything, share their meals and even invite you to stay in their homes. They are among the friendliest people in Africa, with a natural generosity that entirely belies their poverty. They are strictly Islamic nondrinkers but will discreetly enjoy a *chicha* (a water pipe infused with apple or tobacco) after a meal. Frequent street clashes and revolts reflect a city whose people, justifiably or not, remain passionate about past and present conflicts and continue to fight for their beliefs.

DEFINING EXPERIENCE

Eating *ta'amiya* (felafel) while picking through the wares at the souq in Omdurman, watching the colours of the Blue and White Niles swirl into

415

A REFUGEE FROM DARFUR WITH SOMETHING TO SMILE ABOUT.

one from the White Nile Bridge, and then – if it's a Friday – going to Hamed el-Nil Mosque to see the Halgt Zikr, where a colourful local troupe of whirling dervishes stirs up the dust in worship of Allah for the last two hours before sunset.

STRENGTHS

- ◢ Convergence of the Niles
- ◢ Nubian history
- ◢ The National Museum
- ◢ Omdurman

- ◢ The souq
- ◢ The camel market
- ◢ Mahdi's Tomb
- ◢ The Ethnographical Museum
- ◢ Cheap (if basic) hotels
- ◢ Fast, low-priced internet
- ◢ Pyramids

WEAKNESSES

- ◢ War zone
- ◢ Death penalty (maximum) for homosexuality
- ◢ Extreme poverty

- ◢ Nonexistent nightlife
- ◢ 40°C summer heat

GOLD STAR

The souq – this market is a dusty, vibrant relic of Sudanese life. At home in Khartoum's traditional suburb of Omdurman, it is the largest souq in the country.

STARRING ROLE IN...

- ◢ *Khartoum* (1966)
- ◢ *Triumph of the Sun* by Wilbur Smith

LOCAL BOYS SPOT THE CAMERA WHILE FILLING UP THEIR WATER TANKS.

◢ *The Translator* by
  Leila Aboulela

See the sun setting on the narrow pyramids that fill the ancient royal cemetery of Begrawiya.

Eat fuul (beans) and ta'amiya on the riverside at El-Shallal.

Drink fresh fruit juice – fruit is blended with ice and boy you will need it!

Do ride the fast-moving Ferris wheel in the Al-Mogran Family Park for an original perspective of the converging Niles.

Watch the Halgt Zikr stir up the dust in celebration of Allah at the Hamed el-Nil Mosque every Friday afternoon.

Buy almost anything from the amazing variety of wares at the Khartoum souq.

After dark enjoy a postdinner smoke at the tiny chicha terrace on Sharia as-Sayed Abdul Rahman.

Kolkata

NICKNAME CITY OF JOY **DATE OF BIRTH** 1690; WHEN IT WAS FOUNDED
AS A TRADING POST FOR THE BRITISH EAST INDIA COMPANY; IT
LATER SERVED AS THE CAPITAL OF BRITISH INDIA UNTIL 1912
ADDRESS INDIA (MAP 9, C6) **HEIGHT** 6M **SIZE** 1036 SQ KM
POPULATION 15 MILLION **LONELY PLANET RANKING** 065

India's second largest city and its cultural capital is the centre of Bengali intellectual life. Every stage of human life is played out on its teeming streets.

ANATOMY

Kolkata sprawls north–south along the eastern bank of the Hooghly River. South of the Howrah Bridge are BBD Bagh (the hub of the CBD, the central business district) and Chowringhee Sts. A new one-way system with streets flowing in different directions depending on the time of day, mean taxis, crowded trolleybuses or the subway (the oldest in Asia) are the way to get around.

PEOPLE

The majority of the population is Hindu. Muslims and Christians constitute the largest minorities, but there are also Sikhs, Jains and Buddhists, and small Jewish and Christian communities.

TYPICAL KOLKATAN

Kolkatans are the poets and artists of India, with a penchant for art and culture and a level of intellectual vitality and political awareness unsurpassed in the rest of the country. No other Indian city can draw the kinds of thronging crowds to book fairs, art exhibitions and concerts. There is a lively trading of polemics on walls, which has led to Kolkata being dubbed the 'city of posters'. Elsewhere in India, the many millions of poor are largely shut out of this cultural life.

DEFINING EXPERIENCE

Soaking up an education at the Indian Museum and popping down to Park St (Mother Teresa Sarani) for a refreshing cappuccino or hot *kati* roll (marinated fillings in bread) and browsing in the Oxford Bookstore, then strolling along the east bank of the Hooghly River, passing several Hooghly Ghats, and finally, heading to the river for a ferry trip across the Hooghly for views of the Hooghly Bridge before dining at Peter Cat, a Kolkata institution.

SEEN FROM ABOVE, THE FLOWER MARKET BENEATH HOWRAH BRIDGE BLAZES WITH COLOUR.

A CONTEMPLATIVE RICKSHAW WALLAH WAITS FOR A FARE OUTSIDE VICTORIA MARKET.

CURRY AND CONVERSATION AT THE FOOD STALLS IN FRONT OF THE TIPPU SULTAN MOSQUE.

FAMILIES GATHER TO CELEBRATE THE NEW YEAR TOGETHER AT KALIGHAT TEMPLE.

STRENGTHS
- St Paul's Cathedral
- India Museum
- Durga Puja
- Birla Planetarium
- Victoria Memorial
- Academy of Fine Arts
- Graveyard at St John's Church
- Eden Gardens
- Howrah Bridge
- Botanical Gardens

WEAKNESSES
- Traffic jams
- *Bandhs* (strikes), which happen with monotonous regularity
- Flooding

GOLD STAR
The Indian Museum covers an impressive range of subjects, from natural history to modern art. Highlights include a gallery of religious sculptures and a life-sized reproduction of the Barhut Gateway, built by Bihari Buddhists in the 2nd century BC. Also interesting is the gallery on plants and horticulture.

STARRING ROLE IN...
- *The Missionary Position: Mother Teresa in Theory and Practice* by Christopher Hitchens
- *City of Joy* by Dominique Lapierre
- *A Suitable Boy* by Vikram Seth

See a Bengali or foreign art-house film at the Nandan Complex.

Eat Bengali cuisine – a wonderful discovery with a whole new vocabulary of names and flavours.

Drink as the Kolkatans do, making street-side tea stops for minicuppas served in disposable *bhaar* (eco-friendly earthenware thimbles).

Do catch Kolkata's beautiful young things in their finest at Tantra where you can dance.

Watch the crowds stream over the Howrah Bridge and the flower sellers below.

Buy embroidered clothes and fabrics at the Women's Friendly Society.

After dark take in a dance-drama performance or Bengali poetry reading at Rabindra Sadan.

PIGEONS AND FAMILIES ALIKE FLOCK TO MAIN MARKET SQ, THE HEART AND SOUL OF THE CITY.

Kraków

NICKNAME POLAND'S ROYAL CITY **DATE OF BIRTH** 7TH CENTURY; WHEN SETTLEMENT WAS FIRST RECORDED HERE **ADDRESS** POLAND (MAP 4, 010) **HEIGHT** 209M **SIZE** 327 SQ KM **POPULATION** 760,000 (CITY); 1.4 MILLION (METRO AREA) **LONELY PLANET RANKING** 030

Kraków is a whimsical, beautiful city: tatters of the iron curtain can still be found in the city's grey, identikit suburbs, but these only throw into relief the pale, lazy loops of the Vistula River curling around the Old Town, or the flower stalls, which make the centre of the Old Town and its marketplace so vivid.

ANATOMY

Relatively flat, save for some scattered rocky formations, Kraków is bisected by the Vistula River, Poland's longest river (wending its way 1047km to the Baltic). Most districts, including the historic quarter, are on the northern, left bank and very walkable. The Old Town is only 800m wide and 1200m long, with Rynek Główny (Main Square) in the middle. Both buses and trams are used to travel further out.

PEOPLE

Ethnically homogeneous, Poles make up almost all of Kraków's population. The current Jewish population is relatively small, compared with 70,000 in the late 1930s. The majority of the population is Roman Catholic.

TYPICAL KRAKÓW CITIZEN

Residents of Kraków are more conservative than their fellow countrymen in Warsaw and they are firmly religious. They are friendly and hospitable but polite and formal – they are passionate hand-shakers.

DEFINING EXPERIENCE

Reflecting on Poland's long Catholic tradition at St Mary's Church in Rynek Główny, then leisurely strolling around the square, passing through the Cloth Hall, finding an appetising lunch on ul Grodzka, then heading to the Czartoryski Museum before ambling to Wawel Castle and watching the stunning views over the Vistula River.

WAWEL CASTLE IS A GOTHIC MASTERPIECE THAT DATES FROM THE 14TH CENTURY.

STRENGTHS

- ◢ Wawel Castle
- ◢ Wawel Cathedral
- ◢ Czartoryski Museum
- ◢ Rynek Główny
- ◢ Cloth Hall
- ◢ The jazz scene
- ◢ Wieliczka Salt Mine
- ◢ A vast collection of artworks
- ◢ Wierzynek, Poland's oldest restaurant, dating from 1364

WEAKNESSES

- ◢ Weather
- ◢ Nowa Huta
- ◢ Sauerkraut with everything

GOLD STAR

Rynek Główny – the largest medieval town square in Poland (and reputedly in all of Europe) – and the Cloth Hall. The 1257 layout has been retained to this day – the façades might look neoclassical, but most of the buildings are much older. Head beneath the vast square to experience the multimedia Rynek Underground exhibition.

STARRING ROLE IN...

- ◢ *La Double vie de Véronique* (The Double Life of Véronique, 1991)
- ◢ *Schindler's List* (1993)

See the Chapel of Kinga, a church deep in the salt mine at Wieliczka.

Eat obwarzanek (pretzels) – one of the signs you've arrived in Kraków are the

COLD BEER AND WARM ATMOSPHERE DEFINES KRAKÓW'S PERSONABLE PUB SCENE.

stalls placed seemingly at every street corner selling these hefty snacks.

Drink beer (Zywiec, Okocim or EB) or vodka (clear, or flavoured with juniper berries, cherries or rowan berries).

Do make the trip out to Auschwitz, possibly the most moving experience in the whole of Poland.

Watch experimental theatre (knowledge of the language is not necessary).

Buy amber in striking colours – from ivory and pale yellow to reddish and brownish hints.

After dark vaulted cellar pubs and bars are the place to head for; there are hundreds of pubs and bars in the Old Town alone.

Kuala Lumpur

NICKNAME KL **DATE OF BIRTH** 1857; WHEN A TROUPE OF TIN
PROSPECTORS LANDED AT THE JUNCTION OF THE KLANG AND
GOMBAK RIVERS AND DUBBED IT KUALA LUMPUR (MUDDY
CONFLUENCE) **ADDRESS** MALAYSIA (MAP 9, E9) **HEIGHT** 39M
SIZE 243 SQ KM **POPULATION** 1.9 MILLION (CITY); 7.2 MILLION
(METRO AREA) **LONELY PLANET RANKING** 052

**A triumphant and forward-looking city, Kuala Lumpur
accommodates its traditional Malay, Chinese and
Indian cultures with the buzz of industry.**

ANATOMY

KL's traditional heart beats at Merdeka Sq, while the Golden Triangle
represents modern KL; the Petronas Towers are dazzling beacons of
industry. Southeast of Merdeka lies Chinatown and southward is Masjid
Negara (National Mosque) and the historic KL Train Station. Stretching
west is KL's 'green belt', with the Lake Garden and Malaysian Parliament
House. KL's maze of motorways can frustrate pedestrians – it's easier to
nab a cab or ride the slick LRT (Light Rail Transit) system.

PEOPLE

Kuala Lumpur truly is 'Little Asia', with a mix of Malays, Chinese, Indians
and other Asian cultural groups. The official language is Malay; other
languages spoken are Hokkien/Fukien, Cantonese, Hakka, Teochew, Tamil,
Telugu, Hindi and English. Mostly Muslim, Buddhists, Hindus, Sikhs and
Christians form part of KL's tapestry.

TYPICAL KUALA LUMPUR CITIZEN

Kuala Lumpur's citizens are proud, respectful and tolerant of different
beliefs and cultural practices. They have triumphed at building a
metropolis that retains local traditions and colour. Oppressed by dripping
humidity, the citizens know how to relax, be it enjoying great food or
bargain-hunting in air-conditioned malls.

DEFINING EXPERIENCE

Picnicking at the Lake Gardens among butterflies, birds and orchids,
serenading your true love on a Tasik Perdana (Premier Lake) rowing boat,
topped off by a balmy banquet at Chinatown's night market.

RED FOR LUCK AT THE MODERN THEAN HOU TEMPLE OVERLOOKING JALAN SYED PUTRA.

AT PLAY BENEATH THE SOARING PETRONAS TOWERS.

A SALESWOMAN MELTS INTO A BACKGROUND OF EMBROIDERED SCARVES IN LITTLE INDIA'S ARCADE.

STRENGTHS
- Multiculturalism, tolerance and diversity
- Dazzling Petronas Towers
- Hawker markets and foodstalls
- Luscious gardens
- Exquisite pewter

WEAKNESSES
- Dripping humidity (though great for orchids)
- Traffic congestion, narrow streets and lack of sidewalks
- Smog and poor water quality
- The invasion of 'mall culture'

GOLD STAR
Cheap, delicious and culturally diverse food – a memorable meal can be found in any one of KL's nooks, crannies and basements.

STARRING ROLE IN...
- *Entrapment* (1999)
- *The Big Durian* (2004)

See the city lights from the Petronas Towers before getting a ride an hour northwest of KL to see the natural light show of kelip-kelip (fireflies) in the mangroves, best viewed on a river tour from Kuala Selangor.

Eat at the collection of roadside restaurants and stalls lining Jalan Alor – from around 5pm till late every evening, the street transforms into a continuous open-air dining space.

Drink with friendly locals at *mamak* stalls (hang-out spots) dotting the city; run by Muslim Indians they are a great place for night owls to hang out late.

Do brave the indoor rollercoaster at Berjaya Times Sq.

Watch Malay dance, Indian classical dance, Chinese dance and t'ai chi performances every weekend at the open-air Central Market.

Buy electronic gadgets and mobile phones at Low Yat Plaza.

After dark doof-doof into the wee hours at Bangsar, KL's hub for clubs.

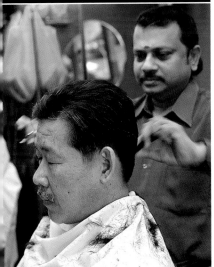

A TRIM AT A HAIRDRESSING SALON IN LITTLE INDIA.

STATELY ST MICHAEL'S MONASTERY IS SURE TO LEAVE A LASTING IMPRESSION.

Kyiv

NICKNAME NORTHERN ROME **DATE OF BIRTH** AD 5–6; THE STORY ABOUT THE ORIGINS OF THE CITY ARE DISPUTED, BUT ACCORDING TO OFFICIAL SOVIET HISTORY THE CITY WAS FOUNDED AT THIS TIME **ADDRESS** UKRAINE (MAP 4, S10) **HEIGHT** 179M **SIZE** 780 SQ KM **POPULATION** 2.8 MILLION **LONELY PLANET RANKING** 145

This ancient city has undergone a facelift in the wake of the nation's independence in 1991, and modern Kyiv is consumerist, cosmopolitan and rich in the treasures of history and culture.

ANATOMY

Situated on the Dnipro River, Kyiv's city centre and old city are on the western bank, while grey residential blocks sit on the eastern bank. The old town lies along the high bank, with the main commercial centre of town sitting behind it. The city's wide boulevards are lined with a curious mix of architecture that reflects the rich historical influences in the capital: plain Stalinist buildings and stunning medieval, baroque, Gothic, Russian and Byzantine monuments and churches. As the main attractions are mostly found beyond the centre of town, the Kyiv metro is a good way to get around, with river cruises, buses and car hire also available.

PEOPLE

The capital's population is composed of a Ukrainian majority, as well as Russians and a few Eastern European immigrants. The majority of the population belongs to one of several national Orthodox churches or to the Russian Orthodox Church, with minority faiths including Roman Catholicism, Judaism and Islam. Ukrainian is the official language, but English is also quite widely spoken in Kyiv.

TYPICAL KYIVAN

The city attracts more than its fair share of wealthy and talented Ukrainians as well as the political elite and stunning fashionistas. These moneyed groups are flashy. They are pushy and don't like to queue. They are fast and frantic and voracious consumers. They love to be seen at the hot clubs, bars and restaurants of Kyiv. They do, however, like the more 'ordinary' people of the city, have strong social connections and are proud of their culture and city.

431

EXTINCT IS FOREVER – SIGNS OF REMEMBRANCE FOR THE MANY TOWNS LOST TO CHORNOBYL.

DEFINING EXPERIENCE

Indulging with breakfast and views of Kyiv's golden church domes at the Premier Palace Hotel, then meeting friends at Independence Sq before watching resident football team Dynamo Kyiv play a match.

STRENGTHS

- Culinary capital of Ukraine where beer is considered a soft drink
- St Andrew's Church
- Mosaics and frescoes at the 11th-century St Sophia Cathedral
- Museum of the Great Patriotic War
- Mariyinsky Palace
- Pyrohovo Museum of Folk Architecture
- Kitsch-themed restaurants
- Wild nightlife

WEAKNESSES

- Wild traffic
- Pushy locals in queues
- High cost of living
- Covert sex industry

GOLD STAR

Caves Monastery – to Orthodox pilgrims this site is holy land and to all other visitors this place is something truly spectacular.

STARRING ROLE IN...

- *Mamai* (2003)
- *A Prayer for Hetman Mazepa* (2002)
- *The White Guard* by Mikhail Bulgakov

See the mummified monks by candlelight in the underground passages of the Caves Monastery.

Eat at Pervak – Kyiv's best Ukrainian restaurant masterfully creates old Kyiv (c 1900) without falling into the schmaltz trap.

Drink 'real coffee' at Kaffa.

Do meet at the ever-lively and noisy, fountain-filled Independence Sq.

Watch the 'walruses' (swimmers) wake up to themselves with a winter swim in the freezing Dnipro River.

Buy tasty Kyivsky Tort (a nutty, layered sponge) at the train-station stalls.

After dark get into the latest tunes at the glam Tchaikovsky club.

Kyoto

DATE OF BIRTH 7TH CENTURY; LITTLE MORE THAN A VAST, FERTILE PLAIN, KYOTO – THEN KNOWN AS YAMASHIRO-NO-KUNI – BECAME HOME TO THE HATA CLAN FROM KOREA **ADDRESS** JAPAN (MAP 9, K2) **HEIGHT** 41M **SIZE** 610 SQ KM **POPULATION** 1.5 MILLION **LONELY PLANET RANKING** 045

Cultural heart of Japan, Kyoto's raked pebble gardens, sensuously contoured temple roofs and latter-day geishas fulfil the Japanese fantasy of every Western cliché hunter.

ANATOMY

The city is divided into five sections designating the central *(raku-chu)*, eastern *(raku-to)*, northern *(raku-hoku)*, western *(raku-sai)* and southern *(raku-nan)* areas, plus *raku-gai*, the city's outskirts. With a rectangular grid system, it's easy to navigate. The business district is in the south and centre; the less populated northern parts have a greener feel, with rice fields sandwiched between apartment buildings. Although many major sights are in the centre, the best sightseeing is on the fringes. It's easy to get around by walking, cycling, taking the bus or subway.

PEOPLE

Kyoto is home to one of the largest concentrations of colleges and universities in Japan, however, the majority of students leave after graduation for the bigger economic centres of Tokyo and Osaka. There are also an estimated 33,000 Japanese-Koreans living here, particularly in the neighbourhood south of Kyoto station.

TYPICAL KYOTOITE

Kyotoites are sometimes described as cold, unnecessarily formal and snobbish towards outsiders, though short-term tourists are made to feel welcome. The Kyoto dialect can be extremely vague, masking true feelings behind veiled smiles and nebulous wording. Known for their sense of style, Kyotoites prefer small and refined over large and flashy.

DEFINING EXPERIENCE

Visiting Nanzen-ji temple and its grounds, including the classic Zen garden, then viewing the cherry blossoms in bloom (April only) in Kyoto Imperial Palace Park, before relaxing in a *sentō* (public bath) as a prelude to an evening stroll around Ponto-chō's restaurants, bars and teahouses.

LIKE A BRUSH PAINTING BROUGHT TO LIFE, THE BLOSSOMING BANKS OF THE KAMO GAWA RIVER PRESENT AN IDYLLIC SCENE.

'AND DON'T FORGET TO PUBLISH YOUR MEMOIRS' – AN APPRENTICE GEISHA RECEIVES ADVICE FROM AN OLDER WOMAN.

STRENGTHS

- Japan's cultural treasure-house – 17 ancient structures and gardens are World Heritage Sites
- More than 1600 Buddhist temples
- Over 400 Shintō shrines
- Three palaces
- Dozens of gardens and museums
- Cherry-blossom festival (April)
- Nightlife in Ponto-chō and Gion's 'floating world'
- Hundreds of *matsuri* (festivals) every year
- Growing environmental awareness among young Kyotoites
- Kyoto station

WEAKNESSES

- Ugly urban development
- Widespread environmental apathy
- Kyoto Tower – great views, not so great to look at

GOLD STAR

Nanzen-ji Temple, for the combination of temple, grounds, Zen garden and hidden shrine in a forest hollow behind the main precinct

STARRING ROLE IN...

- *Katakuri-ke no kôfuku* (The Happiness of the Katakuris, 2001)
- *The Pillow Book* (1996)
- *Ai no corrida* (In the Realm of the Senses, 1976)
- *Rashômon* (1950)

See Kyoto's geisha perform fantastic dances in the spring and autumn, participating in a brief tea ceremony before the show.

Eat *sukiyaki* in a traditional tatami room at Morita-ya.

Drink sake at Ing, a favourite spot for a drink in Kyoto.

Do belt out a number or three at Jumbo Karaoke Hiroba.

Watch a traditional kabuki performance at Minami-za, the oldest kabuki theatre in Japan.

Buy distinctive ceramics at the Kōbō-san market-fair at To-ji temple, held on the 21st of every month.

After dark wander the 'floating world' of traditional entertainment areas Gion and Ponto-chō.

ON THE SHOPPING STRIP OF ARTESANÍA ALLEY IS THE MERCADO DE HECHICERÍA, SPECIALISING IN LLAMA FOETUSES AND DRIED FROGS.

La Paz

DATE OF BIRTH 1548; LA CIUDAD DE NUESTRA SEÑORA DE LA PAZ (CITY OF OUR LADY OF PEACE) WAS FOUNDED AND NAMED BY SPANISH CAPTAIN ALONSO DE MENDOZA **ADDRESS** BOLIVIA (MAP 3, C10) **HEIGHT** 3658M **SIZE** 7 SQ KM **POPULATION** 1 MILLION (CITY); 2 MILLION (METRO AREA) **LONELY PLANET RANKING** 094

Standing at the edge of the canyon, the earth drops away, revealing, 400m below, the sprawling city of La Paz, which fills the bowl and climbs the walls of this gaping valley.

ANATOMY

There's only one major thoroughfare in La Paz, called the Prado, and it follows the Río Choqueyapu canyon. Away from the Prado and its extensions, streets climb steeply uphill and many are cobbled or unpaved. Above the downtown skyscrapers, the adobe neighbourhoods and the informal commercial areas climb towards the city of El Alto, perched on the canyon's rim. La Paz is well served by public transport: basically you can choose between *micros* (buses) and *trufis* (either cars or minibuses).

PEOPLE

More than half of the city's population claims pure indigenous heritage; nearly 1% is of African heritage, mostly descendants of slaves conscripted to work in the Potosí silver mines. The remainder of Bolivia's citizens are largely of European extraction. Not all are descendants of the early Spanish conquerors; there are Mennonite colonies, Jewish refugees from Nazi Europe, Eastern European refugees and hordes of researchers, aid workers and missionaries. Spanish and Quechua are the official languages; Aymara is also spoken.

TYPICAL PACEÑO

The standard of living of most Bolivians is alarmingly low, marked by substandard housing, nutrition, education, sanitation and hygiene. Bolivia suffers from a Third World trifecta: a high infant mortality rate, a high birth rate and a low female literacy rate. Overall, almost 90% of primary-school-aged children are enrolled in classes, but attendance isn't a high priority. The people of La Paz are hard-working but generally underemployed, and many supplement their income by participating in the informal street-market and coca-production economy. Strikes among the public service and farmers are common.

LOCAL BOYS PLAY A HIGH STAKES GAME OF FOOTBALL ABOVE THE CITY.

DEFINING EXPERIENCE

Starting your day with a *salteña* (meat-filled pastry) around Plaza Isabel La Católica – the perfect spot for watching the world's highest city wake up, then strolling the historic cobblestone streets around Iglesia de San Francisco or wandering the nearby Artesanía Alley (or Calle Linares) and Mercado de Hechicería (Witches' Market) while shopping for fine alpaca wear.

STRENGTHS

- ◢ El Alto's sprawling markets
- ◢ Ancient ruins of Tiahuanaco
- ◢ *Peñas* (folk-music venues)
- ◢ Museo de la Coca
- ◢ Trendy Zona Sur
- ◢ Urmiri's hot springs
- ◢ The world's highest downhill skiing on the slopes of Chacaltaya
- ◢ Día de los Muertos (Day of the Dead, or All Souls' Day)
- ◢ Valle de las Ánimas
- ◢ The Cañón de Palca (aka Quebrada Chua Keri) gorge

WEAKNESSES

- ◢ Seventy percent of the population below the poverty line
- ◢ *Soroche* (altitude sickness)
- ◢ Machismo
- ◢ High infant mortality rate
- ◢ Unemployment
- ◢ *Lustrabotes* (shoeshine boys)

GOLD STAR

The Prado. On Sunday afternoon, when traffic is restricted and the city empties out, the Prado hosts promenading families, and the

CHARANGOS FOR SALE IN SMALL SHOP ON CALLE LINARES.

sidewalks fill with balloon and candy-floss sellers, and people renting kites, bicycles and toy cars.

STARRING ROLE IN...

- ◢ *Woman of Courage* (1993)
- ◢ *A Question of Faith* (1996)
- ◢ *Morder el Silencio* (The Biting Silence) by Arturo von Vacano
- ◢ *Los Fundadores del Alba* (The Breach) by Renato Prada Oropeza

See La Paz on a clear, dark night and the cityscape will appear like a mir-rored reflection of the glittering sky.

Eat a dinner of llama medallions with mushroom sauce at Tambo Colonial and enjoy live folk-music performances.

Drink a splendid local coffee at the cheery, little arty café Pepe's Coffee Bar.

Do explore the Mercado de Hechicería and pick yourself up a lucky llama foetus or dried toucan beak.

Watch a folklore show at the Teatro Municipal Alberto Saavedra Pérez –

a great old restored building with a round auditorium, elaborate balconies and a vast ceiling mural.

Buy fine woven wares at Artesanía Alley off Calle Sagárnaga.

After dark attend a *peña*, such as El Calicanto, for a taste of traditional Andean music, rendered on *zampoñas* (panpipe), *quenas* (bamboo flute) and *charangos* (stringed instrument).

Lahore

NICKNAME HEART OF PAKISTAN **DATE OF BIRTH** AD 630; WHILE THE DATE IS OFTEN DISPUTED, THE FIRST RELIABLE REFERENCE TO THE CITY WAS IN THE WRITINGS OF XUAN ZANG, A CHINESE TRAVELLER **ADDRESS** PAKISTAN (MAP 8, K4) **HEIGHT** 214M **SIZE** 185 SQ KM **POPULATION** 11 MILLION **LONELY PLANET RANKING** 188

Although not Pakistan's administrative capital, Lahore wins hands down as the cultural, intellectual and artistic jewel of Pakistan, sparkling with effervescent local culture and studded with historic monuments.

ANATOMY

The second-largest city in Pakistan, Lahore sits high on an alluvial plain near the Ravi River and the Indo-Pakistani border. The city bears the stamp of its former status as the capital of the Mughal Empire, with fearsome Mughal constructions as well as the British Raj legacy of Gothic Victorian styles. A railway and air transport nerve-centre of Pakistan, Lahore's local transport comprises buses and minibuses as well as *tongas* (two-wheeled carriages), taxis and auto-rickshaws.

PEOPLE

As capital of the Punjab province, Lahore is dominated by the Punjabi ethnic group but include other groups, notably Afghan refugees. The city comprises a Muslim majority, with Christian and Hindu minorities. Punjabi is the main language, followed by English and Urdu.

TYPICAL LAHORI

Lahoris are fiercely patriotic and proud of their city and culture. They are highly skilled professionals, sportspeople and craftspeople. They love traditions but embrace many aspects of Western culture, including cricket, and are vocal spectators. Lahori women also fight for civil rights. They are generous, warm and open to travellers but expect visitors to be respectfully dressed. They don't drink but are indulgent eaters.

DEFINING EXPERIENCE

Lazily reading in the restful garden of the gorgeous Jinnah Library, chowing down on calamari and alcohol-free piña colada at Café Aylanto, then firing up for a showcase of electrifying *qawwali* (Islamic devotional singing) at the shrine of Data Ganj Bakhsh Hajveri.

BADSHAHI MOSQUE WAS COMMISSIONED IN 1671.

BEAUTY IN MOTION – HIJRA DANCING IN LAHORE, HIJRA REFERS TO PEOPLE OF THE 'THIRD GENDER' IN PAKISTAN AND INDIA.

STRENGTHS

- Skilled artisanship
- *Qawwali*
- Local music
- Basant – the kite-flying festival
- Mughal architecture of the Old City
- Mela Chiraghan (Festival of Lights)
- Jehangir's Tomb
- Royal Fort
- Shalimar Gardens
- Badshahi Mosque

WEAKNESSES

- Indifferent attitude to the treatment of animals
- Rain, humidity and mosquitoes during the monsoon (July to September)
- Pollution
- Dry zone
- Crowded buses

GOLD STAR

Lahore Museum – touted as the best in Pakistan, if not the subcontinent. It is definitely worth a couple of hours' snooping. Its exhibits span the recorded history of the subcontinent, dating from the Stone Age to the present day and include a haunting statue, the *Fasting Buddha*.

STARRING ROLE IN...

- *Veer Zaara* (2004)
- *Eating Grass* (2003)
- *Bhowani Junction* (1956)
- *The Reluctant Fundamentalist* by Mohsin Hamid

See the wildly ecstatic spectators as you take in an international cricket match at Qaddafi Stadium.

Eat *boti kebab* (meat grilled on a spit) under a clear night sky twinkling with stars at Coco's Den & Café.

Drink up at the upmarket Pearl Continental to celebrate your newly acquired drinking permit.

Do attend 'Sufi Night' and get caught up in the mystical bliss and drumming.

Watch the theatrics of the daily border-closing from the grandstand.

Buy a traditional Punjabi *dhal* (drum) at Langay Mandi.

After dark check out the impromptu rooftop jams at the Regale Internet Inn.

LIGHTS, CAMERA, ACTION – ON FREMONT STREET.

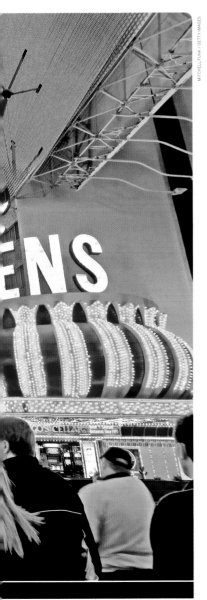

Las Vegas

NICKNAME SIN CITY **DATE OF BIRTH** 1829; WHEN ANTONIO ARMIJO
TOOK A DETOUR EN ROUTE TO LOS ANGELES, BUT NATIVE AMERICAN
SETTLEMENTS HAVE BEEN HERE SINCE ANCIENT TIMES **ADDRESS** USA
(MAP 1, F6) **HEIGHT** 612M **SIZE** 293 SQ KM **POPULATION** 585.000 (CITY);
2 MILLION (METRO AREA) **LONELY PLANET RANKING** 046

There's nowhere like Vegas, baby – come here to marry a stranger, gamble your life savings away or just lap up the glorious oddness and kitsch of the whole place.

ANATOMY
Centred on the world-famous Strip (or Las Vegas Blvd to purists), the city can seem to be little else for those just in town for a few days. Las Vegas proper is centred on Fremont St and the downtown area to the north of the big hotel-casino complexes of the Strip.

PEOPLE
The vast majority of Las Vegans were born outside Nevada. It's impossible to define this mixed bunch. There's a Bible-toting Elvis bumming smokes from the guy hawking his first hip-hop album in what appears to be Tuscany. At the strip joint off the strip the drunken guy on his last fling is throwing dollars at the perky-breasted gal dancing on the pole. She's telling him the money's so good she commutes from the West Coast.

TYPICAL LAS VEGAN
Your typical Las Vegan loves this city, as they've chosen to live here, coming from other towns in the US and beyond. The population loves its sport (particularly golf and tennis) and is oblivious to the tourist crowds on the Strip, avoiding them by living and hanging out downtown, and so experiencing a very different lifestyle (despite many working in the casinos and hotels of the strip) from that enjoyed by most visitors to the city.

DEFINING EXPERIENCE
Strolling down the Strip through the animated crowds in the summer evening heat, wandering from Venice (the Venetian Resort Hotel Casino) to Polynesia (the Mirage, complete with on-site erupting volcano) to Paris (the Paris-Las Vegas) to New York (the New York-New York) to Egypt (the Luxor) in the space of half an hour, constantly being amazed at what an insane place Las Vegas is.

A PINK LIMOUSINE PROWLS FOR A PARKING SPACE UNDER A GAUDY CANOPY OF CASINO LIGHTS.

PAST ITS PRIME, A GIGANTIC W RESTS IN PEACE IN THE NEVADA DESERT.

ALL SHOOK UP ON THE STRIP, UH HUH.

STRENGTHS

- 24-hour gambling and drinking
- Huge choice of hotels, all with their own ridiculous theme
- Delicious food and extraordinarily attentive service
- No need to worry about being rained out

WEAKNESSES

- Sometimes you just want some normality and a little less neon
- The need to take a taxi almost everywhere
- The heat makes staying in an air-conditioned casino such an attractive idea
- There's nothing to make you feel you should be having anything but fun...

GOLD STAR

There's only one reason for Vegas being here – it's the undisputed gambling capital of the world, with more choice and more casinos than anywhere else on earth.

STARRING ROLE IN...

- *Viva Las Vegas* (1964)
- *Rain Man* (1988)
- *Leaving Las Vegas* (1995)
- *Casino* (1995)
- *Oceans Eleven* (1960 and 2001)
- *The Hangover* (2009)

See the incredible dancing fountains outside the Bellagio Hotel.

Eat in vast hotel buffets – the only way Vegas can realistically feed its teeming thousands of hungry gamblers.

Drink for free as you play – just grab a cocktail waitress and don't forget to tip.

Do get married to someone you barely know at short notice in one of the hilarious chapels on the strip.

Watch the neon-clad city from the sky by ascending the Stratosphere at night.

Buy more chips, regularly...and remember, the house always wins.

After dark bring your sunglasses out with you to deal with all the neon.

Lhasa

NICKNAME HOLY CITY; SUNLIGHT CITY **DATE OF BIRTH** 7TH CENTURY;
WHEN LOCAL RULER SONGTSEN GAMPO MADE LHASA HIS CAPITAL
ADDRESS TIBET (MAP 9, D4) **HEIGHT** 3595M **SIZE** 30,000 SQ KM
POPULATION 373,000 **LONELY PLANET RANKING** 089

The resilient heart of a nation and a city of unique heritage, this city on the top of the world is seen by many as the homeland and jewel in the crown of Buddhism.

ANATOMY

The city divides clearly into a western (Chinese) section and an eastern (Tibetan) section. The Chinese side holds most of Lhasa's upmarket accommodation options, along with Chinese restaurants, bars and the Nepali consulate. The Tibetan eastern end of town is more colourful and has all the budget and midrange accommodation popular with independent travellers. The main drag is the east–west Dekyi Nub Lam, which then becomes Dekyi Shar Lam in the east of town (in Tibetan, *nub* means west and *shar* means east). Jokhang Temple and Barkhor Sq are in between Dekyi Shar Lam and Chingdröl Shar Lam (Jiangsu Lu) and are connected to these two main roads by the Tibetan quarter – a web of winding alleyways lined with the whitewashed façades of traditional Tibetan homes. Bicycle is without a doubt the best way to get around (once you have acclimatised to the altitude). Otherwise, you'll find privately run minibuses are frequent on Dekyi Shar Lam and taxis are plentiful.

PEOPLE

The official figures for Lhasa's population are 80% Tibetan and just under 17% Han Chinese, though these are generally discounted by all except the Chinese government, which released them. More realistic estimates put the percentage closer to 50/50. The population of the city before the Chinese takeover was less than 30,000 and the recent influx of Han Chinese has been nicknamed 'China's second invasion'.

TYPICAL LHASAN

Understanding the basics of Buddhism is essential in understanding any Tibetan and the citizens of Lhasa even more so. They are gentle in spirit, deeply religious and quietly unshakable in their resolve. Though they have lost so much to outside influence, they remain remarkably open and generous.

CHRISTOPHER PILLITZ / GETTY IMAGES

MONKS CHANTING AT SERA MONASTERY.

DEFINING EXPERIENCE

Following the flow of pilgrims around the Barkhor circuit with sustenance stops at nearby restaurants for *momos* (Tibetan dumplings) washed down with steaming yak-butter tea.

STRENGTHS

- ◢ Potala, the deserted citadel of the Dalai Lama
- ◢ Jokhang and its shrines
- ◢ Walking tours
- ◢ The nearby Drepung Monastery
- ◢ Buddhist history
- ◢ Tibet Museum
- ◢ Barkhor Sq
- ◢ A plethora of chapels
- ◢ The Norbulingka

WEAKNESSES

- ◢ Chinese cultural dominance
- ◢ Altitude sickness
- ◢ Modernisation
- ◢ Chinese propaganda
- ◢ Limited cuisine

GOLD STAR

To the Tibetans – for holding tight to what's left of Tibetan cultural and religious heritage after half a century of brutal and restrictive Chinese rule.

STARRING ROLE IN...

- ◢ *Windhorse* (1998)

See the Potala, the deserted citadel of the Dalai Lamas.

Eat local fare such as *momos*, *thugpa* (soup) and *shemdre* (potatoes and yak meat) at the Pentoc Tibetan Restaurant.

Drink *bö cha* (Tibetan yak-butter tea).

Do cycle to the Drepung Monastery for an afternoon of exploring what remains of its 6th-century history.

Watch traditional performances at the Tibetan Dance & Drama Theatre.

Buy a prayer wheel from one of the many stalls lining the Barkhor circuit.

After dark head to a Tibetan nangma dance hall, offering a mix of disco, Tibetan line dancing, beer and Chinese karaoke.

NOVICE MONKS AT DREPUNG MONASTERY CROWD IN FOR A GROUP SHOT.

PILGRIMS COMPLETE THEIR RITUAL CIRCUMAMBULATION OF JOKHANG MONASTERY.

A WOMAN SQUINTS AT A CELEBRATION OF LOSAR, THE TIBETAN NEW YEAR.

ONE OF LISBON'S TRADEMARK TRAMS PREPARES TO POUNCE FROM A NARROW STREET CORNER.

Lisbon

DATE OF BIRTH 1200 BC; WHEN THE PHOENICIANS FIRST SETTLED HERE **ADDRESS** PORTUGAL (MAP 5, B5) **HEIGHT** 77M
SIZE 87 SQ KM **POPULATION** 547,000 (CITY); 3 MILLION (METRO AREA)
LONELY PLANET RANKING 050

Lisbon is as romantic as Paris, as fun as Madrid, as laid-back as Rome, but small enough to fit into their handbags.

ANATOMY

Lisbon sits atop seven hills on the northern side of Portugal's finest natural harbour, the wide mouth of the Rio Tejo (Tagus River). On each hill is a castle, church or stunning *miradouro* (viewpoint). Many of the medieval buildings were destroyed in a huge earthquake in 1755 and the city was rebuilt in a baroque style along a formal grid. The ancient mazelike Alfama district, relatively unscathed, still exists near the narrow streets of the Bairro Alto's fin-de-siècle decadence with snaking cobbled streets. Trams, both very old and very new, and funiculars exist alongside an extensive metro system.

PEOPLE

Portugal's population breakdown has seen dramatic changes in the last few decades. The country's emigration rate has long been among Europe's highest, but its immigration rate shot up during the mid-1970s when around one million African *retornados* (refugees) immigrated from former Portuguese colonies. They have especially big communities in Lisbon. Another influx resulting from Portugal's empire building is of Brazilians. There's a small resident Roma (formerly known as Gypsies) population and there are also increasing numbers of immigrant workers from central and Eastern Europe.

TYPICAL LISBONITE

Lisbonites, like most Portuguese, return to home villages in August, drawn by family ties and a longing for home. They are known to suffer bouts of *saudade*, a particularly Portuguese melancholia, or longing, for something past. The city and its inhabitants have benefited greatly from EU membership, with floods of foreign investment and an overhaul of the city centre. Despite this, recent studies have declared the Portuguese the laziest people and heaviest drinkers in Europe. Lisbonites will have none of it.

THE ESTACAO DO ORIENTE BY ARCHITECT SANTIAGO CALATRAVA IS LISBON'S MAIN BUS AND TRAIN STATION.

DEFINING EXPERIENCE

Wandering Baixa (Lower Town), Lisbon's heartbeat, taking a tram to Belém for a custard tart, then spending the afternoon with art and antiquities at the Museu Calouste Gulbenkian before choosing from an eclectic range of restaurants in Bairro Alto (some as big as a dining room).

STRENGTHS

◢ The Lisbon metro – an art gallery in itself

◢ *Azulejos* – the decorative glazed tiles found everywhere
◢ Mosteiro dos Jerónimos
◢ Torre de Belém
◢ Royal Palaces
◢ Gare do Oriente
◢ 17km-long Ponte de Vasco da Gama
◢ African jazz scene
◢ Laid-back clubs
◢ Dining late
◢ Custard tarts
◢ Rickety trams
◢ Cobblestone streets

WEAKNESSES

◢ The rivalry between Cape Verdean and Angolan gangs
◢ *Bacalhau* (salt cod) – there is such a thing as too much
◢ Mateus Rosé

GOLD STAR

A city in thrall to its past, Lisbon has baroque cafés, 1960s diners, velvet-lined bars and Art Deco bakeries. This city has not been renovated into oblivion.

AN ELDERLY LISBONITE RESTS AT THE WINDOW OF HER HOUSE IN BAIRRO ALTO.

STARRING ROLE IN...

- ◢ *The Lisbon Story* (1994)
- ◢ *The Book of Disquiet* by Fernando Pessoa
- ◢ *The Last Kabbalist of Lisbon* (2000)
- ◢ *A Small Death in Lisbon* by Robert Wilson
- ◢ *Caitaes de Abril* (April Captains, 2000)
- ◢ *Requiem* by Antonio Tabucchi

See the central city from the low vantage point of 45m – the frilly, wrought-iron 19th-century oddity, the Elevador de Santa Justa.

Eat custard tarts from a secret recipe – they taste as though made by angels – at Casa Pasteis de Belém.

Drink *vinho verde* (green wine) – light, crisp dry wine (Portugal's signature wine).

Do take a stroll through Alfama, starting on tram 28 to Miradoura da Senhora do Monte to avoid the uphill slog.

Watch free Sunday-morning music and dance performances at Centro Cultural de Belém.

Buy *azulejos* and ceramics, sold all over, but check out styles first at the Museu Nacional do Azulejo.

After dark seek out the *fado* (Portuguese blues) experience in Bairro Alto or Alfama.

Livingstone

NICKNAME MARAMBA **DATE OF BIRTH** 1905; FOLLOWING THE
COMPLETION OF THE RAILWAY BRIDGE ACROSS THE ZAMBEZI RIVER
ADDRESS ZAMBIA (MAP 7, C6) **HEIGHT** 985M **POPULATION** 137,000
LONELY PLANET RANKING 161

Africa's adventure capital, the humble, dusty city of Livingstone is only a stone's throw from the magnificent Victoria Falls, where bungee-jumping, white-water rafting and abseiling end in sunset booze cruises on the mighty Zambezi.

ANATOMY

Livingstone lies only 11km north of one of the world's greatest natural wonders: the Victoria Falls. Mosi-oa-Tunya Rd is the city's tourist mecca, with shops, banks, *bureaux de change*, a post office, the Zamtel public-phone office and, most importantly, travel and tour agents. South of the town centre is Livingstone's main produce market (Maramba Township). Past the train station the town fizzles out but the trail of minibuses and taxis heading south lead to the Zambezi River, Victoria Falls and the Zambia–Zimbabwe border.

PEOPLE

More than half of Zambia's population lives in urban areas such as Livingstone, which lies on the border of the traditional territories of the Lozi, Tonga and Leya peoples. Although the main language group and people are Lozi, English is the official language and widely spoken due to Livingstone having become a major hub for travellers in southern Africa. The dominant religion is Christianity, though the majority also adhere to the traditional Zambian beliefs.

TYPICAL LIVINGSTONIAN

If Zambians have a reputation for being laid-back, Livingstonians are decidedly tranquil. They are notoriously friendly and easy-going and live happily in the present. They are blasé and indifferent to the buzz and hype of the falls and more interested in what tourism has done for Livingstone than what Livingstone has done for the tourist. They party hard and won't begrudge you a space on the dance floor. They are both colonial and very African.

TAKE A TOUR OF THE ZAMBEZI ON AN ELEPHANT.

GRUBBY HANDS GET CLEANED UP BEFORE MEAL TIME.

A STATUE OF DR LIVINGSTONE (WE PRESUME), KEEPING WATCH OVER VICTORIA FALLS.

THE VICTORIA FALLS BRIDGE'S BUNGY-JUMP STATION.

DEFINING EXPERIENCE

Waking up in an oasis, having breakfast with strangers discussing spine-tingling adventures, then sharing a minibus to the adrenalin junkie's paradise, bungee-jumping into the Batoka Gorge, and white-water rafting through the seething turmoil that is the Zambezi.

STRENGTHS

- Victoria Falls
- Gateway to Zambia's wildlife parks
- Vast array of activities
- Laid-back atmosphere
- Tourist-friendly layout
- A raw-edged Africa
- Livingstone Museum
- Mukuni Village
- Great backpacker accommodation

WEAKNESSES

- Regular muggings between Livingstone and Victoria Falls
- Touts
- Rougher-than-usual wilderness
- It-can-wait attitude
- Losing capital-city status (to Lusaka)

GOLD STAR

Victoria Falls on the Zambezi River – the mesmerising waterfall spans nearly 2km, drops a dramatic 100m over a cliff and accommodates an amazing range of activities, from the tranquil to the terrifying.

STARRING ROLE IN...

◢ *Stanley and Livingstone* (1939)

See the natural wonders of the Victoria Falls section of Mosi-oa-Tunya National Park.

Eat African-international cuisine at the open-air Cafe Zambezi.

Drink as much as you can handle on a sunset booze cruise on the Zambezi.

Do a heart-stopping gorge swing over Batoka Gorge.

Watch traditional dance performances from Zambia and neighbouring countries at Falls Craft Village.

Buy wood carved by the Leya people at Mukuni Village craft market.

After dark rock to the roof with Western hits and Zambian live music at the latest club.

UNION OLIMPIJA BASKETBALL FANS AT HALA TIVOLI, LJUBLJANA, SLOVENIA.

Ljubljana

NICKNAME WHITE LJUBLJANA, AFTER THE NUMBER OF PALE-COLOURED CHURCHES AND MANSIONS BUILT BY THE HABSBURGS
DATE OF BIRTH 1144; THE CITY WAS FIRST DOCUMENTED THEN BUT THE AREA HAD BEEN INHABITED FOR AT LEAST THREE MILLENNIA
ADDRESS SLOVENIA (MAP 5, N3) **HEIGHT** 298M **POPULATION** 280,000
LONELY PLANET RANKING 084

Pocket-sized, picture-perfect Ljubljana punches above its weight with a thriving cultural scene, riverside bars and cafés and a photogenic Old Town – you just want to put it in your pocket and take it home with you.

ANATOMY

Ljubljana lies within the Ljubljana Basin, which comprises the Ljubljana Marsh and the Ljubljana Plain. It is positioned between the Polhov Gradec hills to the west and Golovec Hills (including Castle Hill) to the east and southeast. The combination of hills and marsh creates an early-morning fog in autumn and winter. The Ljubljanica River flows under several bridges, including Cobbler Bridge (Čevljarski Most), Triple Bridge (Tromostovje) and Dragon Bridge (Zmajski Most). On the western side of the river is Center, the commercial area, while the Old Town is on the eastern side. You can catch public buses around town.

PEOPLE

A typical native is likely to speak not only Slovenian but also English, German and Italian. Over 80% of the population is Slovene but increasing numbers of Croatians are popping over the border in search of work. Almost 60% of the population is Catholic but as many as 33% are without specified religious beliefs.

TYPICAL LJUBLJANA CITIZEN

Despite the patina of imperial Austria, contemporary Ljubljana has a lively Slavic feel all its own, thanks to the temperament of its residents, which is influenced by central Europe's penchant for orderliness and the Mediterranean's zest for life. Its inhabitants have always taken an active interest in the preservation of their city's character and rich cultural life. They are enthusiastic about the performing arts and are especially proud of their philharmonic academy, one of the oldest in Europe. Outdoor pursuits are also popular, who parade their pets in Tivoli Park and swim at Ilirija pool when not basking in the sauna at Zlati Klub. Over 27,000 students attend Ljubljana's university, which has three art academies.

DEFINING EXPERIENCE

Buying an ice cream in Prešernov trg, licking it across the Triple Bridge and pottering around the Old Town between *burek* (small stuffed pastry) stands and shaded outdoor cafes before heading up to Ljubljana Castle for a spot of lunch outside Bar Ljubljanski Grad and looking at the view.

STRENGTHS

- Proximity to the rest of Slovenia
- Riverside cafes
- Skiing in Krvavec
- Swimming in the Adriatic
- Rafting on the Sava, kayaking on the Ljubljanica
- Union beer
- Very pretty Old Town
- National Gallery
- Slovenian National Opera and Ballet Companies
- Bird-watching
- Slovenian bread *(kruh)*
- Mushroom picking

WEAKNESSES

- Increasing prices
- Confusing queuing system outside restaurants
- Illegal waste dumping

GOLD STAR

Compact charm – simply wandering around the streets seems to be one of the local inhabitants' favourite pastimes, probably because the city still retains its human scale.

STARRING ROLE IN...

- *Sign of the Cross: Travels in Catholic Europe* by Colm Tóibín

See Ljubljana Castle, and peer over the Old Town from the ramparts.

Eat local cuisine at Pri Škofju, a delightful Krakovo restaurant.

Drink award-winning Slovenian wines at the Movia Vinoteka wine bar.

Do go rafting on the Sava and experience the great Slovenian outdoors.

Watch open-air theatre at the Ljubljana Summer Festival.

Buy antiques and trinkets at the tempting Sunday-morning antiques flea market on Cankarjevo nabrežje.

After dark shake your funky stuff at the Top Six Club on the 6th floor of Nama department store.

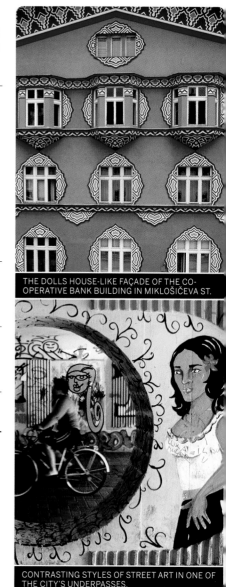

THE DOLLS HOUSE-LIKE FAÇADE OF THE CO-OPERATIVE BANK BUILDING IN MIKLOŠIČEVA ST.

CONTRASTING STYLES OF STREET ART IN ONE OF THE CITY'S UNDERPASSES.

COSMOPOLITAN CAFÉ CULTURE ON THE TRENDY RIVERSIDE STRIP.

London

NICKNAME THE BIG SMOKE **DATE OF BIRTH** AD 43; EMPEROR
CLAUDIUS LED AN ARMY TO ESTABLISH A PORT CALLED LONDINIUM
ADDRESS ENGLAND (MAP 4, F8) **HEIGHT** 5M **SIZE** 1572 SQ KM
POPULATION 8 MILLION (CITY); 13.7 MILLION (METRO AREA)
LONELY PLANET RANKING 005

Britain's economic motor, London is one of the most vibrant, multiculturally diverse spots on earth, where you can listen to any style of music, view any kind of art and sample world cuisines.

ANATOMY

Above ground the River Thames meanders through the capital, while underground is a warren of tube lines. Within the yellow one (Circle Line) you'll find the main tourist sights, nightlife and shops except a few that dot the regenerated South Bank. A third of the city is parkland, making it the greenest city of its size in the world. The skyline is punctured by a few skyscrapers, most notably the Shard (one of Europe's tallest buildings) on the South Bank, and Canary Wharf's flashing pyramid roof.

PEOPLE

London's nonwhite population is the largest of any European city. With an estimated 33 ethnic communities and 300 languages spoken, it's no empty boast when it is referred to as 'a world in one city'.

TYPICAL LONDONER

Londoners work the longest hours in the EU and live in its most expensive city. They are polite (yes, they queue), tolerant and unfazed by outrageous dress or behaviour. They are always in a rush but won't refuse a request for help. They go to the pub after work and will coolly ignore any famous faces. They frequently take weekend breaks in Europe courtesy of discount airlines. They complain about London a lot but wouldn't live anywhere else.

DEFINING EXPERIENCE

Sunbathing in Hyde Park with champagne and strawberries, Coldplay on the iPod, then walking into Notting Hill for a pint outside the Cow to dissect last night's missed penalty before catching an art-house film at the Electric.

THE GOTHIC MASTERPIECE OF THE HOUSES OF PARLIAMENT WITH THE CLOCK OF BIG BEN.

STRENGTHS

- History around every corner
- The Royal Parks
- Pubs and pints
- Cheap flights to Europe
- The congestion charge
- Free museums and galleries
- Notting Hill Carnival (second largest in the world after Rio de Janeiro)
- Ethnic and designer cuisine
- The Tate Modern
- Tower Bridge
- Royal Palaces eg Buckingham Palace, Kensington Palace

WEAKNESSES

- Vertiginous house prices and the high cost of living
- Armpit ambience on crowded rush-hour tubes
- 11pm pub closing time
- Litter
- Friday night traffic leaving London
- 1950s to 1970s architecture
- Its size

GOLD STAR

Theatre – London is still the world leader, with Hollywood stars seeking credibility treading West End boards.

STARRING ROLE IN...

- *Harry Potter and the Half-Blood Prince* (2005)
- *The King's Speech* (2010)
- *Closer* (2004)
- *Bridget Jones's Diary* (2001)
- *28 Days Later* (2002)
- *Lock, Stock and Two Smoking Barrels* (1998)

See the 40km view from the London Eye.

Eat Michelin-star Chinese food in sophisticated Hakkasan.

Drink organic bitter at the 18th-century Jerusalem Tavern.

Do a London walk and discover the haunted corners of the city of London.

Watch Shakespeare performed as it was meant to be at the Globe Theatre.

Buy cutting-edge fashion at Spitalfields Market.

After dark check out the dance floor and amazing DJ line-ups at Fabric.

THE SWISS RE TOWER, BETTER KNOWN AS THE GHERKIN.

ESSENTIAL ACCESSORIES ON OFFER AT THE PORTOBELLO RD MARKET.

A DECKCHAIR DEVOTEE CATCHES UP ON RAYS AND READING IN HYDE PARK.

NOCTURNAL ANTICS ON THE ROOF OF THE STANDARD HOTEL.

Los Angeles

NICKNAME LA; CITY OF ANGELS **DATE OF BIRTH** 1781; SPANISH
MISSIONARIES FOUNDED THE SETTLEMENT **ADDRESS** USA (MAP 1, E7)
HEIGHT 95M **SIZE** 1215 SQ KM **POPULATION** 12.8 MILLION
LONELY PLANET RANKING 049

Los Angeles may be the world capital of myth-making but it thrives beyond its own highly constructed clichés with a mosaic of cultures and a beautiful setting between desert and sea.

ANATOMY

Los Angeles, in fact an enormous concatenation of independent cities, stretches down the Pacific coast, and is sandwiched inland by the Santa Monica and San Gabriel Mountains. Inland, the skyscrapers of Downtown are the only recognisable centre. East LA, a Latino-dominated area, edges against Downtown, as do the historically African-American neighbourhoods of South Central and Compton. Westward are iconic Hollywood, West Hollywood, Bel Air and Beverly Hills. The car is king, but there is a large bus and limited light-rail network.

PEOPLE

Angelinos are a diverse lot. Almost half the population are Hispanic by birth or heritage, and Spanish is spoken almost as widely as English. There is a fast-growing Asian and Pacific Islander population, who join significant African-American and Native American communities.

TYPICAL ANGELINO

Angelinos don't care what the world thinks of them (narcissistic, vapid, flaky and superficial), or their city (dystopian, ugly, soulless) because they are too busy keeping fit, self-actualising, working the room, or just out there enjoying the place. They will admit to their notoriety for aggression behind the wheel, and are all too aware of the appalling economic disparities on display (and the simmering tensions it can generate), but that's because they are generally a tolerant, open-minded and cosmopolitan lot.

DEFINING EXPERIENCE

Running along the beach, then off to morning service at a happening little nondenominational (spirituality is on the list of things to improve this year), grabbing some cheddar enchiladas at La Cabana before going to a Lucha

471

SURFER DUDES CARVE UP THE WEEKEND WAVES WITH PANACHE.

Libre match (those wrestler's masks are *so* hot...), stopping by WordTheatre's reading to check out your actor friend doing Raymond Carver, and then heading home to blog all the latest gossip.

STRENGTHS

◢ 300-plus days of sunshine per year
◢ Excellent contemporary-art museums and galleries
◢ Nuevo-Latino cuisine
◢ Downtown renewal
◢ Walt Disney Concert Hall
◢ LA Metro
◢ Getting into trouble at the Marmont
◢ Hollywood Forever Cemetery
◢ Griffith Park
◢ David Lynch's online weather report
◢ Farmers Market
◢ Midcentury modern furniture
◢ Las Posadas and other Mexican festivals
◢ Thriving alternative art scene
◢ Jacarandas in bloom
◢ Kilometres of beaches
◢ Kelly Wearstler's OTT interiors
◢ Vibrant Latino culture

WEAKNESSES

◢ June gloom
◢ Sprawl
◢ Cooler-than-thou bouncers and shop assistants
◢ Stop-and-go freeways
◢ Persisting racial inequality
◢ Bad pizza
◢ Aggressive surfers
◢ Gang violence
◢ New York 'transplants' who do nothing but criticise
◢ San Andreas fault line

THE SURF-INSPIRED ARCHITECTURE OF THE GETTY CENTER.

GOLD STAR

Built environment – for fans of modernist architecture, LA is the most innovative and diverse city in the USA.

STARRING ROLE IN...

- *Double Indemnity* (1944)
- *The Big Sleep* (1946)
- *Sunset Boulevard* (1950)
- *Rebel without a Cause* (1955)
- *Touch of Evil* (1958)
- *Chinatown* (1974)
- *Boyz n the Hood* (1991)
- *The Player* (1992)
- *Short Cuts* (1993)
- *LA Story* (1991)
- *Pulp Fiction* (1994)
- *LA Confidential* (1997)
- *Mulholland Drive* (2001)
- *Crash* (2004)

See nature *and* culture: the mountain and sea views plus David Hockney's Californian scenes at Richard Meier's glorious Getty Center.

Eat meat and drink vodka, Atkins-style, in the rococo-camp surrounds at the old Santa Monica hangout the Galley.

Drink an apple martini holed up in a poolside pleasure pod on the rooftop at the Standard Downtown.

Do a Friday-night yoga session with live DJs, the ultimate in LA chill.

Watch a Hollywood blockbuster in Hollywood, at the hipster-favoured ArcLight on Sunset Boulevard.

Buy preloved rock-and-roll clothing, perhaps an ultra-rare Ziggy Stardust T-shirt from Kelly Cole Extraordinarium.

After dark be entertained by Marty and Elayne at the Dresden Room.

Luang Prabang

DATE OF BIRTH 1512: WHEN THE CITY-STATE OF MUANG XIENG THONG (CITY OF GOLD) BECAME KNOWN AS LUANG (GREAT OR ROYAL) PHABANG (PRABANG) **ADDRESS** LAOS (MAP 9, E6) **HEIGHT** 287M **POPULATION** 50,000 **LONELY PLANET RANKING** 054

Encircled by mountains and situated at the confluence of the Khan and Mekong Rivers, the city's stunning mix of gleaming temple roofs, crumbling French provincial architecture and multiethnic inhabitants is enthralling.

ANATOMY

Luang Prabang is dominated by Phu Si, a large hill near the middle of the peninsula formed by the confluence of the two rivers. Most of the longer roadways through Luang Prabang parallel the river. Shorter roads – once mere footpaths – bisect the larger roads and lead to the riverbanks, serving as dividing lines between different villages. Most of the historic temples are located between Phu Si and the Mekong, while the trading district lies to the south of the hill. The airport, speedboat landing and northern bus terminal are all northeast of the city, while the southern bus terminal and Sainyabuli terminal are to the southwest. Most of the town is accessible on foot and you can catch *jumbos* (motorised three-wheeled taxis).

PEOPLE

Lao is the official language, but Lao dialects (closely related to Thai) are also spoken, as are French and English. Sixty percent of the population is Buddhist, with 40% made up of animist and spirit cults.

TYPICAL LUANG PRABANG CITIZEN

Laid-back, relaxed, cruisey, slow paced, serene, unfussed and easy-going, the locals commonly express the notion that 'too much work is bad for your brain' and often say they feel sorry for people who 'think too much'. They avoid any undue psychological stress, choosing not to participate in any activity, whether work or play, unless it contains an element of *múan* (fun).

DEFINING EXPERIENCE

A morning spent playing *kátâw* (a game with a cane ball) with the locals, cruising through scenic villages on a motorcycle to the stunning Tat Kuang

MONKS ON *TAK BAAT*, OR ALMS ROUND, COLLECTING FOOD IN THE MORNING.

ENTHUSIASTS WATCH A NIGHT MATCH OF PALENQUE, A POPULAR BOWLING GAME SIMILAR TO BOULES.

Si waterfalls and indulging in a soothing massage at the Lao Red Cross, before enjoying the tasteful chinoiserie décor and a sumptuous dinner of Lao, Thai and Pacific Rim cuisine at one of Luang Prabang's best restaurants, the Apsara.

STRENGTHS

◢ Gilded temple roofs
◢ Multiethnic marketplaces
◢ The ubiquitous Beer Lao
◢ Charming French colonial architecture

◢ The famous Pak Ou caves, crammed with images of the Buddha in all styles and sizes
◢ The wide, many-tiered waterfall of Tat Kuang Si, tumbling over limestone formations into a series of cool, turquoise pools
◢ Peaceful Buddhist traditions
◢ Lao women's more-or-less equal status in the workforce, inheritance, land ownership and so on
◢ Low cost of living/lazing
◢ Picturesque riverside setting
◢ The quaint Royal Palace Museum
◢ Trekking, rafting and cycling

WEAKNESSES

◢ Smoke from slash-and-burn agriculture in the surrounding mountains, causing red, watery eyes and breathing difficulties
◢ Crack-of-dawn roosters
◢ The high number of serious speedboat accidents, including fatalities, on the rivers

GOLD STAR

The traditional herbal sauna and/or hour-long Swedish-Lao massage at the Lao Red Cross.

GOTCHA! A CHEEKY CHILD PICKS A WATER FIGHT DURING CELEBRATIONS FOR THE LAO NEW YEAR.

STARRING ROLE IN...

- ◢ Short story 'The Boatman's Gift' by Pamela Michael
- ◢ *Het Bun Dai Bun: Laos Sacred Rituals of Luang Prabang* by Hans Georg Berger

---

See Wat Xieng Thong, Luang Prabang's most magnificent temple.

Eat *phák nâm* (a delicious watercress that's unique to Luang Prabang) and *khào nĭaw* (the ubiquitous sticky rice).

Drink *khào kam* – a local red, sweet, slightly fizzy wine made from sticky rice.

Do a walking tour around Luang Prabang's northeastern quarter to take in most of the historic attractions and sightseeing spots.

Watch the boat races during Bun Awk Phansa (the End of the Rains Retreat) in October.

Watch local performers put on a show that includes a *bạasĭi* (spirit-blessing) ceremony, traditional dance and folk music at the Royal Theatre.

Buy beautiful handmade *sĭa* (mulberry bark) paper, naturally dyed house-woven Lao silk and cotton, handcrafted silverware, silk-lined cushions and embroidered rice mats.

After dark join a young Lao crowd dancing to bands playing Lao and Thai pop or DJs spinning rap and hip-hop in the cavernous club of Dao Fah.

LIFE'S A BEACH IN LÜBECK.

Lübeck

DATE OF BIRTH AD 1000; WHEN THE WENDS ESTABLISHED A ROYAL
SEAT CALLED LIUBICE **ADDRESS** GERMANY (MAP 4, L8) **HEIGHT** 17M
POPULATION 210,000 **LONELY PLANET RANKING** 131

Lübeck's medieval architecture is as mouth-watering as its marzipan, and for a relatively small city it packs a powerful punch – it's a Unesco World Heritage site and in days gone by its famous Holstentor (gate) used to grace the DM50 note.

ANATOMY

The twin, pointy-roofed circular towers of the Holstentor form the main entry to Lübeck's *Altstadt* (old town) on the western side. The northern and eastern parts of the *Altstadt* belonged to craftspeople in the Middle Ages. Now this area is characterised by small low-rise homes in *Höfe* (courtyards) that are accessed by little *Gänge* (walkways) from the street. Not far from the Holstentor is the *Markt* (marketplace), where you'll find the *Rathaus* (town hall) and the Marienkirche, Germany's third-largest church. The pedestrianised shopping area leads off from here. The whole of the *Altstadt* is surrounded by the Trave River and its canals. Travemunde ferry port is 16km from the *Altstadt*. Buses and trains service the city.

PEOPLE

Lübeck still calls itself a Hanseatic city, referring to the commanding medieval Hanseatic League that united more than 150 merchant cities in an 'association'. It may now be a provincial city, but the people of Lübeck have powerful roots.

TYPICAL LÜBECK CITIZEN

Lübeck is the main attraction for visitors to Schleswig-Holstein, Germany's answer to the Côte d'Azur (weather aside), and inhabitants of Lübeck escape the crowds by sailing to islands offshore and relaxing on the attractive beaches along the coast. The city may be old and picturesque, but it also hums with life, particularly in the warm and inviting bars that are popular with the locals. The people also enjoy culture and the city has connections to two Nobel prize-winning authors – Thomas Mann, who was born in Lübeck in 1875, and Günter Grass, who is a current resident.

A DARK FIGURE CONTEMPLATES THE LIGHT SIDE AS SUN SETS ON HEILIGEN-GEIST-HOSPITAL.

Lübeck

DEFINING EXPERIENCE

Musing on creative genius in the Günter Grass-Haus, then seeking inspiration for your novel among the fairy-tale architecture of the *Altstadt*, before taking the kids to the *Marionettentheater* (puppet theatre).

STRENGTHS

- Holstentor
- Medieval merchant's homes
- 1000 historical buildings
- Hanseatic League
- Marienkirche and its shattered church bells, now a peace memorial
- *Rathaus*
- Literary tradition
- Café Niederegger
- Füchtingshof and Glandorps Gang
- Nearby beaches
- Boat trips through the canals
- Gothmund, a charming fishers' village

WEAKNESSES

- Lots of temptation for those on a diet
- Cold winds and dark clouds (even in summer)

GOLD STAR

Don't you just love those chocolate-covered marzipan delights...

STARRING ROLE IN...

- *The Buddenbrooks* by Thomas Mann
- *Holstentor* by Andy Warhol

See the magical city gate, Holstentor, and imagine letting down your Rapunzel hair from the circular towers.

Eat modern German cuisine in Markgraf, an elegant historic restaurant.

Drink home-brewed beer in Brauberger, which has made its own since 1225.

Do a boat tour of the canals that surround the Altstadt – well, with all that water you have to really, don't you?

Watch a spellbinding organ concert in the Marienkirche, home to the world's largest mechanical organ.

Buy some of that lovely sweet stuff at Café Niederegger – and, yes, we're talking about marzipan.

After dark watch a play in the Art Nouveau Theater Lübeck.

Luxembourg City

DATE OF BIRTH AD 963; WHEN COUNT SIGEFROID OF ARDENNES ERECTED A CASTLE HERE **ADDRESS** LUXEMBOURG (MAP 4, J10) **HEIGHT** 330M **POPULATION** 100,000 **LONELY PLANET RANKING** 179

The entire ancient core of this 1000-year-old city has been preserved and provides spectacular vistas over lush parklands and atmospheric old quarters, spanned by a series of imposing bridges.

ANATOMY

The Alzette River passes through Luxembourg City and gives the capital its geographic charm. A medieval street plan mixes with 18th- and 19th-century buildings in the Old Town. The city's central area is divided by gorges; the lower town is at the base of the Old Town's Bock fortifications. Walking is the best way to get around.

PEOPLE

Lëtzebuergesch, closely related to German, was proclaimed the national language in 1984. French and German are also official languages. Almost the entire population is Roman Catholic. The population is about one-third foreigners, predominantly Italian, French and Portuguese, the highest ratio of any EU country.

TYPICAL LUXEMBOURGER

Luxembourgers are wealthy; the country's per-capita GDP is one of the word's highest and the standard of living consistently rates among the best. Luxembourgers are likely to work in the new service-based economy, as the country has morphed from an industrial producer by wooing big spenders from abroad with favourable banking and taxation laws. Luxembourgers are a confident lot. Their motto? *'Mir wëlle bleiwe wat mir sin'* (We want to remain what we are.)

DEFINING EXPERIENCE

Wandering the pedestrianised heart of the Old Town, investigating history and art in the new Musée National d'Histoire et d'Art, delving into the dark Bock Casemates and taking the lift (elevator) carved into the rock at Plateau du St Esprit to Grund for an apéritif before returning to the Chemin de la Corniche and dining outside for a fabulous view.

JOHN B MUELLER PHOTOGRAPHY / GETTY IMAGES

LUXEMBOURG'S ADOLPHE BRIDGE WAS BUILT BETWEEN 1900 AND 1903.

WAVING THE FLAG IN THE PLACE D'ARMES.

STRENGTHS

◢ Place d'Armes
◢ Musée National d'Histoire et d'Art
◢ Chemin de la Corniche
◢ Breedewee
◢ The equality of three official languages: French, German and Lëtzebuergesch

WEAKNESSES

◢ Conservative attitudes
◢ Very Eurocentric
◢ Eurocratic

GOLD STAR

With its impressive state-of-the-art museums, its Moorish Palais Grand-Ducal, its cathedral and free lift dug into the rock, the pedestrianised centre is a pleasant way to while away the time. Unesco obviously thought so when it added the fortifications and older quarters of the city to its list of World Heritage Sites.

STARRING ROLE IN...

◢ *The Moon of the Big Winds* by Claudine Muno
◢ *Aleng* by Cathy Clement

See the startling white building of the Musée National d'Histoire et d'Art, with collections of prehistoric relics and contemporary local and international artists.

Eat the national dish, *judd mat gaardebounen* (slabs of smoked pork served in a thick, cream-based sauce with broad beans and huge chunks of potato).

Drink local brews Gamorinus, a blond beer, and Diekirche's Grand Cru.

Do promenade on the Chemin de la Corniche and the pedestrianised heart of the Old Town.

Watch history come to life at Luxembourg's fascinating Musée d'Histoire de la Ville de Luxembourg.

Buy porcelain from the House of Villeroy & Boch, the world-famous manufacturer of china and crystal.

After dark try out the techno and house at one of the local clubs.

TRADITONAL TILED ROOFS STAND OUT IN THE SUN.

Lyon

DATE OF BIRTH AD 43; WITH ROMAN LUGDUNUM **ADDRESS** FRANCE (MAP 5, J3) **HEIGHT** 170M **POPULATION** 488,000 **LONELY PLANET RANKING** 053

This unexpectedly sophisticated city near the Alps never fails to surprise – or seduce. So opulent are its fountain-laced squares and 19th-century mansions, so intriguing are its medieval alleys and Roman ruins, so iconic is its outlandishly piggish cuisine that a trip to Lyon only translates one way: as the start of a beautiful love affair.

ANATOMY

With the north–south A6 slicing through the city, France's third-largest metropolis is a place most French only know in a traffic jam. The Seine and Rhône rivers cut its nine arrondissements (districts) into three. The city centre squats the river-framed peninsula (Presqu'île), lorded over by two mythical hills: west, the 'Hill of Prayer' (Fourvière) above the Unesco-protected old town (Vieux Lyon); and east, the 'Hill of Work' (Croix-Rousse) where craftsmen wove some of Europe's finest silk in the 18th century and where Lyon's bohemian cafe culture and nightlife lets rip today.

PEOPLE

Increasingly multicultural, Lyon is home to 70-odd different nationalities, around one-tenth of the population.

TYPICAL LYONNAIS

Lyonnais possess almost as much Gallic snootiness and pride as Parisians, hence the rivalry between the two. Accustomed to world-class opera and theatre on their doorstep, Lyon urbanites are culture-savvy and love going out – and that includes dining well, very well, on meaty dishes typically built from pig, tripe or blood in *bouchons* (traditional bistros). Feasting with fierce passion, friends or family, and much wine is their holy trinity

DEFINING EXPERIENCE

Getting lost in Vieux Lyon, riding the funicular up to the Basilique de Fourvière, drinking in the panorama from its roof, lunching at La Mère Brazier (1921), indulging in a hot chocolate between Presqu'île shops at Grand Café des Négociants (1864), dining after dark in Croix-Rousse.

STRENGTHS

- Unique cuisine
- *Bouchons* (Lyonnais bistros)
- Fine wines: Côtes du Rhone, Mâcon, Beaujolais
- Unesco-listed old town
- Roman amphitheatre used for summer performances
- Musée Lumière, cinema's birthplace
- Outstanding art museums
- Busy clubbing and bar scene
- Cafe culture
- The Alps next door

WEAKNESSES

- The best *bouchons* close at weekends
- Small metro system
- August – the city grinds to a halt as Lyonnais head south *en vacances*

GOLD STAR

Gastronomy – be it bistro, brasserie or Michelin-starred, French dining has never been so good.

STARRING ROLE IN...

- *Exit of the Lumières Factory* (1895)
- *The Clockmaker* (1973)
- *Hôtel Terminus: The Life and Times of Klaus Barbie* (1988)

See masterpieces by Rodin, Rembrandt and Monet at the Musée des Beaux-Arts on Place des Terreaux.

Eat *andouillette* at Café des Fédérations, a *bouchon* that has cooked up Lyon's signature pig-intestine sausage for decades.

Drink a blood-red *communard*, a blasphemous mix of red Beaujolais wine and *crème de cassis* (blackcurrant syrup).

Do the indoor market Les Halles de Lyon or hike uphill to Croix-Rousse's outdoor market – brunch on oysters and white wine on a pavement terrace.

Watch public squares blaze with colour during December's Fête des Lumières (Festival of Lights).

Buy silk and other crafts from galleries and workshops along Montée de la Grand Côte.

After dark hit the left-bank Rhône for drinking and dancing aboard the barge bars beside quai Victor Augagneur.

LIVE TO EAT – LYON IS FAMED FOR ITS CULINARY SCENE.

TRY ON SOME FRENCH FOOTWEAR AT LYON'S SHOE SHOPS.

LAIDBACK IN LYON – THE CITY HAS A SLOWER PACE OF LIFE THAN PARIS.

Macau

DATE OF BIRTH 1557; WHEN IT WAS OFFICIALLY FOUNDED AS
A COLONY OF PORTUGAL; IT WAS REBORN AS THE SPECIAL
ADMINISTRATIVE REGION OF MACAU IN 1999 **ADDRESS** CHINA
(MAP 9, G5) **HEIGHT** 59M **SIZE** 24 SQ KM **POPULATION** 568,000
LONELY PLANET RANKING 121

A rough diamond with a spit-and-polish, Macau fuses the Mediterranean and Asia with its Chinese temples and colonial villas.

ANATOMY

Most of Macau's attractions are clustered round the peninsula's centre – it's a hilly but rewarding walk from church to fort and back again. Taipa Island is linked to the peninsula by two bridges, and a causeway links Taipa with Coloane. Aside from walking, the best way to get around is by air-conditioned bus or minibus.

PEOPLE

The population is about 95% Chinese. Fewer than 2% of Macau residents are Portuguese and the rest are Macanese, with mixed ancestry. Portuguese and Chinese (particularly Cantonese) are the official languages of Macau. Taoism and Buddhism are the dominant religions, followed by Catholicism.

TYPICAL MACAU CITIZEN

Fond of a good meal and a punt, Macau citizens have a hearty, easy-going nature. Residents enjoy relaxed, laid-back pleasures, such as smoking a pipe or having their palm read in Mediterranean-style cafés.

DEFINING EXPERIENCE

Escalating to the Monte Fort at the Macau Museum, followed by a leisurely stroll along Praia Grande before braving a game of baccarat at one of Macau's flashy new casinos (dress classy).

STRENGTHS

⊿ Unique Latin-Sino culture
⊿ Cheap dim sum
⊿ Fascinating cemeteries

YAMEME PHOTOGRAPHY / GETTY IMAGES

WHEN COMPLETE, THIS BUILDING PROJECT WILL CONNECT MACAU, HONG KONG AND ZHUHAI.

TRIPPING THE LIGHT FANTASTIC – LANTERNS DURING CHINESE NEW YEAR CELEBRATIONS IN SENADO SQ.

THE SCENT OF RELIGION KEEPS THE JOSS STICK INDUSTRY IN BUSINESS.

STEAMING DUMPLINGS IN MACAU.

- ◢ Guia Fort
- ◢ High-speed ferries to Hong Kong
- ◢ Kun Iam Temple
- ◢ Ruins of the Church of St Paul
- ◢ Leal Senado
- ◢ Monte Fort

WEAKNESSES

- ◢ Rampant gambling culture – the casino reigns supreme
- ◢ Progress, progress, progress
- ◢ Early dinners (many restaurants are empty by 9pm)

GOLD STAR

Extreme makeover – after years of Macau playing the dowdy Jan Brady to sassy big sister Marcia (Hong Kong), Macau's citizens have dolled her up in a pastel palette, wooing commerce and tourism like never before.

STARRING ROLE IN...

- ◢ *Isabella* (2006)
- ◢ *Fist of Fury* (1972)
- ◢ *Indiana Jones and the Temple of Doom* (1984)

See into your future with one of the many fortune-tellers that throng the incense-infused Kun Lam Temple.

Eat Macanese cuisine (African chicken and Macau sole) at the three-decade old Henri's Galley by Sai Van Lake.

Drink whiskies from around the world in the oak-panelled Macallan Whisky Bar & Lounge.

Do trek to the top of Guia Fort, as there are few better places in Macau to get your bearings (alternatively, ride the teeny cable car).

Watch some soulful blues musicians perform in the basement of Macau Soul.

Buy wonderful Macanese postage stamps, depicting everything from key colonial landmarks to roulette tables.

After dark hit the *Pai kao* (Chinese dominoes) tables at a casino.

Madang

DATE OF BIRTH 1884; WHEN THE GERMAN NEW GUINEA COMPANY BRIEFLY ESTABLISHED A BASE HERE BEFORE MALARIA DROVE THEM OUT **ADDRESS** PAPUA NEW GUINEA (MAP 10, H1) **HEIGHT** 4M **POPULATION** 30,000 **LONELY PLANET RANKING** 199

Often dubbed the 'Prettiest town in the Pacific', Madang has a mega-chilled resort-style feel coupled with excellent facilities, and provides easy access to nearby volcanoes, islands and legendary dive sites.

ANATOMY

This small town of parks and ponds nestles snugly on a lush peninsula surrounded by harbours, bays and nearby islands. Luxuriant vegetation and lily-capped waterways flourish alongside the main thoroughfares. The aquatically inclined will find spectacular scenery beneath the surrounding coastal waters – the perfect accompaniment to this surreally beautiful township. Buses gather around the market at 8am and the door guys yell out their destinations 'LaeLaeLaeLae' and 'HagenHagenHagen' with a great sense of theatre. Once full, they head off.

PEOPLE

As capital of Madang province, the city attracts coastal people, islanders, highlanders, and river-dwellers in search of prosperity. More recently, Europeans and Chinese settlers have entered the mix. There are 30 main tribal languages spoken in Madang, but the official languages are English, Tok Pisin (the Pidgin language) and Motu, with Tok Pisin being the most widely used.

TYPICAL MADANGESE

Each of Madang's 30-plus tribal groups has its own traditional ideas and practices, and belief in supernatural forces and ancestral spirits is strong despite two centuries of missionary activity in the region. In the main, locals are extremely friendly. Petty crime is not uncommon – there is no safety net for those drifting into Madang from nearby villages in search of work, and even unemployed graduates often fall into gangs of *raskols* just to survive.

TRADE ROUTE – PASSENGER BOATS ARE ALWAYS BUSY AS PEOPLE MAKE THEIR WAY TO AND FROM THE MARKETS.

DEFINING EXPERIENCE

Snorkelling in the warmest water ever off Lion's Reserve Beach, drip-drying as you follow the picturesque trail south of the Coastwatcher's memorial, before hitting a slow round of golf at sunset and being treated to one of nature's spectacles as swarms of giant bats take flight from their home among the towering casuarina trees.

STRENGTHS

- ◢ Luxuriant vegetation
- ◢ Jaw-dropping beauty
- ◢ Mabarosa Festival
- ◢ Giant butterflies and bats
- ◢ Volcanic activity
- ◢ Warm coastal waters
- ◢ Unique cultures

WEAKNESSES

- ◢ Malaria zone
- ◢ Spitting locals
- ◢ Volcanic activity
- ◢ Litter

GOLD STAR

Diving – excellent visibility, stunning tropical coral and fish life, plus countless WWII wrecks make the diving and snorkelling world-class.

STARRING ROLE IN...

- ◢ *Robinson Crusoe* (1996)
- ◢ *Bekim* by Rosalie Ann Christensen
- ◢ *The Cannibal Cookbook: Low Cal Meals to Die For* by Liva Kabok

See the truly amazing four-day Mabarosa Festival (held annually in August or September), which features *singsing* (performance/dance) groups from all over the country.

Eat fresh seafood daily at the water's edge at Madang Lodge.

Drink a cocktail as you stroll around the Orchid Gardens at the Madang Resort Hotel.

Do take a photograph of the horizon at sunset.

Watch the canoe race from Krangket Island to Madang during the Mabarosa Festival.

Buy curious artefacts from the carver's hut at the Madang Resort Hotel.

After dark head out to the reefs for an exhilarating night dive.

CROCODILES ARE HAZARD BUT THIS LITTLE FELLOW IS A MANAGEABLE SIZE, JUST.

NEWSPAPER IN HAND, A LOCAL MAN STROLLS PAST THE ELABORATE TILE WORK ON THE FAÇADE OF A CITY SHOP.

Madrid

DATE OF BIRTH AD 854; WHEN MOHAMMED I, EMIR OF CÓRDOBA, ESTABLISHED A FORTRESS HERE **ADDRESS** SPAIN (MAP 5, D5) **HEIGHT** 660M **SIZE:** 607 SQ KM **POPULATION** 3.2 MILLION (CITY); 6.5 MILLION (METRO AREA) **LONELY PLANET RANKING** 036

Madrid's city centre is the most vibrant, versatile and exciting in Europe – La Movida may technically be over, but you'll be hard-pressed to believe it on a weekend night at 4am.

ANATOMY

Madrid is one of Europe's highest capitals. Most major sights are within walking distance of a very short metro ride. The historic centre features a mix of old and new low-rise buildings and hundreds of plazas, with skyscrapers predominantly in the northern part of the city. Madrid's metro is the quickest and easiest way to get around the city, with *cercanías* (regional trains) and buses close runners-up.

PEOPLE

Many locals aren't from Madrid proper, and often come from all over Spain. Some 600,000 foreign migrants live in the Comunidad de Madrid (the region around Madrid) – more than two-thirds of them in the city. The biggest groups include Ecuadorians, Romanians, Colombians and Moroccans. In the working-class neighbourhoods of Lavapiés and around, you will encounter North Africans rubbing shoulders with Pakistanis, black Africans and Latin Americans.

TYPICAL MADRILEÑO

Doesn't seem to need any sleep! They might be *gatos* (born-and-bred locals, from the Spanish word for 'cat') or they might be from somewhere else in Spain or North Africa, but they'll work long hours, spend a fortune on keeping a roof over their heads and appreciate that none of it's worth it without regular tapas-fuelled catch-ups with friends and family.

DEFINING EXPERIENCE

Waking up late, having coffee and *churros* (doughnuts), then browsing for trash (maybe treasure) at El Rastro flea market before enjoying a long Sunday lunch in a restaurant, having a rest in El Retiro afterwards, and then waiting to hear if your plans for the evening come to fruition.

GIGGLING FOR FORGIVENESS – CHEEKY WOMEN PENITENTS AT THE EASTER HOLY WEEK PROCESSIONS.

ROW AWAY YOUR TROUBLES AT RETIRO PARK.

ONLY IN MADRID – THE MUSEUM OF HAM HOSTS MUSIC NIGHTS.

STRENGTHS

- Tolerance
- Chatty locals
- Efficient public transport
- Thousands of tapas bars
- Regional Spanish and ethnic cuisine
- Siesta
- Nightlife
- Major art museums
- Los Austrias, La Latina and Lavapiés barrios (neighbourhoods)
- Plazas brimming with friends and neighbours catching up
- Green parks in the early morning
- Real Madrid
- Acoustics at Teatro Real

WEAKNESSES

- Struggling economy and pervasive unemployment among the young
- Noise pollution including early-morning rubbish collection
- Dog poo on the streets
- Packed peak-hour metro trains in summer
- Freezing winters and hellish summers
- Drunken teens on the streets at weekends
- Trying to score Real Madrid tickets

GOLD STAR

Art – Madrid has three blockbuster museums in the Museo del Prado, the Museo Thyssen-Bornemisza and the Centro de Arte Reina Sofía.

STARRING ROLE IN...

- *Abre los Ojos* (Open Your Eyes, 1997)
- *Amantes* (The Lovers, 1991)
- *Live Flesh* (1997)
- *Bad Education* (2003)

See Picasso's *Guernica* and weep.

Eat tapas every chance you get.

Drink eye-crossingly potent cocktails in any of the party *barrios*.

Do as the locals do and take it easy for the siesta with a long lunch.

Watch a soul-stirring flamenco performance at a backstreet *tablao* (flamenco bar).

Buy a beautiful embroidered silk *mantón* (shawl) from El Corte Ingles.

After dark try staying awake for as long as Madrileños – say 6am.

501

Male'

DATE OF BIRTH 2000 BC; EVIDENCE OF THE EARLIEST SETTLEMENT ON MALE' **ADDRESS** THE MALDIVES (MAP 9, A8) **HEIGHT** 2.1M **SIZE** 2KM **POPULATION** 104,000 **LONELY PLANET RANKING** 147

The only city in this Indian Ocean archipelago nation, Male' is the transit point for divers and honeymooners: a laid-back stop atop a coral reef.

ANATOMY

Two kilometres long and only one wide, the island is flat but half of it has been reclaimed in the last century as the reef has been filled in with dredged coral to create more land. The atoll is now all filled in, packed to the edges with buildings, roads and a few well-used open spaces, and there's nowhere to go but up – high-rises are growing. Taxis are the way to get around, if not on foot. The increasing number of cars is causing the not unexpected but wholly unwelcome inconvenience of traffic jams.

PEOPLE

Male''s citizens are liberal Muslims. They start their families at a young age and population growth is quite high, compounded by urbanisation and by Maldivians flocking to the capital for education and work opportunities. A century ago only 5000 people lived on the much smaller land area of Male'.

TYPICAL MALE' CITIZEN

Maldivians make up at least 75% of the city's population. They are laid-back, friendly, sober and accustomed to living in fairly cramped quarters. Other ethnic groups include South Indians, Sinhalese and Arabs.

DEFINING EXPERIENCE

Strolling around the island on Boduthakurufaanu Magu, one of the loveliest street names, late in the afternoon, watching a game of football, basketball or maybe cricket, on the manmade sports grounds at the eastern end, then stopping for refreshments at a teahouse.

STRENGTHS

▲ The *dhoni* (a traditional all-purpose vessel now usually powered by a diesel engine) ride from the Male' airport island, Hulhule

SAVIS PAPADOPOULOS / GETTY IMAGES

TROPICAL METROPOLIS – MALE' FROM THE AIR.

- The gold-domed Grand Friday Miskiiy (mosque)
- The coral-stone-walled Hukuru Miskiiy, which dates from 1656
- Curious street names rather than numbers – watch for Crabtree, Sweet Rose, Sun Dance, the grand River Nile, the strange Ozone or even Aston Villa
- The Artificial Beach built on reclaimed land at the eastern end of the island

WEAKNESSES
- Traffic
- No alcohol

GOLD STAR
The Hukuru Miskiiy (Old Friday Mosque), which dates from 1656. Its walls, built with coral stones, are intricately carved with Arabic writings, ornamental patterns and expert lacquer works, especially in the domes.

STARRING ROLE IN...
- *The Strode Venturer* by Hammond Innes

See the rounded corners of walls and buildings so vehicles can negotiate tight corners more easily.

Eat *hedhikaa* (short eats) – a selection of sweet and savoury counter items including rice pudding, tiny bananas, curried fish cakes and frittered dough balls, which are usually fishy and mostly spicy.

Drink *raa*, the local brew, a sweet and delicious toddy tapped from the crown of the palm-tree trunk.

Do dive to the wreck of the *Maldive Victory,* with its wheelhouse underwater at around 15m and propeller at 35m.

Watch football or cricket at the National Stadium.

Buy fine-woven *kunaa* (mats) with elegant, abstract geometric patterns and subdued natural colouring.

After dark catch a movie or hang out in a teashop.

OVERCROWDED CITY LIVING CAN'T DAMPEN THE GENEROUS MALDIVIAN SPIRIT.

THE GOLD DOME OF THE GRAND FRIDAY MISKIIY RISES ABOVE THE BUILDINGS.

SHARK JAWS, GET YOUR SHARK JAWS HERE!

CANTONA, SCHOLES, GIGGS, KEANE, BEST – ALL HAVE PLAYED A PART IN THE THEATRE OF DREAMS.

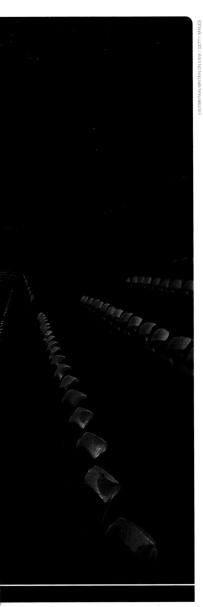

Manchester

DATE OF BIRTH AD 70; WHEN THE ROMANS ESTABLISHED A FORT
CALLED MAMUCIUM **ADDRESS** ENGLAND (MAP 4, F7) **HEIGHT** 73M
SIZE 1286 SQ KM **POPULATION** 500,000 (CITY); 2.7 MILLION (METRO
AREA) **LONELY PLANET RANKING** 126

Manchester's pioneering spirit started the Industrial Revolution and a musical revolution, and its resilience shook off an IRA bomb to rise triumphant, with excellent museums, fine dining and top shopping.

ANATOMY

The city centre is navigable on foot or using the efficient Metrolink. The latter's hub is in Piccadilly Gardens, east of the cathedral. North of here is the hip Northern Quarter. To the southeast you'll find Canal St and the Gay Village, with Chinatown next door. Nineteenth-century canalside industrial buildings have been developed at Castlefield and Deansgate Locks southwest of the centre. Further south are the Salford quays embellished by the fabulous Imperial War Museum North and the Lowry Centre. Old Trafford (the 'Theatre of Dreams') is nearby. If you're not pounding the pavements, catch one of the many buses or trams that weave across the city or one of the trains that skirt the inner city area.

PEOPLE

Manchester's population is predominantly of British heritage, although the number of Pakistani and Bangladeshi inhabitants is increasing.

TYPICAL MANCUNIAN

Mancunians are justifiably proud of their city, from its industrial history as 'Cottonopolis' through to the musical mayhem of 'Madchester'. They believe Manchester is the best city in England, and are friendly and welcoming to visitors. The city of Hacienda fame knows how to party, and people are fun-loving and stylish. Despite housing Manchester United, the hugely successful football club and global brand, most people support Manchester City, its far less successful neighbour. In addition to a general rivalry with London, Manchester and Leeds sit on opposite sides of the historic Lancashire-versus-Yorkshire clash, which is reinterpreted every year with the Roses cricket match. The city bounced back after the 1996 IRA bomb and many now say the city looks much better for it.

507

DEFINING EXPERIENCE

Breathing in the view of the city from Godlee Observatory before heading down for some shopping heaven in the Northern Quarter, followed by a reviving beer in Bar Centro and a spot of live music at the Manchester Roadhouse.

STRENGTHS

- Civic pride
- Successful urban regeneration
- Canals
- Old Trafford
- Imperial War Museum North
- Lowry Centre
- Manchester Art Gallery
- Manchester Smithsonian
- University of Manchester
- Canal St after dark
- Lancashire County Cricket Club

WEAKNESSES

- Weather
- Lack of low-cost airlines
- Manchester–Liverpool rivalry, Manchester–Leeds rivalry

GOLD STAR

Pioneering and resilient spirit.

STARRING ROLE IN...

- *24-Hour Party People* (2002)
- *Cold Feet* (1998–2003)
- *Coronation Street* (1960–)
- *The Queen is Dead* by the Smiths

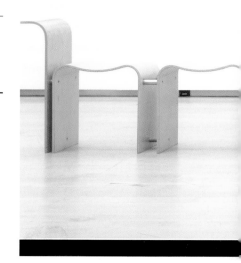

See the Daniel Libeskind–designed Imperial War Museum North and the audiovisual displays inside.

Eat at the best Indian restaurant on Curry Mile, Shere Khan.

Drink a whisky in Temple of Convenience, a converted public toilet.

Do a tour of Old Trafford and imagine wearing one of those red shirts.

Watch the heavens above and the city below from little-visited Godlee Observatory.

Buy stylish clothes and must-have accessories in Millennium Quarter.

After dark prepare for cutting-edge sounds at The Deaf Institute.

ENJOY THE ART AT THE LOWRY GALLERY IN SALFORD QUAYS.

BUDDHA BLESSES THOSE AT SENG GUAN TEMPLE IN MANILA.

Manila

NICKNAME PEARL OF THE ORIENT **DATE OF BIRTH** 1571: WHEN IT WAS FOUNDED BY SPANIARD MIGUEL LOPEZ DE LEGAZPI, ALTHOUGH A MUSLIM SETTLEMENT HAD EXISTED ON THE SITE FOR CENTURIES **ADDRESS** PHILIPPINES (MAP 9, J7) **HEIGHT** 14M **SIZE** 38.55 SQ KM **POPULATION** 11.8 MILLION **LONELY PLANET RANKING** 069

The hub of the Philippines' 7000 islands, Manila is a megacity of skyscrapers, shantytowns and malls with ghosts of a Spanish colonial past lurking in the alleyways.

ANATOMY

Manila is huge. The Metro Manila area is a vast district comprising 17 sprawling municipalities. At the centre is the City of Manila, gazing westward over the ocean. Intramuros is the oldest district, perched on a peninsula that juts into Manila Bay. This was the site of the original Muslim settlement, on top of which the Spanish built their fortress. From here venture east into the metropolis on foot or by *jeepney* (local bus).

PEOPLE

Most Manilans are Catholic, and although the majority belong to the Tagalog ethnic group, Manila has become something of a microcosm of the Philippines since immigrants from the archipelago settled here.

TYPICAL MANILAN

Manilans have a reputation for being warm and relaxed but they're never afraid to express opinions. It's hardly surprising. The city has been occupied by the Spanish, Americans and Japanese, and residents have had to struggle for their sense of self and freedom. The influence of the West remains strong, yet Manilans have adapted rather than surrendered to the outside world. Some locals speak 'Taglish', a dialect of Tagalog that subsumes elements of English.

DEFINING EXPERIENCE

Paying your respects at the bizarre Chinese Cemetery, strolling through the weird and wonderful markets and side streets of Quiapo, Santa Cruz and Binondo, then wandering along the walls of Intramuros to appreciate the sunset over Manila Bay.

STRENGTHS

- *Jeepneys* – multicoloured local buses evolved from ex-US army jeeps
- Dr José Rizal – national hero of the Philippines
- Intramuros – the walled Spanish city
- Fast-changing nightlife of the Malate and Ermita areas
- Fantastic clothing off the rack
- Extraordinary markets
- Trendy eateries
- Karaoke

WEAKNESSES

- Shantytowns, poverty and prostitution
- Stifling heat
- Pollution and traffic
- Overpopulation
- Ferdinand Marcos

GOLD STAR

Sunset – Manila is perfectly poised to witness the brilliant sunsets over the bay, and the pollution in the air only enhances the light show!

STARRING ROLE IN...

- *Seed of Contention* (2006)
- *Homecoming* (2003)
- *Too Hot to Handle* (1977)
- *The Tesseract* by Alex Garland

See Intramuros, the old walled city that guarded Spain's Asian empire.

Eat typical dishes from all over the Philippines at a cheap and cheerful *turo turo* (a fast-food restaurant where you point to what you want to order).

Drink San Miguel beer, the finest in Asia.

Do a tour of the Chinese Cemetery where mausoleums have running water and flush toilets for the deceased.

Watch the sun set over Manila Bay.

Buy anything you can imagine – and much that you'd rather not – at a city market.

After dark hit the karaoke bars with the rest of Manila.

A COLOURFUL JEEPNEY GRIDLOCK ALONG THE MAIN ROAD AT DIVISORIA MARKET.

SOME DHOWS STILL FISH FROM MAPUTO BUT OTHERS OFFER SIGHTSEEING TOURS BY SAIL.

Maputo

DATE OF BIRTH 1787; THE TOWN DEVELOPED AROUND A PORTUGUESE FORTRESS, WHICH WAS COMPLETED AT THIS TIME
ADDRESS MOZAMBIQUE (MAP 7, E8) **HEIGHT** 59M
POPULATION 1.2 MILLION **LONELY PLANET RANKING** 181

One of Africa's most alluring cities for rest and relaxation, Maputo has a distinctly Mediterranean atmosphere, white sandy beaches and friendly locals that give the busy capital a resort feel.

ANATOMY

Set on a small cliff overlooking the large harbour in Maputo Bay, the city is circled by stunning beaches, the scenic Inhaca and Portuguese Islands, the 'reed cities' – the overpopulated slums – as well as coastal wetlands. The city's ample avenues, lined with red acacia and lilac jacaranda trees, are populated by worse-for-wear colonial buildings – the result of almost two decades of civil war – many modern constructions and a lively café culture. The best way to see Maputo is by foot, but minibus tours and car hire are options. Many drivers have a relaxed attitude to road laws.

PEOPLE

Indigenous tribal groups comprise almost the entire population, with Europeans and Indians making up the rest. Around 50% of the population adheres to indigenous beliefs, about 30% is Christian and 20% Muslim. Although Portuguese is the official language, there are many local dialects spoken, and English is quite common in the city.

TYPICAL MAPUTO CITIZEN

Unlike their rural counterparts, many urban Mozambicans have disposable income. Going out for coffee is a popular habit, as is hanging out at the beach. They have strong religious beliefs, are resilient and optimistic, enthusiastic about music and love to dance and play sport.

DEFINING EXPERIENCE

Sunbathing with a book on the white sands of Praia de Maceneta, then taking in the bustling street life over a protracted beer and spicy tiger-prawn feast, checking out the live music at the jazz cafe in the train station and cutting it up almost till dawn at a club... before hot-footing it to the bay to take in a glorious sunrise.

STRENGTHS

- Locals
- Relaxed atmosphere
- Beach weather year-round
- Cheap-as-chips seafood
- Huge, colourful street murals
- Palm tree–lined beaches with excellent water sports
- Lively nightlife
- Maputo Bay sunrises
- Café culture
- Maputo Elephant Reserve
- Colourful markets
- National Art Museum
- Local football matches
- Species-rich wetlands close by
- National Company of Song & Dance

WEAKNESSES

- Street crime; dodgy police officers
- Lawless drivers
- Poverty
- Central Railway Station

GOLD STAR

Pristine beaches – they're full of marine life and coral reefs, are within close reach of the city centre and have heaps of water sports.

STARRING ROLE IN...

- *Ali* (2000)
- *Under the Frangipani* by Mia Couto
- *Half a Life* by VS Naipaul

See the 95m-long mural opposite the Praça dos Heróis Moçambicanos, commemorating the Revolution.

Eat spicy *piri-piri* chicken at the 1960s-feel Restaurante Piri-Piri.

Drink the local beers – Laurentina, Manica and 2M – street-side, under the shade of an acacia tree.

Do a camping trip to Inhaca Island and explore its offshore coral reefs.

Watch a performance of the first-rate National Company of Song & Dance.

Buy up-to-the-minute import items delivered straight from the docks of Maputo Bay to the city's air-conditioned shopping centres.

After dark check out the local jazz scene at Cinema Gil Vicente.

GOING PLACES – YOUNG BOYS ON ROLLER BLADES IN THE BAIXA AREA OF MAPUTO.

Marrakesh

NICKNAME THE RED **DATE OF BIRTH** 1062; WHEN THE CONQUERING ALMORAVID GENERAL YOUSSEF BEN TACHFINE ESTABLISHED A FORTIFIED CAMP **ADDRESS** MOROCCO (MAP 6, D2) **HEIGHT** 460M **SIZE** 70 SQ KM **POPULATION** 1 MILLION **LONELY PLANET RANKING** 042

One of Morocco's most important cultural centres, Marrakesh is a lively former capital famed for its markets and festivals set in breathtaking surroundings.

ANATOMY

Built around an oasis at the foot of the High Atlas Mountains, Marrakesh is a Moroccan rail and road hub. The old city is a maze of red mud-brick buildings. The French-built Ville Nouvelle (New Town) is next door, with its wide boulevards and Art Deco/Moorish architecture, while breeze-block modern suburbs sprawl out to the north and east. Extensive gardens and palm groves preserved within the New Town provide an escape from the bustling centre. Walking is usually the best way to get around, but for longer distances, *petits taxis* (local taxis) are fairly cheap.

PEOPLE

Marrakesh is a Berber town. The Romans called them Barbari, or barbarians, and the Arab conquerors continued the practice. The Berbers themselves prefer the term Amazigh (free men), but they rarely get their own way. The language spoken by the tribes in the area is called Tashilhayt. Arabic is more common among the city's established residents, but Marrakesh is a market town for the Amazigh, and so you will hear Tashilhayt spoken as well. There is also a substantial expat community of French, Germans and English, drawn by the climate and the culture.

TYPICAL MARRAKSHI

Marrakshis are more laid-back than most urban Moroccans. The Berber culture is more relaxed in matters of religion and formality. Marrakshi woman have freedoms that would be frowned upon further north, and the city is relatively gay-friendly. Marrakshis are known for their warmth, directness and sense of humour. But beware, commerce is a passion for Marrakshis, and they have developed the hard-sell haggle to a fine art.

FOOD FOR ALL IN THE MEDINA.

DEFINING EXPERIENCE

Strolling through the souq (market), retreating from the clamour to the shade of the Menara gardens, then sitting on the terrace of Café Glacier, overlooking the Djemaa el Fna, drinking mint tea and watching the sunset turn the mud bricks from red to pink to orange, discussing which of the Gueliz nightclubs is the least touristy.

STRENGTHS

◢ Beautiful architecture
◢ Colourful markets
◢ The Koutoubia
◢ The gardens
◢ The Festival of Popular Arts
◢ Berber music
◢ Sunny winters

WEAKNESSES

◢ Overcrowding
◢ Poverty
◢ Sex tourists
◢ Pickpockets and scammers
◢ Bureaucratic sluggishness

GOLD STAR

Marrakesh has one of the most beautiful and exotic city squares in the world, Djemaa el Fna.

STARRING ROLE IN...

◢ *Hideous Kinky* (1999)
◢ *Marrakesh* by George Orwell
◢ *The Sand Child* by Tahar Ben Jelloun
◢ *Lords of the Atlas* by Gavin Maxwell
◢ *Our Man in Marrakesh* (1966)

See the old city from a rooftop terrace at sunset.

Eat the best couscous at Al Fassia restaurant.

Drink green tea with mint and sugar.

Do a walk through the Ben Youssef Medersa.

Watch the Fantasia horse dance at the Festival of Popular Arts in June.

Buy hand-woven Berber carpets.

After dark dance to the latest hits at Le Diamant Noir.

IN FINE RED ROBES A PERFORMER ENTERTAINS THE PUBLIC IN DJEMAA EL FNA.

SHADOWS LENGTHEN IN THE DUSK AS LOCALS HURRY ABOUT THEIR BUSINESS.

FRAMED BY THE WINDOW OF A STUDENT CELL IN THE ALI BEN YOUSSEF MEDERSA, A BURNOOSE WEARER CONTEMPLATES THE SCENE BELOW.

THE TINY FISHING PORT OF VALLON DES AUFFES HAS A BIG REPUTATION FOR CHARMING SEASIDE RESTAURANTS.

Marseille

DATE OF BIRTH 600 BC; WHEN GREEK MARINERS FOUNDED A TRADING POST CALLED MASSILIA **ADDRESS** FRANCE (MAP 5, J4) **HEIGHT** 4M **POPULATION** 850, 000 (CITY); 1.7 MILLION (METRO AREA) **LONELY PLANET RANKING** 124

Marseille is not pretty or quaint like its Provençal neighbours – it's a real cosmopolitan city with an endearing old port, great seafood and a ticking nightlife.

ANATOMY

Marseille's main artery is the boulevard of La Canebière, which carves through the city east from the Old Port. Bohemian cours Julien buzzes with cafés, restaurants and theatres south of the boulevard. Further south stands the Basilique Notre Dame de la Garde, which surveys the city from its spot on a hill. West from the Old Port and out to sea, boats sail to Corsica, Sardinia, Tunisia, Spain and Algeria. Also out to sea but closer to home stands Château d'If, the 16th-century fortress-turned-jail immortalised in Alexandre Dumas' *Le Comte de Monte Cristo*. Rumbling beneath the city are two metro lines, while buses cruise around above the surface. The overland train station is north of La Canebière.

PEOPLE

Due to its proximity to Tunisia and Algeria, Marseille is France's most North African city, with many immigrants from these countries. Immigrants also come from the Mediterranean basin and Comoros.

TYPICAL MARSEILLAIS

As citizens of France's second city and the capital of Provence, the Marseillais are predictably and justifiably proud. The city used to have a reputation for violence and racial tensions, but development projects and the TGV link to Paris are leaving this image behind. Smart Parisians are snapping up weekend homes and plugging into the cultural scene. In general, people are welcoming of visitors, but they do have a defensive streak, which can allow them to close ranks if they choose to. The people of Marseille were enthusiastic supporters of the revolution, and France's national anthem, 'La Marseillaise', was named after local revolutionaries who sang it on their march to Paris. Finally, the Marseillais are big fans of football and hip-hop.

DEFINING EXPERIENCE

Delving into the city's Greek and Roman past at the Musée d'Histoire de Marseille, before tasting some *pastis* (an anise-flavoured cousin of absinthe) at La Maison du Pastis, grabbing some bouillabaisse at the port and then making for place Jean Jaurès to buy vintage clothing.

STRENGTHS

- ◢ Shopping heaven on rue Paradis
- ◢ Basilique Notre Dame de la Garde
- ◢ Château d'If
- ◢ Sunbathing at the Calanques
- ◢ Musée des Beaux-Arts
- ◢ Musée de la Mode
- ◢ Harbourside restaurants
- ◢ Old Port
- ◢ TGV link to Paris
- ◢ Fiesta des Suds

WEAKNESSES

- ◢ Some street crime
- ◢ Smelly backstreets

GOLD STAR

- ◢ Bouillabaisse.

STARRING ROLE IN...

- ◢ *La Vie est Tranquille* (2000)
- ◢ *Taxi* (1998)
- ◢ *The French Connection* (1971)
- ◢ *Le Comte de Monte Cristo* by Alexandre Dumas

See the view of Marseille from the highest point in the city, the Romano-Byzantine Notre Dame de la Garde.

Eat inventive cuisine at Une Table au Sud; take a break from bouillabaisse.

Drink homemade *pastis* or, if you're brave, absinthe at L'Heure Verte.

Do stroll around the Old Port and spy the fishing craft and pleasure yachts.

Watch or join in a game of *pétanque* (aka boules – similar to lawn bowls but played with heavy metal balls on a sandy pitch) in the late afternoon.

Buy African woodcarved animals at Marseille's best market, Marché aux Puces (flea market).

After dark salsa, samba and prop up the bar at steamy Le Cubaila Café.

STRAIGHT FROM THE BOAT – FRESH FISH FOR SALE AT MARSEILLE'S DOCKS.

SPREADING THE FAITH – RUGS ARE LAID OUT IN PREPARATION FOR MORNING PRAYERS.

Mecca

NICKNAME FORBIDDEN CITY **DATE OF BIRTH** APPROXIMATELY 2000 BC;
POSSIBLY FOUNDED BY THE PROPHET IBRAHIM (ABRAHAM)
ADDRESS SAUDI ARABIA (MAP 8, C6) **HEIGHT** 277M
POPULATION 2 MILLION **LONELY PLANET RANKING** 176

Mecca is an icon of inestimable religious and historic importance; to spend time in Islam's first city is a truly unforgettable experience.

ANATOMY

The ancient city nestles on the slopes of the narrow valley of Abraham, surrounded by dusty hills and mountains on three sides. The Sacred Mosque dominates the centre of the city and contains the Kaaba (the first temple of God constructed by Adam, later rebuilt by Ibrahim). Mecca has a fairly efficient infrastructure to cater for pilgrims, whose numbers are concentrated during the main pilgrimage, known as the haj, when several million Muslims descend on the city.

PEOPLE

By law non-Muslims cannot enter Mecca. The city's permanent residents are mainly Arabs (around 80%) but there is a significant minority of nationals from other Islamic countries, mainly Africa and Asia, who come here to study the Koran. Mecca is Saudi Arabia's third most populous city after the capital, Riyadh, and Jeddah. Arabic is the main language, with English spoken by staff in some hotels.

TYPICAL MECCAN

During the haj you might only get to meet other pilgrims, whose extra-ordinary numbers give real meaning to the term 'sea of humanity'. The city's students give the place a welcoming vibe and everyone who lives here considers themselves blessed. The Arab Meccans have a remarkable ability with languages and may be scornful of those who don't try to begin conversations in Arabic.

DEFINING EXPERIENCE

Dropping your jaw upon realising the size of the Grand Mosque, using sign language to communicate with pilgrims of every nationality, drinking chilled water from the public fountains, and returning to the Grand Mosque at twilight when it is bathed in an eerie blue light.

STRENGTHS

- The Black Stone of Kaaba
- The Sacred Mosque (al-Masjid al-Haram)
- Almost zero crime
- Incredible ornamentation
- Street vendors
- Gates to the Sacred Mosque (there are almost 100)
- Multilevel ablution complex (over 2000 toilets and ablution units)

WEAKNESSES

- Ban on non-Muslims
- Overcrowded
- Stampeding pilgrims
- Public executions
- Judicial amputations
- Zero nightlife
- Expensive
- The bulldozing of historic quarters to make way for ugly towers

GOLD STAR

The Kaaba – Muslims pray in the direction of the Kaaba all their lives and seeing it for the first time is an unforgettable spiritual experience.

STARRING ROLE IN...

- The Koran
- The Bible (the city has been controversially identified as the ancient city Bakkah, the Biblical 'valley of Baca' in Psalm 84)
- *Personal Narrative of a Pilgrimage to Al Madinah and Meccah* by Richard Burton
- *One Thousand Roads to Mecca* edited by Michael Wolfe

See the narrow streets of the old quarter, the original heart of Mecca.

Eat like a local and grab a cheap chicken or camel *shwarma* (meat stuffed in pita-type bread with tomatoes and garnish) from street vendors.

Drink holy water from the Zamzam Well, referred to in the Koran.

Do wander out into the suburbs where you can see enormous excavations as more buildings are cut into the rock.

Watch the *tawaf* (pilgrims circling the Kaaba) from a viewing platform at the Sacred Mosque.

Buy Ajwa Kajoor dates, said to contain healing powers.

After dark visit the Sacred Mosque when it is less crowded and brilliantly lit up by stadium lights.

REZA / GETTY IMAGES

GOING WITH THE FLOW – A SEA OF PILGRIMS CIRCLE THE KAABA IN THE SACRED MOSQUE.

YOU'LL FIND GRAFFITI AND GREAT COFFEE IN MELBOURNE'S HISTORIC TRAFFIC-FREE LANEWAYS.

Melbourne

NICKNAME PARIS OF THE SOUTHERN HEMISPHERE **DATE OF BIRTH** 1835; BY TASMANIAN ENTREPRENEURS KEEN ON A MAINLAND BASE **ADDRESS** AUSTRALIA (MAP 10, G8) **HEIGHT** 35M **SIZE** 2025 SQ KM **POPULATION** 4 MILLION **LONELY PLANET RANKING** 011

Suave, sophisticated and stark-raving sports mad, Melbourne is an arty powerhouse with an eye on the Melbourne Cup and a mouthful of world-class cuisine.

ANATOMY

Melbourne lines Port Phillip Bay and stretches into the plains to the west and east and out to the foothills of the Dandenong Ranges. The city is divided by the muddy Yarra River, with the CBD on the north bank, set in a neat grid that suits its kitschy tram transport perfectly. To the CBD's north is the dining precinct of Carlton and grungy Fitzroy, which vies for coolest-suburb honours with St Kilda to the south of the Yarra with its ace of beaches and backpackers. Trams and trains are the best way to get around the city.

PEOPLE

Melbourne's population is drawn from around the world, with postwar migrations of Italian, Greek and Jewish people giving it a unique cultural make-up. Melbourne, famously, has the highest population of Greeks of any city outside of Greece itself. More recently Vietnamese, Indonesian and Malaysian people have arrived, with Melbourne having a particularly high population of international students (the fourth-largest in the world). Melbourne's original people, the Wurundjeri, have survived all of these waves of immigration.

TYPICAL MELBURNIAN

Dressed in black and swilling a coffee, Melburnians have been known to argue about their city's best restaurant for hours and spend most of Monday talking about how their footy team went. You could say lifestyle is more important than career, but Melburnians are passionate about their politics, with the city holding the largest protests against federal government change to industrial relations reforms. While many talk about the 'great divide' between the north and south side of the Yarra, many more live in suburbs far from the river.

MEET HERE – FEDERATION SQUARE OPPOSITE FLINDERS ST STATION IN CENTRAL MELBOURNE.

DEFINING EXPERIENCE
Running a lap of the Botanic Gardens, then catching a tram to the MCG (Melbourne Cricket Ground) for Saturday's big AFL (Australian Football League) game, hunkering down in a Fitzroy pub to watch a local band, then spotting possums in Carlton Gardens on the way home.

STRENGTHS
- Flinders St Station
- Trams
- Secret city laneways and back alleys
- St Kilda beaches
- Live music
- Federation Sq
- Melbourne Zoo
- Sports-obsessed culture
- National Gallery of Victoria
- MCG, or more simply, the G
- Esplanade Hotel (The Espy)
- Royal Exhibition Buildings and Carlton Gardens
- Snazzy new Docklands
- 'Paris end' of Collins St
- St Kilda bars and restaurants
- Melbourne Museum
- Diverse cuisine
- Funky Fitzroy
- Lygon St cafés
- Artsy Southgate

WEAKNESSES
- Tricky traffic hook turns
- St Kilda beaches
- Tea-coloured Yarra River
- Controversial Crown Casino

GOLD STAR
Multiculturalism – from postwar Italian and Greek immigrants to more recent Vietnamese and Eritrean

WORSHIPPERS CONGREGATE AT THE MCG, THE CATHEDRAL OF AUSTRALIAN RULES FOOTBALL, MELBOURNE'S ORTHODOX RELIGION.

families, Melbourne has a diverse ethnicity.

STARRING ROLE IN...

◢ *Ghost Rider* (2007)
◢ *Three Dollars* (2005)
◢ *The Wog Boy* (2000)
◢ *The Bank* (2001)
◢ *Malcolm* (1986)
◢ *Proof* (1991)
◢ *Crackerjack* (2002)
◢ *The Slap* by Christos Tsiolkas (TV series 2011)
◢ *Mallboy* (2001)
◢ *The Castle* (1997)
◢ *Love and Other Catastrophes* (1996)
◢ *Death in Brunswick* (1991)
◢ *Dogs in Space* (1987)
◢ *Harvie Krumpet* (2003)
◢ *Street Hero* (1984)

See the patchwork design of Federation Sq.

Eat the sumptuous Peking duck at the Flower Drum, Melbourne's foodie apogee.

Drink an espresso (anything else isn't *autentico*) at Pellegrini's or a flat white at that fabulous new place everybody is talking about.

Do the adrenalin rush of kite-surfing at St Kilda Beach.

Watch a local band at the iconic live-music venue, the Corner Hotel.

Buy an edgy outfit on Chapel St, only to spot a bargain knock-off on Bridge Rd.

After dark check out the back alleys that hide bars like the Croft Institute and Double Happiness.

Memphis

NICKNAME THE BLUFF CITY **DATE OF BIRTH** 1739; WHEN THE FRENCH
FORT ASSUMPTION WAS ESTABLISHED, BUT 3000 YEARS AGO THE
LOESS BLUFFS ON THE EASTERN SHORE OF THE MISSISSIPPI RIVER
WERE INHABITED BY NATIVE AMERICAN TRIBES **ADDRESS** USA (MAP 1,
O7) **HEIGHT** 101M **SIZE** 723 SQ KM **POPULATION** 646,000 (CITY); 1.3
MILLION (METRO AREA) **LONELY PLANET RANKING** 098

**Where Elvis Presley lived and Martin Luther King
died, Memphis reclines sleepily on the banks of the
Mississippi, listening to its legendary blues and
rock 'n' roll and watching the steamboats chugging
past cotton mansions.**

ANATOMY
Downtown Memphis hugs the eastern bank of the Mississippi, with
Riverside Dr and a promenade running parallel to the river. Slightly inland
is the main tourist area, roughly bordered by Beale St and Union Ave, 2nd
and 4th Sts. Groovy neighbourhoods with shops, bars and restaurants lie to
the east along Union Ave and Overton Sq. Graceland is 5km south of town
on US51, also known as 'Elvis Presley Blvd'. Trolleys serve Main St
downtown, and riverboat cruises ply the Mississippi.

PEOPLE
Memphis' population is two-thirds black and one-third white. Minority
groups include Native Americans, Asians and Hispanics.

TYPICAL MEMPHIAN
Memphis may be a big city, but Memphians enjoy a relaxed pace of life.
Traffic jams and pollution are not as much of a problem as in other urban
centres. The people are proud of their city and celebrate its musical heritage
with a bevy of concerts and festivals. Outdoor activities are popular, with
boating and water sports available on nearby lakes. Memphis has moved a
long way from the racial tension of Martin Luther King's time and
Memphians enjoy a generally peaceful, soulful existence.

DEFINING EXPERIENCE
Wandering around Sun Studio where Elvis cut his first record, grabbing a
po'boy sandwich (French bread, usually filled with roast beef, oysters or
prawns) before soaking up some blues and soul on Beale St.

BLUES LEGENDS SUCH AS MUDDY WATERS AND B.B. KING HAVE PLAYED ON BEALE STREET.

CLASSIC CARS PRESERVE A SENSE OF HISTORICAL REALISM AT THE LORRAINE MOTEL WHERE MARTIN LUTHER KING JR WAS ASSASSINATED.

STRENGTHS

- ◢ Graceland
- ◢ The Blues Foundation (based in Memphis)
- ◢ Blues on Beale St
- ◢ Memphis Rock 'n' Soul Museum
- ◢ National Civil Rights Museum
- ◢ Mississippi River Museum
- ◢ Sun Studio
- ◢ Steamboats
- ◢ Stax Museum of American Soul Music
- ◢ Victorian Village district on Adams Ave
- ◢ Pink Palace Museum and Planetarium
- ◢ Overton Park
- ◢ Memphis Zoo
- ◢ Pulled barbecue pork butt

WEAKNESSES

- ◢ Street crime
- ◢ Mud Island

GOLD STAR

Elvis!

STARRING ROLE IN...

- ◢ *Elvis by the Presleys* (2005)
- ◢ *21 Grams* (2003)
- ◢ *A Painted House* (2003)
- ◢ *Cast Away* (2000)

See the 5m couch, fake waterfall and more '70s décor at Graceland, and imagine living like the King.

Eat a Memphis staple – charcoal-broiled dry ribs – at the family-owned Rendezvous.

Drink to steady your nerves before a guitar-pickin' contest at Kudzu's.

Do visit the National Civil Rights Museum, where Martin Luther King was shot in 1968, and learn about his contribution to the civil-rights movement.

Watch Memphis Grizzlies basketball action at the FedEx Forum.

Buy Elvis memorabilia and a pair of those gold shades at Graceland.

After dark swing into the clubs of Beale St for the sounds of live soul, rock, country and jazz music.

HARVESTING NEW WORLD GRAPES IN AN OLD-FASHIONED WAY.

Mendoza

DATE OF BIRTH 1561; WHEN IT WAS FOUNDED BY PEDRO DE CASTILLA
ADDRESS ARGENTINA (MAP 3, D14) **HEIGHT** 801M **SIZE** 110 SQ KM
POPULATION 114,000 **LONELY PLANET RANKING** 134

A town that offers wine tasting, a sunny clime, tree-lined streets and parks just made for roaming, mountain jaunts… Mendoza offers all this and more amid the company of relaxed and friendly Mendocinos.

ANATOMY

First you'll notice the trees: giant sycamores forming a canopy over the wide avenues of downtown, shading Mendoza's lively inhabitants from the blistering summer sun. With all those leaves, you'd never know it's a desert. But the *acequias* (open irrigation channels) burbling along every street give it away. They carry snow-melt from the Andes, visible evidence of the city's indigenous and colonial past, even where modern quake-proof construction has replaced fallen historic buildings. Mendoza's architecture, hidden behind the trees, is almost an afterthought. Without the trees, Mendoza would be hell. With them, it's one of Argentina's finest cities, with outdoor cafés crowded with coffee drinkers, five beautiful central plazas, a bustling shopping district and an exciting nightlife. And above the city are the Andes. Mendoza is more spread out than most Argentine cities, so you'll need to tighten your shoelaces or catch a bus to get around.

PEOPLE

Mendocinos are mostly European descendants (especially Spaniards and Italians) and mestizos, with some indigenous people. They speak Spanish, as well as Quechua, Araucanian and Guaraní. They are predominantly Roman Catholic with smaller percentages of Protestant, Jewish, Ukrainian Catholic and Armenian Orthodox communities.

TYPICAL MENDOCINO

Mendocinos have city charm but country tranquillity. They're laid-back but full of passion, their relaxed natures concealing the party animal within. They'll dance until 7am and still make time for a family *asado* (barbecue) for lunch. They'll boast of the surrounding natural wonders but won't bother to leave the city to see them. They believe they're more European than Argentine, except when it comes to World Cup football.

DEFINING EXPERIENCE

Waking up late after a night dancing in a *boliche* (nightclub), starting the day with a maté (Argentina's traditional drink), strolling shaded streets and plazas, gorging on an *asado* until late afternoon, drinking bottle after bottle of Quilmes and dancing the night away to *cumbia* (Colombian dance tunes), then returning home after sunrise to sleep through half the weekend.

STRENGTHS

◢ Damn fine Malbec wines
◢ Laid-back atmosphere
◢ Wide, shady avenues
◢ Sun
◢ Snow
◢ The Italianate character
◢ Inner-city greenness
◢ Proximity to the Andes and all its adventure sports
◢ Outdoor cafés
◢ Open-air and handicraft markets

WEAKNESSES

◢ Wide irrigation channels on both sides of every street
◢ Climatic extremes
◢ Clichéd Argentine egotism and machismo
◢ Earthquakes

GOLD STAR

For being the city that converted Argentina's wine industry from a local shame to an international success.

STARRING ROLE IN...

◢ *The Motorcycle Diaries* (2004)

See the Museo Popular Callejera on Av Las Heras – an innovative sidewalk museum.

Eat *lomitos* (beef sandwiches) on the wide esplanade of the Costanera Sur.

Drink a good Malbec at Mendoza's Vendimia (grape-harvest) festival on the first Saturday of March each year.

Do a relaxing walk around the parks and lakes of Parque General San Martín.

Watch the underwater show at the Acuario Municipal Mendoza (aquarium).

Buy indigenous weavings at the Mercado Artesanal (Handicraft Market).

After dark dine, drink and dance on Av Aristides Villanueva.

MATÉ, A POWERFUL, REJUVENATING TEA, HAS BEEN ENJOYED BY LOCALS FOR CENTURIES.

MODERN MENDOZA UNDER THE NIGHT SKY.

ARGENTINIAN HORSE RIDERS START YOUNG.

Mexico City

CHRIS CHEADLE / GETTY IMAGES

NICKNAME EL DF; CHILANGOTLÁN; CHILANGOLANDIA; LA CIUDAD DE LOS PALACIOS (CITY OF PALACES); LA CIUDAD DE LA ESPERANZA (CITY OF HOPE) **DATE OF BIRTH** 1325; WHEN THE AZTECS RULED IT AS TENOCHTITLÁN, BUT IT WAS REBUILT AS NUEVA ESPAÑA BY THE CONQUISTADORS AROUND 1550 **ADDRESS** MEXICO (MAP 2, C4) **HEIGHT** 2309M **SIZE** 5000 SQ KM **POPULATION** 21.2 MILLION **LONELY PLANET RANKING** 029

Mexico City is North America's oldest metropolis, and its layers of European nostalgia, rich indigenous culture and modern urban energy are exhilarating.

ANATOMY

Set in a high valley, Mexico City's 350 *colonias* (neighbourhoods) sprawl. The heart of the city, El Zócalo, and its surrounding museum-packed neighbourhoods and green expanses of the Alameda, form the Centro Histórico. Architectural styles range from baroque to early-20th-century delights, from millennial-gated communities to the outer rings of slum dwellings. Traffic congestion is terrible, despite a metro, a large network of buses and trolley cars, and countless (and infamous) taxis.

PEOPLE

The majority of *capitalinos* or *chilangos,* as residents are known, are Spanish-speaking mestizos, a typically Mexican melange of Spanish and indigenous ancestry, often with some European or African-slave heritage. The city's huge population continues to be swelled by immigrants.

TYPICAL CAPITALINO

Young *capitalinos* from fashionable inner neighbourhoods tend to be politically engaged (if cynical), culturally switched on, and hedonistic. Although deep-held values – family, machismo, Catholicism – still endure, there are profound shifts in social attitudes. Not all *capitalinos* get to share in a city that is safer than ever, increasingly stylish and certainly cosmopolitan; over 20% live in poverty.

DEFINING EXPERIENCE

Brunching late at El Pendulo, listening to the guitarist, taking a stroll around the Mercado de la Merced with your *abuela* (grandmother), then having a prickly-pear ice cream at Neveria Roxy, stopping by Chic By Accident and bargaining for an antique mirror you've been coveting, followed by drinks on the rooftop at Condesa DF.

A YELLOW VOLKSWAGEN BEETLE TAXI PROCLAIMS ITS INDIVIDUALITY AMONG THE MASSES.

I GOT YOUR BACK – MEXICAN COWBOYS WAIT AT A RODEO.

COLUMNS OF CANDY FLOSS FOR SALE ON A STREET CORNER IN COLONIAL COYOACAN.

MEXICO REMAINS A STAUNCHLY CATHOLIC COUNTRY.

STRENGTHS

◢ Museo Nacional de Antropología
◢ The new 'Mexican chic' epitomised by Hotel Habita and Condesa DF
◢ Palacio de las Bellas Artes
◢ Thousands of taco stands
◢ Photography collection at Galería Casa Lamm
◢ Art Deco in Condesa
◢ Art Nouveau in Colonia Roma
◢ Casa Azul and Museo Casa Estudio Diego Rivera y Frida Kahlo (key cult-of-Kahlo sites)
◢ Church of Santa Veracruz and the baroque Church of San Juan de Dios
◢ The pyramids at Teotihuacán Tenochtitlán

WEAKNESSES

◢ Sprawl and decrepit infrastructure
◢ Pollution
◢ Extreme social inequalities

GOLD STAR

Mexico City's murals, especially those by Rivera, Siqueiros and Orozco.

STARRING ROLE IN...

◢ *Los Olvidados* (1950)
◢ *Love in the Time of Hysteria* (1991)
◢ *Amores Perros* (2000)
◢ *Y Tu Mama Tambien* (2001)
◢ *Frida* (2002)
◢ *The Death of Artemio Cruz* by Carlos Fuentes

See the Gothic, baroque *and* neoclassical Catedral Metropolitana and the Aztec Templo Mayor.

Eat *nueva cocina mexicana* (new Mexican cuisine) at Izote.

Drink *pulque* (maguey liquor) at Las Duelistas, a basic *cantina* (bar).

Do escape to the shaded waterways of pre-Hispanic Xochimilco.

Watch a fútbol match at Aztec Stadium.

Buy vintage dresses and antique silver at Bazar Sábado in San Angel.

After dark get to the Dos Naciones for contemporary sounds and *cantina* atmosphere.

A LIFEGUARD STATION IN MIAMI'S TRADEMARK EYE-CATCHING COLOURS.

Miami

DATE OF BIRTH 1870; WHEN WILLIAM B BRICKELL ESTABLISHED A TRADING POST **HEIGHT** 8M **SIZE** 93 SQ KM **ADDRESS** USA (MAP 1, R10) **POPULATION** 408,000 (CITY); 5.5 MILLION (METRO AREA) **LONELY PLANET RANKING** 032

Miami is a fabulous melting pot of Latin immigrants, A-list celebrities and buffed beauties, all soaking up the city's sexy image and great museums and art galleries – not to mention the sun, sand and sea.

ANATOMY

Miami and Miami Beach are separated by the Intracoastal Waterway – Miami is on the mainland, while Miami Beach sits on a strip of white sand 6km to the east. Miami Beach is home to the world-renowned Art Deco Historic District and South Beach (SoBe). Multicultural Miami has Little Havana, initially populated by Cubans but now home to a pan-Latin community, and Little Haiti, a medley of Haitian markets and eateries. The Miami River runs through downtown Miami. Miami's port regularly welcomes cruise ships. Get around by bus or double-decker train.

PEOPLE

Sixty percent of the population was born outside the USA and the largest community in Miami is Latino (particularly Cuban). The average age of inhabitants is 39. Miami is bilingual (English and Spanish).

TYPICAL MIAMIAN

Miamians are hard-working, style-conscious people who tend to dress casually unless going out in the evening, when they pull out all the stops. It's not unusual to see A-list celebrities in Miami, but Miamians would never let on that they've noticed. Almost 40% of inhabitants own a property and real estate is more expensive in Miami Beach. Luxury condo high-rises are going up all the time. SUVs are the vehicle of choice. Miamians are a tolerant lot; in 2004 a law was passed to allow gay and straight couples living together to register their partnership.

DEFINING EXPERIENCE

Inhaling the odours of cigar shops on Little Havana's Calle Ocho, watching old men playing dominoes in Máximo Gómez Park, then heading to South Beach for a bite in the News Cafe, some time on the beach and cocktails at the Delano Hotel.

LIFE IN THE FAST LANE ON OCEAN DRIVE.

FLASHY NIGHTLIFE AT THE SPIRE LOUNGE.

INSIDE OUT – THE QUIRKY EXTERIOR DECORATION OF A FURNITURE STORE IN THE DESIGN DISTRICT.

STRENGTHS

◢ Art Basel Miami Beach
◢ Carnaval Miami
◢ Art Deco Historic District
◢ Argentine-Italian food in Normandy Isle
◢ Floribbean cuisine (a mix of Caribbean, Latin and local traditions)
◢ Mojitos (rum, lime, sugar, mint and soda water)
◢ Environmentally Endangered Lands (EEL) program
◢ Everglades National Park
◢ Art galleries of the Design District, particularly Moore Space
◢ Museum of Contemporary Art
◢ Latin music
◢ Rollerblading on the Promenade
◢ Photo shoots on Glitter Beach
◢ MiMo architecture eg Fontainebleau Hilton

WEAKNESSES

◢ Lack of affordable housing
◢ High unemployment
◢ Political scandals
◢ Mosquitoes in summer
◢ Hurricanes

GOLD STAR

Fabulousness – beautiful Art Deco architecture and beautiful people.

STARRING ROLE IN…

◢ *Miami Vice* (1984–89)
◢ *The Birdcage* (1996)
◢ *Scarface* (1983)

See contemporary art exhibitions and live music at the Design District's monthly Art and Design Night.

Eat succulent steaks at Prime 112, in the oldest inn on Miami Beach, the 1915 Browns Hotel.

Drink mojitos with famous faces in the upstairs garden at Skybar.

Do a walking tour of the South Beach Art Deco Historic District.

Watch topless men gyrating on dance floors at the gay extravaganza, Winter Party Festival.

Buy, buy, buy at Coconut Grove's popular outdoor malls: Coconut Walk and Streets of Mayfair.

After dark indulge in all-night drinking and dancing at enormous Space.

Minsk

KEREN SU / GETTY IMAGES

NICKNAME THE OUTPOST OF TYRANNY **DATE OF BIRTH** 11TH CENTURY; FOLKLORE SAYS A GIANT NAMED MENESK (OR MINCZ) HAD A MILL ON A NEARBY RIVERBANK, WHEREBY HE MADE BREAD TO FEED HIS WARRIORS **ADDRESS** BELARUS (MAP 4, R8) **HEIGHT** 234M **SIZE** 15 SQ KM **POPULATION** 1.8 MILLION **LONELY PLANET RANKING** 172

With more Soviet iconography and statues than you can shake a sickle at, Minsk offers a refreshing respite from the consumerist glut of Western Europe.

ANATOMY

Most of Minsk's buildings have only been around since 1944 (following the USSR's violent recapture) and it's probably the best standing example of grand-scale Soviet planning. The main drag, praspekt Nezalezhnastsi (formerly praspekt Francyska Skaryny), is a huge and hectic promenade: at the southwestern end sits the 500m-long ploshcha Nezalezhnastsi (Independence Sq), surrounded by government buildings and the attractive Polish Catholic Church of St Simon. Public transport consists of trams, trolleybuses and buses.

PEOPLE

Ethnic Belarusians make up the vast majority of the population, with Russian, Polish and Ukrainian nationals comprising the rest. About 80% of the populace is Eastern Orthodox and the remaining 20% are Roman Catholics. Everyone speaks Russian in public, saving their native Belarusian tongue for home.

TYPICAL MINSK CITIZEN

Urbane and savvy even as their government does its best to block all Western influence, Minsk citizens serve up communism with a cappuccino. Belarusians have a reputation for being exceptionally neat, tidy and law-abiding – even tipsy teens assiduously use rubbish bins for their beer bottles. Many locals have fair hair and piercing blue eyes.

DEFINING EXPERIENCE

Taking snaps of tiny Traetskae Prodmestse (Trinity Suburb) on the eastern bank of the Svislach River, then ogling the best architectural examples of Soviet monumentalism on praspekt Nezalezhnastsi and, after dark, people-watching on the block between vulitsa Lenina and vulitsa Enhelsa.

TRADITIONAL DANCERS KICK UP A STORM.

BRIGHT YOUNG THINGS STROLL IN FRONT OF THE HOLY SPIRIT CATHEDRAL.

BRUCE YUAN-YUE BI / GETTY IMAGES

STRENGTHS

◢ Astounding Soviet architecture
◢ The Red Church
◢ Museum of the Great Patriotic War
◢ Tsentralny Skver (Central Sq)
◢ Booming slogan: The Feats of the People Will Live Forever!
◢ Trinity Suburb
◢ The monument on the Ostrov Slyoz (Island of Tears), a tribute to those who died in war
◢ The Belarusian State Art Museum

WEAKNESSES

◢ Astoundingly ugly Soviet architecture
◢ A long history of human-rights abuses
◢ The Outpost of Tyranny
◢ Rude, blunt service
◢ Paranoia and suspicion
◢ '70s time-warp fashions

GOLD STAR

History – for better or for worse, Minsk is bursting with a rich cultural heritage, bloodstained or not.

STARRING ROLE IN...

◢ *Babi Yar* (2003)
◢ *Mysterium Occupation* (2004)
◢ *The Locals* by Janka Kupala
◢ *Two Souls* by Maxim Haradsky

See Dinamo Minsk, Belarus' top football club, play in its home stadium.

Eat hearty Belarusian fare at Verhniy Gorod and enjoy the great views of the Cathedral of the Holy Spirit.

Drink the city's finest coffee and tea at Stary Mensk on praspekt Nezalezhnastsi as you spy on the KGB building across the street.

Do forgo the romance of cracked hotel walls and goonish doormen by renting your own flat.

Watch the Belarusian Ballet, which during Soviet times was considered second only to Moscow's Bolshoi Ballet.

Buy Belarusian folk art, particularly the wooden boxes intricately decorated with geometric straw patterns, from any of Minsk's department stores.

After dark take in a kick-ass live rock show in the inimitable Graffiti on per Kalinina, where the vibe is garage meets army surplus.

Mombasa

DATE OF BIRTH AD 150; WHEN PTOLEMY PLACED THE CITY ON HIS MAP OF THE KNOWN WORLD **ADDRESS** KENYA (MAP 7, G2) **HEIGHT** 16M **SIZE** 30 SQ KM **POPULATION** 939,000 **LONELY PLANET RANKING** 191

A thriving port city, Mombasa is a steamy, tropical entrepôt where life unfurls languidly.

ANATOMY
Mombasa is an island, connected to the mainland by causeways to the north and west and a ferry to the south. Digo Rd, and its southern extension, Nyerere Ave, is the main north–south thoroughfare. East of Digo Rd is the main market, which leads to the Old Town's warren of streets. On the fringe of the Old Town, overlooking the old harbour, are the fish markets and the bulk of Fort Jesus. Packed *matatus* (minibuses) buzz around, and connect Mombasa to beach resorts north and south.

PEOPLE
As befits a port, Mombasa has seen people – Persian, Portuguese, Omani, all of whom mixed with local African populations – come and go for millennia. The city is now one of the biggest Swahili cities, with a coastal culture that is a melange of African, Asian and Arabic influences. Along with the mosques of the Swahili populace there are Hindu and Sikh temples. There is a sizable English community as well as refugee communities from the Horn of Africa.

TYPICAL MOMBASAN
A tropical people, the Mombasans approach life at a languid pace. The humidity and a laid-back mind-set mean that there is no need to rush. That said, Mombasa is the biggest port in East Africa and it bustles (albeit at its own pace). Locals are convivial and gregarious – life occurs on the street, particularly in the evening as the cool descends. Etiquette is paramount, and greetings are long and elaborate. Mombasa is one of the oldest settlements in Kenya, so locals have a strong sense of identity.

DEFINING EXPERIENCE
Strolling the streets of the Old Town, admiring the carved doorways, window frames and fretwork balconies of the coastal colonial houses, stopping for chai, then exploring the battlements of Fort Jesus, including

AN ELOQUENT TOUR GUIDE ELABORATES ON MOMBASA'S ATTRACTIONS.

GOING FOR A STROLL UNDER DRYING RAIMENTS.

Omani House, heading north to watch the ebb and flow at the dhow harbour, or turning south on Mama Ngina Dr, passing baobab trees and gazing out across the Indian Ocean.

STRENGTHS
- ◢ Chai flavoured with cardamom
- ◢ The scent of frangipani flowers in tropical rain
- ◢ The elaborate (slightly fading) glory of Swahili architecture
- ◢ Starched tablecloths on the Mombasa–Nairobi train
- ◢ Football on the gravel beneath Fort Jesus
- ◢ Lateen sails of dhows putting out to sea
- ◢ Tropical fruits – mangoes, pawpaws, pineapples

WEAKNESSES
- ◢ Street hassle from touts
- ◢ Mosquitoes
- ◢ Humidity during the monsoon
- ◢ Gradual disappearance of dhows
- ◢ Security after dark
- ◢ Sex tourism

GOLD STAR
Coastal indolence – Mombasa is the place to watch the world pass by.

STARRING ROLE IN...
- ◢ *The Portuguese Period in East Africa* by Justus Strands
- ◢ *A Tourist in Africa* by Evelyn Waugh
- ◢ *Lunatic Express* by Charles Miller
- ◢ *The Weather in Africa* by Martha Gellhorn

See the sun rise over the Indian Ocean.

Eat traditional Swahili fare: grilled fish, beans in coconut milk, spiced pilau.

Drink lime soda in Fort Jesus.

Do a luxury dhow cruise around the harbour.

Watch the colourful floats and parades at the annual carnival.

Buy a *kanga* or a *kikoi* (colourful traditional woven cloths).

After dark check out the bars on Moi Ave or Mama Ngina Dr.

Monaco

DATE OF BIRTH 1297: THE BEGINNING OF GRIMALDI RULE, BUT THE AREA WAS PROBABLY SETTLED IN PHOENICIAN TIMES
ADDRESS MONACO (MAP 5, K4) **HEIGHT** 7M **SIZE** 1.95 SQ KM
POPULATION 36,000 **LONELY PLANET RANKING** 102

Tiny but beautiful Monaco has the same relationship with glamour as its residents do with diamonds – easy, effortless and elegant – so be sure to dress appropriately.

ANATOMY

Monaco comprises six main areas: Monaco Ville (south of the port) with its pastel houses and Palais du Prince; Monte Carlo (north of the port), home to the casino and flash shops; La Condamine, southwest of the port; industrial Fontveille, south of Monaco Ville; Moneghetti, west of Condamine; and Larvotto Beach, north of Monte Carlo. Elegant yachts stand proudly in the harbour, lifts (elevators) whisk people up to the higher levels and fast cars roar around before being carefully valet parked.

PEOPLE

Monaco is ruled by the Grimaldi royal family. Residents do not pay income tax so Monaco has become a tax haven for many foreign celebrities. Only 7000 residents are Monégasque – most of the others are French and Italian.

TYPICAL MONACAN

The citizens of Monaco live a lovely, tax-free, low-crime life. They have their own flag (red and white), national holiday (19 November), national anthem and country dialling code. The official language is French, but many street signs also appear in the local dialect, Monégasque. This dialect, which is a mixture of French and Italian, is taught in schools. Finally, of course, they are glamorous and expensively dressed, drive super-cars and own luxury yachts.

DEFINING EXPERIENCE

Coasting your private helicopter onto a friend's huge catamaran to drink cosmopolitans and fine dine, followed by a spot of blackjack in a private room at the casino.

CAROL WILEY / GETTY IMAGES

THE CITY'S BEACH IS PACKED IN THE HIGH SEASON.

STRENGTHS

- Monaco Grand Prix
- Casino de Monte Carlo
- Palais du Prince
- Musée Océanographique de Monaco
- No income tax
- Low crime rate
- Grace Kelly
- Royal family
- Personal lives of Princesses Stéphanie and Caroline
- Chic shops
- Being a sovereign state
- Lifts up through the rock
- The Mediterranean
- Jardin Exotique
- Collection des Voitures Anciennes
- Local beaches – Plage du Larvotto and Plage de Monte Carlo
- Glitz and glamour

WEAKNESS

- If you don't have a platinum card, this place will not be as much fun

GOLD STAR

Glamour – Monaco never goes out of style.

STARRING ROLE IN...

- *GoldenEye* (1995)
- *Herbie Goes to Monte Carlo* (1977)
- *L'Inconnue de Monte Carlo* (1938)

See a slice of life under the sea at the world-famous aquarium Musée Océanographique de Monaco.

Eat fine cuisine at Alain Ducasse's three-Michelin-starred restaurant, Louis XV.

Drink champagne and play count-the-limousines at the Café de Paris.

Do visit the lush Jardin Exotique and breathe in the incredible view.

Watch one of the most thrilling car races in the world – Monaco's Grand Prix.

Buy designer goods and precious jewels in the lavish boutiques on ave des Beaux-Arts.

After dark be like James Bond and have a flutter in the beautifully ornate Casino de Monte Carlo.

PORT HERCULE CAN BE VIEWED FROM THE BALCONY ROOMS OF THE HERMITAGE HOTEL.

SERVICE AT THE CASINO MONTE-CARLO ALWAYS COMES WITH A SMILE.

POMP AND CEREMONY IN MONACO.

HORSEMANSHIP IS A BRUISING PART OF THE URUGUAYAN NATIONAL CHARACTER.

Montevideo

DATE OF BIRTH 1726; WHEN THE SPANISH FLEET ESTABLISHED A
CITADEL IN THE SHELTERED PORT OF MONTEVIDEO REACTING TO THE
BURGEONING PORTUGUESE IN THE RIO DE LA PLATA AREA
ADDRESS URUGUAY (MAP 4, F14) **HEIGHT** 22M **POPULATION** 1.3 MILLION
LONELY PLANET RANKING 138

**A picturesque blend of colonial Spanish, Italian
and Art Deco styles paired with superb sandy
beaches on the city's outskirts, Montevideo is
South America's well-kept secret.**

ANATOMY

Lying almost directly east of Buenos Aires on the west bank of the Río de la
Plata (River Plate), Montevideo's Ciudad Vieja (Old Town) attracts most
visitor attention. The Rambla (riverfront road) rambles eastward past
numerous public parks (including Parque Rodó) at the southern end of
bulevar Artigas. Well within the city limits are the sandy beaches, a little
further east. Montevideo's bus fleet is reliable, but most stop running by
11pm. If you're out late, taxis are safe and on the meter but a little pricey.

PEOPLE

Predominantly white with around 8% mestizo (with mixed Spanish and
indigenous blood) and 4% black, Montevideo's population includes many
European immigrants, mostly from Spain and Italy. Economic stagnation
and political decline in the mid-20th century also saw many rural folk flood
into Montevideo's city slums.

TYPICAL MONTEVIDEANOS

A city of lovers (of the arts and big drinking) not fighters (bar-room brawls
are rare), Montevideanos pride themselves on being the opposite of the
hot-headed Latin-American stereotype. Sunday is family day, a time to
throw half a cow on the *asado* (spit roast), sip some maté and stroll along
the river.

DEFINING EXPERIENCE

Perusing the opulent furnishings of Montevideo's 19th-century elite at the
Museo Romántico, riding bus 64 along the riverfront Rambla, then tucking
into a seriously sumptuous steak in the Mercado del Puerto.

STRENGTHS
◢ Historical Ciudad Vieja
◢ Laid-back atmosphere
◢ Museo Histórico Nacional
◢ White sandy beaches
◢ Mercado del Puerto
◢ Rich artistic and cultural heritage
◢ Teatro Solís (superb acoustics and a quality roster of local and international performers)
◢ Spanish, Art Deco and Italian styles
◢ The neoclassical Palacio Legislativo (Parliament)

WEAKNESSES
◢ A throbbing decades-old hangover from economic stagnation
◢ Dependency on Argentine tourism
◢ Increasing social divide
◢ Shabby (not chic) city appearance
◢ Rising street crime

GOLD STAR
Montevideo's port market, Mercado del Puerto – it was the continent's finest when it opened back in 1868. The impressive wrought-iron superstructure bustles with craftspeople, street musicians, outstanding seafood restaurants and traditional *parrillas* (steakhouses).

STARRING ROLE IN...
◢ *State of Siege* (1972)
◢ *Burnt Money* (2000)
◢ *Between the Moon and Montevideo* (2001)

See the crumbling vestiges of grand 19th-century neoclassical buildings, legacies of the beef boom, in Ciudad Vieja.

Eat obscenely big steaks at *parrillas* inside the Mercado del Puerto.

Drink *medio y medio* (a knockout blend of local sparkling and white wines) in Bartolomé Mitre, Montevideo's most happening bar precinct.

Do ride bus 64 along the riverfront Rambla – Montevideo's beaches get better the further you go.

Watch local football rivals Nacional and Peñarol at Montevideo's Estadio Centenario.

Buy everything from antique knick-knacks to fried fish at Montevideo's sprawling outdoor market, the Feria de Tristán Narvaja.

After dark whip that rose between your teeth and take on the tango at Fun Fun in the Mercado Central.

MICHAEL COYNE / GETTY IMAGES

A SOLITARY PALM LENDS SOME SHADE TO THOSE WORKING WITHIN THE INDEPENDENCE BUILDING AT PLAZA INDEPENDENCIA.

CHECKING OUT THE CITY FROM MONT ROYAL VIEWPOINT.

Montréal

DATE OF BIRTH 1642; WHEN THE LURE OF FUR AND SOULS IN NEED OF SAVING – IN THIS CASE IROQUOIS – SAW PAUL DE CHOMEDEY DE MAISONNEUVE FOUND VILLE-MARIE **ADDRESS** CANADA (MAP 1, R2)
HEIGHT 57M **SIZE** 449 SQ KM **POPULATION** 3.8 MILLION
LONELY PLANET RANKING 020

As the locals say, it's Europe and America rolled into one: achingly hip, proudly diverse, bilingual, and all set in a rousing frontier landscape.

ANATOMY

Montréal occupies an island on the north shore of the St Lawrence River. Skyscrapers mix with 18th- and 19th-century greystones in the distinct neighbourhoods that cluster around Mont Royal, known locally as 'the mountain'. 'The Main', busy rue Saint Denis and blvd Saint Laurent, delineates traditional French–English boundaries. Its grid pattern streets don't often see gridlock, with commuters happy to use the metro and bus system or pedal power.

PEOPLE

Although two thirds of Montréalers claim French as their first language, today half speak both French and English. Traditional boundaries are fast eroding, due to a younger global generation and a large number of migrants. Montréal has a diverse ethnic profile: 10% have Italian heritage and there are also significant Haitian, Chinese, Portuguese, Jewish, Greek and various Middle Eastern communities.

TYPICAL MONTRÉALER

They don't earn as much as their Toronto counterparts, but Montréalers are increasingly happy to stay put, citing charming but affordable housing, a fantastic festival calendar, a sense of cultural renaissance and business confidence. Many grew up with traditional values – over 70% are Roman Catholic – but are also laid-back. Montréalers are stylish and fanatical about food. They love the outdoors. Hockey is the favourite spectator sport.

DEFINING EXPERIENCE

White-water rafting at the Lachine rapids, agonising over the outfit (Kamkyl or Marc Jacobs?) for a meal at a Plateau *bistrot*, finishing with Québécois *lait cru* (raw milk) cheese, nabbing a sofa at Jello.

STRENGTHS

◢ The Mountain
◢ Nightlife
◢ Underground City (all 29km of it)
◢ Habitat 67, architect Moshe Safdie's iconic vision of urban life
◢ Tam Tams on summer Sundays
◢ Basilique Notre Dame
◢ Franco-frontier cuisine
◢ Mile End and Plateau
◢ Musée d'Art Contemporain
◢ Thriving indie band scene
◢ Quartier Latin
◢ Festival International de Jazz

WEAKNESSES

◢ Second-fiddle chip on shoulder
◢ Spiralling rents
◢ Subarctic cold snaps of -40°C
◢ Anglophone–Francophone tension on St Jean-Baptiste Day
◢ Gas-guzzling habits

GOLD STAR

Multicultural cuisine – affordable, eclectic and sophisticated.

STARRING ROLE IN...

◢ *Jesus of Montreal* (1989)
◢ *The Score* (2001)
◢ *Les Invasions barbares* (The Barbarian Invasions, 2003)
◢ *Le Survenant* (2005)
◢ *Bonheur d'Occasion* by Gabrielle Roy

See the Old Port from the observation tower of the Chapelle Notre Dame de Bonsecours, the Sailors' Church.

Eat *poutine foie gras* (French fries with cheese curds and foie gras) at the Plateau's Au Pied de Cochon.

Drink a Païenne (blond ale) at the Brasserie Dieu du Ciel.

Do an icy lap at the blissfully bucolic Lac Aux Castors rink.

Watch Cinémathèque québécoise's Ciné-Jazz program, part of the behemoth annual Jazz Fest.

Buy fur without the guilt: recycled pelt products from stylish Harricana.

After dark and, in true Montréal style, after day has dawned, shake your thing at Stereo.

STREET GARDENS, LIKE THESE IN THE QUARTIER LATIN, LINE THE CITY'S RESIDENTIAL AREAS.

THE 40-YEAR-OLD BIOSPHERE REMAINS THE CITY'S CENTRE OF ENVIRONMENTAL AWARENESS.

THE FLAGS OF MONTRÉAL, QUÉBEC AND CANADA APPEAR THROUGH THE COLOURED FAÇADE OF THE MONTRÉAL CONVENTION CENTER.

Moscow

NICKNAME THE THIRD ROME **DATE OF BIRTH** 1147; THE CITY WAS
FIRST MENTIONED IN THE HISTORIC CHRONICLES WHEN PRINCE
YURY DOLGORUKY INVITED HIS ALLIES TO A BANQUET THERE
ADDRESS RUSSIA (MAP 4, U6) **HEIGHT** 156M **SIZE** 1035 SQ KM
POPULATION 11.5 MILLION **LONELY PLANET RANKING** 061

**Russia's relentless economic motor and the
biggest city in Europe by several million people,
brutal, over-whelming, fascinating Moscow is an
absolute must for anyone wanting to see what's
happened to Eastern Europe since the end
of communism.**

ANATOMY

The Moscow River weaves its way through the enormous city, with
the Kremlin and Red Sq on the northern bank. The centre is defined by
the enormous garden ring road around which you'll find many of the
city's most important buildings. Controversial former Mayor Luzhkov
was a big fan of modern buildings and had little or no interest in
heritage, which led to a shocking policy of destroying any building
getting in the way of more high-rise apartment blocks or mega casinos
for Moscow's new rich.

PEOPLE

With nearly three million unregistered inhabitants from elsewhere in
Russia, it's hard to give an accurate breakdown of who lives here, but the
city is fairly homogeneously Russian (and unlike other large European
cities, it's almost entirely white). Despite this, there are significant and
well-established groups of Caucasians, Central Asians and Ukrainians, not
to mention a huge expat population of mainly businesspeople living and
working in the city.

TYPICAL MUSCOVITE

Dour, mordant, sardonic – it's hard to overstate the initial hardness of your
average Muscovite and this often skews the perception of locals for anyone
here for just a few days. However, break the ice with a Muscovite (as with
any Russian) and you'll be shown an entirely new set of characteristics:
funny, warm, interested and welcoming.

DMITRY MORDVINTSEV / GETTY IMAGES

A TRAIN PULLS INTO A REFINED METRO STATION OF CHANDELIERS AND DECORATIVE ARCHES.

MUSCOVITES THAW OUT IN THE STEAMING OPEN-AIR THERMAL SWIMMING POOL.

A STUDENT GETS EMERGENCY WARDROBE ASSISTANCE AT THE MOSCOW CIRCUS SCHOOL.

DEFINING EXPERIENCE

Red Sq in the snow, with flurries around the domes of St Basil's, soldiers goose-stepping around Lenin's pyramidal mausoleum, and escaping in the warmth of a side-street bar for some warming borscht.

STRENGTHS

- The efficient and aesthetically impressive Moscow metro
- The city's architectural wealth
- The smell of power in the air

WEAKNESSES

- The weather
- The city's sheer inhuman size
- The vast expense
- The economic disparity

GOLD STAR

The Moscow metro. Hands down the best in the world – over 180 stations, used by nine million people a day and breathtakingly efficient. Moreover, it's a joy to travel on, with chandelier and marble-clad platforms, socialist realist art and political sculpture.

STARRING ROLE IN...

- *The Saint* (1997)
- *The Barber of Siberia* (1998)
- *Night Watch* (2004)

See the magnificent cathedrals inside the Kremlin.

Eat wonderful Russian and Ukrainian peasant food at Shinok.

Drink vodka – pretty much every bar or shop has a huge and unusual selection.

Do not miss your chance to see Lenin up close and personal at his mausoleum.

Watch the offerings at the world-famous Bolshoi Theater.

Buy everything and anything in Moscow's commercial heart, the Novy Arbat.

After dark head to friendly clubs Kitaysky Lyotchik or Propaganda for clubbing without the attitude.

Mumbai

NICKNAME GATEWAY TO INDIA **DATE OF BIRTH** 1661; WHEN THE
HARBOUR AND FISHING VILLAGES WERE ACQUIRED BY THE BRITISH
ADDRESS INDIA (MAP 9, A6) **HEIGHT** 11M **SIZE** 440 SQ KM
POPULATION 12.4 MILLION (CITY); 20.7 MILLION (METRO AREA)
LONELY PLANET RANKING 077

**India's most liberal city is irrepressibly vibrant, with
grand colonial and Art Deco architecture, double-
decker buses, teeming bazaars, an unparalleled range
of restaurants and Bollywood starlets and wannabes.**

ANATOMY

The city sprawls across seven islands fused into an artificial isthmus. The
principal part of the city is concentrated at the southern end of the island
known as South Mumbai and the southernmost peninsula is Colaba.
Further north, across Mahim Creek, are the suburbs of Greater Mumbai,
where many of the best restaurants and nightspots can be found. Taxis,
double-decker buses on major routes, ferries and two suburban train lines
are the way to get about.

PEOPLE

The majority of Mumbai's millions are Hindu, but there is a sizable
Muslim minority. There are also Christians, Buddhists, Jains and Parsis.
About a third of the population lives in squalid *chawls* (cramped,
makeshift, miserable hovels) and many live on the streets.

TYPICAL MUMBAIKAR

Hustling Mumbaikars lead India with amazing wealth and astonishing
poverty. They enjoy the most liberal and cosmopolitan city of India.
Wealthier citizens work in Bollywood, nuclear research, commerce, the
media and advertising – and work is their focus; poorer citizens make of
life what they can. Mumbaikars are relaxed and vivacious.

DEFINING EXPERIENCE

Taking a boat out to the Elephanta Caves from the Gateway of India,
walking over to the Chhatrapati Shivaji Museum and Jehangir Art Gallery,
wandering through the Chor (Thieves) Bazaar, eating at the Revolving
Restaurant and then driving Marine Dr in the evening.

LIGHTS, CAMERA, SONG! ACTORS IN GLITTERY COSTUMES PREPARE FOR ANOTHER TAKE ON THE SET OF A BOLLYWOOD FILM.

MUSLIM WOMEN IN VIBRANT CLOTHING PRAY AT A CITY MOSQUE.

ABSTRACT TABLES AND CHAIRS ON THE LAWNS OF THE MUMBAI CRICKET CLUB.

THE GREAT PANI PURI SALESMAN UPHOLDS HIS REPUTATION ON CHOWPATTY BEACH.

STRENGTHS

◢ Chhatrapati Shivaji Museum
◢ Rajabai Clocktower
◢ Gothic-style buildings
◢ Crawford Market
◢ Chowpatty Beach
◢ Mahatma Gandhi Museum
◢ Hanging Gardens
◢ Cricket on the *maidan* (an open grassed area in a city)

WEAKNESSES

◢ Traffic
◢ Enormous wealth disparities
◢ Vicious gang warfare controlled by underworld dons
◢ The religious fault-line

GOLD STAR

Mumbai's transposed European building styles are fascinating. Many Victorian buildings were constructed on the edge of Oval Maidan in the 1860s and '70s. The western edge of the *maidans* out towards Marine Dr is now lined with an impressive collection of Art Deco apartment blocks.

STARRING ROLE IN...

◢ *Midnight's Children* by Salman Rushdie
◢ *Maximum City: Bombay Lost and Found* by Suketu Mehta
◢ *Shantaram* by Gregory David Robert
◢ *Slumdog Millionaire* (2008)

See the sun setting into the Arabian Sea from Marine Dr.

Eat *puri* (flat dough that puffs up when deep fried) with chickpeas.

Drink chic cocktails at Flavours in the Ambassadors Hotel in Churchgate.

Do take a boat trip out to Elephanta Island for the caves and carved temples.

Watch flamboyant wedding parties on Chowpatty Beach.

Buy silks and saris from all over India at Sheetal on B Desai Rd.

After dark spot Bollywood stars at the nightclub of the moment.

Munich

DATE OF BIRTH 1158; WHEN HEINRICH DER LÖWE (HENRY THE LION) BECAME RULER **ADDRESS** GERMANY (MAP 5, M2) **HEIGHT** 524M **SIZE** 310 SQ KM **POPULATION** 1.3 MILLION **LONELY PLANET RANKING** 037

Regularly voted by Germans as the most desirable place to live, the Bavarian capital's beguiling résumé includes grand architecture, world-class museums, beer halls, well-dressed people and the world-famous Oktoberfest.

ANATOMY

The *Altstadt* (old town) is home to most of the city's major attractions, which unfurl from the central Marienplatz. North of here is the museum and theatre district, the Residenz. East of the Residenz buzzes bohemian Schwabing and the enormous Englischer Garten. Across the Isar River, which runs through the eastern part of the city from south to north, are trendy Haidhausen and moneyed Bogenhausen. The Olympiapark, captivating Schloss Nymphenburg and multicultural Neuhausen, lie to the northwest. Besides walking, Munich's public-transport network (MVV) is the best way to get around.

PEOPLE

Munich is Germany's third-largest city. Around one in five is not of German origin, with the largest ethnic groups from Turkey and Eastern Europe. The majority are Catholic, but there are also many Lutherans.

TYPICAL MÜNCHENER

Müncheners are a mix of cultural sophistication and traditional values. They are proud of their Bavarian heritage and assert their traditions by wearing *Tracht* (lederhosen for the men and dirndls for the ladies). They are characterised by an independent streak, with Bavaria holding a special legal status as a 'free state'. The people of Munich are known for being affluent, polite and groomed but are not averse to nude bathing and sunbathing in the Englischer Garten.

DEFINING EXPERIENCE

Admiring the Renaissance art at the Alte Pinakothek then soaking up the sun in the Englischer Garten and cooling off with a stein at the Chinesischer Turm, before hitting the shops on Maximilianstrasse.

RECIPE FOR TROUBLE – A MERRY-GO-ROUND AT THE OKTOBERFEST BEER FESTIVAL.

STRENGTHS

- Sausages, particularly the *Weisswurst* (veal sausage)
- Breweries (half of Germany's breweries are in Bavaria), beer halls (eg Hofbräuhaus), beer gardens and steins
- Marienplatz
- Schloss Nymphenburg
- Lenbachhaus
- Pinakothek museums
- *Blaue Reiter* art
- Residenzmuseum and Museum Brandhorst
- Low unemployment rate
- Low air-pollution levels
- The Wittlesbachs, who ruled Bavaria for over 700 years
- Opera and Bayerische Staatsoper
- Münchener Philharmoniker
- *Jugendstil* (German Art Nouveau)
- Skiing in the Bavarian Alps

WEAKNESSES

- Meat-heavy cuisine
- The Föhn – static-charged wind from the south that gives people headaches and makes them irritable

GOLD STAR

Bavarian culture.

STARRING ROLE IN...

- *Munich* (2005)
- *Marlene* (1999)
- *Herr und Hund* by Thomas Mann

See the stunning Schloss Nymphenburg with its majestic interiors and sculpted gardens.

Eat traditional Bavarian fare in the tiny but authentic Hundskugel (Munich's oldest restaurant), founded in 1440.

Drink as much beer as you can bear at the mammoth Oktoberfest.

Do take a stroll around the endlessly enticing Englischer Garten and feel free to strip off and sunbathe.

Watch the characters of the delightful glockenspiel (carillon) dance and celebrate on Marienplatz.

Buy funky street fashion in the boutiques of Schwabing and Haidhausen.

After dark pick your best party clothes and mix with celebs at P1.

QUENCH YOUR THIRST IN THE BEER GARDEN OF THE AUGUSTINER BREWERY.

THE STYLISH ENTRANCE HALL OF THE PINAKOTHEK DER MODERNE.

BICYCLES ARE A POPULAR WAY OF GETTING AROUND MUNICH.

YOUNG MEN AND THEIR FAITHFUL DONKEYS IN MUSCAT.

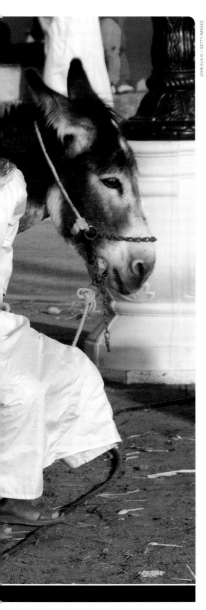

Muscat

NICKNAME THE THREE CITIES **DATE OF BIRTH** 1741; IMAM AHMED BIN SAID, HAVING EXPELLED IRANIAN RULE, MADE MUSCAT THE CAPITAL OF THE NEWLY INDEPENDENT OMAN **ADDRESS** OMAN (MAP 8, G7) **HEIGHT** 5M **POPULATION** 734,000 **LONELY PLANET RANKING** 107

Elegance in a concealed harbour – Muscat is a dichotomy of tradition and progression, where camels cruise through the city on the back of Toyota pick-ups and the domed buildings of the walled city are inhabited by modern Omanians with mobile phones.

ANATOMY

Wedged between the sea and a jagged spine of mountains, Muscat comprises a string of suburbs, each with its own attractions. The gated city of Muscat sits on a natural harbour and is flanked on the coast by Mutrah, which stretches along an attractive corniche of latticed buildings and mosques. Inland lies Ruwi, Oman's 'little India', the commercial and transport hub of the capital. Plentiful public transport (buses) runs through the three cities. The highway parallels the coast and passes through its main attractions.

PEOPLE

Although the city's population is predominantly Arab and Arabic speaking, an Indian merchant community has existed in Muscat for at least 200 years, and English is also enthusiastically spoken. Muscatians follow the Ibadi sect of Islam and are tolerant of other religious groups. Under the auspices of a progressive leader, Sultan Qaboos, the city has reawakened into a modern culture.

TYPICAL MUSCATIAN

Muscatians are as paradoxical as their beloved three cities. They will fashionably wear a headscarf and silk *abeyya* (black outer robe) over Western clothing; receive text messages on eating well while becoming increasingly obese on fast food; and contemplate genetically modified crop rotations, while looking at the cloudless sky and realising that they haven't been praying loud enough. They are hard-working and modern, the women motivated and politically active. They embrace rapid change with a healthy scepticism.

CUBS AND SCOUTS FIND COMMON GROUND THE WORLD OVER.

THE ART OF MARRIAGE – A BRIDE CELEBRATES LAYYAT AL-HENNA ON THE EVE OF HER WEDDING.

THE WATCHTOWER MONUMENT ONCE FORMED PART OF THE CITY'S ANCIENT FORTIFICATION.

DEFINING EXPERIENCE

Visiting the Marina at dawn to inspect the daily catch, enjoying fresh juice and *shwarma* (meat stuffed in a pocket of pita-type bread with chopped tomatoes and garnish) at the souq (market), then stocking up on savoury pastries, *halwa* (halva) and dates to picnic by the water, discussing the afternoon's wet-pitch football game.

STRENGTHS

- Sultan Qaboos
- (Almost) endless stretches of beach
- Domed buildings
- International-standard health care
- Walled city of Muscat
- Mountain walks
- Water sports
- The Muscat Festival (mid-January to mid-February)
- Excellent bird-watching
- Spotlessly clean streets
- Progressive attitudes

WEAKNESSES

- High cost of living
- Public beaches (which may make women feel uncomfortable)
- Limited shopping and entertainment
- Lack of Arabic coffee

GOLD STAR

Mutrah's souq – an outdoor warren of aisle-like alleyways selling everything from frankincense to fruit juice.

STARRING ROLE IN...

- *The Icarus Agenda* by Robert Ludlum

See 125 years of graffitied records left by sailors on the harbour walls.

Eat sizzling kebabs at the Khargeen Café.

Drink snake coffee, which the head waiter performs by setting fire to an orange peel, at Mumtaz Mahal.

Do visit the perfect bathing spot at picturesque Jissah Beach.

Watch the fireworks and dance displays at the fabulous Muscat Festival.

Buy and bargain for frankincense in Muscat's Mutrah souq.

After dark pop down to Al-Ghazal for some pub grub and a quiz night.

THAT'S HOW WE ROLL – REAL LIFE ON THE RAILWAY.

Nairobi

NICKNAME SAFARI CAPITAL OF THE WORLD **DATE OF BIRTH** 1901:
AFTER EMERGING AS THE ADMINISTRATIVE CENTRE FOR THE
UGANDA RAILWAY, NAIROBI BECAME THE CAPITAL OF THE BRITISH
PROTECTORATE **ADDRESS** KENYA (MAP 7, F2) **HEIGHT** 1820M
SIZE 680 SQ KM **POPULATION** 3.1 MILLION (CITY); 4.2 MILLION (METRO
AREA) **LONELY PLANET RANKING** 135

**From a rugged iron-roofed frontier town with rhinos
and lions roaming in the streets, Nairobi has, in the
last 100 years, emerged as a bustling cosmopolitan
city set amid the vast wilderness of Africa.**

ANATOMY

As the gateway to East Africa, the Kenyan capital is surrounded by the
snowcapped Mt Kenya and the plains of the Masai Mara National Reserve.
This young city, with its modern skyline and few remaining colonial-era
buildings, spreads out from the centre – where the main touristy sights are
located – into the working-class suburbs, the wealthy garden suburbs of
expats and the sprawl of shantytowns. Getting around Nairobi is easy, but
often treacherous: there are crowded but cheap and plentiful speed-demon
matatus (shared minibus taxis), trains and buses.

PEOPLE

The population comprises indigenous tribes, a significant number of expats
and an increasing number of refugees from surrounding nations. Besides
English (the official language) and the widely spoken Swahili, there are also
many ethnic languages. Most of the population is either Protestant, Roman
Catholic or Muslim; a small percentage are animist.

TYPICAL NAIROBIAN

Nairobians are largely working-class, even though there are rich and poor
elements of society. They like going out for a drink and socialising in cafés,
restaurants and clubs. Sport is popular – athletics, golf, rugby and cricket –
as are Indian and mainstream movies, and shopping.

DEFINING EXPERIENCE

Sharing a table with locals and enjoying coffee, cake and a newspaper at the
Nairobi Java House, then heading *Out of Africa* to wander around the
colonial house and gardens of the Karen Blixen Museum before heading
down the road to the pub in the Karen Blixen Coffee Garden.

587

MAASAI FOR THE MASSES – BRIGHT BEADWORK ADORNS BRACELETS AND BELTS.

STRENGTHS

- Excellent nightspots and good music scene
- Hot, but not extreme, temperatures (due to the high altitude)
- Westlands Triangle Curios Market
- White-water rafting on the Tana River
- Many craft emporiums
- Good selection of restaurants and bars
- Text Book Centre (one of the best bookshops in East Africa)
- Excellent outdoor activities

WEAKNESSES

- Poverty
- Rampant crime (the city is referred to as Nairobbery by the locals)
- Political instability (and attendant violent demonstrations)
- Ever-present prostitutes
- AIDS epidemic

GOLD STAR

Proximity to Africa's natural wonders – just a few kilometres from the air-conditioned luxury of the city is the species-rich Nairobi National Park, full of famous African beasts, hundreds of species of birds and exotic plant life, while only an hour out of town the thrills and spills of white-water rafting await the adventurous. Trekking and mountain-climbing fun on Mt Kenya (5199m) is also close by – only a couple of hours out of town.

STARRING ROLE IN...

- *Nowhere in Africa* (2003)
- *Nairobi Affair* (1988)
- *Out of Africa* (1985)
- *Present Moment* by Marjorie Oludhe Magoye

See a gleeful group of baby elephants being bottlefed at the David Sheldrick Wildlife Trust.

Eat excellent Swahili stews and curries at a local restaurant.

Drink an ice-cold Tusker as the heat of the day begins to fade.

Do learn how much of Nairobi lives by taking a tour of Kibera, the world's second-largest shanty town.

Watch a range of African bands at popular bar-restaurant Simmers.

Buy good quality *kikoi* (cotton sarongs) from shops on Biashara St.

After dark join the steamy drinkin' and dancin' mayhem at the bizarre spacecraftlike New Florida, locally known as the 'Mad House'.

NAIROBIAN CHILDREN CLAP TO THEIR OWN TUNE.

SHARE A DRINK AT THE LORD DELAMER BAR IN THE NORFOLK HOTEL.

Naples

DATE OF BIRTH 474 BC; WHEN GREEKS FROM NEARBY CUMAE
FOUNDED NEOPLIS **ADDRESS** ITALY (MAP 5, N7) **HEIGHT** 110M
SIZE 117 SQ KM **POPULATION** 1 MILLION (CITY); 4.5 MILLION (METRO
AREA) **LONELY PLANET RANKING** 097

Naples is a city for those who relish the intense urban experience: raucous, polluted, crowded and chaotic, but never dull.

ANATOMY

Naples has a heart-wrenchingly beautiful, if precarious, setting. Facing a crescent-shaped bay, Italy's largest port is overlooked by Mt Vesuvius. The chaotic *centro storico* (inner city) follows the grid of its ancient counterpart that lies below: Via Toledo, Naples' main street, leads north from Piazza Trieste e Trento, next to the waterfront's landmark, Castel Nuovo. Funiculars and the metro service residential neighbourhoods; elsewhere foot and scooter are more efficient than bus or cars.

PEOPLE

Naples' history is one of both occupation (as the local dialect flush with Arabic, Spanish, French and English words attests) and emigration. Neapolitans now stay, and though they imagine themselves as a homogeneous Italian-born group, they are increasingly joined by immigrants from Asia, North Africa and Eastern Europe.

TYPICAL NEAPOLITAN

Neapolitans embrace the Italian stereotype – theatrical, food-obsessed and passionate. They don't earn as much as most other Italians, but that doesn't stop them eating out and staying up. They also go to the theatre, rack up astronomical mobile-phone bills and drive maniacally. The notion of family is still strong; once young Neapolitans marry and move out of home, they will have more children than other Italians.

DEFINING EXPERIENCE

Waking after a siesta to a sweet, strong espresso, a chat with the barista, hopping on your Piaggio to Mergellina for the evening *passeggiata* (promenade), grabbing a pizza and folding it in quarters, eating it as you stroll along staring out to Capri, then trying a new flavour of gelato.

SIGHTSEEING AT THE NAPLES CATHEDRAL.

A GREENGROCER AMONG HIS PRODUCE IN THE ANCIENT ROMAN MARKETPLACE OF VIA TRIBUNALI.

STRENGTHS

- *Sfogliatella* – the *dolce* (sweet) of Naples, flaky and ricotta-filled
- The late-night *passeggiata*
- A Unesco-listed *centro storico* that's historical but also vividly alive
- Ferries to Capri, Genoa, Palermo or Tunisia
- *Mozzarella di bufala* (buffalo-milk mozzarella)
- Feeling like you have the Museo Archeologico Nazionale to yourself
- Leg- and lung-saving funiculars
- Ospedale delle Bambole – the delightfully kooky doll's hospital

PIAZZA PLEBISCITO'S OBSTACLES INCLUDE PERFORMERS AND HERDS OF NERVOUS TOURISTS.

WEAKNESSES

- The Camorra (Naples' home-grown Mafia)
- Cavalier attitude to the preservation and display of artefacts
- Filthy and crumbling historic treasures
- Chaotic traffic
- Street hustlers and petty criminals
- Air pollution

GOLD STAR

Street life – Neapolitans take to the piazze and the *vicoli* (backstreets) for breakfast, lunch and dinner, and for a lot of the time in between.

STARRING ROLE IN...

- *Paisà* (Paisan, 1946)
- *L'Oro di Napoli* (The Gold of Naples, 1954)
- *Vito e gli altri* (Vito and the Others, 1991)
- *Il Postino* (The Postman, 1994)
- *The Talented Mr Ripley* (1999)
- *Gomorrah* by Roberto Savian
- *Midnight in Sicily* by Peter Robb

See the chaos below, and Vesuvius beyond, from the peaceful piazze of the Vomero.

Eat a *margherita* at Da Michele; why can't pizza always be this good?

Drink a local *limoncello* (lemon-based liqueur) on ice at Bar Lazzarella.

Do a run around Parco di Capodimonte.

Watch the dancing to electro-pop on the beach at Arenile Reload on a hot July night.

Buy *presepi* (nativity scene) figures in Via San Gregorio Armeno.

After dark stumble across the Argentinian tango dancers in the Galleria Umberto, and join them if your tango is up to it.

THE EXCLUSIVE 16TH-CENTURY PROMENADE OF SANTA LUCIA.

New Orleans

NICKNAME THE BIG EASY **DATE OF BIRTH** 1718; WHEN SIEUR DE BIENVILLE FOUNDED NOUVELLE ORLÉANS **ADDRESS** USA (MAP 1, O9) **HEIGHT** 2M **SIZE** 468 SQ KM **POPULATION** 1.1 MILLION **LONELY PLANET RANKING** 039

New Orleans will always seduce with soulful jazz wafting out of saloon doors, people leaning over wrought-iron balconies on sultry summer nights and masked party-goers turning up the heat at Carnival.

ANATOMY

New Orleans lies in reclaimed swampland sandwiched between the Mississippi to the south and Lake Pontchartrain to the north. The heart of the original city is the historic French Quarter (the Vieux Carré). Southwest of here is the Central Business District (CBD). The arty Warehouse District and bohemian Lower Garden District are upriver (paradoxically this is south) of the French Quarter. Adjacent to the Lower Garden District are the historic homes of the Garden District. Faubourg Marigny to the east attracts a mostly gay crowd, while the mainly black neighbourhood of Faubourg Tremé to the north is known for its music. Catch a local bus or streetcar to get around town.

PEOPLE

Well over half of New Orleans' population is black. Whites make up one third and Hispanics are a growing minority. A group of Asian immigrants lives mainly in the Versailles area and on the West Bank. Thanks to its French and Spanish heritage, the population is largely Roman Catholic.

TYPICAL NEW ORLEANIAN

New Orleans is a fairly poor city with a small tax base to support its social services and education. Wages in Louisiana, as measured in income per capita, are the lowest in the USA after Mississippi and Arkansas, and one in four people live on or near the poverty line (most of the poor people are black). New Orleanians are a friendly bunch and welcoming towards visitors (although you're not really part of the club unless you have generations of New Orleans blood coursing through your veins). Life in the Big Easy is for enjoying and service can occasionally be slow. But New Orleanians don't worry about that – they know that having a good time is more important than having a quick time!

THE FURIOUS SOUNDS OF NEW ORLEANS JAZZ RAISING THE ROOF AT PRESERVATION HALL.

CARNIVAL BEADS AND JAZZY TRINKETS OVERLAY AN EMBLEMATIC IMAGE OF MARDI GRAS.

JAMMING IN THE SUNSHINE.

DEFINING EXPERIENCE

Starting the day with a coffee at Café du Monde before wandering around the French Quarter, relaxing in Jackson Sq and gearing up for an evening of live music at one of the French Quarter's many excellent venues.

STRENGTHS

- New Orleans Jazz & Heritage Festival
- Mardi Gras
- The beautiful Garden District
- Riverboat calliope music
- St Charles Ave streetcar
- The balconies and courtyards of Royal St
- St Louis Cemetery No 1
- Creole restaurants of Royal St and Bourbon St
- The French Quarter
- Ursuline Convent
- Tranquil Bayou St John
- New Orleans Museum of Art

WEAKNESSES

- Racial inequality during the Civil War and Reconstruction
- Risks of flooding – Hurricane Katrina devastated the city in 2005

GOLD STAR

Jazz.

STARRING ROLE IN...

- *JFK* (1991)
- *Dead Man Walking* (1995)
- *Easy Rider* (1969)
- *A Streetcar Named Desire* (1951)
- *The Big Easy* (1986)

See the city from aboard a riverboat.

Eat gumbo at local favourite K-Paul's Louisiana Kitchen.

Drink in the candlelit Lafitte's Blacksmith Shop, allegedly an old pirate haunt.

Do wander through the French Quarter, discovering New Orleans' history at the Louisiana State Museum and soaking up the atmosphere.

Watch the parades, floats, revellers and debauchery of Mardi Gras.

Buy local tunes from the Louisiana Music Factory, which also has live music on Saturday.

After dark check out the nightly jazz jams at Preservation Hall on St Peter.

BOURBON STREET'S BALCONIES.

NEW YORK BY NIGHT – THE SKYLINE HAS CHANGED BUT THE SPIRIT HASN'T.

New York City

NICKNAME THE BIG APPLE; THE CAPITAL OF THE WORLD; GOTHAM
DATE OF BIRTH 1609; WHEN DUTCH WEST INDIA COMPANY EMPLOYEE
HENRY HUDSON ARRIVED **ADDRESS** USA (MAP 1, S4) **HEIGHT** 96M
SIZE 1572 SQ KM **POPULATION** 18.9 MILLION **LONELY PLANET RANKING** 002

Not much about New York City is subtle – it boasts vibrant architecture, world-class art, fashion and entertainment, snarling traffic, spirited politics, and a rich and radical history infused with the tradition of immigration that endures today.

ANATOMY

New York Harbor has 105 sq km of inland waterways and 1240km of direct shoreline. Grid systems are at work on the city streets in the five boroughs of this fairly flat city. Transport is a mixture of subway, buses, honking cabs and ferries all crammed into roads, tunnels and bridges.

PEOPLE

New York is a city for the young; the median age of residents is 34. Less than half of the population is white, a third is Latino and a quarter is black. Asians comprise less than a tenth. One-third of New Yorkers are foreign-born and hundreds of languages are spoken. Religiously, New York is much more Semitic than the rest of the country: about 2% of the national population is Jewish, but in the city it's about 12%. Around 70% are Christian.

TYPICAL NEW YORKER

New Yorkers have attitude, and they're not afraid to use it. They're tough, brave, jaded, overworked and intensely focused. Ask one of those blank-faced strap-hanging subway travellers for directions, however, and they'll respond with explicit instructions and a smile, and perhaps even escort you themselves if it's on the way to where they're headed. A lot of it is drama: barking into mobile (cell) phones, marching down the street – these are citizens for whom being swamped with work becomes a point of pride, frequently trying to one-up each other with tales of endless responsibilities and deadlines.

DEFINING EXPERIENCE

Hopping on a subway and heading to Little Italy in the Bronx, going for a sunset run around the sparkling Central Park reservoir, and kicking off the evening with a martini somewhere fabulous.

TAXIS TAKE OFF LIKE RACE CARS IN THE WORLD'S MOST IMPATIENT CITY.

STRENGTHS

- Restaurant week
- US Open tennis tournament
- New York City Marathon
- Macy's Thanksgiving Day Parade
- Rockefeller Center Christmas tree lighting
- Dean & DeLuca
- Lower Broadway
- Central Park
- The Dakota Building
- Brownstone streets in Brooklyn that look like Sesame St
- Greenwich Village
- Alphabet City
- Gourmet delivery
- Sylvia's on Lenox in Harlem
- Narrow skyscraper canyons

WEAKNESSES

- The Donald and his glitzy buildings
- The coffee
- Aggressive cab drivers and territorial contests over parking spaces
- The relentless keeping up
- Exposed, heavily populated coastal areas with little protection from major storm surges

GOLD STAR

Manhattan, the isle of joy, is a thing of wonder. Nothing quite beats the pleasure of walking out onto the streets to be surrounded by the incredible variety of life, the brusqueness and the energy.

STARRING ROLE IN...

- *Sex and the City* (1998–2004)
- *Underworld* by Don DeLillo
- *Breakfast at Tiffany's* by Truman Capote
- *The Catcher in the Rye* by JD Salinger

WEST SIDE STORY – MANHATTAN'S NEW HIGHLINE PARK RUNS ALONG A DISUSED ELEVATED TRAIN LINE.

- *The Great Gatsby* by F Scott Fitzgerald
- *New York, New York* (1977)
- *Basketball Diaries* (1995)
- *Desperately Seeking Susan* (1985)
- *Kids* (1995)
- *Manhattan* (1979)
- *Midnight Cowboy* (1969)
- *Saturday Night Fever* (1977)
- *Taxi Driver* (1976)

See the 360-degree view from the Empire State Building.

Eat good on-the-go grub from street vendors hawking everything from hot dogs and tacos to homemade soups and felafel sandwiches.

Drink New York State wine from the excellent wine bar Il Posto Accanto.

Do visit the Metropolitan Museum of Art, with extensive collections of American, European, Asian, African, Egyptian and Graeco-Roman art.

Watch conspicuous consumption all over Manhattan.

Buy quirk at the gallery stores at the Museum of Modern Art (MoMA) or cutting-edge fashion in the streets around Lower Broadway.

After dark New York truly never sleeps, so find somewhere locally or jump in a cab for downtown.

601

Nuuk

NICKNAME GODTHÅB (LITERALLY 'GOOD HOPE' IN DANISH) **DATE OF BIRTH** 1728; THE TOWN WAS FOUNDED BY THE NORWEGIAN MISSIONARY HANS EGEDE AS THE FIRST ALL-YEAR EUROPEAN COLONY AND TRADING POST IN GREENLAND **ADDRESS** GREENLAND (MAP 4, A2) **HEIGHT** 20M **SIZE** 690 SQ KM **POPULATION** 16,000 **LONELY PLANET RANKING** 165

Nuuk is the perfect base for discovering Greenland and Inuit culture – then head off into the mountains or onto the fjords for spectacular adventure tourism.

ANATOMY
Situated on the mouth of the Godthåbsfiord, Nuuk commands an impressive fjord system and is backed by a panorama of mountains, particularly Mt Sermitsiaq. The architecture is a mix of older homes of real Greenlandic charm and rows of spirit-crushing modern housing. Explore the world's northernmost capital city by boat and snowmobile.

PEOPLE
This city's population is bicultural, with Greenlanders (Inuit) forming the majority and Danes the minority. The two thought systems are often diametrically opposed, but Greenlanders of Danish, Inuit and mixed origin share a bond of objective, philosophical realism, and they mock incoming Danes and foreigners alike for their unrealistic belief in clocks, appointments and deadlines. Danish is the official language.

TYPICAL NUUK CITIZEN
Nuuk's inhabitants have adapted to the shift from traditional Greenland society to a modern industrial town. The economy functions because of administrators, but tools lie where they're dropped once the cash arrives on payday. Time will be spent with friends, but in comfortable silence – the key is in the body language. Smiles are common, but don't always mean pleasure. Your race will be observed, but you'll be judged on your actions. Nuuk is the place to be for family, friends and the hunt.

DEFINING EXPERIENCE
Morning fishing on the fjords, then *kaffemik* (coffee, cakes or biscuits) with the community, sitting in blissful silence with friends and leaving when you've had your second cup of coffee, eating your day's catch, then heading out for a night of live music and dancing at the pub.

ANDERS BLOMQVIST / GETTY IMAGES

BASKING IN THE AFTERNOON SUN – UNIFORM APARTMENT BLOCKS ARE A COMMON SIGHT IN NUUK.

GOLFERS DO IT TOUGH AGAINST A BACKDROP OF SERMITSIAQ PEAK.

STRENGTHS

- ◢ Vibrant Inuit culture
- ◢ Aurora borealis
- ◢ Braedet Market
- ◢ Photogenic Qornup Suvdula fjord
- ◢ Traditional costumes worn on the first day of school
- ◢ Snow, ice and water sports galore
- ◢ Humpback whales in the harbour
- ◢ Greenlandic modern art

WEAKNESSES

- ◢ Long-slab apartment blocks
- ◢ Pervasive economic apartheid
- ◢ Children on the streets all night from parental neglect
- ◢ Alcoholism
- ◢ *Perlerorneq* ('the burden' in Greenlandic) – depression during the long, dark winters

GOLD STAR

The Nuuk Marathon – Nuuk hosts a challenging marathon through Old Nuuk and the surrounding hills every August.

STARRING ROLE IN...

- ◢ *Nuuk* (2004)
- ◢ *Miss Smilla's Feeling For Snow* by Peter Høeg
- ◢ *Smilla's Sense of Snow* (1977)
- ◢ *Last Places* by Lawrence Millman
- ◢ *Tales and Traditions of the Eskimo* by Henry Rink
- ◢ *Eskimo Folk-tales* collected by Knud Rasmussen

See Kolonihavn – an 18th-century fishing village in the heart of Nuuk.

Eat gourmet Arctic gastronomy (like musk steak) at Restaurant Nipisa.

Drink genuine Greenlandic coffee at Café Tuap.

Do explore ancient and modern Inuit art at the Katuaq Cultural Centre.

Watch snow sculptors at work at the annual Nuuk International Snow Festival.

Buy a piece of black *Nuummiit*, the 'Greenland opal', found only in the Nuuk region.

After dark drink up in Kristinemut, Greenland's first pub.

Oaxaca City

NICKNAME IN THE NOSE OF THE SQUASH; THE LITERAL MEANING OF 'HUAXYÁCAC', OAXACA'S EARLIER AZTEC NAME **DATE OF BIRTH** 1529; WHEN THE SPANISH OFFICIALLY FOUNDED THE CITY, ALTHOUGH AN INDIGENOUS SETTLEMENT HAD ALREADY EXISTED AT THE SITE OF PRESENT-DAY OAXACA CITY FOR SEVERAL MILLENNIA **ADDRESS** MEXICO (MAP 2, E5) **HEIGHT** 1550M **POPULATION** 265,000 **LONELY PLANET RANKING** 079

At once relaxed and energetic, remote and cosmopolitan Oaxaca City is one of Mexico's cultural capitals where ancient indigenous culture and modern artistic innovation intermingle in a charming colonial setting.

ANATOMY

Situated at a comfortable altitude at the juncture of three valleys, the city enjoys a sunny and stable climate, which suits its cheerful vibe. Oaxaca's Spanish colonial heritage is visible as much in the stunning stone buildings as in the city's gridlike planning. Streets open onto public gardens and plazas then disappear into cobbled lanes and back alleys. The city's heart and soul is the *zócalo* (town square), a meeting place and venue for cultural events. Most points of interest in the city are within walking distance of each other, but use buses if your feet tire.

PEOPLE

Almost all of Oaxaca City's citizens are descended from the indigenous Zapotec and Mixtec peoples who remain fiercely proud of their heritage; many continue to observe pre-Hispanic traditions, from cooking and music to healing practices.

TYPICAL OAXACAN

Oaxacans have the best of everything. They are well educated (thanks in part to the town's historic hero, Benito Juárez), artistically appreciative, discerning in matters culinary and lacking in the macho boisterousness that tends to confront visitors in other parts of Mexico. Locals are as comfortable yelling at a football match as they are chatting at a café or wandering quietly through an art gallery. Nobody is in much of a hurry in Oaxaca. With thousands of years of colourful history, what's the rush?

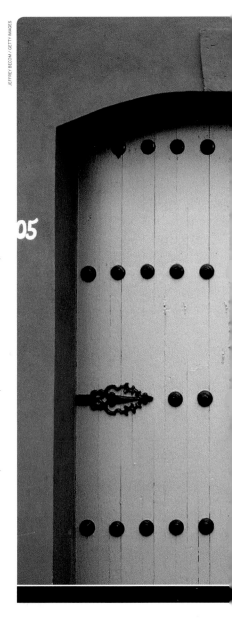

COWBOY-HATTED LOCALS FRAMED AGAINST THE CHARACTERISTIC PASTEL COLOURS OF A CITY DWELLING.

SANTO DOMINGO CATHEDRAL RISES ABOVE THE PALM-LINED ZOCALO IN THE CITY CENTRE.

PLASTIC BASKETS FOR SALE AT OAXACA MARKET.

IN A BLUR OF MOVEMENT A DANCER STEPS TO THE BEAT.

DEFINING EXPERIENCE

Getting up early and heading for the rowdy market to enjoy a bowl of hot *cacao* (chocolate) and sweet bread, stepping out again into the clear light that has inspired some of Mexico's most respected contemporary artists, crawling the galleries and the cafés for the rest of the day before losing yourself in the joyful mania of a festival.

STRENGTHS

- ◢ Chocolate
- ◢ Extraordinary arts and crafts
- ◢ Stunning galleries and modern art
- ◢ Indigenous culture
- ◢ Explosive festivals
- ◢ Unbeatable local cuisine
- ◢ Día de los Muertos (Day of the Dead) celebrations
- ◢ Colonial architecture
- ◢ Benito Juárez

WEAKNESSES

- ◢ Heavy-handed police
- ◢ Political unrest
- ◢ Former dictator Porfirio Díaz
- ◢ Traffic

GOLD STAR

Nowhere is the Mexican festival Día de los Muertos taken more seriously than in Oaxaca City and the surrounding villages. In this Zapotec celebration, which has fused with Catholic traditions, Oaxacans honour their dead by setting off fireworks in cemeteries, eating sugared skulls and dressing up in outrageous costumes.

STARRING ROLE IN...

- ◢ Día de los Muertos iconography

See the Iglesia de Santo Domingo, the best of Oaxaca's many churches.

Eat spiced grasshoppers from a street stall.

Drink sickly sweet hot chocolate with cinnamon and crushed almonds.

Do a round of the contemporary art museums and wind up in a café.

Watch frenetic dancing at the Guelaguetza festival.

Buy Mexico's best folk art.

After dark hit Candela to catch some of the best salsa you'll ever see.

609

Panama City

NICKNAME PANAMÁ, THE NAME OF THE FORMER CITY, RAZED TO THE GROUND BY THE PIRATE HENRY MORGAN IN 1671 **DATE OF BIRTH** 1519; WHEN IT WAS FOUNDED ON THE SITE OF AN INDIAN FISHING VILLAGE BY THE SPANISH GOVERNOR PEDRO ARIAS DE ÁVILA **ADDRESS** PANAMA (MAP 2, M8) **HEIGHT** 13M **SIZE** 275 SQ KM **POPULATION** 880,000 **LONELY PLANET RANKING** 108

The bottleneck of the world's shipping routes, Panama City is a teeming capital in the heart of Latin America, touched by transient influences from all over the globe – sooner or later, everything comes to town.

ANATOMY

Panama City stretches about 20km along the Pacific coast, with the Bahía de Panamá to the south, the Panama Canal to the west, protected forest to the north and the stone ruins of Panamá Viejo (Old Panama, the city's original site) to the east. You can trace the history and personality of the city by walking from the crumbling old town neighbourhood of Casco Viejo through the hotel district of La Exposición to arrive eventually at the vertiginous skyscrapers of El Cangrejo, the thriving banking district. Panama City has a good network of local buses (nicknamed *diablos rojos* – or red devils). Taxis are also plentiful.

PEOPLE

Most of Panama City's population is mestizo (of mixed Spanish and indigenous ancestry). There is also a sizable Chinese community, and a considerable proportion of the population is descended from English-speaking West Indians.

TYPICAL PANAMANIAN

Just as the colonial decay of old-town Casco Viejo is thrown into sharp relief by the modern excess of new-town El Cangrejo, your typical citizen of Panama City is equally contradictory. The exceptionally tolerant Panamanian character weathers many disjunctions – the old and the new, the grave disparity between rich and poor, and the gorgeous natural environment and its rapid destruction. Much of this tolerance begins in the family, which is the cornerstone of Panamanian society and plays a role in nearly every aspect of a person's life.

JOHN COLETTI / GETTY IMAGES

THE MUNICIPAL PALACE'S STATUES GAZE OVER THE METROPOLITAN CATHEDRAL IN CASCO VIEJA.

ALL THE WORLD'S A STAGE – THE NATIONAL THEATRE IN CASCO VIEJA.

THE SPARKLING VIEW DOWN BALBOA AV.

STRIKING A POSE, PANAMA-STYLE.

DEFINING EXPERIENCE

Wandering aimlessly through the heavily atmospheric old-town district of Casco Viejo, peering in the doorways of old churches to admire the altar displays and escape the midday sun, rambling on towards the bustling market and finishing up with a sangria or coffee at an outdoor café.

STRENGTHS

- Bicycle-riding police
- Fabulously decorated public buses
- Mireya Moscoso, the country's first female president
- Artistic postage stamps
- Scrumptious international food
- The Panama Canal
- Diverse museums

WEAKNESSES

- High crime
- Psychotic drivers
- General Manuel Noriega
- Unemployment
- Government corruption

GOLD STAR

The Panama Canal, one of the seven wonders of the industrial world, is just a short distance from the city. Its construction was considered as early as 1524 and its early-20th-century system of giant lock gates remains a marvel of engineering.

STARRING ROLE IN...

- *The Tailor of Panama* (2001)

See a ship passing through the giant locks of the Panama Canal.

Eat cuisine from all over the world.

Drink sangría in Casco Viejo.

Do a dance course at the Latin Dance Company; this skill will get you places.

Watch the thunderous, booty-shaking *carnaval* parade.

Buy bargain jewellery.

After dark hit one of Panama City's pumping clubs and be prepared to dance till you drop.

PLACE DE LA CONCORDE – THIS CITY OF LOVERS COMES ALIVE AT SUNSET.

STEPHANIE BENJAMIN / GETTY IMAGES

Paris

NICKNAME CITY OF LIGHT **DATE OF BIRTH** 52 BC; WHEN JULIUS CAESAR ESTABLISHED LUTETIA ON THE BANKS OF THE SEINE **ADDRESS** FRANCE (MAP 4, G10) **HEIGHT** 75M **SIZE** 105 SQ KM **POPULATION** 2.3 MILLION **LONELY PLANET RANKING** 001

Paris has it all: celebrity monuments, manicured parks, taste-bud-tingling cuisine, endless museums, frenetic flea markets and haute couture – and like its well-groomed citizens, it always looks good, without a hair out of place.

ANATOMY

Ringed by the blvd Périphérique, France's capital city is made up of 20 *arrondissements* (districts). The Seine River flows through the city and around two islands, Île de la Cité (site of Notre Dame) and Île St-Louis. The arty, intellectual Left Bank (south of the Seine) houses the Sorbonne University, the vibrant, touristy Latin Quarter and upmarket St-Germain. The Right Bank is home to the Champs-Élysées and the Louvre, as well as trendy shopping in the Marais, nightlife in the Bastille district and Paris's two opera houses. Overlooking the city to the north is the 126m-high Butte de Montmartre (Montmartre hill), the Moulin Rouge and Pigalle (the red-light district). The Eiffel Tower is directly south of the Arc de Triomphe on the southern side of the Seine. Walk or take the wonderfully efficient Métro.

PEOPLE

Almost one-fifth of Paris' population are immigrants, with the largest numbers arriving from Algeria, Portugal, Morocco, Tunisia, China and Mali (in descending numerical order). The rest are French.

TYPICAL PARISIAN

Parisians are typically crazy drivers and park with their handbrakes off to allow their neighbouring parker the inevitable bumping. They are stylish, chic and will wear lipstick for putting the rubbish out. They can come across as snooty and see the rest of France as rather provincial. Etiquette is very important and one false move will meet a barely detectable raising of the eyebrows and semiaudible sigh. They are well educated and ambitious, but never brash. They are also expert conversationalists and very respectful and proud of French cuisine and culture. Finally, despite burgeoning nonsmoking laws, Parisians still smoke.

LIFE IMITATES ART IN THE CAFE OF THE MUSÉE GREVIN.

DEFINING EXPERIENCE

Coffee and croissants on Place de la Contrescarpe, then strolling through the Latin Quarter and over the river to the quietly charming Île St-Louis, on to the Marais for some retail indulgence then lunch and a *vin rouge* (red wine) on Place des Vosges.

STRENGTHS

▲ Successful modern masterpieces, eg the Eiffel Tower, the Louvre Pyramid and the Centre Pompidou
▲ Musée du Louvre

▲ Musée d'Orsay
▲ Sacré Cœur
▲ Dazzling department stores – Printemps, Galeries Lafayette
▲ Shakespeare & Co bookshop
▲ Haute couture
▲ Cathédrale de Notre Dame de Paris
▲ Cimetière du Père Lachaise
▲ Château de Versailles
▲ Café terraces
▲ Quirky museums, eg the Musée des Égouts de Paris (sewers) and Catacombes de Paris (catacombs)
▲ Philosophers and intellectuals

▲ Paris Plage
▲ French Open
▲ Compulsory cleaning of building façades every 10 years
▲ Art in the Métro
▲ Heavenly food and wine
▲ The Vélib bike-share scheme

WEAKNESSES

▲ Underwhelming Eurostar terminal
▲ Tiny, expensive hotel rooms
▲ Dog poo
▲ August – much of Paris closes as Parisians flee the city

SWEET TREATS ON DISPLAY AT A PARISIAN PÂTISSERIE.

GOLD STAR

Landmarks – so much of Paris is iconic.

STARRING ROLE IN...

- ◢ *Midnight in Paris* (2011)
- ◢ *Before Sunset* (2004)
- ◢ *Le Fabuleux Destin d'Amélie Poulin* (Amélie, 2001)
- ◢ *Ronin* (1998)
- ◢ *Last Tango in Paris* (1972)
- ◢ *À Bout de Souffle* (1959)
- ◢ *Les Misérables* by Victor Hugo

See Leonardo da Vinci's *Mona Lisa* at possibly the world's best art gallery, the Louvre.

Eat delectable patisseries and confections at Ladurée on rue Royale, founded in 1862.

Drink with the city's in-the-know crowd at the Experimental Cocktail Club on rue Saint-Sauveur.

Do sunbathe by the Seine at Paris Plage (artifical sand beaches complete with plastic palm trees).

Watch the Eiffel Tower light up from the balcony of Georges restaurant in the Centre Pompidou.

Buy Hermès and Yves Saint Laurent on rue du Faubourg St-Honoré.

After dark catch a classical recital at the restored Salle Pleyel on rue du Faubourg St-Honoré.

UPWARDLY MOBILE – PERTH IS DUE TO GROW ONE-THIRD IN SIZE BY 2025.

Perth

NICKNAME CITY OF LIGHTS **DATE OF BIRTH** 1829; WHEN THE SWAN RIVER SETTLEMENT WAS FOUNDED ON LAND OCCUPIED BY THE ABORIGINAL NYOONGAR TRIBE **ADDRESS** AUSTRALIA (MAP 10, B7) **HEIGHT** 60M **SIZE** 1075 SQ KM **POPULATION** 1.7 MILLION **LONELY PLANET RANKING** 047

This city on sand epitomises the wild frontier character of Australia's emptiest and largest state, but despite its isolation, easy-going Perth rivals its east-coast brethren for quality of life, with top-class food and wine, vibrant nightlife, and more days of sunshine than any other capital city in the country.

ANATOMY

Perth's compact city centre sits on a sweeping bend of the Swan River. Shoppers buzz through the Hay St and Murray St Malls, while the city's suits wheel and deal along St George's Tce, the centre of Perth's business district. Jump on a Transperth bus or train and head west to the sprawling Kings Park or cross the railway line to the north, and you'll find Northbridge, heart of the city's nightlife. West and northwest of the city are the popular Indian Ocean beaches, Cottesloe and Scarborough.

PEOPLE

The city is home to people born in more than 200 different countries, speaking 170 languages and practising more than 100 religious faiths.

TYPICAL PERTH CITIZEN

Sandgropers (as residents of Western Australia are known) just have to 'get out', but once away they pine for their unspoilt west coast and sleepy small-town values. Everyone plays something, be it tennis, football, golf or a Fender. There are enough baby-boomer Poms to fill the Burswood Lyric Theatre for Gerry and the Pacemakers three nights running. And the America's Cup *will* come back to the Royal Perth Yacht Club.

DEFINING EXPERIENCE

Heading down to Scarborough Beach for a surf, breakfasting at Cottesloe, then walking through the wildflowers at Kings Park, making sure you have time to catch the sardine fishermen unloading at Fremantle before barbecuing the catch overlooking the Swan as the sun sets in the west.

STRENGTHS

⊿ Stunning city beaches and the sunshine to enjoy them
⊿ Federation Walkway through the tree tops in Kings Park
⊿ Fremantle
⊿ Maritime Museum
⊿ Subiaco on a Saturday
⊿ The Fremantle Doctor
⊿ Indonesian food
⊿ A drive into Margaret River
⊿ The boutique brews
⊿ Proximity to Asia

WEAKNESSES

⊿ The empty seats at the opera
⊿ The ballot for a place on Rottnest
⊿ Lack of iconic buildings
⊿ Cost of flights

GOLD STAR

Perth locals swear they have the best city beaches in Australia, and with that clean white sand and warm aquamarine water, who can argue?

STARRING ROLE IN...

⊿ *The Shark Net* by Robert Drewe
⊿ *Japanese Story* (2003)

See the sun rise as you go for a morning jog along one of the city's many picture-perfect beaches.

Eat Malay king-prawn curry, or hand-pick your fish from the market adjoining Kailis Bros Fish Café in groovy Leederville.

Drink a pale ale on the outside deck at Little Creatures in Fremantle.

Do catch the ferry to Rottnest for a day of cycling around the island.

Watch humpback whales pass by on their annual journey to Antarctic waters.

Buy a case of Margaret River wine.

After dark grab a mate and trawl for prawns in the shallows of the Swan.

PERTH'S BELLTOWER HOUSES 14TH-CENTURY BELLS BROUGHT OVER FROM ENGLAND.

THE CHAMELEON BRASS BAND PERFORMING AT THE FUNK CLUB IN PERTH.

SUN WORSHIPPERS PERFORM THEIR ABLUTIONS OUTSIDE INDIANA TEA HOUSE ON COTTESLOE BEACH.

ON THE EDGE OF THE CITY, WORKERS HARVEST RICE UNDER A RAIN-LADEN SKY.

Phnom Penh

NICKNAME PENH **DATE OF BIRTH** 1430S; ANGKOR WAS ABANDONED AND PHNOM PENH WAS CHOSEN AS THE SITE OF THE NEW CAMBODIAN CAPITAL **ADDRESS** CAMBODIA (MAP 9, F7) **HEIGHT** 12M **SIZE** 290 SQ KM **POPULATION** 2.3 MILLION **LONELY PLANET RANKING** 056

At times beautiful and beguiling, at times chaotic and charmless, Phnom Penh is a crossroads of Asia's past and present, a city of extremes of poverty and excess, but one that never fails to captivate the visitor.

ANATOMY

Many of the city's most popular restaurants and bars are located along Sisowath Quay, which hugs Tonlé Sap river. The major boulevards of Phnom Penh run north–south, including Samdech Sothearos Blvd near the riverfront, which passes the Royal Palace, Silver Pagoda and National Assembly building. Most buses, taxis and pick-ups arrive in the centre of town around Psar Thmei. The train station is a couple of blocks northwest.

PEOPLE

At first glance, Cambodia appears to be a nation full of shiny, happy people. But scratch the surface and you'll hear stories of endless personal tragedy, of dead brothers, mothers and babies, from which Cambodians have never had the chance to recover. The hellish years of the Khmer Rouge left a people in shock, suffering inside, stoical on the outside.

TYPICAL PHNOM PENHOIS

Older Phnom Penhois place family, faith and food at the centre of life, remembering when families were destroyed, food was scarce and faith got them through. The younger generation, however, are creating feisty friction. Teens, raised in a post-Communist period of relative freedom, dress as they like, date whom they choose and hit the town until late.

DEFINING EXPERIENCE

Strolling along the dawn-lit riverfront to see the mass t'ai chi sessions, taking in the dazzling treasures of the Silver Pagoda at the Royal Palace and the wondrous Khmer sculpture at the National Museum, shopping for treasures at Psar Tuol Tom Pong, listening to soothing jazz, G&T in hand, at the Foreign Correspondents Club, cruising the Mekong at sunset then hitting the dance floor at the heaving Heart of Darkness.

THE CHAN CHAYA PAVILION AT THE ROYAL PALACE.

BEFORE HITTING TOWN, A WOMAN TAKES TIME FOR ESSENTIAL HAIR CARE AT A BEAUTY SALON.

CHILDREN ESCAPE THE MIDDAY SUN IN THE COOL WATERS OF TONLE SAP RIVER.

STRENGTHS

- The Mekong riverfront, lined with palms and billowing flags
- 5000 silver floor tiles at the Silver Pagoda
- Art Deco Psar Thmei, Phnom Penh's central market
- Great nightlife and restaurants
- French colonial architecture
- Foreign Correspondents Club
- Phnom Penh Water Park on a stinking hot day
- Chaul Chnam (Khmer New Year), when the capital grinds to a halt for a huge celebration, with a lot of water and talc being thrown
- Bon Om Tuk (Water Festival), when Tonlé Sap river comes alive with boat races and up to two million people flood the capital

WEAKNESSES

- Risk of robbery
- Poverty
- The highest rate of HIV infection in Southeast Asia
- Air pollution

GOLD STAR

The Tuol Sleng Museum, a savage reminder of Cambodia's past, and the Killing Fields of Choeung Ek, where prisoners from Security Prison 21 were taken for execution – a grim experience, but essential for understanding just how far Cambodia has come.

STARRING ROLE IN...

- *City of Ghosts* (2002)
- *One Night After the War* (1997)
- *The Killing Fields* (1984)

See an impressive traditional shadow-puppet performance at Sovanna Phum Arts Association.

Eat the *amoc* (baked fish wrapped in banana leaf with coconut, lemongrass and chilli).

Drink the cheap and tasty Angkor beer, and make sure it's on the rocks!

Do jump on the back of a *moto* (motorcycle) and zoom around the city.

Watch the passing parade, including elephants, beggars, and occasionally the king, from the balcony of the Foreign Correspondents Club.

Buy handicrafts and textiles from shops raising money for projects to assist disadvantaged Cambodians.

After dark brave the happening Heart of Darkness, the place to be in Phnom Penh come midnight.

Prague

NICKNAME MATIČKA PRAHA (LITTLE MOTHER PRAGUE)
DATE OF BIRTH 4000 BC; WHEN FARMING COMMUNITIES WERE
ESTABLISHED BY GERMANIC AND CELTIC TRIBES; THE SLAVS ARRIVED
AROUND AD 600 **ADDRESS** CZECH REPUBLIC (MAP 4, M10)
HEIGHT 262M **SIZE** 496 SQ KM **POPULATION** 1.2 MILLION (CITY);
2.3 MILLION (METRO AREA) **LONELY PLANET RANKING** 014

With its fairy-tale cityscape, solid cultural heritage and perfect pilsner, Prague continues to captivate.

ANATOMY

Prague straddles the Vltava River, its two halves joined by the Charles Bridge, one of the world's loveliest. The centre consists of five towns: Hradčany, the castle district; Malá Strana (Little Quarter), between the river and castle; Staré Město, the Gothic 'Old Town' on the east bank; adjacent Josefov, the former Jewish ghetto; and Nové Město (New Town; new in the 14th century), to the south and east. This maze is best seen on foot, aided by Prague's fine Soviet-era metro, tram and bus system.

PEOPLE

Prague has a significant Czech population, as well as Slovak and Roma groups – the latter are often the target of racism. Significant numbers of German and American expatriates also call Prague home.

TYPICAL PRAGUER

Praguers pay dearly for the privilege of living in one of Europe's best-preserved and most-visited cities – at least half their wages can go to rent, and many restaurants, bars and consumer goods are out of their reach. They still manage to drink enormous amounts of beer, and indulge decidedly highbrow cultural tastes (and dress up for the symphony). First impressions may suggest mild manners and old-fashioned values, but Praguers often harbour a surreal sense of humour, and a steely sense of their rights and their place in history.

DEFINING EXPERIENCE

Taking the dog for a run through Vrtbovska Gardens and up Petřín Hill, refuelling on strudel and browsing for antique books in Staré Město, then drinking beer and scoffing sausage at riverside Letenske sady, laughing about David Černý's latest stunt and deciding whether it's to be an all-nighter at Akropolis or a jazz jam at Little Glen's.

MASSIMO PIZZOTTI / GETTY IMAGES

PRAGUE'S SKYLINE INSPIRES LOVE IN THOSE LUCKY ENOUGH TO VIEW IT.

STRENGTHS

- A thousand years of well-preserved European architecture
- Pilsner, pilsner and more pilsner
- Poignant, picturesque Josefov
- Old Town Sq, despite the tack
- Fab futurist metro stations
- The Velvet Revolution
- The Havel/Pistek-designed uniforms of the castle guards
- Jan Švankmajer
- The morally instructive Astronomical Clock

WEAKNESSES

- Shuffling crowds of camcorder-wielding tourists
- Jazz-fusion fanatics
- Grumpy service
- Pickpockets
- Meter-meddling taxi drivers

GOLD STAR

Romance – despite the tourists, Prague's riverside setting and architectural heritage cannot fail to pull the heart strings.

STARRING ROLE IN...

- *Comfortably Numb* (2005)
- *Van Helsing* (2004)
- *A Knight's Tale* (2001)
- *Mission: Impossible* (1996)
- *The Unbearable Lightness of Being* (1988)
- *Metamorphosis* by Franz Kafka

See the semiprecious stones in the Chapel of St Wenceslas in St Vitus Cathedral.

Eat traditional pork and dumplings at Kolkovna in Staré Město, a fresh take on the beer hall.

Drink light, dark or flavoured Czech lager, made on the premises at Nové Město's Pivovarský Dům.

Do a Sunday afternoon football match at AC Sparta Praha's stadium.

Watch Smetana performed at the glorious Národní Divadlo, a living monument to the Czech National Revival.

Buy a 16th-century aquatint of an angel at Antikvariát U Karlova Mostu.

After dark dance with the bohemians, or discover the lethal combination of *pivo* (beer) and poetry, at Radost FX.

LOCALS CROSS CHARLES BRIDGE INTO MALA STRANA AT THE FOOT OF PRAGUE CASTLE.

THE DANCING BUILDING BY VLADO MILUNIĆ AND FRANK GEHRY.

THE RED ROOFS OF THE CITY'S OLD TOWN.

A MAN WAITS FOR A BUS FROM BEHIND A CURTAIN OF TROPICAL RAIN IN ZONA CENTRO.

Puerto Vallarta

NICKNAME PARTY VALLARTA; PV **DATE OF BIRTH** 1851; WHEN THE SÁNCHEZ FAMILY MOVED TO THE AREA FARMERS AND FISHERFOLK SOON FOLLOWED **ADDRESS** MEXICO (MAP 2, A4) **HEIGHT** 2M **SIZE** 1300 SQ KM **POPULATION** 255,000

Formerly a quaint fishing village, Mexico's most picturesque coastal city with its happy-go-lucky vibe has become a popular playground for tourists worldwide.

ANATOMY

Set among palm-covered mountains and languid white beaches on the Bahía de Banderas (Bay of Flags), the old town centre features cobbled streets and whitewashed buildings. There are two main thoroughfares and the *malecón* – the seaside promenade – lined with shops, restaurants and nightspots. The small island of Cuale is downtown, surrounded by the two forks of Río Cuale. Amid the quaintness of the city are modern hotels and resorts, with attendant high-rises, reaching to the city fringes. Walking is the best way to see the hilly city, but buses, rental cars or taxis service the weary; water taxis also operate in the area.

PEOPLE

While there are hundreds of thousands of international visitors to this township in the state of Jalisco every year, the live-in population is predominantly Mexican. They largely belong to the Roman Catholic faith, with around 5% Protestant and a smaller percentage belonging to other religions. Due to tourism, most of the population is bilingual: Spanish and English.

TYPICAL PUERTO VALLARTA CITIZEN

Most Mexicans here work in tourism – there is no other industry. They are religious. They are often poor. They are mainly young. They have been dubbed by international film crews and travel magazines as 'the friendliest people in the world'. They are keen to preserve their home from excessive development, but happy to share it with the world.

DEFINING EXPERIENCE

Exploring the coral reefs and underwater caves of pristine Isla Marietas, then refuelling at a beachside taco stand before heading out to the Malecon (the boardwalk) for some ice-cold *cerveza* (beer).

STRENGTHS

- ◢ Tree-top canopy tour
- ◢ Great boutique shopping
- ◢ Excellent water sports
- ◢ The depths of the jungle close by
- ◢ Stunning views
- ◢ A few great fine art galleries
- ◢ Casa Kimberley (the house Richard Burton bought for Elizabeth Taylor)
- ◢ Gorgeous nearby villages
- ◢ Beach of the Spirits
- ◢ Local festivals
- ◢ Good variety of restaurants
- ◢ Friendly locals
- ◢ Abundant marine life
- ◢ Street stalls

WEAKNESSES

- ◢ Mega-luxury resorts destroying the view
- ◢ Lots of trashed tourists
- ◢ Hurricane and cyclone risks

GOLD STAR

Every activity you could possibly hope for in a tropical paradise is here by land or by sea.

STARRING ROLE IN...

- ◢ *Kill Bill Vol 2* (2004)
- ◢ *Predator* (1987)
- ◢ *Herbie Goes Bananas* (1980)
- ◢ *The Night of the Iguana* (1964)

See the city from the reproduction galleon *Marigalante* – the cruise climaxes in a mock pirate attack!

Eat jumbo shrimp at the hillside restaurant El Palomar de los González.

Drink a strong coffee or yummy smoothie at the artsy Café San Angel.

Do try a freshly rolled cigar from one of the city's specialist cigar stores.

Watch a performance of contagious mariachi sounds.

Buy the delicious mango slices seasoned with salt and chilli from the small-cart vendors on the beach.

After dark show the young things how it's done with some table-top dancing at the club du jour.

A MARIACHI BAND SIZES UP THE COMPETITION.

Pyongyang

DATE OF BIRTH AD 427; WHEN THE GOGURYEO DYNASTY MOVED ITS CAPITAL HERE **ADDRESS** NORTH KOREA (MAP 9, H2) **HEIGHT** 27M **SIZE** 200 SQ KM **POPULATION** 3.2 MILLION **LONELY PLANET RANKING** 187

Monumental and monolithic, the North Korean capital is one of the most impressive and unique cities on earth.

ANATOMY

Clustered around the massive Taedong River, Pyongyang's streets are eerily empty of traffic – most people walk or take buses, only the privileged few have access to private motor cars. The centrepiece is Kim Il Sung Sq, the vast public space where military parades of fanatic precision take place under the gaze of the cherubic-faced Kim Jong-un, the third-in-line in North Korea's Communist dynasty.

PEOPLE

Pyongyang must be one of the most homogeneous cities on earth. Its scant foreign population is billeted in the restricted diplomatic quarter, while the Chinese workers who run some of the city's hotels are unable to leave the establishments they work at as it is feared they may adversely influence the locals. Pyongyang inhabitants are therefore fascinated by any foreigner, and will wave and smile, but rarely dare speak to you. Only those of an ideologically pure background are given permits to live in the capital, so the people you see here are among the most privileged in the country.

TYPICAL PYONGYANGER

Despite their relatively high status in North Korean society, the vast majority of Pyongyang's inhabitants live austere lives. Every household will have a portrait of Kim Il Sung and his son Kim Jong Il. While food is no longer scarce, most people will live on a frugal diet of rice and noodles. Electricity is in short supply and the capital is often pitch black at night. Whenever the lights go off, locals shout 'blame America!' in response.

DEFINING EXPERIENCE

Finding Pyongyang's heart and soul is challenge indeed. So much of what you see is facade designed to interpret the government's vision of the country, but often bearing nothing in common with reality. In itself this is the defining experience of the city – trying to see through the cracks and chinks in the city's ideological armour.

THE STRANGE BALLET OF THE MASS GAMES IS A WELL CHOREOGRAPHED SPECTACLE.

STRENGTHS

◢ The North Koreans, when you are lucky enough to spend time with them, are delightful
◢ Lack of traffic pollution
◢ No crime problems

WEAKNESSES

◢ Appalling human-rights record
◢ No contact with locals (you'll mainly speak to your North Korean guides)
◢ You can't leave the hotel without your guide
◢ Little nightlife beyond pool and karaoke in your hotel
◢ Bugged hotel rooms

GOLD STAR

Monumental buildings: few cities can compete with Pyongyang's exceptional ability to produce vast socialist-realist-meets-Asia architecture.

STARRING ROLE IN...

◢ *The Game of Their Lives* (2002)
◢ *State of Mind* (2004)

See the view of this incredible city from the top of the Tower of the Juche Idea.

Eat at the Pyongyang Number 1 Boat Restaurant, which cruises the Taedong River while you eat.

Drink Taedong beer, and reflect that it was made in a factory bought and shipped wholesale from Trowbridge, England.

Do make an effort to learn the Korean for 'hello' and 'thank you', as it will mean the world to any North Korean with whom you do have fleeting contact.

Watch the annual 'Mass Games' – a weird North Korean team sport in which thousands of participants perform ideological worship as ballet.

Buy plenty of propaganda, including exquisite hand-painted agitprop posters.

After dark enjoy the facilities in your hotel, as you're unlikely to be going anywhere else.

ON GUARD IN THE DEMILITARISED ZONE – NORTH KOREAN SOLDIERS ON PATROL AT TRUCE VILLAGE.

A LONE WORKER WALKS BY JUCHE TOWER, THE SYMBOL OF NORTH KOREAN COMMUNISM.

FORMER LEADER KIM JONG IL IS A CULT FIGURE IN NORTH KOREA.

THE SPIRE OF CHALMERS-WESLEY UNITED CHURCH IN VIEUX QUÉBEC DOMINATES THE SKYLINE.

Québec City

DATE OF BIRTH 1608; FOUNDED BY SAMUEL DE CHAMPLAIN ON THE
SITE OF STADACONA, A FIRST NATIONS SETTLEMENT **ADDRESS** CANADA
(MAP 1, S1) **HEIGHT** 90M **SIZE** 93 SQ KM **POPULATION** 516,000 (CITY);
765,000 (METRO AREA) **LONELY PLANET RANKING** 095

Cradle and protector of French culture in North America and the heart that first beat the province's blood, captivating, historic Québec City is Canada's most European-flavoured destination.

ANATOMY

Québec City is small, with nearly everything of interest packed into one compact, walkable district. Part of the city sits atop the cliffs of Cap Diamant (Cape Diamond), and part lies below. The city is thus divided into Haute Ville and Basse Ville (Upper and Lower Town). The Citadelle, a fort and landmark, stands on the highest point of Cap Diamant. Together, the 10 sq km of these upper and lower areas, within the stone walls, form the Vieux Québec (Old Town). Québec City is covered by a reasonably priced and efficient bus system.

PEOPLE

Québec City has a predominantly European population of French, British, Italian and Irish origin. Most people are white, with a small percentage of Arab, Hispanic and Asian inhabitants. Many residents are bilingual, though most speak French and claim French ancestry.

TYPICAL QUÉBÉCOIS

In general French Québécois tend to be down-to-earth and not big on ceremony. There is a sense of not wanting to seem better than others, and many project an earthy straightforwardness often missing in their Anglophone counterparts. Francophones also have a reputation for being more fun-loving and raucous at get-togethers.

DEFINING EXPERIENCE

Breakfasting at Casse Crêpe Breton; exploring Haute Ville's fortifications, Parc des Champs de Bataille (Battlefields Park) and the Citadelle; then wandering the old Basse Ville, before drinking beer at L'Oncle Antoine and later dining at a Basse Ville patio.

WINTRY SCENES AND SNOWY SHOPS IN THE PRELUDE TO CHRISTMAS.

QUÉBEC – PRETTY AS A PICTURE.

STRENGTHS
- Winter Carnival
- La Citadelle
- Musée du Québec
- Fortifications of Québec National Historic Site
- Parc de l'Artillerie
- Cathedrale de la Sainte Trinité (Cathedral of the Holy Trinity)
- Latin Quarter
- Basilica Notre Dame de Québec
- Musée de l'Amérique Française
- Le Château Frontenac
- Terrasse Dufferin
- Place Royale
- Antique shop district

WEAKNESSES
- Exploitation of fauna reserves by the forest industry
- World's second-largest exporter of asbestos
- Xenophobic government hiring policies

GOLD STAR
With its striking architecture and well-organised permanent and temporary exhibits that cover both historical and contemporary concerns, the Musée de la Civilisation is not to be missed.

STARRING ROLE IN...
- *Le Confessional* (1995)
- *Black Robe* (Robe Noire, 1991)

See newcomers or the occasional big name at Les Yeux Bleus, one of the best *boîtes à chansons* (informal singer-songwriter clubs).

Eat provincial fare including pea soup, duck or trout followed by maple-syrup pie at Aux Anciens Canadiens.

Drink a selection of beers at L'Inox in the Old Port area.

Do tweak snowman/mascot Bonhomme's nose at the Winter Carnival (January).

Watch a classical concert at the Grand Théâtre de Québec.

Buy Inuit art from Galerie Art Inuit Brousseau et Brousseau.

After dark chill out (literally) at North America's first Ice Hotel, half an hour from central Québec City.

NORTH AMERICA'S OLDEST GROCERY STORE, JA MOISAN, FOUNDED IN 1871.

AND THE BAND PLAYED ON – A DISPLAY OF DANCING IN QUITO.

Quito

DATE OF BIRTH PRE-COLUMBIAN; EARLY INHABITANTS OF THE AREA WERE THE PEACEFUL QUITU PEOPLE, WHO GAVE THEIR NAME TO THE CITY **ADDRESS** ECUADOR (MAP 3, A6) **HEIGHT** 2879M **SIZE** 17KM LONG AND 4KM WIDE **POPULATION** 2.2 MILLION **LONELY PLANET RANKING** 104

Tucked amid a high Andean valley and flanked by majestic mountains – when it comes to setting, Quito has it made.

ANATOMY

Quito lies along the central valley in a roughly north–south direction. It can be divided into three segments: the centre (El Centro) is the site of the old town, with its whitewashed, red-tiled houses and colonial churches; north is modern Quito, the new town, with its major businesses, airline offices, embassies, shopping centres and banks; and south of Quito consists mainly of working-class residential areas. The local bus network runs north–south. The speedy and efficient *El Trole* (the trolleybus) is Quito's most comfortable and useful transportation system. Trolleys run along Av 10 de Agosto, through the old town to the northern end of the southern suburbs.

PEOPLE

About 25% of the population is Indian, and another 65% is mestizo (of mixed Spanish and indigenous ancestry). Most of the rest of the population is either white or black, with a small number of people of Asian descent. Quechua and Spanish are spoken.

TYPICAL QUITEÑO

Quiteños are warm, welcoming and polite. Class division is an issue and blacks and indigenous people are sometimes discriminated against and treated as second-class citizens. While most of the population is Catholic, the Indians tend to blend Catholicism with their traditional beliefs.

DEFINING EXPERIENCE

Strolling along the old-town streets, then stopping at the hole-in-the-wall Heladería San Agustín, a 140-year-old ice-cream parlour, for a couple of scoops of nourishment before walking from the narrow colonial streets of the old town into the openness of Plaza San Francisco, revealing one of the finest sites in Ecuador – a sweeping cobblestone plaza backed by the long whitewashed walls and twin bell towers of Ecuador's oldest church, the Monasterio de San Francisco.

643

A HILLSIDE DESCENT REVEALS SPOTLIT QUATRERS OF THE OLD CITY.

ALISON WRIGHT / CORBIS

CANDIED APPLES RIPE FOR THE PICKING.

STRENGTHS
- Plaza San Francisco
- Vibrant indigenous cultures
- Spectacular setting
- World Cultural Heritage Site status
- Virgin of Quito on El Panecillo
- Avenue of Volcanoes
- *Salsotecas* (salsa nightclubs)
- Museo del Banco Central
- La Mitad del Mundo (The Middle of the World) monument
- Well-preserved colonial architecture

WEAKNESSES
- Altitude sickness
- Political unrest
- Pickpockets, especially in the Ipiales market area
- Economic instability
- Deforestation

GOLD STAR
El Panecillo ('The Little Bread Loaf') – from the summit of this much-loved hill there are marvellous views of the city stretching out below, as well as views of the surrounding volcanoes.

STARRING ROLE IN...
- *Between Marx and a Naked Woman* (1996)
- *Proof of Life* (2000)
- *The Villagers* by Jorge Icaza

See marvellous views of Quito by climbing the tower of La Basílica high on a hill in the northeastern part of the old town.

Eat *yaguarlocro* (potato and blood-sausage soup) for lunch at Tianguez, under the Monasterio de San Francisco.

Drink the local firewater, *aguardiente* (sugar-cane alcohol), at the cosy La Taberna del Duende while listening to *música folklórica* (folk music).

Do take a few salsa dance lessons at Ritmo Tropical before hitting the dance floor of one of Quito's *salsotecas*.

Watch the Ballet Folklórico Nacional Jacchigua at Teatro Aeropuerto.

Buy Andean textiles on the weekend at Quito's biggest crafts market and sidewalk art show at the northern end of Parque El Ejido.

After dark head to Reina Victoria, around Santa María and Pinta, where there are several popular bars.

TRADITIONAL DANCERS GET IN THE SWING OF IT.

645

BATHERS AT THE LAUGARDALUR COMPLEX DEMONSTRATE WHY ICELAND IS SO POORLY NAMED.

Reykjavík

DATE OF BIRTH AD 874; ACCORDING TO ARI THE LEARNED, NORWEGIAN VIKING INGÓLFUR ARNARSON SET UP HOUSE NEXT TO A SET OF GEOTHERMAL VENTS, NAMING THE SETTLEMENT REYKJAVÍK (SMOKY BAY) **ADDRESS** ICELAND (MAP 4, J2) **HEIGHT** 18M **SIZE** 275 SQ KM **POPULATION** 120,000 (CITY); 201,000 (METRO AREA) **LONELY PLANET RANKING** 128

Tiny and often very cold, Reykjavík surprises with its exuberance, cultural savvy and otherworldly setting.

ANATOMY

The world's northernmost capital lies on a small peninsula, framed by the icy Mt Esja and the Atlantic. Recent generations of architects have filled the capital with intriguing modern buildings, which sit juxtaposed against the tin-clad houses. The old town centre lies between the harbour and a large pond, the Tjörn, to the southwest. Reykjavíkers bike, bus or traverse their city on foot, but favour 4WDs for the suburbs.

PEOPLE

Reykjavíkers usually know each other and are often distantly related. Around 94% are of mixed Scandinavian and Celtic stock – a legacy of early settlement. The remaining 6% are either transplanted spouses or temporary workers, mainly from Poland (as immigration is strictly controlled). Most Reykjavíkers will be fluent in English.

TYPICAL REYKJAVÍKER

National traits of self-reliance and reserve may well apply, but young Reykjavíkers also tend to be somewhat bohemian. They are more likely to be interested in poetry, painting or their band's upcoming performance than outdoor pursuits. They work hard but love nothing more than to go out for long drinking sessions come the weekend.

DEFINING EXPERIENCE

Belly-flopping into the warm waters of the Laugardalur thermal pool, hoping to forget how late you stayed out the night before, then browsing the Kolaportið flea markets, grabbing the obligatory hot dog with *remúladi* (a mayonnaise sauce) and crispy-fried onion from Bæjarins Bestu before heading off to an opening of contemporary sculpture at Hafnarhúsið with friends just back from New York.

STRENGTHS

- Long summer days
- The Raðhús
- Surprisingly short flying times to New York, London or Oslo
- Perlan parkland
- Alternative attitude
- Hallgrímskirkja
- Eco-consciousness
- Geothermal swimming pools and beaches
- Ingibjörg Pálmadóttir's Icelandic-minimal interiors
- Unique moonscapes close to town

WEAKNESSES

- Summer temperatures that never leave the teens
- Everyone hears what you got up to last weekend
- Economic instability
- Ubiquitous corrugated iron

GOLD STAR

Friday nights: for a small, chilly city, it's amazingly energetic and uninhibited.

STARRING ROLE IN...

- *Reykjavík Guesthouse: Rent a Bike* (2002)
- *101 Reykjavík* (2000)
- *Icelandic Dream* (2000)
- *Children of Nature* (1992)
- *Rokk í Reykjavík* (Rock in Reykjavík, 1982)

See, as you sit by the harbour at midnight, the summer sun dip slightly below the horizon before it makes its way up again.

Eat cod throats at Við Tjörnina, still one of the best Icelandic seafood restaurants after 25 years.

Drink vodka-spiked beer with the Friday night *runtur* (literally, 'round tour') crowd around Laugavegur in the centre – the ultimate pub-crawl.

Do a walking tour of the city's modernist architecture.

Watch an international rock act, preferably from the comfort of a geothermal pool, during the Iceland Airwaves Festival in October.

Buy Icelandic CDs at Japis or Skifan who stock the entire Björk back catalogue.

After dark discuss the sagas or the songs of Sigur Rós, at the volcanic-monochrome bar of the 101 Hotel.

GAZING OVER AT REYKJAVÍK AND TJORN FROM CITY HALL.

Rīga

NICKNAME THE PARIS OF THE BALTICS; PARIS OF THE EAST **DATE OF BIRTH** 1201; WHEN BISHOP ALBERT OF LIVONIA FOUNDED THE LIVONIAN KNIGHTS **ADDRESS** LATVIA (MAP 4, P6) **HEIGHT** 3M **SIZE** 307 SQ KM **POPULATION** 700,000 **LONELY PLANET RANKING** 116

The Baltic States' biggest and most cosmopolitan city, Rīga exudes both medieval charm and contemporary cool, combining these qualities seamlessly in a welcoming environment that has not gone unnoticed by European tourists, who flock here for weekend breaks.

ANATOMY

Rīga lies slightly inland from the massive Bay of Rīga, on the massive Daugava River. On the eastern bank is Vecrīga (Old Rīga), the city's historical heart, with a skyline dominated by three steeples: St Peter's, Dome Cathedral and St Jacob's. The river is crossed by three huge bridges, and joins Vecrīga to the city's more modern left bank and to the nearby seaside resort of Jūrmala. You can get around by bus, minibus, tram or trolleybus.

PEOPLE

Just as Latvia is the most Russian of the Baltic States, Rīga is the most Russian of the Baltic capitals, with close to half of the city's residents being ethnic Russians. Many of the Latvians resident in the city also speak fluent Russian, too, so unlike Tallinn or Vilnius the city has an extremely Russian feel. Most Latvians are Lutheran, while the Russian population is generally Russian Orthodox Christian.

TYPICAL RĪGAN

Despite a very real Latvian feeling of colonisation and resentment towards Russians in general, anti-Russian feeling is hardly ever expressed by Rīgans – a rare case of two very different peoples sharing a city in almost total harmony. While Latvians have a very Scandinavian approach to life – and this is evident in the incredible pace of change over the past two decades – the Eastern-looking Russian Rīgans have also been caught up in the developmental frenzy and profited from it equally. Your typical Rīgan will have both Russian and Latvian friends, be confident in both languages and be extremely proud of Rīga's pre-eminent position among the Baltic capitals.

BRUCE YUAN-YUE BI

UP THE NIGHTLIFE OUTSIDE THE RĀTSLAUKUMS (TOWN SQUARE), WITH THE HOUSE OF BLACKHEADS LIT UP IN THE BACKGROUND.

THE HOUSE OF THE BROTHERHOOD OF BLACKHEADS, AN ASSOCIATION OF MERCHANTS.

CONNIE COLEMAN / GETTY IMAGES

THE NEW GENERATION OF LATVIANS ARE MEMBERS OF THE EUROPEAN UNION.

BRUCE YUANYUE BI / GETTY IMAGES

LATVIA'S RIFLEMAN STATUE STANDS IN FRONT OF OCCUPATION MUSEUM.

DEFINING EXPERIENCE

Wandering the charming streets of Vecrīga, stumbling across ancient churches and colourful houses, always being surprised by something.

STRENGTHS

- Extremely clean streets
- Friendly people
- Easy to negotiate
- Superb Art Nouveau architecture

WEAKNESSES

- Some would say that Rīga has been cleaned up and restored into sterility
- Those freezing winters limit most visitors to just a few sunny months during the summer
- The stodgy and greasy national cuisine of Latvia leaves many people cold

GOLD STAR

The cleanliness of the city, its charming inhabitants and their extraordinarily good manners – this is a city where people clean up after themselves, always open doors for you and drivers bend over backwards to give way to each other at junctions. If nothing else, this will convince you just how Scandinavian Rīga is.

STARRING ROLE IN...

- *The Dogs of Riga* by Henning Mankell
- *The Merry Baker of Riga* by Boris Zemtzov

See the stunning Art Nouveau architectural creations that line the streets of Vecrīga.

Eat everything infused with garlic (including dessert) at Kiploku Krogs.

Drink the local lethal tipple, Rīga Black Balsam, only if you dare...

Do visit the Dome Cathedral, the largest in the Baltics.

Watch a production at the stunning National Opera House.

Buy exquisite amber jewellery from the Rīga Central Market.

After dark enjoy the sleek restaurants and cool bars of Vecrīga.

THE BEACH AT COPACABANA IS INHABITED BY AN ODD SPECIES OF DANGLING PRIMATE.

Rio de Janeiro

NICKNAME CIDADE MARAVILHOSA (MARVELLOUS CITY)
DATE OF BIRTH 1565: THE PORTUGUESE SET UP THE FIRST
SETTLEMENT; RIO BECAME THE CAPITAL IN 1763 **ADDRESS** BRAZIL
(MAP 3, H11) **HEIGHT** 61M **SIZE** 1200 SQ KM **POPULATION** 6.3 MILLION
(CITY): 12.3 MILLION (METRO AREA) **LONELY PLANET RANKING** 017

With renowned beaches, green mountainous surrounds and streets that seethe with sensuality, Rio has more than its fair share of natural and cultural riches.

ANATOMY

Rio is a tale of two cities: the upper and middle classes reside in the Zona Sul, the lower class in the Zona Norte. *Favelas* (shantytowns) cover steep hillsides on both sides of town. Most industry is in the Zona Norte. The beaches are in the Zona Sul. Buses are easily caught, but they're crowded, slowed by traffic and driven by maniacs. The excellent subway system is limited to points north of the middle-class neighbourhood of Botafogo.

PEOPLE

The racial composition of Rio's population reflects its past: a mix of Africans, Europeans and Indians who have intermarried since colonial times. The Portuguese gave the country its religion and language, Indian culture provided the legends. The influence of African culture is also prominent as the early slaves brought with them their religion, music and cuisine, which shaped Brazilian identity. Rio's melting pot is also a product of immigrants who began arriving in the 19th century – Italians, Spaniards, Germans, Japanese, Russians and Lebanese among others.

TYPICAL CARIOCA

The Cariocas – as Rio's inhabitants are called – thrive on dance, drink, the beach, sport and sun. They are spontaneous, friendly and prone to kicking footballs. However, it is class more than anything that separates Rio's citizens. At least one in five Cariocas live in a *favela*.

DEFINING EXPERIENCE

Celebrating with Fluminense fans over a hard-won football match at a sidewalk café in Flamengo, then heading to Lapa and wandering among the bars and old music halls in search of the soul of samba, and, finally, dancing in the streets with fellow Friday-night revellers.

STRENGTHS

- Ipanema Beach
- Catedral Metropolitana
- *Bolo* (cake) and thick *cafezinho* (little coffee)
- Samba clubs in Lapa
- Antique stores of Rua do Lavradio
- A game of *futebol* at the Maracanã
- *Cristo Redentor* (Christ the Redeemer) on Corcovado (Hunchback) mountain
- Centro Cultural Banco do Brasil, which hosts some of the city's best exhibitions
- Riding the *bonde* (tram) to the lovely hilltop neighbourhood of Santa Teresa
- Rio's weekend Feira Nordestina

WEAKNESSES

- Pollution
- Poverty, street kids and *favelas*
- Drug trade and police corruption
- Violence

GOLD STAR

The birthplace of bossa nova today hosts samba, jazz, reggae, funk, electronic music and Música Popular Brasileiro (MPB).

STARRING ROLE IN...

- *Pixote* (1981)
- *Motorcycle Diaries* (2004)
- *The City of God* (2002)

See the city unfold beneath the arms of the *Cristo Redentor*.

Eat the best *churrasco* (barbecued meat) in Rio at Porcão.

Drink cocktails and take in the ambient sounds (mixed by a changing crew of house and drum and bass hands) at the sleek Sitio Lounge.

Do take a *voleibol* (volleyball) class on Ipanema Beach.

Watch Rio's new breed of hip-hop (pronounced hippie-hoppie) aficionados at a jam in Humaitá or Botafogo.

Buy vintage vinyl at the open-air Feira de Música market in Centro.

After dark check out a *baile* (literally a 'dance' or 'ball') and try on your best dance moves alongside 10,000 locals.

THE STATUE OF CRISTO REDENTOR ON CORCOVADO.

A VOLLEYBALL ECLIPSE IN FRONT OF SUGARLOAF MOUNTAIN.

A SAMBA DANCER SHOWS HOW IT'S DONE DURING A CARNAVAL PARADE.

Rome

NICKNAME THE ETERNAL CITY **DATE OF BIRTH** 21 APRIL 753 BC;
WHEN ANCIENT ROMANS DATED THE CITY FOUNDATION
ADDRESS ITALY (MAP 5, M6) **HEIGHT** 17M **SIZE** 150 SQ KM
POPULATION 2.7 MILLION **LONELY PLANET RANKING** 006

Whether they're romantics, art-lovers, gourmands or historians, when you tell people you're going to Rome, they'll sigh – even if they haven't been there.

ANATOMY

Rome's best-known geographical features are its seven hills: the Palatine, Capitoline, Aventine, Caelian, Esquiline, Viminal and Quirinal. Two other hills, the Gianicolo, which rises above Trastevere, and the Pincio, above Piazza del Popolo, were never part of the ancient city. From the Gianicolo you can see how the River Tiber winds through town. Rome's bus routes cover the city; a semi-useless two-line metro system (Linea A and Linea B) traverses the city in an X-shape.

PEOPLE

The majority of Romans (over 80%) still consider themselves Catholic, though church attendance isn't what it used to be. Of the non-Catholics in the city, it's the Muslims who are making the furthest inroads – 36.5% of immigrants to Italy are Muslim. The Muslim community in Rome is based around the city mosque, inaugurated in 1995.

TYPICAL ROMAN

The typical Roman works for the government, drives rather than taking public transport, lives at home with the family despite being over 30 years old and is fairly conformist when it comes to matters of style, preferring to look like most other Romans – stylish, groomed and labelled. They share their city with millions of tourists and 150,000 stray cats.

DEFINING EXPERIENCE

Taking your morning espresso at Caffè Sant'Eustachio, walking the streets and getting lost only to stumble upon the perfect trattoria and losing all sense of time over *saltimbocca alla romana* (jump-in-the-mouth veal) and a good wine, crossing Piazza del Popolo and having your breath taken away by Caravaggio's the *Calling of St Matthew*.

MARTIN MOOS / GETTY IMAGES

BERNINI'S COLONNADE, THE GRAND GATEWAY TO THE VATICAN, PIAZZA DI SAN PIETRO.

THE COBBLED DISTRICT OF TRASTEVERE IS ALWAYS A BLUR OF ACTION.

TWO OLD FRIENDS BASK IN THE SUNSET GLOW OF PIAZZA GARIBALDI.

STRENGTHS

- History everywhere you look
- Stylish dressing as an art form
- Gelato
- Passeggiata di Gianicolo walk for beautiful views of the city
- AS Roma
- The Pantheon
- The Forum
- Via del Governo Vecchio
- Villa Borghese
- Baroque architecture
- Morning coffee on a piazza
- Crossing the Tiber on foot
- Al dente pasta
- Trastevere

WEAKNESSES

- Overcrowded buses and an all but useless metro
- Too many menus in English/French/German
- Bureaucracy
- Tame nightlife
- Trying to walk in heels on cobblestones (unless you're a local)

GOLD STAR

History – Rome knows that no-one's coming here for the modern architecture, so a lot of money gets spent on keeping the past alive.

STARRING ROLE IN...

- *Roma, città aperta* (Rome, Open City, 1945)
- *Ladri di biciclette* (The Bicycle Thief, 1948)
- *Roman Holiday* (1953)
- *La Dolce Vita* (1961)

See the Vatican.

Eat Rome's favourite pizza at Da Baffetto.

Drink a glass of Torre Ercolana, an opulent local red from Anagni, in a little *enoteca* (wine bar).

Do as the Romans do.

Watch some of the tightest reverse parking you'll ever see.

Buy something beautiful from a household name on Via dei Condotti.

After dark go sightseeing when everyone's in bed – you won't get inside the big sights, but you will get to see the outside with no hassles.

THE TIMELESS FACE OF THE DIOSCURI STATUE LOOKS TO ROME'S GLORIOUS PAST.

Saint-Denis

DATE OF BIRTH 1669; FOUNDED BY THE GOVERNOR REGNAULT, WHO NAMED THE SETTLEMENT AFTER A SHIP THAT RAN AGROUND HERE **ADDRESS** RÉUNION (MAP 7, K7) **HEIGHT** 12M **SIZE** 423 SQ KM **POPULATION** 145,000 **LONELY PLANET RANKING** 196

Dominating life on the tropical island, Saint-Denis is Réunion's historic cosmopolitan capital with a chilled vibe and wicked café culture that is unparalleled anywhere in the Indian Ocean.

ANATOMY

The city centre, conveniently arranged in a grid pattern, is built on a coastal plain that drops gently north towards the sea. Life revolves around the vibrant seafront area, Le Barachois, with its cafés and bars, and Ave de la Victoire, the main thoroughfare heading inland that leads to the grand Creole mansions along Rue de Paris. St-Denis is relatively small and getting around the centre on foot is a breeze, but there is nevertheless a good and comprehensive city-bus service.

PEOPLE

The population of Saint-Denis is predominantly descended from 17th-century French settlers and successive waves of migrants from Madagascar, East Africa, India and Southeast Asia who were either brought to the island as slaves, arrived as mutineers, or came to trade. The official language is French but Creole is widely spoken. Creoles (people of Afro-French ancestry) are the largest ethnic group, comprising around 40% of the population.

TYPICAL SAINT-DENISIAN

The city is a veritable melting pot and over the years has supported an abundance of interracial marriages that led to the emergence of its unique Creole culture. Whatever their ethnicity, locals tend to share a strong sense of community and family values, which bind them together. Most would refer to themselves as Creole, not in the narrow sense of having Afro-French ancestry, but simply meaning one of 'the people'. Saint-Denisians have a casual approach to life and often come across as being reserved, although they are disarmingly polite when approached. In this town it's very much a case of 'you have to show respect, to get respect'.

WALTER BIBIKOW / GETTY IMAGES

THE CITY, SEEN FROM LA MONTAIGNE, GETS READY FOR THE NIGHT.

DEFINING EXPERIENCE

Marvelling at the *Cathédrale* sculpture as you drive in from the airport, sniffing your way through the perfumed plants at the Botanical Gardens, filling up on pastries from Le Castel, then heading to Le Barachois to knock back a few evening tumblers of rum while swapping fantasies about what you'd like to do to the mosquitoes.

STRENGTHS

- Creole mansions
- *Pétanque* (boules played with heavy metal balls on a sandy pitch)
- Culturally diverse
- Bird-watching
- Hearing Creole spoken
- Jurassic Park backdrop
- *Bonbons piments* (deep-fried balls of lentils and chilli)
- Botanical Gardens
- Amazing ice cream

WEAKNESSES

- Mosquitoes
- Everything's expensive
- Cyclones
- Finding a seat in a restaurant at lunchtime

GOLD STAR

Food – thanks to the French passion for *la gastronomie* (gastronomy), there's a restaurant or café around virtually every corner.

STARRING ROLE IN...

- *Paul and Virginie* by Bernardin de Saint-Pierre

See the Creole mansions on Rue de Paris, many of which feature elaborate verandas and intricate *lambrequins* (ornamental window and door borders).

Eat a storming traditional Creole curry at the funky-cool Cyclone Café.

Drink blinding mojitos (a cocktail made of rum, lime, sugar, mint and soda water) while posing at the ultra-modern Moda Bar.

Do play *pétanque* before sunset at the seafront park at Le Barachois.

Watch a Hollywood blockbuster that's been hilariously dubbed into French at Gaumont cinema.

Buy the luscious *rhums arrangés* (flavoured rums) from Le Petit Marché.

After dark get into the groove by taking an Afro-Caribbean dance class.

THE COLOURFUL EXTERIOR OF THE HINDU TEMPLE LOOKS AT ITS BEST IN THE SUNSHINE.

AT A COCOA PLANTATION, THREE HORSES AWAIT THEIR NEXT CARGO.

Salvador da Bahia

NICKNAME BAHIA; SALVADOR; BLACK ROME **DATE OF BIRTH** 1549; WHEN TOMÉ DE SOUSA LANDED ON PRAIA PORTO DA BARRA UNDER PORTUGUESE ROYAL ORDERS TO FOUND BRAZIL'S FIRST CAPITAL **ADDRESS** BRAZIL (MAP 3, J9) **HEIGHT** 19M **SIZE** 324 SQ KM **POPULATION** 2.7 MILLION **LONELY PLANET RANKING** 062

Salvador da Bahia is the African soul of Brazil, where descendants of African slaves have preserved their cultural roots. This beautiful city thrives with culinary, religious, musical, dance and martial-art traditions.

ANATOMY

Salvador's one-way roads wend their way around the hills and valleys. The centre is on the bay side of the peninsula and is divided by a steep bluff in two parts: Cidade Alta (Upper City) and Cidade Baixa (Lower City). The heart of historic Cidade Alta is the Pelourinho (or Pelô), the base for Salvador's nightlife. Cidade Baixa contains the Comércio (the commercial centre), and port. Linking Cidade Alta and Cidade Baixa are the Elevador Lacerda (four lifts that shuttle 28,000 passengers daily) and the Plano Inclinado Gonçalves (funicular railway).

PEOPLE

Bahia is Brazil's most Africanised state, and many inhabitants were forcibly brought here as part of the slave trade; other ethnic groups were lured by the Portuguese to mine for gold. About 70% of the population is Roman Catholic, with a significant proportion either belonging to cults or practising Indian animism. Portuguese is the official language.

TYPICAL SALVADORENOS

Fun-loving, joyous, sensual and mystical all describe Salvadorenos, as does paradoxical. They are spiritual people who devoutly dedicate time to the activities of their church or *terreiro* (place of worship). On Sunday everyone dons something skimpy and heads out to ogle and be ogled.

DEFINING EXPERIENCE

Drinking in a panoramic bay view from the Praça Municipal, then marvelling at the off-kilter icons in the baroque Igreja e Convento de São Francisco before attending a Candomblé (an African-American religion, chiefly practised in Brazil) service at a *terreiro* in Casa Branca.

SPONTANEOUS DRUMMING AND DANCING IN THE FORMER SLAVE DISTRICT AS A PRELUDE TO CARNAVAL.

BOYS LEAP INTO THE BAY AS THE SUN SETS.

MAKING A CALL FROM A PHONE BOOTH SHAPED LIKE A CAPOEIRA INSTRUMENT.

STRENGTHS
- Exciting, exhilarating *carnaval*
- Forbidden dances
- Capoeira
- Churches, churches, churches
- Idyllic white-sand beaches
- Colourful colonial façades
- Warm waters
- Enthusiastic, energetic locals
- Charming cobblestone streets

WEAKNESSES
- Sleazy, dangerous, volatile *carnaval*
- Rampant poverty and begging
- Scams, muggings and pickpockets
- Sexual harassment
- Dengue fever

GOLD STAR
Mojo – Salvador da Bahia has a culture rich in hypnotic drum beats, fragrant spices, inherent sensuality and *axé* (divine energy that brings good luck).

STARRING ROLE IN...
- *That's My Face* (2002)
- *Dona Flor e Seus Dois Maridos* (1976)
- *Tenda dos Milagres* (1977)
- *Robinson Crusoe* by Daniel Defoe

See city streets from the windows behind the lift (elevator) entrances at the beautifully restored Art Deco Elevador Lacerda.

Eat steaming plates of *bobó de camarão* (shrimp in yucca cream) lowered down to you on a tray from the kitchen in tiny Dona Chika-ka.

Drink cocktails on the open-air patio at popular Cantina da Lua.

Do attend Salvador's raucous *carnaval*, the second largest in Brazil.

Watch Bahia's beautiful people, skimpy togs and all, on beachside Praia Porto da Barra, bustling with vendors along the clear, calm waters.

Buy local handicrafts ranging from embroidery to musical instruments at Mercado Modelo on Praça Cayru.

After dark a long evening of Candomblé in Casa Branca, Salvador's oldest *terreiro*, is quite an experience.

San Cristóbal de las Casas

NICKNAME SAN CRISTÓBAL **DATE OF BIRTH** 1528; WHEN DIEGO DE MAZARIEGOS FOUNDED THE CITY AS A SPANISH REGIONAL BASE **ADDRESS** MEXICO (MAP 2, F5) **HEIGHT** 2163M **POPULATION** 186,000 **LONELY PLANET RANKING** 086

In the heart of Mexico's southernmost state, San Cristóbal de las Casas is a light and airy city; indigenous communities trade goods and ideas among crumbling colonial churches and pastel-coloured houses.

ANATOMY

Although San Cristóbal de las Casas is a couple of kilometres above sea level, it manages to rest in a fertile valley. The town grid is framed by a chain of low hills dotted with indigenous villages. The serene heart of the city is Plaza 31 de Marzo where craft sellers and lunch-breakers mill around in the sun. Commerce has not left a strong architectural imprint: the tallest structures are the lovely Spanish municipal buildings and cathedrals. Combis go up Av Crescencio Rosas from the Pan-American Hwy to the town centre. You can catch taxis within town.

PEOPLE

Due to their custom of wearing their hair in pony tails, the men of San Cristóbal earned the nickname *coletos* (from the Spanish word *cola* or 'tail'). The word is still used to refer to a resident of the city although most citizens are mestizo (of mixed Spanish and indigenous ancestry). From its beginnings the town has been a meeting point for Tzotzil and Tzeltal peoples, who continue to define the soul of the city.

TYPICAL COLETO

San Cristóbal wears its history on its sleeve, and residents have a strong sense of both their ancestry and their place in the unfolding narrative. Largely untouched by the land reforms of 1917, the region's inhabitants continued to suffer under a punishing colonial structure until relatively recently. Indigenous pride is strong in the area and it's not unusual to see locals in their traditional dress in the heart of the city. *Coletos* are confident but wary – cheerful faces veil simmering social tensions.

LOUIS GRANDADAM / GETTY IMAGES

THE CROSS CASTS A SHADOW ON SAN CRISTÓBAL'S CATHEDRAL.

DEFINING EXPERIENCE

Getting up early to enjoy the freshest coffee from the city's own Museo Café (Coffee Museum), heading to the hills on a caffeine high to observe the unique lifestyles of San Cristóbal's neighbours, making it back to the market for an open-air lunch in the middle of the madness then winding down in the late afternoon sun at Plaza 31 de Marzo.

STRENGTHS

◢ Bartolomé de las Casas (early defender of indigenous rights)
◢ Zapatista iconography
◢ Cobbled streets
◢ Clear highland light
◢ Plaza 31 de Marzo
◢ Mercado Municipal – the wonderfully chaotic city market
◢ Organic coffee

WEAKNESSES

◢ Foreign missionaries
◢ Heavily armed soldiers
◢ Political tensions
◢ Intransigent councils
◢ Religious intolerance

GOLD STAR

Weaving – Tzotzil weavers are some of the most skilled in Mexico and their distinctive needlework can be seen everywhere you wander.

STARRING ROLE IN...

◢ *A Place Called Chiapas* (1998)

See the charming Templo de Santo Domingo, a fine example of Spanish colonial architecture.

Eat rustic tortillas containing microscopic amounts of ground limestone.

Drink organic coffee from locally harvested beans.

Do take an excursion to the nearby indigenous villages of San Lorenzo Zinacantán and San Juan Chamula.

Watch Mexican and Latin American cinema, political documentaries and art-house movies at Kinoki.

Buy expertly woven indigenous garments.

After dark there's always something going on at Café Bar Revolution.

A WOMAN HAULS HER LOAD HOME.

SMILES ALL ROUND AT THE TIENDA DONA PANCHITA ON CALLE DIEGO DUGELAY.

A PUPPETEER IN A CROW COSTUME ACTS OUT A SCENE FROM A MAYAN MYTH.

CHEERING ON THE GIANTS AT SAN FRANCISCO'S BASEBALL STADIUM.

San Francisco

NICKNAME FRISCO (ALTHOUGH NOBODY FROM SAN FRANCISCO WOULD EVER SAY THIS); CITY BY THE BAY **DATE OF BIRTH** 1776; WHEN A MILITARY POST WAS ESTABLISHED BY SPANISH MISSIONARIES FROM MEXICO **ADDRESS** USA (MAP 1, D5) **HEIGHT** 16M **SIZE** 121 SQ KM **POPULATION** 805,000 (CITY); 4.3 MILLION (METRO AREA) **LONELY PLANET RANKING** 107

Post dot-gone, the City by the Bay sparkles on with literary luminaries, artsy stars and an array of cultures.

ANATOMY

The city is on the tightly packed tip of a peninsula bordered by the Pacific Ocean and San Francisco Bay. The central part resembles a slice of pie, with Van Ness Ave and Market St marking the two sides and the Embarcadero bend serving as the crust. Squeezed into this compact area are Union Sq, the Financial District, Civic Center, Chinatown, North Beach, Nob Hill, Russian Hill and Fisherman's Wharf. San Francisco's public transport system is Muni, which operates nearly 100 bus lines, streetcars and cable cars. BART is the limited subway system.

PEOPLE

Long ago an Anglo-Celtic town, the face of San Francisco has changed since the early days. Though still predominantly a white population, the Asian community follows at a close second. The balance of the city's residents are Latino and black, with a significant 10% who classify themselves as 'other'. Best estimates say about one sixth of residents are gay. San Franciscans are also young, with a median age of 36.5 years old.

TYPICAL SAN FRANCISCAN

Native San Franciscans are few and far between. San Francisco is a city of transplants, and the city attracts free spirits. Everyone you meet will be writing a novel, producing a film or performing their interpretive dance. They usually do it in between wine tasting in Sonoma Valley, being dazzled by the bay and bracing themselves for the next big one.

DEFINING EXPERIENCE

Hanging out in Haight Ashbury, browsing the latest works at the 826 Valencia bookstore, grabbing a burrito on Mission St, making new friends with leather chaps and handle-bar moustaches at Harvey's, chowing down on dim sum in Chinatown then spying the Golden Gate in the fog.

STRENGTHS

- Golden Gate Bridge
- Mexican food
- Diverse sexuality
- Eccentricity
- The Ferry Plaza Farmers Market
- San Francisco 49ers and Giants
- City Lights bookstore
- Haight Ashbury

WEAKNESSES

- Haight Ashbury
- Panhandlers
- The Tenderloin
- San Andreas Fault
- Real-estate prices

GOLD STAR

Hanging out – Kerouac came here to learn how to do nothing and the city is still a great place to just tune into the universe, man.

STARRING ROLE IN...

- *Tales of the City* by Armistead Maupin
- *Basic Instinct* (1992)
- *Dirty Harry* (1971)
- *American Graffiti* (1973)
- *Birdman of Alcatraz* (1962)
- *The Joy Luck Club* (1993)

See the almost inescapable Alcatraz, which hosted Al Capone and a bird fancier or two.

Eat a juicy burrito at La Taquería on Mission St.

Drink an American pale ale straight from the cellar at Magnolia Pub & Brewery.

Do the cycle around the Presidio as a warm-up for mountain biking in Marin County.

Watch and heckle a spoken word performance (that's poetry reading to you and me) at Café Du Nord.

Buy a vinyl copy of the Grateful Dead at Amoeba Records on Haight St.

After dark grab a brew and rock to the blues at the Boom Boom Room.

LETTING HIS HAIR DOWN AT GAY PRIDE.

DANCERS HIT THE SPIN CYCLE AT THE CARNIVAL ON MEMORIAL DAY WEEKEND.

THE NEON WONDERLAND OF CHINATOWN BY NIGHT.

San Juan

DATE OF BIRTH 1511; WHEN THE SPANISH COLONISED THE CITY
ADDRESS PUERTO RICO (MAP 2, R2) **HEIGHT** 25M **SIZE** 300 SQ KM
POPULATION 2.4 MILLION **LONELY PLANET RANKING** 113

Fulfilling all fantasies about tropical Caribbean coastal cities, San Juan offers all the fun and drama of a Latino holiday haven, played out against the backdrop of the spectacular fortressed walls of the old city.

ANATOMY

The city stretches from San Juan Bay across a coastal plain. The city's centre (Old San Juan) is crammed with Spanish colonial architecture. This walled city occupies the end of a small island on the eastern side of the entrance to the bay. East of Old San Juan are the resort districts of Condado and Isla Verde, with greater San Juan stretching south, east and west of the main centre. Walking is the best way to get around Old San Juan and the immediate vicinity, though there is a handy and free tourist trolley. There are also many *públicos* (shared taxis) available.

PEOPLE

The majority of the population is of Spanish or mixed Spanish descent; around 20% are of African descent. Most locals are Roman Catholic, with around 10% being Protestant and a small percentage following other faiths. The official language is Spanish, but English is widely spoken.

TYPICAL SAN JUAN CITIZEN

San Juan's citizens work mainly in manufacturing industries or tourism. Despite the fact that Puerto Rico is a US territory, the hourly wage is significantly lower than in the USA, although many work for US firms. They are increasingly prosperous. They have small families, are religious, love quick tempos and hot moves, and are friendly. After work they hang out at restaurants and bars that pulse with the rhythm of the night.

DEFINING EXPERIENCE

Sipping coffee and scrawling inspired notes for 'the novel' at the popular meeting place for writers and artists (Cuatro Estaciones Cafe in Old San Juan), then heading to the beach for a splash and some well-deserved shut-eye before sprucing up for a sizzling night of salsa at La Rumba.

JOHN NEUBAUER / GETTY IMAGES

STEP BACK IN TIME – SPANISH COLONIAL ARCHITECTURE IS A FEATURE OF OLD SAN JUAN.

Hijos de Boringuen

CALLE
DE
SAN SEBASTIAN

FOR SALE
WILTON CANCEL
REALTY
721-1040 [R]

D A LUIS N. Falcon XI
Denis Mario
1982

MUSEO
SIN
TECHO
A SOL
Y
AGUA

SI TE SORPRENDO
VANDALIZANDO LAS
OBRAS DE ARTE
TE
CASTIGARÉ

JORGE

THE PUERTO RICO FLAG EMBODIES THE NATION'S PRIDE.

CAFES AND BARS SERVE UP FINGER-LICKING FOOD AND A LIVELY SOCIAL SCENE.

THEY'RE NOT CUBAN BUT SAN JUAN'S CIGARS ARE STILL WORLD-CLASS.

STRENGTHS

- Coral reefs offshore
- Thriving nightlife
- Rainforest nearby
- Gardens of the Casa Blanca
- World Heritage Site of Old San Juan
- Beach weather year-round
- Coconut limber (homemade icy-pole in a cup)
- Radio Sol (good salsa station)
- Cronopios (The Bookstore)

WEAKNESSES

- Traffic jams (and carjacking)
- Dangerous areas in and around the city
- Many restaurants closed on Sunday or Monday
- Drug dealers
- Heaps of tourists, virtually everywhere, most of the time

GOLD STAR

The walled city of Old San Juan – within its walls are the charms of over 400 years of Spanish colonial history, fine cultural institutions, a spirited community and a thriving nightlife. This fortress of fun offers travellers more entertainment per square kilometre than New York City, at a pace that is laid-back and distinctly Latin.

STARRING ROLE IN...

- *Bad Boys 2* (2003)
- *Amistad* (1997)
- *GoldenEye* (1995)
- *Assassins* (1995)

See the salsa heroes of tomorrow perform on the streets.

Eat your fill of fresh, cheap exotic fruits as you peruse the market stalls of the colourful Mercado de Río Piedras.

Drink free rum on a tour at the factory of world-famous Bacardi Rum.

Do devote as many days as possible to exploring Old San Juan – to fully soak up its bubbling tropical atmosphere and bold beauty.

Watch surfers battle the swells east of the broad tropical beach of Isla Verde in the dusk of early evening.

Buy new-season items at the Ralph Lauren store in Old San Juan.

After dark hear live salsa along Calles San Sebastian and Forteleza.

IN FULL VOICE – LUBRICATED BY RUM AND LIME AT ONE OF THE CITY'S BARS.

San Salvador

NICKNAME SAN SAL **DATE OF BIRTH** 1525; WHEN IT WAS FOUNDED BY SPANISH CONQUISTADOR PEDRO DE ALVARADO
ADDRESS EL SALVADOR (MAP 2, H7) **HEIGHT** 682M **SIZE** 75 SQ KM
POPULATION 2.4 MILLION **LONELY PLANET RANKING** 170

You can come to be one of the few tourists to see San Salvador's spectacular natural sights, or to watch Salvadoran society reconstruct itself after the ravages of civil war, but really, just come to meet the people.

ANATOMY

Built on a volcanic slope that parallels the Pacific coast, the city of San Salvador is El Salvador's largest and its crossroads. It's the hub of the nation, and is home to over one-third of its population and half of the wealth. Crossed by the Pan American Hwy, the city's modern downtown area has many high-rise buildings, but sadly earthquakes have destroyed the majority of historic landmarks. San Salvador's extensive bus network can get you just about anywhere you need.

PEOPLE

San Salvadorans are among the more European-looking Central Americans – the vast majority is undoubtedly mestizo (of mixed Spanish and indigenous ancestry), but fair skin and green and blue eyes are not unusual. Around 10% of San Salvadorans are considered of full European ancestry, while 1% are indigenous. Spanish is the official language.

TYPICAL SAN SALVADORAN

San Salvadorans are straight-talking, strong-minded and hard-working. They're extremely helpful and almost universally friendly, with a powerful sense of justice; few are shy about expressing their opinion. The civil war still looms large for many, but they're genuinely dismayed to learn that foreigners know little about their country *other* than war, and will talk with pride about El Salvador's natural virtues.

DEFINING EXPERIENCE

Beginning the day with bread and *cafecito* (short black coffee), stocking up on food in the Mercado Central, cooking a beans-and-rice lunch then snoozing away the siesta, drinking Pilsener and getting down to some *cumbia* (Colombian dance tunes) and salsa.

STRENGTHS

⬛ San Salvadorans' positivity
⬛ The Mayan community
⬛ Creative street vendors
⬛ The Festival of El Salvador del Mundo
⬛ Museo de Arte de El Salvador
⬛ Post–civil war unity
⬛ Adventure of travelling a relatively unvisited city
⬛ Great literary history
⬛ Year-round summer climate

WEAKNESSES

⬛ Petty theft
⬛ High population growth
⬛ Poverty and shanty towns
⬛ Guns everywhere
⬛ Pollution and traffic
⬛ Earthquakes
⬛ Bitter political history
⬛ Environmental destruction

GOLD STAR

San Salvadorans have a strong work ethic and have quickly raised their country from the wreckage of civil war to close to the top of Central America's economic ladder.

STARRING ROLE IN...

⬛ *Salvador* (1986)
⬛ *Romero* (1989)
⬛ *Salvador* by Joan Didion
⬛ *San Salvador* by Roque Dalton

See the view of the city from the rim of Boquerón volcano.

Eat *pupusas* (meat or cheese pastries) from a street stall.

Drink Pilsener beer at a bar with the locals.

Do check out the MARTE (the Museo de Arte de El Salvador).

Watch the maelstrom of crowds scurrying through sprawling markets, music blaring from every direction and buses zipping around at breakneck pace.

Buy handicrafts, hand-woven textiles and ceramics at the Mercado Ex-Cuartel.

After dark see live jazz and salsa at La Luna Casa y Arte.

WHISPERED PRAYERS RISE UP TO MEET THE CEILING OF IGLESIA LA CIBA DE GUADALUPE.

A LOCAL WOMAN HAS SEEN SAN SALVADOR CHANGE FOR THE BETTER.

THE PALM SUNDAY PROCESSION THROUGH THE CENTRE OF SAN SALVADOR.

San Sebastián

BASQUE NAME DONOSTIA **DATE OF BIRTH** 1174; SAN SEBASTIÁN WAS GRANTED SELF-GOVERNING STATUS BY THE KINGDOM OF NAVARRA, FOR WHOM THE BAY WAS THE PRINCIPAL OUTLET TO THE SEA
ADDRESS SPAIN (MAP 5, F4) **HEIGHT** 7M **POPULATION** 186,000
LONELY PLANET RANKING 111

One of the oldest and most famous beach resorts in the world, San Sebastián's breathtaking natural beauty, warm inhabitants and extraordinary cuisine ensure that the gloss never wears off this quintessential haunt of the bronzed and beautiful.

ANATOMY

San Sebastián has three main centres. The modern centre surrounds the Catedral del Buen Pastor, while the heart of San Sebastián beats in the Parte Vieja (Old Town), squeezed below Monte Urgull Parque on the eastern spur of the Bahía de la Concha. The third area is Gros, east across the Río Urumea, which also has a good beach, and is home to the Renfe train station. The main bus station is about 1km south of the cathedral.

PEOPLE

The Basque people have become one of Europe's most prominent yet least-understood minorities. The Basques have retained a language, and with it a separate identity, whose origin still puzzles linguists.

TYPICAL SAN SEBASTIÁN CITIZEN

Chic, hard-working and fond of food and drink, the typical citizen of San Sebastián speaks both Castilian (Spanish) and Euskara (the Basque language) and keeps a pragmatic but proud grip on local traditions. Older men will often be members of a *txoko* (all-male eating societies) and capable of wearing berets with much style. Younger men will often be keen surfers of the nearby beaches.

DEFINING EXPERIENCE

Starting the day with a refreshing dip at the beach to get the blood pumping after the night before, which saw you tripping between *pintxos* (Basque tapas) bars until the wee hours, then spending the morning sussing out some of the edgy graphic arts on display around the city, followed by a very, very satisfying Michelin-starred lunch.

FAST-PACED *JAI-ALAI* ACTION IN PLAZA DE LA TRINIDAD.

STRENGTHS

- ◢ Burying of the Sardine ritual at the end of *carnaval*
- ◢ Great local beaches
- ◢ Stylish places to stay
- ◢ San Sebastián Film Festival
- ◢ Innovative nouvelle cuisine
- ◢ International Jazz Festival
- ◢ Views from Monte Igueldo
- ◢ Eduardo Chillida's *Peine de Vientos* sculpture
- ◢ Mesmerising Euskara

WEAKNESSES

- ◢ Crowds in summer
- ◢ Trying to get a good night's sleep in the Parte Vieja
- ◢ Angry young drunks around closing time on some of the Parte Vieja streets
- ◢ Unmentionable politics
- ◢ Impenetrable Euskara

GOLD STAR

Food – Basque *pintxos* are the greatest snacks in the world and San Sebastián's are the best of the lot.

STARRING ROLE IN...

- ◢ *The Sun Also Rises* by Ernest Hemingway
- ◢ *The Red Squirrel* (1993)
- ◢ *A Social Parade* (2004)

See the world's prettiest city beach at Playa de la Concha.

Eat at Juan Mari Arzak's triple Michelin-starred Arzak.

Drink red wine from nearby La Rioja.

Do a walk to the top of Monte Urgull by taking a path from Plaza de Zuloaga or from behind the aquarium.

Watch hot cinema at the San Sebastián Film Festival.

Buy cutting-edge Basque fashion from the Loreak Mendian label.

After dark go bar-hopping in the Parte Vieja.

BASQUE *PINTXOS* USE FRESH PRODUCE FROM THE SEA AND THE LAND.

A STREET SCENE IN THE OLD TOWN.

A SURFER WANTS TO SPREAD HIS WINGS ON PLAYA DE LA ZURRIOLA.

ANCIENT STREETS PAVE THE WAY FOR MODERN SAN'A.

San'a

NICKNAME SAM CITY **DATE OF BIRTH** BIBLICAL TIMES; LEGEND SAYS IT WAS FOUNDED BY NOAH'S SON SHEM **ADDRESS** YEMEN (MAP 8, C8) **HEIGHT** 2250M **POPULATION** 1.9 MILLION **LONELY PLANET RANKING** 160

San'a is the capital of one of the last untouched corners of Arabia; the Old City is a perfectly preserved realm of traditional architecture with the stone foundations of some houses thought to date back 1000 years.

ANATOMY

San'a expands vigorously in all directions from its original heart, the walled Old City. The clamorous Midan al-Tahrir sits at the western edge of the Old City, while Az-Zubayri St defines its southern limits. Bab al-Yaman leads into the vibrant Souq al-Milh. Traffic is frantic and anarchic; to enter the fray your best options are taxis and motorbike taxis.

PEOPLE

The population of San'a is almost exclusively Arab – residents are said to have descended from different stock from the tribes that live in the rest of Yemen. The city's once-notable Jewish community has departed for Israel. A small and eclectic population of expats calls San'a home.

TYPICAL SAN'ANI

As a rule, San'anis are welcoming, spontaneous and gregarious to a fault. They are noted throughout the Middle East for their quick sense of humour. Tribe still plays an important role in the consciousness of Yemenis, although less so in San'a, but all Yemenis are proud of their distinctive culture.

DEFINING EXPERIENCE

Starting the day with a strong coffee at a Turkish coffee house near the Bab al-Yaman; pondering the exhibits, including examples of San'ani building styles, at the Museum of Traditional Arts and Crafts; diving in and getting lost in the labyrinth of the Souq al-Milh; chewing *qat* (a mild stimulant) with the locals in the afternoon; getting soapy and washing away the grit of the desert in a *hammam* (bathhouse).

SAN'ANIS WEAR THEIR CULTURE WITH PRIDE AND IN THEIR BELTS.

THE LOCAL ARCHITECTURE STANDS OUT.

THE GRACIOUS SMILE OF AN OLDER SAN'ANI.

STRENGTHS

◢ History around every corner
◢ Free of touts and other tourism-related hassles
◢ Easy-going traders in the souqs (markets) – no hard sell

WEAKNESSES

◢ Dust
◢ Traffic and exhaust fumes
◢ Monsoon rains
◢ Kidnappings (only occasional!)
◢ Stray dogs
◢ Everything closing down every afternoon for the daily *qat*-chewing session

GOLD STAR

Architecture – San'a is home to prototypical skyscrapers built of mud and stone; the entire Old City has been declared a Unesco World Heritage Site.

STARRING ROLE IN...

◢ *Arabian Nights* (1974)
◢ *A New Day in Old San'a* (2005)
◢ *Travels in Dictionary Land* by Tim Mackintosh Smith
◢ *Eating the Flowers of Paradise* by Kevin Rushby
◢ *The Southern Gates of Arabia* by Freya Stark
◢ *Motoring with Mohammed* by Eric Hansen

See the Museum of Traditional Arts and Crafts.

Eat *shwarma*, or *salta*, a fiery stew of lamb, peppers and coriander.

Drink coffee flavoured with cardamom, but don't come here for an alcoholic tipple.

Do a course in the Arabic language or Islamic culture at the San'a Institute for Arabic Language.

Watch the sun set over the domes and towers of the Old City.

Buy spices, fabrics, incense or coffee in the Souq al-Milh.

After dark wander the Old City – the stained-glass windows of the traditional buildings illuminate the city like a mass of coloured lanterns.

Santiago de Chile

NICKNAME SANTIAGO **DATE OF BIRTH** 1541; FOUNDED BY
CONQUISTADOR PEDRO DE VALDIVIA **ADDRESS** CHILE (MAP 3, C15)
HEIGHT 520M **SIZE** 140 SQ KM **POPULATION** 5.2 MILLION (CITY); 7.1
MILLION (METRO AREA) **LONELY PLANET RANKING** 066

**Santiago de Chile is a modern metropolis with a shiny
face, but at the same time, struggling street vendors
board city buses to hawk everything from pins to ice
cream, and housemaids commute for hours to scrub
floors and change nappies in exclusive suburbs.**

ANATOMY

Greater Santiago is an immense bowl-shaped city jammed between the
Andes and the coastal cordillera. The most important axis is the east–west
thoroughfare Av O'Higgins (the Alameda) that in the east becomes Av
Providencia and, further east, Av Apoquindo and Av Las Condes. The
metro's Línea 1 follows this axis, leading 'up' to the residential areas at the
foot of the mountains and 'down' towards the coast.

PEOPLE

Santiago's people are mainly of Spanish ancestry, but the Irish and English
also made a mark. Other immigrants came from Germany, France, Italy,
Croatia and Palestine. Spanish is the official language.

TYPICAL SANTIAGUINO

Santiaguinos tend to be polite, well-dressed and somewhat restrained,
despite their predilection for staying out late. They are hard-working,
prosperous and business-minded. Divorce has not been made legal, but
this hasn't kept families together as much as it has increased the
acceptance of couples living together and having children out of wedlock.
While most Chileans are quite proud of their heritage, there's an obvious
lack of patriotism and an increasing level of individualism.

DEFINING EXPERIENCE

Meandering in the city's historic centre, Plaza de Armas, bordered by
colonial and neoclassical buildings, and stopping off in an arcade flanking
the square for an *empanada de queso* (cheese-filled turnover), then heading
to Museo Chileno de Arte Precolombino or Parque de las Esculturas, a
sculpture garden on the banks of the Río Mapocho.

ENRIQUE SIQUES / GETTY IMAGES

IN THE WAR AGAINST AIR POLLUTION, THE PEAK-HOUR SUBWAY SCRAMBLE IS A REAL BATTLE.

THE SKYSCRAPERS OF THE VITACURA NEIGHBOURHOOD ARE DWARFED BY THE CITY'S NATURAL BOUNDARY, THE ANDES.

STRENGTHS

◢ Bellavista's hip, energetic restaurant and club scene
◢ Quirky architecture in Barrios París Londres, Concha y Toro and Brasil
◢ Barrio Santa Lucía's bars and cafés
◢ Renowned wineries
◢ Skiing at Portillo
◢ Proximity to the Andes
◢ High literacy rate
◢ Cerro San Cristóbal, whose 863m summit is crowned by a dazzling white statue of the Virgin Mary

WEAKNESSES

◢ Pollution
◢ History of human-rights violations
◢ Poor environmental record
◢ Past dictatorships
◢ Pickpockets, especially in Centro

GOLD STAR

There's something great about being smack in the middle of a metropolis and looking up and seeing the second highest mountain range in the world.

STARRING ROLE IN...

◢ *Johnny 100 Pesos* (1994)
◢ *El Chacotero Sentimental* (1999)
◢ *Taxi Para Tres* (2001)
◢ *House of the Spirits* by Isabel Allende
◢ *Passions and Impressions* by Pablo Neruda

See the Barrio Brasil, whose centrepiece is the Plaza Brasil and its quake-damaged, neo-Gothic Basílica del Salvador.

Eat lunch at Galindo, a traditional place that was one of Neruda's favourites.

Drink a *pisco* sour while taking in local theatre, poetry or music at La Casa en el Aire.

Do catch the glass *ascensor* (lift) up the hillside to the gardens, footpaths and fountains of Cerro Santa Lucía.

Watch a Chilean-style rodeo at Club de Huasos Gil Letelier.

Buy handicrafts from all over the country at the artisans' village Centro Artesanal de Los Dominicos.

After dark head to the Pablo Salvador, where hip folk go after drinks at Etniko.

FRIENDSHIP IS ONE OF LIFE'S RICHES – A MOTORCYCLIST CHATS WITH NEIGHBOURS.

Santo Domingo

DATE OF BIRTH 1498; WHEN IT WAS FOUNDED BY BARTOLOMÉ COLOMBUS, BROTHER OF CHRISTOPHER **ADDRESS** DOMINICAN REPUBLIC (MAP 3, C1) **HEIGHT** 17M **POPULATION** 965,000 (CITY); 3 MILLION (METRO AREA) **LONELY PLANET RANKING** 185.

The oldest Spanish city in the Americas has luscious natural surroundings, is profoundly festive and full of joyous, welcoming souls.

ANATOMY

Santo Domingo began as the birthplace of European colonies in the New World, and is now the political and economic centre of the Dominican Republic, which occupies the eastern side of the island of Hispaniola (Haiti occupies the western side). It revolves around green-blue waters crashing against its cliff-lined coast, couples overlooking the surf, whispering sweet everythings to each other, and buses belching long trails of spent diesel. It's a city with a vast cave system beneath it, an old fort and a park that fills daily with hundreds of joggers and cyclists.

PEOPLE

Santo Domingans may have adopted the Spanish language and the Catholic religion of their founders, but racially they're predominantly mulattos (with one white and one black parent), with the rest of the population comprised of those of African and European descent.

TYPICAL SANTO DOMINGAN

Maintaining family ties and cultivating friendships are priorities for Santo Domingans, and the merengue (folkloric dance of the Dominican Republic) is a tool for fostering relationships. Santo Domingans are flexible enough to live with contrasts, such as the wealthy coexisting with those mired in poverty. They maintain traditions and revere their history, yet most watch American TV with awe. It's a city of Catholics with no shortage of brothels, five-star hotels that function despite power outages, and oppressive heat, but locals remain optimistic and patient.

DEFINING EXPERIENCE

Strolling and dining on Dominican food on the *malecón* (waterfront promenade), watching Licey play at Quisqueya Stadium, then dancing merengue in a club until dawn.

699

STRENGTHS

- Not one, but two crazy carnivals a year – in February and August
- Two merengue festivals
- Historic buildings
- Baseball games
- Obelisco del Malecón
- Calle de las Damas (Ladies' Street)
- All-night, or anytime, dancing
- Fantastic views over the cliffs
- Roba La Gallina (an enormous chicken character in carnivals)

WEAKNESSES

- Petty crime
- Hurricanes
- Exterminated Arawak Indians
- Violent political history
- Aggressive police
- One-third below the poverty line

GOLD STAR

Most mobile 'founding city' – Santo Domingo was originally located in La Villa de Navidad in Haiti and finally settled on the Ozama River's west bank.

STARRING ROLE IN...

- *The Brief Wondrous Life of Oscar Wao* by Junot Diaz
- *Santo Domingo Blues* (2004)
- *In the Time of the Butterflies* by Julia Álvarez
- *Sucre amer* (Bitter Sugar) by Maurice Lemoine

See *tabacos* (cigars) being rolled at the Boutique del Fumador or the Museo del Tabaco.

Eat *empanadas* (pastry stuffed with meat or cheese) and *pastelitos* (meat- and cheese-filled pastries) from street stalls.

Drink rum at sunset at Plaza de Hispanidad.

Do bargain at the Pulga de Antigüedades (Antique Market) on Sunday.

Watch baseball played by Licey or Escojido at Quisqueya Stadium.

Buy amber or *larimar* (an opaque blue stone found only in the Dominican Republic) jewellery in the Zona Colonial.

After dark dance to a wide range of music at one of the city's clubs.

BLENDING IN AS ONLY A LOCAL CAN.

MIXED MESSAGES – LIFE ON DUARTE AVE.

BE ENCHANTED BY SANTO DOMINGO'S OLD-WORLD CHARM AND LATIN CHARISMA.

Sarajevo

DATE OF BIRTH 1461: TURKISH SARAJEVO WAS FOUNDED BY ISABEY ISAKOVIC AND LATER BECAME A MILITARY AND COMMERCIAL CENTRE
ADDRESS BOSNIA & HERCEGOVINA (MAP 5, P4) **HEIGHT** 630M
SIZE 142 SQ KM **POPULATION** 411,000 **LONELY PLANET RANKING** 043

The crossroads of East and West since antiquity, Sarajevo stands by the Miljacka River, surrounded by hills and mountains, and encompasses the essence of Bosnia and Hercegovina's cultural diversity, merging dance, music, food and hope after centuries of war.

ANATOMY

Sarajevo lies in a valley created by the Miljacka River. The mountains of Jahorina and Bjelašnica (host to the 1984 Winter Olympics) flank the city to the south. From the airport, 6.5km to the southwest, the main road runs up to the suburb of Ilidža, then swings east through Novo Sarajevo. The bus and train stations are to the north. Near the centre the road runs beside the Miljacka River, before leaving it at Baščaršija (the old Turkish Quarter), which occupies the east end of town.

PEOPLE

Serbs, Croats and Bosnian Muslims are all Southern Slavs of the same ethnic stock. Physically they are indistinguishable. The prewar population was incredibly mixed and intermarriage was common. Ethnic cleansing has concentrated Muslims in Sarajevo, but there are also high numbers of people who are Orthodox and Roman Catholic. Inhabitants are known as Bosnian Serbs, Bosnian Croats or Bosniaks (Muslims). Across Bosnia and Hercegovina, churches and mosques are being built (or rebuilt) at lightning speed. This is more symptomatic of strong nationalism than religion, as most people are fairly secular.

TYPICAL SARAJEVAN

For any city it's a stretch to summarise the general character of its denizens, and that goes for Sarajevo tenfold. Their differences are both their greatest challenge and greatest strength. What is certain is that they are proud, patriotic and traditionally minded but also very cosmopolitan and friendly. Given the speed and diligence with which they are rebuilding their city, to say that they were hard-working and determined would be an understatement.

THE CROWDED SKYLINE TELLS OF THE CITY'S RICH PAST AND ITS ASPIRATIONS FOR THE FUTURE.

A YOUNG MUSLIM WOMAN PLANS HER DAY FROM THE STEPS OF GAZI-HUSREVBEY MOSQUE.

MAKING HIS OWN FUN, A YOUNG BOY PLAYS AMONG THE PIGEONS IN THE MAIN SQUARE.

A BURLY BROLLEY SELLER WAITS FOR CLOUDS TO GATHER IN THE TURKISH QUARTER.

DEFINING EXPERIENCE

Exploring the cobbled laneways of Baščaršija, shopping for a hand-made watch, then spending the afternoon cycling the old road beside the Miljacka River towards the Turkish bridge (Goat Bridge).

STRENGTHS

- Fresh *burek* (filo-pastry balls stuffed with beef or spinach and feta)
- Baščaršija
- National Museum
- The indoor and outdoor markets
- 20km ski run at Mt Jahorina
- The Sebilj fountain
- Latin Bridge
- Morića Han

WEAKNESSES

- Land mines
- Nationalism
- Confusing street-numbering system

GOLD STAR

Survival – for enduring a war that took it to the cusp of destruction and remaining a strong and enigmatic mix of cultures.

STARRING ROLE IN...

- *No Mans Land* (2001)
- *The Perfect Circle* (1997)
- *Welcome to Sarajevo* (1997)

See the Sarajevo roses (skeletal handlike indentations where a shell has exploded) on the pavements – some are accompanied by a brass plaques giving the names of those killed by that shell.

Eat Turkish ćevapčići (grilled minced lamb or beef) with a half-loaf of spongy somun bread, in one of the many restaurants in Baščaršija.

Drink shots of šlivovica (plum brandy) or loza (grape brandy) savoured with a meal at the Bosanska Kuća.

Do take in some of the local art at the art gallery and National Museum.

Watch the dance, music and street theatre of Baščaršija Noći (Nights of Baščaršija) – an annual festival in July.

Buy colourful woven items in Baščaršija.

After dark indulge in a local beer at the bar of the Sarajevo Brewery.

Savannah

DATE OF BIRTH 1733; AS A BUFFER AGAINST SPANISH INTERESTS IN FLORIDA **ADDRESS** USA (MAP 1, Q8) **HEIGHT** 14M **SIZE** 388 SQ KM **POPULATION** 139,000 (CITY); 355,000 (METRO AREA) **LONELY PLANET RANKING** 164

Savannah is rich in charm and Southern hospitality, with one of the largest historic districts in the USA. It features lots of beautiful buildings, with examples of Federal, Italianate and Victorian architecture.

ANATOMY

The city lies on the Savannah River, 29km from the Atlantic Coast amid moors and mammoth oak trees dripping with Spanish moss. Careful urban design, both widely studied and admired, makes for a livable, beautiful and expandable city, with a gridlike pattern of streets, and houses and public buildings built around tree-filled squares. The city is pedestrian-friendly and there are also plenty of buses.

PEOPLE

This is the South, so about one third of the population is African-American. Demographic changes across the continent are felt here too, with Latino and Asian-Americans becoming a growing force. Disease, war and forcible removal have meant that Native Americans form only 1% of modern-day Savannah's populace.

TYPICAL SAVANNAH CITIZEN

The majority of voters are conservatives, although in the early 1960s the city drew on its liberal traditions and became perhaps the first fully integrated city in the South. While the city is almost as cosmopolitan as Miami Beach or San Francisco, the legendary hospitality remains, as does a certain formality and politeness – opening doors for women is expected and the locals like to dress up for special events.

DEFINING EXPERIENCE

Starting the day with a breakfast in the Historic District at Clary's Café then visiting the Savannah History Museum and taking a walking tour before the day heats up too much, eating lunch at an outdoor café then beating the heat by heading out onto the river aboard a paddle wheeler.

GEORGIA'S GRACE – SAVANNAH IS ONE OF THE MOST HANDSOME CITIES OF THE SOUTHERN USA.

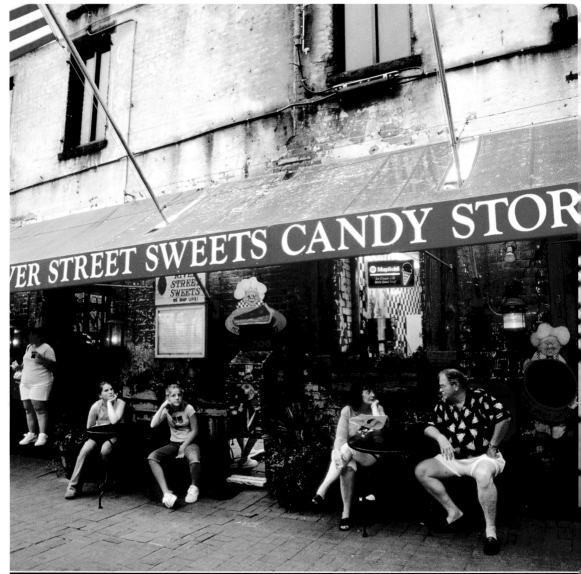

WAITING FOR SWEET SNACK BEFORE SEEING THE REST OF SAVANNAH.

SOUTHERN GOTHIC – THE HAUNTING BEAUTY OF BONAVENTURE CEMETERY.

PADDLE STEAMERS RIDE THE TIDE OF HISTORY.

STRENGTHS

- Riverfront
- Paddle-wheeler trips on the river
- Cobblestone streets
- Carriage rides around town
- City Market
- History Museum
- Mercer House
- Wonderful African Baptist churches and the oldest Reform Judaism temple in the USA (dating from 1733)
- Great tours at all times of day and night
- Telfair Museum of Art

WEAKNESSES

- The sticky height of summer
- Petty crime

GOLD STAR

Savannah's historic districts show off extraordinary collections of 18th- and 19th-century buildings and immense Victorian townhouses.

STARRING ROLE IN...

- *The Gift* (2000)
- *The Legend of Bagger Vance* (2000)
- *The General's Daughter* (1999)
- *Midnight in the Garden of Good and Evil* by John Berendt
- *Forrest Gump* (1994)
- *Glory* (1989)
- *The Return of Swamp Thing* (1989)
- *Roots* (1977)

See the city, river and Tybee Island by riverboat from River St.

Eat Southern cuisine at Mrs Wilkes' Dining Room.

Drink with pleasing ease – drinking alcohol outdoors is OK on city streets, unlike other cities in the South.

Do take a tour of the houses to see mansions and secret gardens.

Watch great drama at the Savannah Shakespeare Festival or listen to musicians at the Savannah Jazz Festival.

Buy antiques from more than 100 registered dealers, or Civil War artefacts from True Grits.

After dark go clubbing at City Market and the Riverfront or catch a drag show at Club One Jefferson.

709

Seattle

NICKNAME THE PACIFIC NORTHWEST'S EMERALD CITY
DATE OF BIRTH 1851; WHEN NEW YORKERS ARTHUR AND DAVID
DENNY LED A GROUP OF SETTLERS HERE **ADDRESS** USA (MAP 1, E2)
HEIGHT 38M **SIZE** 85 SQ KM **POPULATION** 620,000 (CITY);
3.5 MILLION (METRO AREA) **LONELY PLANET RANKING** 055

Mother of Microsoft, Nirvana and Starbucks, Seattle enjoys a cornucopia of outdoor activities and a varied cultural scene.

ANATOMY

Seattle is sandwiched between the Olympic Range to the west and the Cascade volcanoes, including Mt Rainier, to the south and east. The city is surrounded by water with Lake Washington eastward, Puget Sound to the west, and Lake Union and the Lake Washington Ship Canal slicing through the city. Downtown Seattle is compact and contains Pike Place Market and the Waterfront. The Space Needle is in Seattle Center, north of downtown. Adjoining Seattle Center is the residential Queen Anne area. The U district, home to the University of Washington, is on the north side of Lake Union. Metro Transit buses cover the area.

PEOPLE

Almost three-quarters of Seattle's population are white. The rest are Asian-American, African-American, Hispanic and Native American. Seattle has one of the lowest percentages of children in an US city.

TYPICAL SEATTLEITE

Seattleites are laid-back and dress casually, even for the office. But long hours and high pressure are the norm and people tapping on laptops in coffee shops are a common sight. Bars are also full much of the time. As well as drinking, book readings are popular. Seattleites care about their environment and love outdoor pursuits; it's not unusual for locals to head to the mountains for skiing or hiking. Even if it's raining (and Seattleites swear it's more of a drizzle), you'll spot them outside.

DEFINING EXPERIENCE

Zooming up to the top of the Space Needle for views of the Olympic and Cascade Mountains, the water and the city, then grabbing a tall, skinny, hazelnut latte in Pioneer Sq, before walking in Discovery Park.

THE SUN SETS BEHIND THE MONUMENTAL MARKET SIGN AT PIKE PLACE.

STRENGTHS

- Outdoor activities on tap
- Discovery Park
- Lakeside mega homes
- Opening Day of Yacht Season
- High salaries for tech types
- Easy recycling
- Public art in Fremont
- Pacific Northwest Ballet
- The Space Needle
- Brewpubs
- Strong, tasty, ubiquitous coffee
- Skiing at nearby Whistler

WEAKNESSES

- Rain – and lots of it
- Traffic snarls
- Home of Starbucks
- Racial segregation
- Climbing real estate prices
- Struggling public transport

GOLD STAR

Coffee – Starbucks takes over the world but the coffee is good.

STARRING ROLE IN...

- *Sleepless in Seattle* (1993)
- *Singles* (1992)
- *Say Anything* (1989)
- *Snow Falling on Cedars* by David Guterson
- *Frasier* (1993–2004)

See market traders playing catch with live fish at Pike Place Market.

Eat scrumptious seafood at Belltown neighbourhood favourite Queen City Grill.

Drink seasonal beers at the Elysian Brewing Company on Capitol Hill.

Do take advantage of all that water and try windsurfing on Lake Washington.

Watch hydroplane races, an airshow, a carnival and the arrival of a naval fleet at Seafair.

Buy weird and wonderful music from the owners at Wall of Sound.

After dark attend a reading at Seattle's top bookstore, Eliot Book Company.

CARNIVAL RIDES WHIRL BENEATH SEATTLE'S ICONIC SPACE NEEDLE.

GET YOUR CAFFEINE FIX – SHOPFRONT DETAIL OF ONE OF SEATTLE'S HIP CAFES.

FIRST OF THE SEASON
FRESH
JUMBO
ALASKAN WHOLE COOKED DUNGENESS CRABS

FRESH OYSTER KNIVES $10.00

PAPER LANTERNS FLOAT INTO THE BRANCHES OF A TREE AT THE CHOGYE TEMPLE.

Seoul

DATE OF BIRTH 57 BC; DURING THE THREE KINGDOMS PERIOD, WHEN IT WAS RULED BY THE BAEKJE AND SILLA DYNASTIES
ADDRESS SOUTH KOREA (MAP 9, J2) **HEIGHT** 87M **SIZE** 65 SQ KM
POPULATION 10.5 MILLION (CITY); 23.5 MILLION (METRO AREA)
LONELY PLANET RANKING 085

Seoul is the 600-year-old capital of an economic powerhouse and a representation of a true rags-to-riches story – in every aspect of life and culture it is a fascinating melting pot of old and new, East and West.

ANATOMY

Bisected by the Hangang River, Seoul is surrounded by eight mountain peaks. The main historical, sightseeing and accommodation part of Seoul is the downtown area, with Namsan and Seoul Tower forming the southern perimeter. The touristy shopping and entertainment area of Itaewon is on the south side of Namsan. South of Itaewon, the Hangang River winds its way through the city. Within the river, to the west, is the small island of Yeouido, an important administrative centre. The Gangnam district, south of the river, is where upwardly mobile citizens aspire to live. To the east is Jamsil, home to the giant COEX Mall, Lotte World and Olympic Park. Seoul's subway system is modern, fast, frequent, clean, safe and cheap. There are also buses around the city.

PEOPLE

Birth rates are low, the population is getting older and there is a shortage of young females. Korea is ethnically and linguistically homogeneous and, although the number of foreigners working in Seoul is increasing, expats comprise a very small percentage of the population.

TYPICAL SEOULITE

Seoulites work long hours, but also enjoy socialising and are generally more than kind to foreign visitors. Korean relationships are complicated by social hierarchy, and social status is very important. The concept of losing face is integral to Korean society. As a result Koreans are seemingly overly agreeable and pleasant, doing anything to smooth over potential disagreements or arguments that could lead to losing face. Seoulites are always very respectful and will greet each other with a short bow or nod. Seoul has over 40 top universities, and the Koreans' inexhaustible obsession with education and the social status it brings is nowhere more prevalent than here.

YOUNG BUDDHIST MONKS PUT THEIR HANDS TOGETHER TO MARK BUDDHA'S BIRTHDAY AT CHOGYE TEMPLE.

TEMPLE TRADITIONS SURVIVE IN
ULTRA-MODERN SEOUL.

A WOMAN IN A TRADITIONAL GOWN
ACCESSORISES WITH A HANDBAG.

DEFINING EXPERIENCE

Exploring the palaces and War Memorial Museum and Seodaemun
Prison for an introduction to Seoul's complex history, then sipping on
ginseng tea in a stall at Dongdaemun Market before adding the
finishing touches to your wardrobe, and then climbing Inwangsan to
the shamanist shrine at dusk to contemplate the lights of the city.

STRENGTHS

- Low crime rate
- High standard of living and clean streets
- Korean cuisine
- Ancient sculpture and architecture
- Millions of trees (planted to try to improve the city's environment)
- Well-developed bicycle paths and sports facilities

WEAKNESSES

- Seoul is one of the world's most expensive cities
- Summer monsoon season
- Sometimes conservative approach to mixed relationships

GOLD STAR

Seoul is a fascinating melting pot of old and new, East and West.

STARRING ROLE IN...

- *Chihwasun* (2002)
- *Taegukgi* (2003)
- *Sunday Seoul* (2005)
- 'Gangnam Style' (2012)

See the palaces of Gyeongbokgung and Deoksugung to soak up the
atmosphere of the feudal royal court.

Eat temple food and take part in a tea ceremony with Buddhist monks
at Jogyesa or Bongeunsa.

Drink Geumsan Insamju, a rice wine made from a 600-year-old recipe.

Do a hike around the fortresses of Bukhansanseong and Namhansan-
seong that were built in the forest-covered mountains around Seoul.

Watch the royal ancestral rites festival at Jongmyo, as well as historical
re-enactments that reveal an Asian society with its distinctive style.

Buy anything made of leather – it's a Seoul speciality.

After dark head to one of the many tiny underground venues in
Hongkik, Seoul's live indie-music hot spot.

Seville

DATE OF BIRTH MID-2ND CENTURY BC; WHEN IT BECAME A SIGNIFICANT TRADING PORT FOR THE ROMANS **ADDRESS** SPAIN (MAP 5, C7) **HEIGHT** 9M **SIZE** 5.2 SQ KM **POPULATION** 703,000 (CITY); 1.2 MILLION (METRO AREA) **LONELY PLANET RANKING** 044

The historic heart of the city retains the picturesque decay that attracted 19th-century Romantics.

ANATOMY

Seville straddles the Río Guadalquivir, with most places of interest on the east bank. The central area is mostly a tangle of narrow, twisting old streets and small squares. Spain's fourth-largest city is easily walkable, and with the concentration of motor vehicles, foot traffic is preferable. Seville has an extensive and affordable bus network that covers the whole of the greater city area.

PEOPLE

Seville's citizens are quite homogeneously Andalucian, with a Spanish and Moorish heritage. Seville has the largest concentration of *gitanos* (Roma people, formerly known as Gypsies) in Spain. Spanish (Castilian) is the official language. About 80% of the population is Roman Catholic.

TYPICAL SEVILLANO

Sevillanos when comparing themselves to other Spaniards, and more particularly to their Andalucian neighbours in Granada, declare themselves to be more *simpáticos* (genial) and more polite in everything. They love socialising and partying – thought of as gregarious, emotional and in love with colour and action, they have helped set a universal Spanish stereotype. Their southern outlook – lethargic, with a fondness for their afternoon siesta – is balanced by their tendency to spontaneity, exaggerated sense of tragedy and robust sense of humour. They have a strong sense of tradition and are very family-oriented, with gender roles being fairly strict.

DEFINING EXPERIENCE

Visiting the cathedral then wandering through the Barrio de Santa Cruz and enjoying lunch at the Corral del Agua, then in the afternoon heading over to the Río Guadalquivir and visiting Plaza de Toros and the Museo de Bellas Artes before devoting the evening to a relaxed tour of a few tapas bars.

THE TIMELESS FACADE OF THE PLAZA DE ESPANA.

PIG TAILS AND PIROUETTES – AN INSTRUCTOR CALLS THE ROLL FOR SEVILLE'S UP-AND-COMING BALLERINAS.

STRENGTHS
◢ The mix of Muslim and Hispanic building styles
◢ Chocolate and *churros* (Spanish doughnuts) for breakfast
◢ Plaza de España
◢ Traditional Moorish-influenced sweets
◢ Street life on balmy evenings
◢ Flamenco
◢ Alcázar – the palace-fortress
◢ La Giralda – the remaining minaret of the 12th-century mosque
◢ Archivo General de Indias – Spanish late-Renaissance architecture
◢ Spectacular modern bridges over the Guadalquivir
◢ Bullfighting

WEAKNESSES
◢ Traffic
◢ Parking
◢ Drunk teenagers at weekend *botellon* (street party)

GOLD STAR
The sultry nightlife is wondrous. To be out and about till the small hours with this sense of gaiety and brilliance, appreciated for its theatricality and intensity of life, is an unforgettable experience.

STARRING ROLE IN...
◢ *Novelas Ejemplares* (Exemplary Novels) by Cervantes
◢ *Lawrence of Arabia* (1962)
◢ *Mission: Impossible II* (2000)
◢ *Nadie conoce a nadie* (Nobody Knows Anybody, 1999)

See the paintings from the Siglo de Oro (Golden Century) in the Museo de Bellas Artes.

Eat tapas in one of 4000 bars throughout the city.

Drink local wines Aljafe and Los Palacios, when you tire of sherry.

Do climb La Giralda, the minaret of the former mosque, to see the view over the largest Gothic cathedral in the world.

Watch spectacular and slightly creepy Santa Semana (Holy Week) processions, with candlelit parades of hooded penitents going by with grotesque solemnity.

Buy, or at least browse through, all manner of goodies at the Sunday-morning *mercadillo* (flea market) in Alamede de Hercules.

After dark nightlife is jumping – wander the streets and find what's happening – flamenco, jazz, dance...

Shanghai

NICKNAME PEARL OF THE ORIENT; PARIS OF THE EAST
DATE OF BIRTH 11TH CENTURY AD; WHEN THE NAME SHANGHAI FIRST
APPEARED **ADDRESS** CHINA (MAP 9, H4) **HEIGHT** 7M **SIZE** 6341 SQ KM
POPULATION 23 MILLION **LONELY PLANET RANKING** 048

China's most chichi city wows with its sharp fashion and dazzling architecture but manages to keep it traditional.

ANATOMY

Central Shanghai is divided into Pudong (east of the Huangpu River) and Puxi (west of the Huangpu River); downtown is centred around leafy People's Square. Most attractions are in Puxi, including the Bund, the tourist hub. West of the Bund is the former international settlement and Shanghai's main shopping street, Nanjing Rd. South of the Bund is the Chinese city, a maze of lanes. West of the old town and hidden in the backstreets north and south of Huaihai Rd (a top shopping street) is the former French Concession, with the largest collection of bars and restaurants in the city. Western Shanghai is dominated by Hongqiao, a hotel/conference centre/office zone. East of the Huangpu, Pudong is a special economic zone of banks and tower blocks. Walking and taking buses is a nightmare, but the metro and light railway system work well.

PEOPLE

Many Shanghainese residents are the descendants of poor migrants who came to the city from the adjacent provinces of southern Jiangsu and Zhejiang, where Wu Chinese is the dialect. Recent immigration from other parts of China means that Mandarin is now the lingua franca, however. A growing number of Shanghainese speak English, but given the size of the city, they are still an overwhelming minority.

TYPICAL SHANGHAINESE

Chinese people from other parts of China describe the Shanghainese as pragmatic and stingy. Observing those very same traits that others see in them, Shanghainese describe themselves as modern and individualistic. Shanghainese women are regarded as the most on-trend within China, and the city has long served as a filter through which foreign ideas and trends enter Chinese culture. The Shanghainese are proud of their cosmopolitan history, and the city continues to swell with new arrivals looking for opportunities and a taste of the fabled Shanghai glamour.

EXPRESS TO THE FUTURE – TAKE A TRIP THROUGH THE PSYCHEDELIC BUND TUNNEL.

DEFINING EXPERIENCE

Boutique hunting in the French Concession backstreets, queuing for fried dumplings at Yang's, shooting up to the top of a skyscraper in Pudong, exploring the Shanghai Museum and then sipping cocktails on the Bund.

STRENGTHS

- ◢ French Concession
- ◢ The Bund
- ◢ Pudong skyscrapers
- ◢ Fabulous art deco architecture
- ◢ *Longtangs* (traditional lane housing)
- ◢ Yuyuan Gardens and Bazaar
- ◢ Exciting cuisine

WEAKNESSES

- ◢ The cultural scene still has a ways to go
- ◢ Pollution
- ◢ Little personal space
- ◢ Spitting

GOLD STAR

Architecture – from the stunning Pudong skyscrapers to art deco relics like the Fairmont Peace Hotel, there's plenty to dazzle.

STARRING ROLE IN...

- ◢ *Lust, Caution* (2007)
- ◢ *Empire of the Sun* (1986)
- ◢ *Shanghai Triad* (1995)
- ◢ *The Blue Lotus* by Hergé
- ◢ *When We Were Orphans* by Kazuo Ishiguro

See the Shanghai Museum after a stroll along the ritzy Bund.

Eat the braised pork *(hongshao rou)* at any Shanghainese restaurant in town.

Drink martinis in the Glamour Bar enjoying evening views of the Bund.

Do get a traditional Chinese massage for the price of a cocktail or two.

Watch the gymnastic genius of the Shanghai Acrobatics Troupe, bending most nights at Shanghai Centre Theatre.

Buy a *qipao* (cheongsam) tailored to any figure on South Maoming Rd.

After dark head for Yongfu Rd, a hip stretch of bars and clubs in the French Concession.

SHANGHAI'S WINDOW WASHERS LET IT ALL HANG OUT.

THE SCIENCE FICTION CITYSCAPE OF NANJING LU SHOPPING PRECINCT.

FANS OF T'AI CHI SHOW POISE DURING MORNING EXERCISES ON THE BUND.

WINNING SMILE – GIRLS IN ROMAN GOWNS JOIN CELEBRATIONS IN HONOUR OF IL PALIO.

Siena

Stunning Gothic architecture, medieval city walls, the charmingly winding streets and that famous piazza (Il Campo) make peaceful Siena a Tuscan joy.

ANATOMY

At the heart of Siena is the large sloping Piazza del Campo, from which fan out the streets of the medieval town. Two of its main streets reveal Siena's history as a banking town – Banchi di Sopra and Banchi di Sotto. They form part of the Via Francigena pilgrims' route to Rome. Via di Città, another important thoroughfare, joins the other two behind Piazza del Campo. The town is enclosed by its original walls, which are punctured by eight city gates. There are no cars or motorbikes in Siena's city centre, which makes wandering through the streets a rare pleasure. Your only other option is to jump on a bus.

PEOPLE

Italy has one of the lowest birth rates in Europe and Siena's population is slowly dwindling. The majority of its citizens are Roman Catholic, with a small percentage made up of Jewish, Muslim and Protestant communities.

TYPICAL SIENESE

Siena is one of Tuscany's main university towns, and the Sienese are a well-educated, hard-working bunch. Family is very important to them and small family-run businesses are common. Loyal to their neighbourhood, they are more likely to fly the flag of their *contrada* (town district) than the Italian colours. They are gastronomes and very proud of Tuscan wine and cuisine. Politically, they tend towards the left, and finally, like all Italians, they like to look good.

DEFINING EXPERIENCE

Tucking into a dish of *pici* (thick Sienese spaghetti) at Il Carroccio before getting lost in the snaking streets of the town and miraculously ending up at a recognisable landmark, the Palazzo Communale.

STRENGTHS

- Sienese-Gothic architecture
- Il Palio (Siena's famous horse race)
- The Sienese school of painting
- First European city to ban motorised traffic in its centre
- Rivalry with Florence
- The Council of Nine
- Slow Food movement
- Marble font by Jacopo della Quercia in the Battistero (baptistry)
- Museo dell'Opera Metropolitana
- Sienese art in the Pinacoteca Nazionale
- Frescoes depicting Santa Caterina's life in the Chiesa di San Domenico
- Settimana Musicale Senese (July)
- Stunning Tuscan countryside
- Nannini, the best place to buy cakes and ice cream
- *Cantucci* and *biscottini di Prato* (almond-based biscuits)

WEAKNESSES

- Accommodation is elusive in summer, particularly during Il Palio
- It's easy to get lost in the medieval town

GOLD STAR

Gothic architecture.

STARRING ROLE IN...

- *The English Patient* (1996)
- *Stealing Beauty* (1996)
- *Prince of Foxes* (1949)

See the marble- and mosaic-clad cathedral, one of Italy's great Gothic churches.

Eat what you fancy from the *menu degustazione* (a seven-course tasting menu) at Cane e Gatto.

Drink a pricey glass of Brunello di Montalcino at a bar on Il Campo – you're paying for the view but it's worth it.

Do a jazz course at the prestigious Fondazione Siena Jazz.

Watch 10 horses fiercely hauling their riders around Il Campo and see who wins the *Palio* (silk banner).

Buy cheese, sausages and porcini mushrooms from Pizzicheria de Miccoli.

After dark watch a concert at the Settimana Musicale Senese.

PIAZZA DEL CAMPO FRINGED BY THE CREEPING SHADOW OF THE PALAZZO PUBBLICO AND THE TORRE DEL MANGIA.

THE VERTICAL GARDENS OF SINGAPORE'S SUPERTREE GROVE ARE A VISION OF THE FUTURE.

PAUL KENNEDY / GETTY IMAGES

Singapore

NICKNAME THE LION CITY **DATE OF BIRTH** MID-13TH CENTURY; WHEN THE REGION WAS ESTABLISHED AS A MINOR TRADING POST FOR THE POWERFUL SUMATRAN SRIVIJAYA EMPIRE
ADDRESS SINGAPORE (MAP 5, F9) **HEIGHT** 10M **SIZE** 682.3 SQ KM
POPULATION 5.1 MILLION **LONELY PLANET RANKING** 025

An island city that's a land unto itself all tricked-out with Southeast Asia's latest tech toys, Singapore is at a cultural crossroads that includes Indian, Malay and Chinese communities best served up at a hawker stall.

ANATOMY

The Singapore River weaves through the city centre, with the hippest dining and club spots lining the riverbanks at Boat, Clarke and Robertson Quays. Change into a suit to head south of the river to the central business district, or switch to a sari further north for Little India and Kampung Glam, the Muslim quarter. The southern island is the plastic theme park of Sentosa, while the eastern stretch of coast hosts the airport. The far north offers Bukit Timur, the last chunk of surviving wilderness. The west keeps it wild with Jurong's bird sanctuary but is largely industrial. Singapore's public transport is plentiful and varied.

PEOPLE

Predominantly Chinese (three quarters of the population), Singapore's population follows many customs of mainland China, including speaking Mandarin or dialect languages. Neighbouring Malaysia has contributed 14% of the population, bringing an Islamic influence, while India has brought 9% of the population, many from the south. The loud minority are expats who have made English the most spoken language.

TYPICAL SINGAPOREAN

Singaporeans love gadgetry and their traditional cultures so a Mass Rapid Transit (MRT) ride will usually feature kids listening to Goan hip-hop while texting for the latest Chinese horoscopes. The stomach of the Lion City roars for the best food and everyone has an opinion on the best hawker stalls. Privately, Singaporeans might hold opinions on the government and its tough policies, but publicly they're too busy filling their mouths with

THE PAINTED FACES OF BEIJING OPERA PERFORMERS AT THE CHINESE THEATRE CIRCLE IN SINGAPORE.

excellent cuisine to speak out. Shopping rivals eating as a national passion, with many Singaporeans jetting over to China or Indonesia on low-cost flights for bargains. The Hokkien word *kiasu* (afraid to lose) is a philosophy along Orchard Rd around sale times, when bargain frenzies dismiss notions of reserve.

DEFINING EXPERIENCE
Breakfasting on *roti paratha* (grilled stuffed flat bread) in Little India and grabbing a discounted sari before heading over for some shopping in Orchard Rd, chilling out in the Botanic Gardens, then working up an appetite by strolling along the river to Boat Quay, where you'll find tasty Malay satays.

STRENGTHS
- Redeveloped Clarke Quay
- Hyper-efficient MRT
- Hawker food at budget prices
- Cable-car ride from Mt Faber to Sentosa
- World-class Changi Airport
- Cheap, abundant hawker cuisine
- Hi-tech gadgetry at Sim Lim Sq and the Tekka Centre
- Bargain flights to China, India and Southeast Asia
- Limited traffic
- Little India

WEAKNESSES
- Censorship
- Fines for jaywalking, eating on the MRT and chewing gum
- Freezing air-con
- High-priced booze

HINDU RELIGIOUS OFFERINGS AT SRI VEERAMAKALIAMMAN TEMPLE.

- Sentosa's overpriced rides
- Touts hounding you along Temple St

GOLD STAR

Changi Airport – it has churches of every denomination, cinemas, restaurants and free internet, plus it's got zippy public transport straight to the city centre.

STARRING ROLE IN...

- *Army Daze* (1996)
- *Rogue Trader* (1999)
- *King Rat* by James Clavell
- *Saint Jack* by Paul Theroux

See Clarke Quay lit with red lanterns on a romantic evening cruise.

Eat garlic stingray from a hectic Newtown Circus hawker stall.

Drink a Singapore Sling at the Long Bar at Raffles Hotel – a compulsorycliché.

Do a wet and weird Duck Tour on the river and through the colonial district.

Watch a lion dance in front of Ngee Ann City on the lunar New Year.

Buy a Slurping Ape T-shirt from the hippest outlets along Orchard Rd.

After dark dance the night away at the multilevel institutional club, Zouk.

НАРОДНО

THE PARTY HOUSE – UNTIL 1990 THIS SOBER BUILDING WAS THE SEAT OF THE COMMUNIST PARTY, NOW ITS AN EVENTS HALL.

DOUG MCKINLAY / GETTY IMAGES

Sofia

DATE OF BIRTH AD 29; WHEN THE ROMANS FOUNDED ULPIA SERDICA
ADDRESS BULGARIA (MAP 5, R5) **HEIGHT** 160M **POPULATION** 1.2
MILLION **LONELY PLANET RANKING** 122

Glittering onion-domed churches, fascinating museums, leafy parks, gleaming hotels, Communist monuments, tacky casinos and seedy strip clubs – Europe's highest capital is a dynamic mix of old and new, East and West.

ANATOMY

Pl Sveta Nedelya, home to the church of the same name, is at the heart of the city. North of here bul Maria Luisa passes the Central Hali Shopping Centre and the Banya Bashi Mosque on the way to the main train and bus stations. To the south, Sofia's main shopping street, bul Vitosha, points the way to Yuzhen Park and the National Palace of Culture (NDK). East of the centre are pl Nezavisimost (aka the Largo) and bul Tsar Osvoboditel, overlooked by the former royal palace. Bul Tsar Osvoboditel continues past pl Narodno Sabranie and the Parliament building towards Borisova Gradina Park. Various forms of public transport (trams, buses, minibuses, trolleybuses, and the underground metro) operate.

PEOPLE

Around 15% of the national population lives in Sofia. Bulgarians are of Slavic origin, and comprise the majority of the country's people. The Turks and the Roma (formerly known as Gypsies) are the largest ethnic minorities.

TYPICAL SOFIA CITIZEN

The high unemployment and low living standards of the 1990s are on their way out and Sofia is slowly smartening up. The rich-poor divide remains evident and the sight of pensioners begging outside shops frequented by the young and wealthy is not uncommon. Despite the high literacy rate the average wage is very low. People hope EU membership will go some way to rectifying this. Bulgarians are warm, friendly people who like to party with friends and family. They are also cynical, and distrustful of bureaucrats and politicians (perhaps due to decades of totalitarian rule and corruption). Bulgarian stereotypes range from images of shot-putters to Cold War assassins and now that the country is becoming more outward looking, Bulgarians are frustrated by their lack of a tangible international image.

DEFINING EXPERIENCE

Sipping coffee alfresco in the City Garden before discovering Bulgarian folk art at the Ethnographic Museum, then taking in a show at the NDK.

STRENGTHS

- The beautiful Aleksander Nevski Memorial Church
- Archaeological Museum – a real treasure-trove
- Enormous Borisova Gradina Park
- Skiing at Dragalevtsi
- National Museum of History
- Day-tripping to Koprivshtitsa
- The changing of the guard at the President's Building
- Sofia Municipal Gallery of Art
- The murals inside the Church of St George
- Sveta Nedelya Cathedral
- The five gold domes of St Nikolai Russian church
- Monument to the Soviet Army

WEAKNESSES

- Crazy drivers who ignore pedestrian crossings and traffic lights
- Potholed pavements
- Beggars
- Toxic emissions from rather decrepit vehicles

GOLD STAR

Churches – stunning ecclesiastical domes are everywhere.

STARRING ROLE IN...

- *The Other Possible Life of Ours* (2004)
- *Mila from Mars* (2003)
- *You're So Pretty, My Dear* (2004)

See the elaborate interior of Aleksander Nevski Memorial Church (the symbol of Sofia and Bulgaria) and the huge array of religious icons in the crypt.

Eat the best Bulgarian food in Sofia at rustic tavern Pri Yafata and enjoy the evening entertainment.

Drink and dance in the so-hip-it-hurts Buddha Bar.

Do a spot of skiing on the slopes of Mt Vitosha.

Watch the best of Bulgaria's warblers at the National Opera House.

Buy books on Bulgarian culture and Bulgarian novels at the Open-air Book Market on pl Slaveikov.

After dark go mad for the party nights and live music at Chervilo.

WOJTEK BUSS / GETTY IMAGES

SCOUR SOFÍA'S FLEA MARKET FOR AN ICONIC SOUVENIR.

St Petersburg

NICKNAME PETER; THE NORTHERN CAPITAL; VENICE OF THE NORTH
DATE OF BIRTH: 1703; WHEN PETER THE GREAT FOUNDED THE CITY AS
RUSSIA'S 'WINDOW ON EUROPE' **ADDRESS** RUSSIA (MAP 4, R3)
HEIGHT 4M **SIZE** 600 SQ KM **POPULATION** 4.8 MILLION
LONELY PLANET RANKING 057

Hands down Russia's most stunning city, St Petersburg was built on a bog just three centuries ago, and has been relentlessly honed over 200 years to become one of Europe's most breathtaking cities.

ANATOMY

Laid out over 44 islands on the delta of the wide Neva River, St Petersburg is a city of water (and ice for about six months of the year). People zip under the rivers and canals on the super-efficient metro, and slightly less efficiently over them by bus, car, tram and trolleybus. The city centre is focused on Palace Sq and the Winter Palace, as well as the vast central boulevard, Nevsky Prospekt.

PEOPLE

The very homogeneous local population is almost entirely Russian, although there are significant Caucasian, Central Asian and Ukrainian minorities. There's also a large foreign community living and working in the city.

TYPICAL PETERSBURGER

Petersburgers are snobs, there's no other way of saying it. Polite, kind, welcoming snobs, but snobs nonetheless. Moscow, with its heady capitalism and fathomless size just strikes locals here as monstrous and best left to the 'big village' as they like to call their rival city. The Northern Capital is a city of culture and locals spend much of their time (or so they'd have you believe) visiting the stellar artistic entertainment on offer – from ballet at the Mariinsky Theatre to drama at the Maly Theatre.

DEFINING EXPERIENCE

Wandering along the Neva embankment, beer in hand, during the White Nights in late June, the sun dipping below the horizon but never far enough for it to get properly dark, and watching the vast bridges raised to allow boats to pass through the river delta into the Baltic Sea.

BILL LYONS / GETTY IMAGES

POET VLADIMIR MAYAKOVSKY MUSES ON THE STATE OF POST-SOVIET PUBLIC TRANSPORT FROM THE WALL OF MAYAKOVSKY STATION.

STRENGTHS

- The city never sleeps, especially in summer
- Every corner reveals breathtaking beauty
- The metro is super-fast and rather incredible looking
- Fantastic food and drink
- Every car is potentially a taxi (just hold your arm out and see them stop)

WEAKNESSES

- Insufficient public transport
- Collapsing/neglected buildings
- The foreigner pricing system (Russians usually pay up to 90% less for museums, the theatre and ballet)
- Drunks
- The general surfeit of men in uniform
- Nevsky Prospekt is ridiculously long and you are always at the wrong end!

GOLD STAR

The view downriver from the Troitsky Most, with the Winter Palace to one side, the magnificent Peter and Paul Fortress to the other and the Strelka of Vasilevsky Island straight ahead, is unforgettable.

STARRING ROLE IN...

- *October* (1928)
- *Golden Eye* (1995)
- *Brother* (1997)
- *Russian Ark* (2002)

See the mind-blowing art collections of the Hermitage and the Russian Museum.

Eat gourmet Russian food at the plutocrat's favourite, Onegin.

Drink cheap Russian champagne with a cheap Russian crowd at Tsynik.

Do take a *banya* (wet steam bath) for the ultimate Russian experience.

Watch world-class ballet and opera at the Mariinsky Theatre.

Buy the inevitable Russian nesting dolls for your friends.

After dark hang out at Dacha with the cool kids.

THE CITY'S SAILORS SAY A PRAYER BEFORE ST ISAAC'S CATHEDRAL.

A BEGGAR'S MODEST SIGN COMPETES WITH A GIANT BILLBOARD.

THE WARM SMILES OF RUGGED-UP SOUVENIR VENDORS ON THE CITY'S ICY STREETS.

RIDDARHOLMEN AND THE OLD TOWN FROM ABOVE DURING A GORGEOUS WINTER SUNSET.

Stockholm

NICKNAME VENICE OF THE NORTH **DATE OF BIRTH** 1252; WHEN CHIEFTAIN BIRGER JARL ORDERED A FORT CONSTRUCTED ON A STRATEGICALLY PLACED ISLET **ADDRESS** SWEDEN (MAP 4, N4) **HEIGHT** 44M **SIZE** 188 SQ KM **POPULATION** 872,000 (CITY); 2.1 MILLION (METRO AREA) **LONELY PLANET RANKING** 051

Without a doubt, Stockholm is one of the most beautiful national capitals in the world, and walking around the city's waterways and parks is a glorious way to spend a week-long stretch of European summer.

ANATOMY

Stockholm is built on islands, except for the modern centre (Norrmalm), which is focused around the ugly Sergels Torg. This business and retail hub is linked by a network of subways to Centralstationen (central train station); the popular gardens of Kungsträdgården lie just to the east. The island of Stadsholmen and its neighbours house Gamla Stan, separated from Norrmalm by the channels of Norrström near the royal palace, but connected by bridges. On the south side of Stadsholmen, Centralbron (the main bridge) and the Slussen interchange connect with the southern city, Södermalm, and its spine, Götgatan. East of Gamla Stan is the small island of Skeppsholmen, and further down Strandvägen you cross to Djurgården, topped by the Skansen Museum.

PEOPLE

Most of Stockholm's population is of Nordic stock. There are also about 80,000 foreigners of more than 80 nationalities. The single largest group of foreigners are Finns, who form almost one fifth of the total population. The next four largest groups are made up of Iraqis, Somalis, Turks and Iranians, including many Kurds who fled Kurdistan.

TYPICAL STOCKHOLMER

Naturally reserved and often shy, Stockholmers' lack of effusiveness in greeting strangers can seem rude but is seldom intentional. Extremely proud of their city, the populace is uniformly well educated and gender equality is advanced: families where the mother works while the father handles most childcare duties are common. Queuing by number is a favourite pastime, commonly done in shops, bakeries, banks, government offices, police stations and post offices. Rural connections are still strong: the summer cottage is almost de rigueur.

SWEDISH PUBLIC TRANSPORT IS TYPICALLY CLEAN AND EFFICIENT.

DEFINING EXPERIENCE

Breakfasting on *lussekatt* (saffron bun) and coffee at Thelins Konditori before visiting Moderna Museet, strolling along Strömkajen and through Kungsträdgården then lunching at Café Panorama, catching the changing of the guard at Kungliga Slottet, refuelling on *fika* (coffee and cake) prior to visiting the Hornspuckeln galleries, dining at Östgötakällaren, drinking at Kvarnen and taking in some live music at Sodra Teatern.

STRENGTHS

◢ Compact but beautiful city
◢ 608-room Kungliga Slottet (Royal Palace)
◢ Quality of light
◢ Winding streets of Gamla Stan
◢ World leader in design and architecture
◢ Underground art – paintings, sculptures etc in over 90 *tunnelbana* (subway) stations
◢ *Fika*
◢ Salvaged 17th-century flagship *Vasa*
◢ Riddarhuset
◢ Ecological consciousness
◢ Stadshuset's mosaic-lined Gyllene Salen (Golden Hall)
◢ Shopper's paradise
◢ Haga Park
◢ Skogskyrkogården – World Heritage–listed cemetery
◢ Bohemian Södermalm
◢ Progressive political landscape
◢ Gay- and lesbian-friendly
◢ Eating out in Långholmen

WEAKNESSES

◢ A night on the town can be expensive

NOT THE RED-LIGHT DISTRICT BUT A NIGHTSPOT IN MOSEBACKETORG.

- Dumbed-down media/increased commercial influence
- Grim human filing-cabinet–style buildings, courtesy of the Million Program
- Kulturehuset – symbol of demolished history and soulless modern architecture

GOLD STAR

Skansen – step into another time at the world's first open-air museum, featuring around 150 traditional houses (inhabited by staff in period costume) showing how Swedes lived in previous times.

STARRING ROLE IN...

- *Ondskan* (Evil, 2003)
- *Songs from the Second Floor* (2000)
- *The Seventh Seal* (1956)
- *The Girl with the Dragon Tattoo* by Stieg Larsson

See Stockholm's waterways by boat.

Eat your fill of classic *husmanskost* (home cooking) at Den Gyldene Freden.

Drink Staropramen at the steeped-in-history Pelikan.

Do lose yourself in the winding streets of Gamla Stan.

Watch the changing of the guard at Kungliga Slottet.

Buy a variety of goods (and bads) from Skansen's market.

After dark rock the boat on warship-turned-restaurant/nightclub *Lady Patricia*.

THE SACRED HEART CATHEDRAL STANDS ON PRATT STREET IN SUVA.

Suva

DATE OF BIRTH 1882: WHEN THE FORMER CAPITAL, LEVUKA, WAS DEEMED TOO SMALL BY THE BRITISH COLONIALISTS **ADDRESS** FIJI (MAP 10, N4) **HEIGHT** 6M **SIZE** 15 SQ KM **POPULATION** 175,000 **LONELY PLANET RANKING** 150

An island city with a youthful edge, Suva is laid-back yet tainted by the trappings of Western society; but the mix of Fijian and Indo-Fijian cultures, a beautiful landscape and a generous people outweigh these pitfalls.

ANATOMY

A lush and bustling port on the island of Viti Levu, Suva is Fiji's political and administrative centre. Suva houses the University of the South Pacific; the fascinating Fiji museum; Fiji's tallest building, the Reserve Bank of Fiji; and interesting colonial-era buildings. Much of Suva's city centre was built on former mangrove swamps. Express buses run from Suva to major cities and towns, and local buses stop at every village they pass. For island-hopping, ferries are cheap, frequent and reliable.

PEOPLE

Suva is an interesting blend of Melanesian, Polynesian, Micronesian, Indian, Chinese and European cultures. Of these groups, around half are indigenous Fijian and most of the others are Indo-Fijian. The population is predominantly Christian; other religious groups include Hindus, Muslims and Sikhs. The official language is English, with Fijian and Hindi widely spoken.

TYPICAL SUVA CITIZEN

Savvy, good-humoured and proud, Suva's citizens have held onto their traditional rights and practices, including *meke* (traditional dance), *bure* (house construction), kava ceremonies, tapa-cloth making and pottery. Most citizens are young: about half of the Fijian population is under 20, with about two-thirds aged under 30.

DEFINING EXPERIENCE

Listening to uplifting Sunday gospel Fijian-style at a local church, hitting the markets for tropical fruit, vegetables, kava, saris and handicrafts, and later, marvelling at the collection of cannibal curios at the Fiji Museum.

SHOOTING THE BREEZE ON A LOCAL BUS.

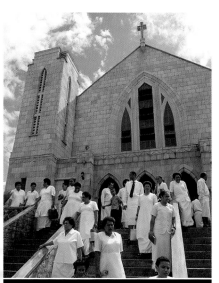

LISTENING TO A SUNDAY GOSPEL CHOIR IS A COMMUNITY EVENT.

BUY FRESH FRUIT AND VEG AT SUVA'S MUNICIPAL MARKET.

STRENGTHS

- ◢ *'Bula!'* (Cheers!) with a smile
- ◢ Easy to navigate on foot (daytime only)
- ◢ The Government Craft Centre
- ◢ Suva Municipal Market
- ◢ Victoria Parade on a Friday or Saturday night
- ◢ Colo-i-Suva Forest Park
- ◢ Hole-in-the-wall curry joints
- ◢ Hibiscus Festival (August)
- ◢ Surf-break near Suva lighthouse
- ◢ Trips to Bega Lagoon

WEAKNESSES

- ◢ Racial strife
- ◢ Political and economic uncertainty
- ◢ Turtle meat and turtle shells freely available at Suva market
- ◢ Polluted waters around Suva
- ◢ Skyrocketing youth unemployment
- ◢ Pickpockets
- ◢ Changeable and inclement weather

GOLD STAR

Suva Municipal Market – *the* place to buy kava and local delicacies, as vendors jostle to sell exotic fruit and vegetables, *nama* (seaweed), fish, bound crabs, pungent spices and neon Indian sweets.

STARRING ROLE IN...

- ◢ *Blue Lagoon* (1979)
- ◢ *Contact* (1997)
- ◢ *Cast Away* (2000)
- ◢ *Anacondas: The Hunt for the Blood Orchid* (2004)

See glorious views of Suva and its surrounds from Mt Korobaba.

Eat scrumptious seafood at one of Suva's most atmospheric nosheries, Tiko's Floating restaurant, anchored at the sea wall across from Ratu Sukuna Park.

Drink fruit concoctions from the tanks at the Suva Municipal Market.

Do experience a touch of Indiana Jones with rope swings and stone steps across streams and natural swimming holes in Colo-i-Suva Forest Park.

Watch rugby (and the fervent spectators!) at Suva's National Stadium.

Buy souvenirs from the Government Craft Centre and support rural artisans.

After dark shake your groove thang at one of the many establishments on Victoria Pde.

Sydney

NICKNAME SIN CITY **DATE OF BIRTH** 1788; WHEN CAPTAIN ARTHUR PHILLIP LANDED THE FIRST FLEET AT SYDNEY COVE **ADDRESS** AUSTRALIA (MAP 10, H7) **HEIGHT** 42M **SIZE** 1800 SQ KM **POPULATION** 4.6 MILLION **LONELY PLANET RANKING** 003

Sparkling in the sunlight and revelling in the limelight, Sydney is all glitz and glam – and catching sight of Sydney Harbour for the first time is one of life's memorable experiences.

ANATOMY

Sydney sits on Australia's populous east coast and is centred on Port Jackson, spreading south to Botany Bay, north to Palm Beach and west to the foothills of the Blue Mountains. It's a hilly city, with numerous bays and headlands and sits atop a sandstone shelf. Its architecture is predominantly modern, although some sandstone gems from the 19th century remain. It is crisscrossed by a bus and train network, with light rail and a monorail in the city centre.

PEOPLE

Sydney is avowedly multicultural, although before WWII most Sydneysiders were predominantly of British or Irish stock. English is the official language, although a growing number of people speak a different language (such as Greek or Vietnamese) at home. Sydney's Aboriginal population is about 1% of the total population.

TYPICAL SYDNEYSIDER

'Work hard, play hard' is a mantra for Sydneysiders. So is the phrase 'smart casual'. People are expected to combine such things at work and still find time to cultivate a buffed, bronzed body, a binge-drinking habit, an ability to cook fusion cuisine and have a wide circle of friends. All this and finding a place to park your car means that they are always talking (on mobile phones) about how busy they are.

DEFINING EXPERIENCE

Starting your day with a dip in an ocean beach such as Bronte then scoffing breakfast with colleagues who've become mates, cruising around one of the markets such as Balmain before late-afternoon beers on a pub's veranda, then seeing a performance at the Opera House.

OLIVER STREWE / GETTY IMAGES

ENDLESS SUMMER – CATCHING A WAVE AT ONE OF SYDNEY'S MANY BEAUTIFUL BEACHES.

STRENGTHS

- Glorious sunshine when you need it most
- The world's best harbour at your tippy toes
- Beachside swimming pools
- Mardi Gras
- 2500 shows a year at the Sydney Opera House
- Sydney Film Festival
- BYO restaurants
- Museum of Contemporary Art
- Friendly locals
- Hills and vantage points

WEAKNESSES

- Ridiculous housing prices
- Crowded (and late) public transport
- GDP-style bills at trendy eateries
- Incessant mobile phone usage
- Narcissism
- Pollution
- Trying to get a cab at 3am changeover time
- Brashness

GOLD STAR

Accessibility – Sydney understood long ago that the great outdoors should be enjoyed by as many people as possible, hence the ease of access to beaches, national parks and walking paths.

STARRING ROLE IN...

- *Lantana* (2001)
- *Finding Nemo* (2003)
- *Puberty Blues* (1981)
- 'Love This City' by The Whitlams

See the view from on high at the Sydney Tower.

Eat fabulous Thai food at Longrain.

Drink schooners at the Hollywood Hotel.

Do the Bondi to Coogee walk.

Watch the stars of the theatre scene at a Company B performance.

Buy the best swimsuit from a local designer at a funky Paddington boutique.

After dark watch movies under the stars at the annual OpenAir cinema in the Domain.

G'DAY POSSUMS! SYDNEY HAS ONE OF THE WORLD'S LARGEST GAY COMMUNITIES.

THE AUSTRALIAN CRAWL IS ALIVE AND KICKING AT THE BONDI BEACH ROCK POOL.

SYDNEY'S MONORAIL PASSES THROUGH CHINATOWN BEFORE ARRIVING AT DARLING HARBOUR.

MYSTICAL SCENES AS LOCALS RELEASE LANTERNS TO BRING BLESSINGS AND GOOD FORTUNE AT THE CHINESE LANTERN.

Taipei

NICKNAME CITY OF AZALEAS **DATE OF BIRTH** 1709; WHEN SETTLERS FROM CHINA'S FUJIAN PROVINCE RECEIVED PERMISSION FROM THE QING GOVERNMENT TO EMIGRATE TO TAIWAN **ADDRESS** TAIWAN (MAP 9, H5) **HEIGHT** 9M **SIZE** 270 SQ KM **POPULATION** 2.6 MILLION (CITY); 7 MILLION (METRO AREA) **LONELY PLANET RANKING** 087

The commercial, cultural and technological heart of Taiwan, Taipei is regarded by many visitors as the friendliest big city in Asia – not to mention one of the world's great food capitals.

ANATOMY

Taipei city is divided into 12 districts that are then divided into neighbourhoods. It is also divided into compass points, much like most American cities. It's dissected at its north and south points by Zhongxiao and Bade Rds, while its east and west grids are bisected by Zhongshan Rd. Cab it, walk or take the MRT (Metropolitan Rapid Transit).

PEOPLE

Close to half of Taiwan's population live in the Taipei area. The vast majority of Taiwanese are of Han Chinese origin; the most recent wave of immigrants from mainland China came following the Communist Revolution. Of the indigenous minorities, the nine main tribes are Ami, Atayal, Bunun, Paiwan, Puyuma, Rukai, Saisiyat, Thao and Yami.

TYPICAL TAIPEI CITIZEN

Taiwanese are welcoming and friendly, particularly the younger set. Until the borders were relaxed in 1987, the typical Taipei citizen suffered from a severe case of workaholic behaviour. But they, too, are coming to learn the value of the 38-hour week.

DEFINING EXPERIENCE

Catching the 37-second lift (elevator) to the 89th floor of Taipei 101 (among the world's tallest buildings), picking up some Hello Kitty merchandise, retreating from the noisy city to the beautiful lotus pond in the Botanical Gardens, then getting a late-night snack at the Shihlin Night Market.

ELDERLY BUDDHIST NUNS KNEEL IN PRAYER AT LUNG SHAN TEMPLE, ONE OF THE OLDEST IN TAIPEI.

A TAXI TAKES OFF IN A BLUR.

TAIPEI 101 REACHES TOWARDS THE STARS.

STRENGTHS
- Subtropical weather
- Excellent (if expensive) seafood
- Excellent Chinese food available 24/7
- Traditional teahouses
- Lively night markets
- Wonderful shopping

WEAKNESSES
- Hazy skyline
- Summer typhoons

GOLD STAR
The National Palace Museum is home to the world's largest collection of Chinese artefacts – around 690,000 pieces. Around 15,000 pieces are on display at any given time and are rotated every three months. At that pace it would take something like 16 years to see everything. Bring a thermos and a packed lunch.

STARRING ROLE IN...
- *Eat Drink Man Woman* (1994)
- *The Red Lotus Society* (1994)
- *In Our Time* (1982)

See the city at your feet from the 89th floor of Taipei 101.

Eat stinky tofu (tofu that has been fermented, deep-fried and served with pickled cabbage and hot sauce).

Drink extra sugary milky tea from one of Taipei's teahouses (check out the Wisteria Tea House, where Ang Lee filmed *Eat Drink Man Woman*) or hot soy milk from a street vendor.

Do visit snake handlers at the Huaxi Night market (aka Snake Alley).

Watch a show by the Contemporary Legend Theatre established by Wu Hsing-kuo, famous for his adaptations of Shakespeare's plays.

Buy shoes, bags, electronics and Hello Kitty paraphernalia from one of the markets or shopping centres.

After dark buy, eat, drink, sniff and join the street peddlers at the Shihlin Night Market.

Tallinn

NICKNAME KOLUVAN; LINDANISA; REVALIA; REVEL; TALLSINKI
DATE OF BIRTH 9TH CENTURY; WHEN AN ESTONIAN TRADING
SETTLEMENT SPRANG UP **ADDRESS** ESTONIA (MAP 4, Q4) **HEIGHT** 44M
SIZE 158 SQ KM **POPULATION** 418,000 **LONELY PLANET RANKING** 088

Fairy-tale architecture and cobblestone streets, which seem made to give Hansel and Gretel a sugar rush, are sweetened by the quaint bay and gooey liqueurs.

ANATOMY

On the southern shore of the Gulf of Finland, Tallinn Bay protects this small city. The Old Town is the city's heart, divided into historic Upper Town on Toompea (the hill dominating Tallinn) and Lower Town, on the eastern side of Toompea. The centrepiece of the Old Town is the magnificent Raekoja plats (Town Hall Sq) hemmed by most of its 2.5km medieval wall. Around the Old Town is a belt of green parks following the line of the city's old defence moat. Radiating outwards from this old core is the New Town, dating from the 19th and early 20th centuries. Trams, trolleybuses and buses are the best way to get around.

PEOPLE

In the post-Soviet era the population has fallen, with immigration to Finland or Western Europe being popular. Predominantly still Estonian, Tallinn has seen new arrivals from Russia and to a lesser extent the Ukraine and Byelorussia. Estonian is the official language, with the related language of Finnish usually understood. Russian is common, though it can be perceived as an uncomfortable reminder of the city's occupation.

TYPICAL TALLINER

Talliners have developed a strong sense of identity since independence when they peacefully ejected the Soviets in protests that became known as the 'Singing Revolution'. The spoils of the free market have been slow to arrive, with unemployment high and most Talliners still living in apartments. Working Talliners do get more in their pay packets than other Estonians, mainly due to large amounts of foreign investment and tourism. Some have dubbed the city Tallsinki for its multilingual leanings and large e-industry. Tourists and Russian immigrants are tolerated by Talliners who still recall the Soviet's control over the city.

THE ALEXANDER NEVSKY CATHEDRAL ON THE LEFT OF TALLINN'S SKYLINE IS AN EXAMPLE OF RUSSIAN REVIVAL ARCHITECTURE.

FOLK DANCERS BLOW THEIR HORNS AT A FESTIVAL IN TALLINN.

TRUDGING THE STREETS OF TOOMPEA IN THE OLD TOWN.

THE SHARP SPIRE OF THE PUHAVAIMU KIRIK.

DEFINING EXPERIENCE

Hopping off the ferry from Helsinki, breakfasting in Raekoja plats at a streetside café, strolling through the Old Town, hopping on a rattling tram across town, then lunching at the romantic Gloria restaurant, which once hosted Soviet canoodlers from St Petersburg, wandering along the docks then pausing for a midafternoon coffee and cake, taking dinner at the latest Thai or Nepali place, then finishing off the night with honey-brewed beer.

STRENGTHS

- Medieval buildings
- Historic trams
- Toompea
- Alexander Nevsky Cathedral
- Art Museum of Estonia
- Art Deco bars
- Backstreets of Pikk

WEAKNESSES

- Drunken Finns
- Street crime
- Cold, dark winters
- Reconstruction in Old Town

GOLD STAR

History – in 1997 Tallinn's Old Town was made a Unesco World Cultural Heritage Site, so there are monuments in every alleyway.

STARRING ROLE IN...

- *Fender Bender* (2003)
- *Lilja 4-ever* (2002)
- *Among the Russians* by Colin Thubron

See the sun setting over the Old Town from atop Toompea.

Eat a vampiric feast of blood sausage at the meaty Kuldse Notsu Kõrts, which has vegetarian (nonbloodsucking) options.

Drink *Vana Tallinn* in the cosy ambience of Gloria Veinikelder.

Do sail the pretty Tallinn Bay or island-hop through the Gulf of Finland.

Watch a play at the epicentre of fringe, Von Krahl Theatre.

Buy a bargain snowflake sweater at the Kadaka Turg market.

After dark shake it with starlets at Hollywood inside the Sõprus Cinema.

THE FADED BEAUTY OF TBILISI.

Tbilisi

DATE OF BIRTH NEOLITHIC PERIOD; ALTHOUGH LOCALS LIKE TO BELIEVE IT WAS FOUNDED IN THE 5TH CENTURY, ACCORDING TO A MUCH-LOVED LOCAL LEGEND **ADDRESS** GEORGIA (MAP 8, 1E) **HEIGHT** 490M **SIZE** 350 SQ KM **POPULATION** 1.5 MILLION **LONELY PLANET RANKING** 151

Hands down the most beautiful city in the Caucasus, the mysterious and historic Georgian capital enchants with its beautiful old town, dramatic cliffside setting and wealth of historic churches.

ANATOMY

A long, slim city built into the gorge of the Mtkvari River, Tbilisi is eminently manageable on foot. The right bank of the river is home to the charming old town, the sulphur baths and the dramatic *Mother Georgia* monument, while the more modern left bank is perched on a clifftop giving views of the old town. An efficient Soviet-built metro system connects the city to the suburbs.

PEOPLE

The cultural centre of Georgia, Tbilisi has large Russian, Armenian, Azeri and Jewish minorities living peacefully side by side. Most people speak both Russian and Georgian, and often more languages.

TYPICAL TBILISIAN

Just as likely to speak Russian as Georgian, your typical resident of this city is a hardened cynic, having lived through a turbulent two decades and seen pretty much everything in that time, from food shortages and starvation to civil war and mass protest. Used to days without electricity, running water and gas, they never lose their sense of humour about the post-Communist chaos into which Georgia was plunged under former president Eduard Shevardnadze. Things might be looking better today, but locals still need to be convinced.

DEFINING EXPERIENCE

Having an invigorating bath and massage at the famous Tbilisi sulphur baths (where Pushkin and Dumas both took the waters), then a bracing walk up to *Mother Georgia*, the vast metallic lady who overlooks the city, and the fascinating Narikala Fortress, before finding the way back down

COLOURFUL OLD HOUSES CROWD TBILISI'S HILLSIDES.

through the old town, checking out some of the beautiful churches and then settling on a traditional Georgian restaurant for the full Georgian culinary experience.

STRENGTHS
- Food, oh! the food...
- Decent wines
- Kind people
- Sioni Cathedral, dating from the 6th century
- Ancient Narikala Fortress
- Famous and long-established theatres
- Paliashvili Opera House
- Gorgeous architecture
- Fascinating history

WEAKNESSES
- Petty crime and street muggings
- Navigationally difficult alphabet
- Steep hills
- Potential instability

GOLD STAR
Dominating the skyline, Narikala Fortress is a symbol of Tbilisi's defensive brilliance. Its walls date from the 4th-century Persian citadel. The tower foundations and the present walls were commissioned by Arab emirs in the 8th century.

STARRING ROLE IN...
- *Since Otar Left* (2003)

See the astonishing collection at the Simon Janashia Museum of Georgia.

Eat as much as you can – try a full Georgian feast at Dzveli Sakhli.

Drink some of the country's wine – start with the very palatable Saperavi.

Do take a day trip to nearby religious centre Mtskheta.

Watch a show at the beautifully ornate Paliashvili Opera House, founded in 1851.

Buy cha cha (Georgian firewater) from the market if you want a memorable introduction to Tbilisi.

After dark head down to Akhvlediani kucha for the late-night bars.

Tel Aviv

NICKNAME THE WHITE CITY; THE BIG ORANGE **DATE OF BIRTH**
1909; WHEN IT WAS FOUNDED BY 60 FAMILIES AS A JEWISH
NEIGHBOURHOOD NEAR JAFFA **ADDRESS** ISRAEL (MAP 8, B3)
HEIGHT 34M **SIZE** 52 SQ KM **POPULATION** 405,000 (CITY); 3.2
MILLION (METRO AREA) **LONELY PLANET RANKING** 132

**While Jerusalem is considered the spiritual centre
of Israel, Tel Aviv, conversely, is the pop-cultural
centre, with its cafés, Mediterranean beaches and
Israeli trance music, which is loud and unavoidable.**

ANATOMY

Hayarkon St, Herbert Samuel Rd and Ibn Gabirol St are the main streets
of Tel Aviv, running north–south and parallel to the seafront. Dizengoff
Sq, Rabin Sq and Hamedina Sq are critical reference points. The New
Central Bus Station is among the world's biggest bus stations and buses
will take you practically everywhere in Israel.

PEOPLE

More than a third of Israel's population lives in greater Tel Aviv. It is a
predominantly Jewish city.

TYPICAL TEL AVIVIAN

Tel Avivians are youthful and brash and totally unlike their neighbours
in Jerusalem, which is only around 45 minutes away but may as well be
on another continent. As a Tel Aviv shopkeeper once said, 'In Jerusalem
they like their religion, in Tel Aviv we like our drugs'. It may not ring
true for the entire city, but it certainly provides an insight.

DEFINING EXPERIENCE

After you've taken in the spiritual teachings of the kabbalah and eaten an
icy pole (ice lolly) on the beach, head over to Nachalat Binyamin (street of
artists) for a look at the work of the city's artisans and street performers.

STRENGTHS

◢ Weather
◢ Beaches
◢ Proximity to the country's amazing sights and relics

FISHING BOATS RETURN TO PORT AFTER WORKING IN THE MEDITERRANEAN.

- Museum of the Jewish People
- Cafés spilling out onto the streets and beaches
- More than 100km of dedicated bike paths
- Citywide bike-rental scheme

WEAKNESSES
- Young soldiers carrying machine guns
- Drivers on mobile phones
- The occasional market-place bombing

GOLD STAR
Behind some drab façades is an incredible collection of Bauhaus buildings along Rothschild Blvd, Ahad Ha'am St, Engel St, Nachmani St, Melchett St and Balfour St, making it the Bauhaus capital of the world.

STARRING ROLE IN...
- 'Tel Aviv' by Duran Duran
- *For my Father* (2008)
- *Walk on Water* (2004)
- *The Flower of Anarchy* by Meir Wieseltier

See fresh-faced soldiers, lads and lasses in shopping malls and nightclubs bandying about their machine guns.

Eat halva ice cream down along Ibn Gabirol and Frishman Sts.

Drink home-brewed ale at the Dancing Camel.

Do walk along powder-fine sand beaches – you'll find sand in every nook and cranny for days to come.

Watch avant-garde and new wave films at the Cinematheque.

Buy secondhand goods at Shuk Hapishpeshim, Jaffa's flea market.

After dark take your *darbuka* (drum) and pound the night away on drum beach.

A YOUNG RABBI SPREADS THE WORD.

COEXISTENCE – OLD AND NEW CONVERGE IN TEL AVIV.

NIGHT FALLS OVER DOWNTOWN TEL AVIV.

HOPES AND DREAMS SPIN IN A RIOT OF COLOUR ON GIANT PRAYER WHEELS.

Thimphu

NICKNAME SHANGRI-LA **DATE OF BIRTH** 13TH CENTURY; WHEN A HUGE FORTRESS WAS BUILT, BUT THE SMALL TOWN ONLY BECAME THE NATIONAL CAPITAL IN 1961 **ADDRESS** BHUTAN (MAP 9, D5) **HEIGHT** 2300M **POPULATION** 99,000 **LONELY PLANET RANKING** 173

With one foot in the past and one in the future, the last Buddhist Himalayan kingdom strolls confidently towards modernisation on its own terms.

ANATOMY

Thimphu lies in a beautiful, wooded valley, sprawling up a hillside on the bank of the Thimphu Chhu River. Several north–south streets run through the town, and numerous smaller streets weave their way uphill to government offices and the posh suburb of Motithang at the top of the town. In the central district, numerous lanes and alleys lead off the north–south streets to provide access to the new shopping centres as well as shops, bars and small restaurants. For those on a normal tourist visa, you will have a car, driver and guide available throughout your stay in Bhutan; and it's easy to pop out for a drink on foot.

PEOPLE

Thimphu's people, like that of the country, are fairly homogeneous, comprising Drukpas (Ngalops and Sharchops) and indigenous or migrant tribes. The main language is Dzongkha, but Tibetan and Nepali are also spoken. The religious divide is nominally Buddhist (three quarters) and Hindu (one quarter).

TYPICAL THIMPHUITE

Bhutanese people are very friendly, open and polite. Despite the fact that Bhutan is not a rich country, the Bhutanese people seem to be content – full of inner and outer beauty, dignity and power. Thimphu, as the capital and only real city, also has the lion's share of bureaucrats, diplomats, politicians and non-governmental organisations (NGOs).

DEFINING EXPERIENCE

Wandering Norzin Lam, lined with shops, restaurants and retail arcades, taking in the view of the river and climbing the telecom tower to see the valley below before letting your guide choose a restaurant and bar followed by a good night's sleep.

THE CITY HAS EXPANDED SINCE 1961 BUT ITS TRADITIONAL BUILDINGS HAVE BEEN PROTECTED.

TIME IS SLOW TO CATCH UP WITH THE PAST IN THIS BEAUTIFUL CITY.

MASKED DANCERS RETELL ANCIENT FOLK STORIES IN A BHUTANESE *TSHECHU*, OR FESTIVAL.

STRENGTHS

- Weekend market
- Tourism as a low-volume, high-cost affair
- Trashi Chhoe Dzong (Fortress of the Glorious Religion)
- Pristine mountain air
- No advertising
- Mobile phones have arrived, but are blissfully rare
- Rugged mountains
- Enchanting valleys and rivers
- Crystal lakes
- Dense forests

WEAKNESSES

- The cost of getting there
- The cost of being there

GOLD STAR

The weekend market – village people jostle with well-heeled Thimphu residents, housewives and monks from nearby monasteries. In one section of the market is an odoriferous collection of dried fish, beef and balls of *datse* (homemade soft cheese that is used to make sauces). During the winter you can even pick up a leg of yak. At the northern end of the market is a collection of indigenous goods and handicrafts. Here you will find locally made goods, including religious objects, cloth, baskets and strange hats from various minority groups.

STARRING ROLE IN...

- *Travellers and Magicians* (2003)
- *The Other Final* (2003)
- *Dreams of the Peaceful Dragon* by Katie Hickman and Tom Owen Edmonds

See the spectacular view of Thimphu Valley from the telecom tower.

Eat green chilli for breakfast – or maybe not.

Drink Tsheringma, a safflower-based herbal tea.

Do take a day walk up to Tango Goemba or Cheri Goemba monastery.

Watch a *tsechu* (festival) at a *dzong* (monastery) in honour of Guru Rinpoche, who brought Buddhism to Bhutan.

Buy contemporary paintings and handmade paper at the Jungshi Handmade Paper Factory.

After dark stay up late and sample Bhutanese nightlife in Thimphu's friendly discos and bars.

ENJOYING SUNSHINE AND GOSSIP IN THE BLLOKU AREA, FORMERLY THE DOMAIN OF THE COMMUNIST ELITE BUT NOW A PLAYGROUND FOR LAD

LUNCH.

Tirana

DATE OF BIRTH 1614; WHEN THE CITY WAS FOUNDED BY A TURKISH PASHA **ADDRESS** ALBANIA (MAP 5, P6) **HEIGHT** 89M **SIZE** 41 SQ KM **POPULATION** 763,000 **LONELY PLANET RANKING** 149

The proud and plucky capital of Albania is charming and surprising, with colonial Italian villas interspersed with monolithic Communist-era structures and traditional Turkish mosques.

ANATOMY

The tiny Lana River is little more than a stream that runs unobtrusively through the city, barely noticed by most people. The central square is the busy Sheshi Skënderbeg (Skënderbeg Sq) from where streets radiate like spokes on a wheel. The city's main street, Bulveardi Dëshmorët e Kombit (Blvd of Heroes and Martyrs) runs from here to Tirana University, hiding ministries and hotels behind its plentiful trees. Near here is the Blloku – once the closed-off residential area of Tirana's Communist elite and now the trendy bar and nightclub quarter. Crowded city buses operate in Tirana.

PEOPLE

Traditionally Tirana has been almost entirely Albanian, particularly as foreigners were almost barred from even visiting until the end of communism in 1990. Since then, though, Tirana has been swamped by a succession of outsiders. First came ethnic Albanian refugees from the conflict in Kosovo and second the waves of aid workers and military peacekeepers who used Tirana as a base in the aftermath of the crisis created. Both have had a large influence on what was in many ways a total backwater and – for better or worse – have contributed to the rapid modernisation and Westernisation of Tirana.

TYPICAL TIRANA CITIZEN

Tirana continues to breed surprisingly conservative people – although this is doubtlessly changing. The influence of both Muslim and Christian mores and the later wave of extremist Stalinism since the end of WWII has had an effect, and while being exceptionally kind and friendly, Tirana's residents are far more easily shocked than their cousins in other European capitals.

DEFINING EXPERIENCE

Wandering the pleasant tree-lined avenues on a summer evening when everyone's out for their evening stroll, and soaking up the charming atmosphere of this friendliest of European capitals.

STRENGTHS

◢ Compact city
◢ Undiscovered by the tourist hordes
◢ A great base for exploring this totally overlooked European country

WEAKNESSES

◢ Still a large amount of poverty despite the progress
◢ Litter is a huge problem – civic pride is still something that very few people attach importance to
◢ Plenty of petty crime
◢ Gaping potholes in the streets to twist ankles

GOLD STAR

Mt Dajti, the mountain overlooking the city, has some beautiful walking and great spots for weekenders leaving the heat of the capital for more alpine climes.

STARRING ROLE IN...

◢ *Slogans* (2001)

PASSING THE TIME OF DAY IN TIRANA.

See the impressive Et'hem Bey Mosque – one of the few religious buildings in the city to survive the Hoxha dictatorship.

Eat pretty much anything you want in Tirana's ever-evolving restaurant scene.

Drink Albanian *rakia* (similar to cognac) if you want a truly rough hangover.

Do make an effort to visit Kruja, the pleasant mountain town a short trip out of Tirana, for an insight into the Albanian struggle for independence.

Watch the nightly processions of Skënderbeg Sq as the entire city takes an evening stroll during the summer months.

Buy anything and everything emblazoned with the Albanian flag – this is one proud country.

After dark head to the Blloku area for bar-hopping, outdoor cocktails or a boogie at the latest nightspot.

THE INSPIRING ET'HEM BEY MOSQUE, SHESHI SKENDERBEG

THE MURAL ON TIRANA'S NATIONAL HISTORY MUSEUM TELLS THE STORY OF ALBANIA.

Tokyo

NICKNAME EASTERN CAPITAL **DATE OF BIRTH** 10,000–300 BC; DURING THE JŌMON PERIOD, WHEN PEOPLE ENJOYED GOOD HUNTING IN THE MARSHY REGION **ADDRESS** JAPAN (MAP 9, K2) **HEIGHT** 6M **SIZE** 616 SQ KM **POPULATION** 13.1 MILLION **LONELY PLANET RANKING** 026

Japan's metropolis rises manga-style from economic ashes and earthquake angst to take on the world by transforming from business-as-usual salaryman to gadget-wielding monster and guardian of Edo's tradition.

ANATOMY

Tokyo's massive size is illustrated by the spaghetti-tangle rail map that includes three different train systems. Tourists stick to the Japan Railway's (JR) Yamanote line, which takes in the Imperial Palace with Ginza and Marunouchi (business district) in the east. To the west lies Roppongi and then more nightlife in Shibuya and Shinjuku. Addresses are determined not by street name but by indicating the *ku* (ward), then the *chō* or *machi* (suburbs) and then *chōme* (roughly a couple of blocks). It's no wonder even taxi drivers ask for directions.

PEOPLE

Japan's famous homogeneity is only slightly disturbed by cosmopolitan Tokyo. Non-Japanese number 400,000 and form a *gaijin* (foreigner) population of business visitors, English-language teachers and Koreans. Some Japanese speak English, but many know only their native tongue.

TYPICAL TOKYOITE

In a city with half a vending machine for every citizen, consumer culture is an obsession. Foreigners often snap up bargains of last-season electronics. The bursting of the economic bubble means real estate is finally becoming more affordable. Expressing *honne* (personal views) is frowned upon socially with a need for *tatamae* (or safer views)…unless the sake is flowing, when even karaoke seems like a good idea.

DEFINING EXPERIENCE

Breakfasting on sushi in gumboots with the fisherfolk at Tsukiji Central Fish Market, striking a pose with the *Cos-play-zoku* (dress-up gangs) near Meiji Shrine, getting spiritual at the shrines of Sensō-ji, then ending the night with beer and snacks at an *izakaya* (pub/eatery).

TOM BONAVENTURE / GETTY IMAGES

LIFE MOVES PRETTY FAST IN TOKYO – STOP AND LOOK AROUND ONCE IN A WHILE.

A MODERN GEISHA'S DUTIES INCLUDE SIGNING AUTOGRAPHS FOR FANS.

INSPECTING ROWS OF TUNA AT TSUKIJI FISH MARKET.

IT'S A WIRED WORLD IN SHINJUKU DISTRICT.

STRENGTHS
- *Cos-play-zoku*
- Ginza
- Ueno Park
- 'Bullet' trains
- Tokyo National Museum
- Bonsai Park
- Shinjuku
- Mt Fuji
- *Kaijū* (monster movie)
- Imperial Palace
- Meiji Shrine and surrounding Harajuku and Aoyama areas
- Kabuki-za Theatre
- *Hanami* (cherry-blossom viewing) in spring

WEAKNESSES
- Impossible traffic
- Distant Nairita airport
- Yakuza (Japanese mafia)
- Earthquakes

GOLD STAR
Low crime – people will stoop to help if you drop your wallet.

STARRING ROLE IN...
- *Lost in Translation* (2003)
- *Kill Bill: Vol 1* (2003)
- *Shinjuku Boys* (1995)
- *Tora! Tora! Tora!* (1970)

See the Meiji Shrine, a tranquil Shinto sanctuary.

Eat the after-work favourite, *yakitori* (grilled skewers of chicken or vegetables), at the ever-busy Akiyoshi

Drink *shōchū* – distilled liquor used as a disinfectant during the Edo period – at any trendy Shinjuku bar.

Do soak and scrub your cares away at Jakotsu-yu, an Edo-era *onsen* (traditional bathhouse).

Watch sumo at the Ryōgoku Kokugikan Stadium, though you'd have to join the *yakuza* to get a seat.

Buy Big Boss coffee from a vending machine, undrinkable but *very* Tokyo.

After dark hang out with Tokyo's creative types in SuperDeluxe, a lounge-club-gallery-venue in Roppongi.

Toronto

NICKNAME THE MEGACITY; HOGTOWN; TO **DATE OF BIRTH** 1793; WHEN LOYALISTS FROM THE AMERICAN REVOLUTIONARY WAR FLED NORTH **ADDRESS** CANADA (MAP 1, Q3) **HEIGHT** 116M **SIZE** 641 SQ KM **POPULATION** 2.6 MILLION (CITY); 5.6 MILLION (METRO AREA) **LONELY PLANET RANKING** 031

Toronto is Canada's boldest metropolis, where the world is available at the cost of a subway token and tolerance is a reigning virtue.

ANATOMY

Toronto was once under the waters of Lake Iroquois. Today the city sits beside Lake Ontario, part of the chain of Great Lakes. Quiet residential blocks around the city centre boast shady trees, one-way streets and Victorian row houses. Overall, Toronto is flat. It has a model public-transport system of integrated subway, bus and streetcar services.

PEOPLE

Toronto is one of the world's most multicultural cities, with almost half of its population comprising minorities. The remainder is of European origin, chiefly of British, Irish, French, Italian and Portuguese descent. Chinese and South Asian communities each make up about 12% of the population. Half of all black Canadians live in Toronto, comprising 8% of the population. Over 100 languages and dialects are spoken, and one third of Toronto residents speak a language other than English at home.

TYPICAL TORONTONIAN

Torontonians think seriously about how to live their daily lives, meaning everything from recycling to how to treat one's neighbour. Although locals are less hesitant to speak their mind than other Canadians, tolerance remains a virtue. Eating and drinking are major pursuits, with life lived outdoors as much as possible, especially during summer.

DEFINING EXPERIENCE

Having a breakfast at the St Lawrence Market, strolling down to the Harbourfront and catching the ferry over to Centre Island, then cycling along the boardwalk and admiring the flowers on Ward's Island before heading back to the mainland, riding the subway north from Union Station and walking to leafy Baldwin Village for lunch at a café.

WITH ITS BEST AND BRIGHTEST ON DISPLAY, ST LAWRENCE MARKET HAS ATTRACTED SATURDAY SHOPPERS FOR OVER 100 YEARS.

IN FRONT OF UNION STATION FRANCESCO PERILLI'S MONUMENT TO MULTICULTURALISM CELEBRATES THE CITY'S DIVERSITY.

PUNK STYLE NEAR KENSINGTON MARKET.

THE CN TOWER STANDS PROUD.

STRENGTHS
- Art Gallery of Ontario
- Royal Ontario Museum
- Toronto Jazz Festival
- Toronto Star Bluesfest
- Toronto International Film Festival
- Toronto Islands
- St Lawrence Market
- Harbourfront
- Queen West
- Legalised gay marriage

WEAKNESSES
- Winter weather
- Summer humidity
- Snarled traffic on expressways

GOLD STAR
Location, location, location. This lakeside city has its very own islands in the waters of the lake, facing off against the downtown skyline, and a string of beaches. Just beyond the city limits are the fertile vineyards of the Niagara Peninsula, and of course, the mighty falls themselves.

STARRING ROLE IN...
- *Queer as Folk* (2003–2005)
- *X-Men* (2000)
- *Good Will Hunting* (1997)
- *Bulletproof Monk* (2003)
- *Chicago* (2002)

See the view from the CN Tower.

Eat Canadian nouvelle cuisine at Canoe and Auberge du Pommier – unusual, fresh (often organic) local ingredients with classic French stylings and daring fusion from Asia.

Drink Niagara Peninsula wines, particularly ice-wine vintages.

Do make the trip to Niagara Falls for a good drenching.

Watch a baseball game at the Rogers Centre or ice hockey in winter.

Buy from the eclectic shops on Queen St W – west of Spadina the street gets funkier the further you go.

After dark sample the variety at Cameron House; get down with soul, R&B, acid jazz and other music at this veteran Queen West venue.

TRADITIONAL YURTS FORM A SUBURB WITH A DIFFERENCE.

Ulaanbaatar

NICKNAME UB **DATE OF BIRTH** 1693; ALTHOUGH THE CITY WAS LARGELY
NOMADIC, SO IT ACTUALLY CHANGED LOCATIONS REGULARLY UNTIL
THE 20TH CENTURY **ADDRESS** MONGOLIA (MAP 9, E1) **HEIGHT** 1325M
SIZE 1368 SQ KM **POPULATION** 1.2 MILLION **LONELY PLANET RANKING** 157

**Definitely one of the most unusual capitals, UB is
the furthest capital city in the world from the sea;
it's the decidedly rough-and-ready hub of a
seminomadic nation.**

ANATOMY

The city is a sprawl without much natural definition. It's centred around
vast Sükhbaatar Sq, named after Mongolia's former Stalinist leader. The
Trans-Mongolian railway runs through the city parallel to the Dund River,
and provides a useful landmark. Public transport is reliable and
departures are frequent, but buses can get crowded. Green minivans run
along similar routes, and for short trips it's just as cheap to take a taxi.

PEOPLE

UB is bursting at the seams, with people from the countryside coming in
to find work. More than one third of the country's population lives here,
which, given the country is twice the size of France, is indicative of how
empty the Mongol plains are. The background of the capital's population is
almost entirely Mongolian.

TYPICAL ULAANBAATAR CITIZEN

This city's residents differ from most other urban dwellers. On the city's
outskirts are *ger* (tent) suburbs, where mongrels patrol unpaved lanes and
locals still live in circular felt tents. Some districts still serve their
traditional role as the protective ring around a monastery. But the lanes
off Sükhbaatar Sq are undergoing an influx of fashion shops and cafés. The
city is still spirited, with a cross section of society – crimson-robed monks
rub shoulders with suited politicians and businesspeople, while mobile-
phone–toting teens skip past nomads fresh off the steppes.

DEFINING EXPERIENCE

Visiting the market to see the colours and the bartering, wandering the
unusual streets of this extraordinary city as the houses give way to *ger*,

where you'll as likely as not be invited in by one of the families living there, then checking out some Mongolian throat singing or the circus in the evening after some hearty fare in a traditional Mongolian restaurant.

STRENGTHS

- Extremely friendly locals
- Very well set up for tourism
- You really do feel like you've reached the end of the earth
- Superb trips to the surrounding stunning countryside

WEAKNESSES

- Unbelievable litter – Mongolians aren't used to nonbiodegradable materials and still simply throw everything onto the ground once they've done with it
- UB has become such a huge tourist draw that sometimes you feel you're in India or Thailand come the summer months

GOLD STAR

The monasteries are spectacular. Visiting the Gandantegchinlen Khiid is a humbling and memorable experience, as is seeing the interior of the Winter Palace of the Bogd Khaan.

STARRING ROLE IN...

- There have been several very successful films shot in Mongolia including *Urga* (1991) and *The Weeping Camel* (2003), but they tend to focus on rural life and as such have not been shot in Ulaanbaatar.

See wrestling and other traditional sports during the Nadaam Festival in July.

Eat *buuz* (steamed mutton dumplings) and *khuushuur* (fried mutton pancakes) for a taste of Mongolia.

Drink the ubiquitous local brew, Chinggis Beer.

Do not miss the staggering exhibits of dinosaurs at the National History Museum.

Watch extraordinary performances of unique Mongolian throat singing.

Buy traditional Buddhist good-luck trinkets at the shops around any monastery or religious building.

After dark be aware that much of the city isn't lit at night!

A BUDDHIST LAMA AT THE GANDEN MONASTERY.

WRESTLING FOR INDEPENDENCE – IT'S ALL ABOUT THE SHOWMANSHIP

A GAME OF DRAUGHTS KEEPS THE FINGERS AND BRAIN ACTIVE.

Ushuaia

NICKNAME THE CAPITAL CITY OF ANTARCTICA; THE END OF THE WORLD **DATE OF BIRTH** 1884; WHEN A MISSION WAS FOUNDED **ADDRESS** ARGENTINA (MAP 3, D19) **HEIGHT** 14M **POPULATION** 57,000 **LONELY PLANET RANKING** 153

This southernmost city in the world has brightly coloured houses sitting toylike against the dramatic backdrop of the Cerro Martial and the Fuegan Andes, and is surrounded by awesome scenery.

ANATOMY

The harbour city, whose name means 'bay overlooking the west' in the local Yamaná language, is situated on the Beagle Channel and sprawls untidily along the coast. It's easy to walk around the town, as all its sights are close together, but you can also catch local buses or taxis.

PEOPLE

The citizens of Ushuaia are mostly descendants of pioneers who came here to settle, explore or serve prison terms. Only artefacts, shell mounds, Thomas Bridges' famous dictionary of the Yamaná language and memories remain of the Yamaná people who once flourished here. The populace is augmented by Antarctic researchers. The majority of the population is Roman Catholic.

TYPICAL USHUAIAN

Ushuaians tend to be easy-going, laid-back and sociable. While they are friendly and passionate, they can also have a subtle broodiness to their nature. Argentina has a large middle class, though it has struggled greatly since the recession that began in 1999. Many locals work as fishers or in the tourism industry. A devotion to family is something all Argentines have in common.

DEFINING EXPERIENCE

Walking around town and checking out the many mansions, then exploring the national park and spotting geese, Magellanic woodpeckers and austral parakeets, before taking a boat out to the penguin colony on Isla Martillo and then eating at any one of the excellent fish restaurants.

THE TRAIN STATION AT THE END OF THE WORLD IS ONE OF USHUAIA'S TOP ATTRACTIONS.

STRENGTHS

⊿ Mansions throughout the city
⊿ Casa Beban Exhibition Centre – built in 1911, prefabricated from a Swedish catalogue
⊿ Museo del Fin del Mundo (The End of the World Museum) – a very Wim Wenders name
⊿ Museo Penitenciario
⊿ The End of the World Train – the world's southernmost steam train
⊿ Estancia Haberton – the oldest sheep station in Tierra del Fuego

WEAKNESSES

⊿ The long, cold winters
⊿ The short, cool summers
⊿ The difficulties getting here
⊿ The rough trip on the Beagle Channel

GOLD STAR

Museo Marítimo & Museo del Presidio are housed in the national prison, which was built by convicts who were moved from New York's Staten Island to Ushuaia in 1906. The spokelike halls of single cells were designed to house 380 prisoners, but during the prison's most active period it held up to 800 inmates. It closed as a jail in 1947 and now houses the museums. It makes a fine port of call on a blustery day. Some of the more illustrious prisoners included author Ricardo Rojas and and Russian anarchist Simón Radowitzky. Halls showing penal life are intriguing, and on the upper floor of one hall is a display on Antarctic exploration.

STARRING ROLE IN...

⊿ *Happy Together* (1997)
⊿ *Uttermost Part of the Earth* by Lucas Bridges

See the museum in the old prison.

Eat Tierra del Fuego *centolla fueguina* (spider crab) at Kaupé.

Drink the traditional beverage of yerba maté.

Do take a trip to the Beagle Channel – the majestic, mountain-fringed sea passage to the south of the city – for sea lions' lairs and cormorant colonies.

Watch the surroundings from the Cerro Martial chairlift.

Buy duty-free goods at Atlantico Sur.

After dark make an appointment with the sunset views over the water from Küar Resto Bar.

NATURE SUPERCEDES ST MARTIN, THE CITY'S MAIN STREET.

WATCHING THE WORLD GO BY FROM VOLVER RESTAURANT

THIS ARTWORK CAN'T HAVE BEEN INSPIRED BY THE CITY'S CHILLY WEATHER.

VALLETTA'S BAROQUE ARCHITECTURE HAS SEEN BETTER DAYS.

DOUG SCOTT / PHOTOLIBRARY

Valletta

DATE OF BIRTH 1566; VALETTA WAS BUILT BY THE KNIGHTS OF THE ORDER OF ST JOHN **ADDRESS:** MALTA (MAP 6, J1) **HEIGHT** 70M **SIZE** 0.6 SQ KM **POPULATION** 7000 **LONELY PLANET RANKING** 192

The capital of Malta is a World Heritage Site whose neat streets are crammed with signs of its history, including enlightening museums; forts and monuments testifying to a valiant past; and remnants of British rule.

ANATOMY

Perched on the tip of the Sceberras Peninsula, Valetta's gridlike pattern of streets makes it easy to navigate. Entering through City Gate, where you'll find the bus terminus and the main street, Triq ir-Repubblika (Republic St), which runs northeast to Fort St Elmo. Parallel with Repubblika run Triq ir-Merkanti (Merchant St) to the southeast and Triq ir-Ifran (Old Bakery St) to the northwest. Triq ir-Repubblika and Triq ir-Merkanti are on the highest point of Valetta and the side streets run downhill. The main landmarks, St John's Co-Cathedral and the Grand Master's Palace, are on Triq ir-Repubblika. Valletta is easily explored on foot, although there is a bus service if you're feeling lazy.

PEOPLE

Over 95% of Malta's population was born on the island. The majority of the foreign community is British but there is a growing North African Muslim community.

TYPICAL VALETTA CITIZEN

The Maltese are proud of their country's history. Since independence from Britain in 1964, they have shown themselves to be politically engaged (around 90% of people vote). The Roman Catholic Church has a large but declining influence; family values are strong. Unemployment is low and there is free education for under-16s. Most people are friendly towards tourists and speak English; the native language is Malti. Football, horse racing and water polo are popular spectator sports.

DEFINING EXPERIENCE

Remembering Malta's WWII experiences in the National War Museum and spying that George Cross medal, before walking around the fortifications past the Siege Bell Memorial then into town for a coffee at Caffè Cordina and a trip around the Grand Master's Palace.

STRENGTHS
- Grand Harbour
- 300 days of sunshine per year
- Mediterranean film studios – Europe's biggest film-set water tanks
- The city's fortifications
- The Grand Master's Palace
- National War Museum
- Maltese folk music at the St James Cavalier Centre for Creativity
- Excellent scuba-diving, a warm sea and rich marine life
- Kinnie orange-and-herb soft drink
- Cisk lager
- Hopleaf beer
- Agius Pastizzerija for pastries
- Carnival (February/March)
- National Museum of Archaeology

WEAKNESSES
- The Maltese Falcon – not spotted since the 1980s
- Rubbish in landfill sites

GOLD STAR
History.

STARRING ROLE IN...
- *Troy* (2004)
- *Gladiator* (2000)
- *The Spy Who Loved Me* (1977)

See where the knights used to worship, St John's Co-Cathedral, and admire Caravaggio's paintings in the Cathedral Museum.

Eat seasonal Maltese cuisine at local favourite Rubino.

Drink and taste local wines in the Castille Wine Vaults underneath the stock exchange.

Do walk around the city's fortifications for views of the Grand Harbour and the Three Cities.

Watch historical pageants and re-enactments at Fort St Elmo.

Buy locally made glassware, lace and ceramics at the Malta Crafts Centre.

After dark see concerts, plays and art-house films in the St James Cavalier Centre for Creativity.

THE CITY IS THE COMMERCIAL HEART OF MALTA.

COLOURFUL MALTESE BUSES MAKE A STATEMENT.

A SMALL CHILD MEETS A MALTESE TERRIER.

VICTORIAN CLAPBOARD HOUSES OVERLOOKING THE BUSY PORT TERMINAL STILL SURVIVE.

Valparaíso

NICKNAME VALPO, LA PERLA DEL PACÍFICO (THE PEARL OF THE PACIFIC) **DATE OF BIRTH** 1536; WHEN IT WAS FOUNDED BY THE SPANISH CONQUISTADOR JUAN DE SAAVEDRA, THEN PERMANENTLY ESTABLISHED IN 1544 WHEN PEDRO DE VALDIVIA MADE IT HIS OFFICIAL PORT **ADDRESS** CHILE (MAP 3, C15) **HEIGHT** 40M **POPULATION** 267,000 **LONELY PLANET RANKING** 096

Valparaíso is a city of dramatic nature – wave-cut terraces with steep, labyrinthine roads and crumbling mansions, precipitous cliffs and a rugged Pacific coast.

ANATOMY

Chile's principal port and second-largest city, Valparaíso occupies a narrow strip of land between the waterfront and nearby hills. Its convoluted centre (known as El Plan) has distinctive, sinuous cobblestone streets and is overlooked by precipitous cliffs and hilltop suburbs, which are accessed by funicular railways and stairway footpaths. It is conducive to mazelike strolls and rides on the funicular, and its natural history, fine arts and maritime museums are justly famed. Muelle Prat, the redeveloped pier, is a lively market area.

PEOPLE

The lineage of Valpo residents is strongly European, particularly Spanish, English and German. The Catholic Church has a great deal of political power, and as a consequence many porteños, as locals are known, are quite conservative in their views.

TYPICAL PORTEÑO

Porteños are laid-back and cultured. They are known for their fine taste in seafood and wine, their prolific cultural output in films and literature, and their pride in their port city. They boast of their individuality but are as conservative as most other Chileans. Their parties are as raucous as their family feuds, and they love both. They explore their own town and take the time to share it with visitors.

DEFINING EXPERIENCE

Having a *cafecito* (short black coffee) for breakfast, then a *paseo* (walk) through the streets and parks, shopping at the fresh fish market on the port and cooking up a *caldillo* (seafood soup), having a siesta in the afternoon and dancing until the small hours on the waterfront.

IF YOU'RE NOT GOING UP IN THIS HILLY CITY, YOU'RE ON THE WAY DOWN.

MODERN HOUSING HAS LOST A LITTLE ELEGANCE.

THE MONUMENT OF THE HEROES OF IQUIQUE.

STRENGTHS
- *Ascensores* (funicular lifts) and the quirky people who operate them
- Generally mild climate
- Views from the *cerros* (hills)
- Tangled, cobbled backstreets
- Spectacular Pacific coastline
- Excellent seafood
- Rich literary history
- Brightly coloured *barrios* (neighbourhoods) on the hillsides
- *Porteños* and their pride in their city's history
- The murals at the Museo a Cielo Abierto (Open-Sky Museum)

WEAKNESSES
- Social conservatism following the Pinochet years
- Earthquakes
- Shantytowns
- Machismo
- Petty theft
- Northern gales in winter

GOLD STAR
Often described as Chile's most distinctive city with its unique, faded grandeur and spontaneous, bohemian charm, the entire city has been named a Unesco World Heritage Site.

STARRING ROLE IN...
- *El Wanderers de Valparaíso* (2003)
- *Valparaíso* (1994)
- *Valparaiso, Valparaiso* (1971)
- *Canto General* and *Confieso que he vivido* (I Confess That I Have Lived) by Pablo Neruda
- *Azul* by Rubén Darío

See the final steps of 500,000 pilgrims walking the Virgen de lo Vasquez Pilgrimage in December each year.

Eat *curanto* – a stew of fish, shellfish, chicken, meat and potato.

Drink wine in the 350-year-old cellar of Trabuxu.

Do ride the *ascensores* to Cerro Concepción, both for the view and the neighbourhood.

Watch the fireworks over the harbour on Año Nuevo (New Year).

Buy antiques in the market at Plaza O'Higgins.

After dark check out the live music at one of the pubs in town.

Vancouver

NICKNAME HOLLYWOOD NORTH; HONGKOUVER; CITY OF GLASS
DATE OF BIRTH 1867; FIRST NAMED GASTOWN, A SALOON WAS OPENED NEXT TO A SAWMILL AND A TOWN SPRANG UP AROUND IT
ADDRESS CANADA (MAP 1, E1) **HEIGHT** 14M **SIZE** 107 SQ KM
POPULATION 2.3 MILLION **LONELY PLANET RANKING** 015

Casual but cosmopolitan, freewheeling Vancouver is framed by mountains with the sea kissing its edges.

ANATOMY

Straddling the lowlands of the Fraser River and the Coast Mountains of southwest British Columbia, Vancouver sits atop the most active earthquake zone in Canada. There are many bays, inlets and river branches shaping the city and coastline. Skyscrapers, big business and high finance sit just blocks from Stanley Park's thick rainforest. The city spreads east and north, and is well served by an elevated skytrain, buses, trains and the sea-bus crossing to North Vancouver.

PEOPLE

Vancouver's population comes from all over the world. By the end of the 20th century it had the largest Asian population in Canada with an influx of Hong Kong Chinese. Forty percent of Vancouver residents are foreign-born.

TYPICAL VANCOUVERITE

With the knowledge that they live in an all-round 'top foreign city' known for its 'best quality of life', Vancouverites have a laid-back mind-set, happy to be part of a pioneering Pacific Rim city where marijuana is tolerated and the foodie scene has exploded. Vancouverites are aggressively outdoors oriented, skiing in the winter but also biking, blading, paddling on False Creek and sailing on English Bay.

DEFINING EXPERIENCE

Strolling through Stanley Park, lunching on the terrace at the Vancouver Art Gallery, taking the sea bus across to North Van and watching for seals in the harbour before heading out to the university campus and the collection of First Nation artefacts at the Museum of Anthropology then finishing the day by dining on Pacific Northwest cuisine on Granville Island.

SKIING ON VANCOUVER'S GROUSE MOUNTAIN, WHAT BETTER WAY TO END THE DAY?

ON THE WATERFRONT – THE TELUS WORLD OF SCIENCE BY BUCKMINSTER FULLER.

STRENGTHS

- Vancouver Art Gallery
- Wreck Beach
- Stanley Park
- Museum of Anthropology
- The startling Coast Mountains north of the city
- Coal Harbour Seawalk
- Eating outside all year round
- Star-spotting on film sets
- Dr Sun-Yat Sen Garden
- Illuminares Lantern Festival
- Bare Buns Fun Run
- The tiny ferries across to Granville Island

WEAKNESSES

- The rain – 170 days a year
- Rapid gentrification
- Ubiquitous Gore-Tex
- Blocked-off streets for film sets

GOLD STAR

Granville Island – not really an island but an enclave of artists, artisans, theatre companies and restaurants.

STARRING ROLE IN...

- *The X Files* (1993–98)
- *Double Jeopardy* (1999)
- Douglas Coupland novels

See the steam-powered clock in Gastown.

Eat Pacific Northwest food – salmon with a hazelnut and maple crust?

Drink Maple Cream Ale at Granville Island Brewery.

Do explore Dr Sun Yat-Sen Park, a tranquil oasis where every pebble and brook has its place.

Watch First Nations carvers working at the Museum of Anthropology.

Buy up-and-coming local fashion on the decidedly inappropriately named Main St.

After dark catch some jazz or blues at Café Deux Soleil or Bukowski's on Commercial Drive.

HINDU PILGRIMS IN VIVID SARIS ON DARBHANGA GHAT.

Varanasi

NICKNAME THE ETERNAL CITY; THE CITY OF SHIVA **DATE OF BIRTH** 1400 BC; VARANASI HAS BEEN A CENTRE OF LEARNING AND CIVILISATION SINCE THIS TIME **ADDRESS** INDIA (MAP 9, C5) **HEIGHT** 81M **SIZE** 74 SQ KM **POPULATION** 1.6 MILLION **LONELY PLANET RANKING** 072

India's holiest city attracts masses of Hindu pilgrims and visitors to the mighty Ganges to bathe, offer blessings, do yoga, wash clothes, get a massage, play cricket and witness cremations; and to drink in the spectacle of life's vibrancy on the riverbanks.

ANATOMY

The old city of Varanasi is situated along the western bank of the Ganges and extends back from the riverbank ghats in a labyrinth of alleys called *galis* that are too narrow for traffic. The *galis* can be disorienting but the hotels are usually well-signposted and however lost you become, you will eventually land up at a ghat where you can get your bearings. Catch crowed buses or a cycle-rickshaw or autorickshaw.

PEOPLE

As you'd expect, the majority of Varanasi's inhabitants are Hindu. Uttar Pradesh is an important political state and has produced half the country's prime ministers.

TYPICAL VARANASI CITIZEN

Despite Uttar Pradesh's prominent political position, poor governance has not made life for the citizens of Varanasi easy. Economic progress is slight, the erratic electricity supply causes problems and the state's overall literacy rate is low. Varanasi, however, has an excellent university and is a well-respected centre of learning. Family is important for Indian society and the birth rate is high – it is rare for people in their thirties to be unmarried or childless. Most Hindu marriages are arranged and although dowries are illegal, they are often still supplied.

DEFINING EXPERIENCE

Watching pilgrims perform *puja* (prayer) at dawn on the ghats, before buying some *paan* (betel nut and leaves concoction) and heading to the Yoga Training Centre for a hatha lesson.

A DEVOUT PILGRIM WADES INTO THE RIVER TO PRAY AT SUNRISE.

LIKE NOTES ON A STAVE, GOATS RECLINE ON THE MULTICOLOURED TULSI GHATS.

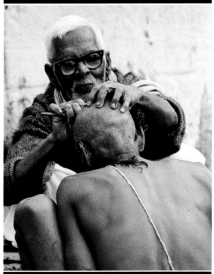

BEFORE DESCENDING INTO THE GANGES, A MAN HAS HIS HEAD SHAVED BY THE RIVERSIDE.

STRENGTHS

- The Ganges
- People-watching at Dasaswamedh Ghat
- Manikarnika Ghat – an auspicious place for a Hindu to be cremated
- The Ganges *susu* (dolphin)
- The particularly holy water between the turrets of Trilochan Ghat
- Vishwanath Temple
- Ramnagar Fort & Museum
- Steam baths and massages
- Silk
- Noise and colour
- Yoga Training Centre
- Hotel Ganges View
- Ram Lila (September/October)

WEAKNESSES

- Pollution of the Ganges
- Blackouts caused by the power-hungry sewage treatment plants
- Rickshaw-wallahs and touts
- Street crime after dark
- Fishing the Ganges *susu*

GOLD STAR

Religious tradition.

STARRING ROLE IN...

- *Ganges Dreaming* (2005)
- *Ganges: River to Heaven* (2003)

See the gold dome and tower of Vishwanath Temple – from the shop over the road if you're not Hindu, or from inside the temple if you are.

Eat local specialities at one of the city's best restaurants, Varuna Restaurant, and enjoy live sitar and tabla music.

Drink a glass of history at Prinsep Bar, named after James Prinsep, illustrator of Varanasi's temples and ghats.

Do an uplifting boat trip down the Ganges from Dasaswamedh Ghat to Harishchandra Ghat at dawn.

Watch cremations at Manikarnika Ghat.

Buy different types of beautiful silk at Ganga Silk.

After dark watch a sitar concert at the International Music Centre Ashram, and take lessons there if you feel inspired.

Venice

NICKNAME LA SERENISSIMA; THE QUEEN OF THE ADRIATIC
DATE OF BIRTH 5TH AND 6TH CENTURIES; WHEN THE ISLANDS OF
THE VENETIAN LAGOON WERE FIRST SETTLED DURING THE
BARBARIAN INVASIONS **ADDRESS** ITALY (MAP 5, M3) **HEIGHT** 1M
SIZE 458 SQ KM **POPULATION** 62,000 (CITY); 270,000 (INCLUDING
MAINLAND) **LONELY PLANET RANKING** 022

There's no city on earth whose visual impact has the same power as Venice – the Adriatic island republic is reluctantly part of Italy, but in reality belongs to the entire world as one of the great cultural treasures anywhere on the planet.

ANATOMY

Spread across 117 islands, connected by over 400 bridges and divided by some 150 canals, Venice is in many places a cramped and dark city whose astonishing colours and vibrancy become apparent in the open spaces and along the Grand Canal, the city's artery, which hums with traffic day and night. Few cities reward walkers so generously as Venice. A vaporetto is the other essential method of getting around, and it can be equally rewarding: you won't find many public transport routes as unforgettable as vaporetto No 1's trip along the Grand Canal. Taking a ride in a gondola is corny, expensive, embarrassing and...well, if you really want to, why not? Water taxis are almost as expensive as gondolas, but their pilots don't wear stripy shirts or sing 'O Sole Mio'.

PEOPLE

Venetians are a declining breed, if not necessarily a dying one. The lack of jobs outside the tourist industry has led to many young people leaving the city for the mainland at the earliest opportunity. House prices – high enough already – are forced higher by large numbers of non-Venetians purchasing second homes here.

TYPICAL VENETIAN

Defined by their own dialect of Italian, a separate history and an island mentality, Venetians are somewhat reluctant Italians and define themselves far more in terms of their city than in terms of their country. It's a love-hate relationship – Venetians will tell you the disadvantages of living in their unique, overpriced and sinking city, but will expect nothing but praise from you as a visitor!

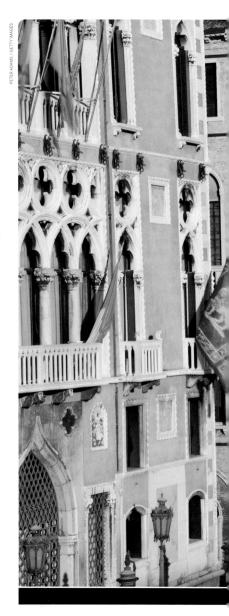

PETER ADAMS / GETTY IMAGES

A VIEW OF THE CHURCH OF SANTA MARIA DELLA SALUTE ALONG THE GRAND CANAL.

DEFINING EXPERIENCE

Taking a trip across the lagoon at dawn to see San Marco before the crowds, stopping off at a café to sip coffee, getting lost in the back alleys, discovering a magnificent church, vaporetto-hopping up and down the Grand Canal and munching top-notch seafood for dinner.

STRENGTHS

◢ Discovering that despite the crowds, the smells and the high prices there's absolutely nowhere like this remarkable city
◢ The Giardini – Venice's green lung beyond San Marco
◢ The Lido – roads! And a beach!
◢ The annual film festival: Hollywood stars rub shoulders with locals
◢ The Venice Biennale, one of the greatest art shows on earth

WEAKNESSES

◢ The crowds
◢ The smelly canals (particularly foul when they are being dredged)
◢ The high prices

GOLD STAR

The Venice Carnival is a once-in-a-lifetime experience that will thrill and exhaust in equal measure. Held in February or March, the city parties nonstop, although you'll feel out of place if you haven't spent a lot of time and money on your costume.

STARRING IN...

◢ *Death in Venice* (1971)
◢ *Don't Look Now* (1973)
◢ *The Merchant of Venice* by Shakespeare
◢ *Everyone Says I Love You* (1996)
◢ *The Talented Mr Ripley* (1999)
◢ *The Aspern Papers* by Henry James

See the extraordinary interior of the Basilica di San Marco early in the morning before the crowds arrive.

Eat superb seafood, but avoid anywhere with a *menu turistico*.

Drink the world's most expensive espresso on Piazza San Marco.

Do try to get there for the Carnival, or one of Venice's other big celebrations.

Watch opera at the stunningly rebuilt La Fenice opera house.

Buy Murano glass (admittedly an acquired taste) at bargain prices.

After dark enjoy a world-famous Bellini (Venice's native cocktail, made with champagne and peaches) at Harry's Bar.

WASHING DAY NEAR CATHEDRAL SAN PIETRO DI CASTELLO.

THE CAT ON THE HAT.

SAN MARCO CAMPANILE – WALK TO THE TOP FOR VIEWS OVER THE WATER-LOGGED CITY.

VIENNA'S NIGHTLIFE HAS MOVED ON A BIT SINCE MOZART.

Vienna

DATE OF BIRTH AD 8; WHEN VINDOBONA WAS FOUNDED BY THE ROMANS **ADDRESS** AUSTRIA (MAP 5, O2) **HEIGHT** 203M **SIZE** 415 SQ KM **POPULATION** 1.7 MILLION (CITY); 2.4 MILLION (METRO AREA) **LONELY PLANET RANKING** 040

Once a gem in the Hapsburg crown, Vienna remains a city of culture, class and beauty, famous for its opera and classical music; but peer beneath this tradition and you'll see experimental arts, world food and green living.

ANATOMY

The Danube runs through Vienna, nudging the old city and most tourist attractions to the west. Heading south from the river, the Danube Canal creates one rim of the historic centre (Innere Stadt). The Donauinsel promises fun with beaches and playgrounds. The beloved Wienerwald (Vienna Woods) undulates appealingly to the west and north of the city. Trams trundle through the city, while the U-Bahn whizzes below ground.

PEOPLE

Almost a quarter of today's population hails from outside Austria, with the largest ethnic communities being from Eastern Europe and the Balkans. The majority of the population is Roman Catholic and there are also significant groups of Protestants and Muslims.

TYPICAL VIENNESE

Despite their reputation for being grumpy, the dark sense of humour of the Viennese is often self-deprecating. Politeness is important – look your co-drinker in the eye when clinking glasses. Employees receive extra salary payments for the summer and Christmas holidays. Around 8% of households own a dog, which approximates to 65,000 dogs. The Viennese are politically engaged. Not surprisingly, they are also cultural, enjoying their theatre, music, opera, art, food and wine.

DEFINING EXPERIENCE

Gazing at Schiele's work in the Leopold Museum, before lapping up some sun and coffee in the MuseumsQuartier's courtyard, then heading to the Old Danube for a leisurely swim and refuelling at a *Heuriger* (wine tavern) in Stammersdorf.

A VIEW OF CLASSICALLY VIENNESE TILES FROM STEPHANSDOM SOUTH TOWER.

CANS OF BEER WEREN'T PART OF TRADITIONAL AUSTRIAN ATTIRE.

THE FACADE OF THE SCHLOSS BELVEDERE ROYAL BIDS FOR BEST POSTCARD VIEW IN VIENNA.

STRENGTHS

- ◢ Magnificent imperial palaces, eg Schönbrunn
- ◢ Gothic Stephansdom (St Stephen's Cathedral)
- ◢ Otto Wagner's metro stations
- ◢ *Heuriger*
- ◢ *Würstelstände* (sausage stands)
- ◢ The Danube
- ◢ Christmas markets
- ◢ The Spanish Riding School and its Lipizzaner stallions
- ◢ Staatsoper (the opera house)
- ◢ *Sacher Torte* (a rich chocolate cake)
- ◢ Hapsburg history
- ◢ Abundant cycle lanes
- ◢ The Vienna Philharmonic
- ◢ Low crime
- ◢ Efficient trams

WEAKNESSES

- ◢ Occasional xenophobia
- ◢ Bureaucratic hoops for budding entrepreneurs
- ◢ Labyrinthine one-way system
- ◢ Grumpy waiters

GOLD STAR

Opera and classical music.

STARRING ROLE IN...

- ◢ *The Piano Teacher* (2001)
- ◢ *Before Sunrise* (1995)
- ◢ *The Man with Two Brains* (1983)
- ◢ *The Third Man* (1949)

See as many museums as you can on Museum Night *(Lange Nacht der Museen)*, usually in September or October.

Eat *Kaffee und Kuchen* (coffee and cake) in Konditorei Oberlaa Stadthaus.

Drink in the Palmenhaus, a beautifully renovated Palm house, complete with high, arched ceilings, glass walls and steel beams.

Do a gentle but illuminating bicycle tour of Vienna's parks and waterways.

Watch the Vienna Boys' Choir in the Hofburg's Royal Chapel.

Buy exquisite porcelain from the Wiener Porzellanmanufaktur Augarten.

After dark throw some shapes on the dance floor at Flex to the soundtrack of Viennese and international DJs.

Vilnius

DATE OF BIRTH 1323; WHEN IT WAS FOUNDED BY THE LITHUANIAN DUKE GEDIMINAS **ADDRESS** LITHUANIA (MAP 4, Q7) **HEIGHT** 189M **SIZE** 401 SQ KM **POPULATION** 554,000 **LONELY PLANET RANKING** 137

Vilnius is kooky, spooky and mysterious with eerie shadowy courtyards, a thriving bohemian community of artists, and beautiful baroque buildings.

ANATOMY

The centre of Vilnius is on the south side of the Neris River. Its heart is Katedros aikšatė (Cathedral Sq), with the cathedral on the north side and Gedimino kalnas (Gediminas Hill) rising behind. South of Katedros aikštė are the cobbled Old Town streets *(senamiestis)*; to the west, Gedimino prospektas cuts straight across the newer part of the centre to Parliament. The train and bus stations are beyond the Old Town's southern edge, 1.5km from Katedros aikštė. The city has tourist signs in English and Lithuanian pointing to sites around the Old Town, making it impossible to get lost!

PEOPLE

Lithuania has the most ethnically homogeneous population of the three Baltic countries, with Lithuanians accounting for about 80% of inhabitants – Russian, Polish and Jewish groups make up the rest. Lithuanian is the official language, though locals are willing to speak English, German and even Russian (in stark contrast to Latvia and Estonia).

TYPICAL VILNIUS CITIZEN

Living in a self-proclaimed (albeit unofficial) independent republic, the typical Vilnius citizen is spirited, artistic, bohemian, fiercely proud of their bizarre, beautiful and bewitching city, and, as well as being a purveyor of rockin' baroque, is also a committed custodian of the world's first ever bronze bust of Frank Zappa.

DEFINING EXPERIENCE

Cruising the blue lagoon around Trakai Castle in a yacht before getting lost in the cobbled streets of the Old Town and hiking up Gedimino kalnas to the tower for a sublime sunset over the city spires.

THE SCULPTURE OF THE FEAST OF THE THREE MUSICIANS AT THE NATIONAL DRAMA THEATRE IN VILNIUS.

GOTHIC BEAUTY – ST ANNE'S CHURCH IS PART OF THE LARGER ST FRANCIS AND BERNARDINE CHURCH.

STRENGTHS

- Baroque Old Town
- World Heritage Site status
- Bohemian locals
- Strange bars in dim courtyards
- Gates of Dawn
- Pilies gatvė (Castle St)
- Applied Art Museum
- World's only Frank Zappa statue
- English signage (easy to navigate)
- The artists' Republic of Užupis
- Great sense of humour

WEAKNESSES

- Some echoes of anti-Semitism
- Uncomfortable KGB jokes
- Western excesses – burgeoning strip clubs and casinos

GOLD STAR

Chocolate-box baroque – decadent and fragile, bohemian and tough, devilishly attractive Vilnius seduces visitors with its Old Town charm and a warm, wizened soul.

STARRING ROLE IN...

- *Koridorius* (The Corridor, 1995)
- *The Necklace of Wolf's Teeth* (1998)
- *The Book of Sorrow* by Josif Levinson
- *Bohin Manor* by Tadeusz Konwicki

See the treasure-trove of religious jewels on display at the Applied Art Museum.

Eat smoked pigs' ears at Ritos Smuklė while the spit roast turns.

BMX BOYS PRACTISE THEIR TRICKS AGAINST THE BACKDROP OF VILNIUS CATHEDRAL.

Drink a craft beer from Avilys microbrewery in the Old Town.

Do catch a performance of the Vilnius String Quartet at various venues around town.

Watch the sun set over Vilnius' Gothic-steepled skyline from the tower on Gediminas Hill.

Buy pottery bells, woven wicker baskets, wooden toys and painted eggs from the artisan stalls that line the length of Vilnius' Pilies gatvė.

After dark head to avant-garde Bix, formed by the eponymous Lithuanian hard-rock band.

PLAYING BALL – HIGH SCHOOL FOOTBALLERS PLAY A FAST-PACED MATCH, CHEERED ON BY SUPPORTERS.

Washington, DC

NICKNAME DC, CAPITAL CITY **DATE OF BIRTH** 1791; WHEN CONGRESS CHOSE THE SITE FOR THE NEW FEDERAL CAPITAL **ADDRESS** USA (MAP 1, R5) **HEIGHT** 22M **SIZE** 177 SQ KM **POPULATION** 618,000 (CITY); 5.6 MILLION (METRO AREA) **LONELY PLANET RANKING** 103

Washington, DC is full of great monuments and museums but it's also one of North America's culinary capitals.

ANATOMY

The city lies at the last navigable point on the Potomac River, where the coastal plain meets a higher, rockier plateau. The latter is the setting for DC's wealthy residents; monumental Washington sits on the coastal lowlands. It's a city of gridded streets and diagonal avenues radiating from ceremonial squares and elegant circles. The city proper is quite small, with much of the metropolitan population living in the Virginia and Maryland suburbs. The centre has wide sidewalks and few highways, ideal for walking to many destinations, and the subway is excellent, uncrowded and convenient.

PEOPLE

Washington is a predominantly black and segregated city. The majority is of African-American descent; there are growing numbers of Asians and Hispanics. A high proportion of the residents are foreign-born.

TYPICAL WASHINGTONIAN

This being a company town, and the industry being politics, there isn't one typical Washingtonian, although about a third of all residents work in government. Whites and blacks don't mix much socially or professionally. Driven and secular (although less so of late), the largely white political class is in stark contrast to the majority. Poverty affects one-fifth of the population, which is way above the national average – and this in a town with the second-highest per-capita income in the USA.

DEFINING EXPERIENCE

Breakfasting at Jimmy T's diner on Capitol Hill, wandering down the mall past the Capitol, picking a museum to explore before blowing your mind in the National Sculpture Garden, strolling along the Potomac to lunch at Dean & Deluca in Georgetown, and then taking in blues at Madam's Organ.

A FULL MOON OVER THE NATIONAL MALL HIGHLIGHTS CAPITOL HILL.

STRENGTHS

- Smithsonian Institution
- Vietnam Veterans Memorial
- Lincoln Memorial
- National Gallery of Art
- International Spy Museum
- Capitol Hill
- The White House
- Library of Congress
- The buzz of Dupont Circle
- Union Station
- The subway – it's a pleasure to ride
- DC Blues Festival
- Arlington National Cemetery
- Funky jazz bars in Adams-Morgan
- Townhouses and cafés of Georgetown
- Watergate complex
- National Cherry Blossom Festival
- National Arboretum
- Eastern Market
- Black Fashion Museum

WEAKNESSES

- Politicians
- The contrived grandeur of Graeco-Roman monuments
- Segregation
- The murder rate
- The government (white, conservative)/populace (black, liberal) divide
- The long ride in from Dulles airport
- The hot air – humidity in summer and from the politicians

GOLD STAR

The National Mall has monuments and museums to occupy visitors for days. It's a history lesson in sod and stone, with a wide expanse of green that stretches from the Potomac in the west to Capitol Hill in the east. It is the scene of protests and celebrations, lined with gravel paths and bordered by tree-shaded avenues.

THE LIVELY STREETS OF GEORGETOWN MAKE CELEBRITIES AND POLITICIANS LOOK DISTINCTLY TWO-DIMENSIONAL.

STARRING ROLE IN...

- *All the President's Men* (1976)
- *Mr Smith Goes to Washington* (1939)
- *Wag the Dog* (1997)
- *The Pelican Brief* (1993)
- *Enemy of the State* (1998)
- *In the Line of Fire* (1993)
- *Patriot Games* (1992)
- *Primary Colors* (1998)
- *Thirteen Days* (2000)
- *Advice & Consent* (1962)
- *Dave* (1993)
- *Being There* (1979)
- *Legally Blonde 2* (2003)
- *The Contender* (2000)
- *The West Wing* (1999–2006)
- *Lost in the City* by Edward Jones
- *Far East Suite* by Duke Ellington
- *In this Land* by Sweet Honey in the Rock

See the suits arriving on Capitol Hill of a morning.

Eat adventurously – choose food from around the world at Dupont Circle or Adams-Morgan, or Southern cuisine at Georgia Brown's, a Clinton fave.

Drink a fiery red Martini at trendy Degrees Bar & Lounge in Georgetown.

Do have your photograph taken under the Alexander Calder sculpture in the National Gallery of Art.

Watch Watch a game of football (Redskins) or baseball (Nationals).

Buy souvenirs, from rubber Nixon masks to shredded money, at the Bureau of Printing & Engraving.

After dark hit the sidewalks of Adams-Morgan and go clubbing: Heaven & Hell to tempt fate or vigorous Latino at Habana Village.

Wellington

NICKNAME WINDY WELLY **DATE OF BIRTH** 1840; EUROPEAN SETTLERS ARRIVED TO BUY LAND OFF THE MAORIS **ADDRESS** NEW ZEALAND (MAP 10, N9) **HEIGHT** 127M **SIZE** 290 SQ KM **POPULATION** 393,000 **LONELY PLANET RANKING** 083

Hosting the *Lord of the Rings* world premieres put New Zealand's beautiful and blustery capital on the map, but you don't have to be a filmstar to enjoy 'Wellywood' – the bohemian vibe, café scene and outdoor pursuits make it as attractive to civilians as it is to hobbits.

ANATOMY
The harbour sits between two peninsulas at the southern tip of New Zealand's North Island. Ferries cross the Cook Strait from here to South Island. The main street, Lambton Quay, used to sit on the waterfront but is now separated from the sea by reclaimed land. The city centre is bounded by the train station at the northern end of Lambton Quay, and Cambridge and Kent Tce to the southeast. Historic Thornton lies north of the centre. Wellington has efficient buses and suburban trains.

PEOPLE
New Zealand is a bicultural nation and Maori and English are the official languages. For most of Wellington's population at least one of these (probably English) is their mother tongue, but the number of Asian inhabitants in the city is on the increase.

TYPICAL WELLINGTONIAN
Wellingtonians enjoy a healthy rivalry with capital Auckland. Like all Kiwis they are passionate about rugby and feel a great loyalty to New Zealand. Wellington is New Zealand's wealthiest region. Locals love outdoor activities and sports; they are also New Zealand's most culturally engaged people. The OE (overseas experience) is a rite of passage, although Australia is overtaking Britain as the top destination.

DEFINING EXPERIENCE
Taking a stroll around the Botanic Gardens before riding the cable car down to town for a cup of coffee, grabbing your sailboard for some windsurfing in the harbour and going drinking later on Courtenay Pl.

WELLINGTON IS A CITY THAT TAKES ITS COFFEE SERIOUSLY, HERE AT THE COUNTER OF CAFE L'AFFARE.

STRENGTHS

- Radio New Zealand, based in Wellington
- Te Papa (Museum of New Zealand)
- City Gallery Wellington
- Old St Paul's Cathedral
- Government Buildings – among the world's largest all-wooden buildings
- Museum of Wellington City and Sea
- National Cricket Museum
- Beehive – the architectural emblem of New Zealand
- Katherine Mansfield's birthplace
- Botanic Gardens
- Red cable car
- Bill Manhire's creative writing course at Victoria University
- Live gigs on the local music scene
- View of the city from Mt Victoria
- Mountain biking at Makara Peak Bike Park
- Windsurfing
- Great café scene (more cafés per capita than New York City)

WEAKNESSES

- Many houses are not insulated and have no central heating
- Wellington is on a fault line
- Windy weather
- Mad bus drivers

GOLD STAR

Cultural and physical activities on tap.

STARRING ROLE IN...

- *King Kong* (2005)
- *Lord of the Rings trilogy* (2001, 2002, 2003)

See exhibits revealing New Zealand's history, and experience an earthquake at the fabulous Te Papa museum.

Eat a slap-up breakfast at one of the city's many cafés.

Drink pinot noir and sauvignon blanc at Toast Martinborough, a food, wine and music bonanza.

Do take a ride in Wellington's red cable car up to the Botanic Gardens.

Watch rock, Latin and soul in Wellington's oldest live-music venue, Bodega.

Buy retro fashion and funky furniture on Cuba St.

After dark take your pick of the bars and clubs on Courtenay Pl.

POST-INDUSTRIAL REFERENCES ON THE EDGE OF WELLINGTON HARBOUR.

CATCHING A WAVE AT LYALL BAY.

THE WELLINGTON CABLE CAR CONNECTS THE CITY CENTRE AND THE NEIGHBOURHOOD OF KELBURN.

THE GLORIOUS SHWEDAGON PAGODA IS ONE OF THE OLDEST IN MYANMAR AND ITS CROWN IS TIPPED WITH MORE THAN 5,000 DIAMONDS.

Yangon

NICKNAME THE GARDEN CITY OF THE EAST **DATE OF BIRTH** 1755; WHEN KING ALAUNGPAYA CONQUERED CENTRAL MYANMAR AND BUILT A NEW CITY ON THE SITE OF YANGON, WHICH AT THAT TIME WAS KNOWN AS DAGON **ADDRESS** MYANMAR (BURMA) (MAP 9, D7) **HEIGHT** 6M **SIZE** 400 SQ KM **POPULATION** 4.3 MILLION **LONELY PLANET RANKING** 139

Situated in the fertile delta country of southern Myanmar on the Yangon River, Yangon is a city of golden pagodas, colonial edifices and wide boulevards that come alive at night with hordes of stalls selling delicious food and piles of huge cigars.

ANATOMY

Located in the Irrawaddy Delta, Yangon is a lush paradise compared to most of its Southeast Asian counterparts. Central Yangon is easy to navigate. The main streets are set in grids and the best way to plot a course is to flag down a trishaw, walk or catch one Yangon's battered, crowded but colourful buses.

PEOPLE

By far the majority of Yangon's citizens are Bamar. A small portion of the population is of Shan and even fewer are Karen, Rakhine, Indian, Mon and Chinese. While Buddhists comprise most of the population, Muslims, animists and Christians make up the rest of its religions, along with a handful of other indigenous beliefs.

TYPICAL YANGONESE

The release of Aung San Suu Kyi in 2010 and the official dissolution of the military junta the following year has given Yangon's citizen's hope for a better future. The Yangonese are optimistic and it shows in their questions and relaxed conversations.

DEFINING EXPERIENCE

Handling some of the finest lacquerware in the world at the Bogyoke Aung San Market followed by a moment's reflection inside a prayer hall of the Shwedagon Paya, then taking a class in Burmese kick boxing at Yangon University and winding down with a cup of syrupy tea and *mohinga* (a fish-based noodle soup) in the balmy afternoon at one of Yangon's famous teashops.

PINK-CLAD FEMALE MONKS IN YANGON.

BUSINESS IS PLEASURE FOR THIS SHOP OWNER.

ANAW RA HTA PLAYS HOST TO THE
EVENING MARKETS.

STRENGTHS
◢ Unspoilt by mass tourism
◢ Shrines to *nat* (animist spirits)
◢ British colonial architecture on leafy streets
◢ Shwedagon Paya
◢ Teashops and sickly sweets

WEAKNESSES
◢ The government
◢ A virtually nonexistent nightlife
◢ No ATMs, credit-card or travellers-cheque facilities
◢ Censorship and the ban on foreign films
◢ Soaring HIV rates
◢ Teak logging

GOLD STAR
Shwedagon Paya, the most sacred of Buddhist sites in Myanmar, is a highlight. Kipling called it 'a golden mystery…a beautiful winking wonder'. The gold-leaf covered stupa is said to house eight of Buddha's hairs.

STARRING ROLE IN…
◢ *Beyond Rangoon* (1995)
◢ *Burmese Days* by George Orwell
◢ *Secret Histories: Finding George Orwell in a Burmese Tea Shop* by Emma Larkin
◢ *Letters from the East* by Rudyard Kipling
◢ *True Love* (2005)

See t'ai chi practised at the crack of dawn at Mahabandoola Garden.

Eat *lethouq* – a spicy salad of raw vegetables dressed with lime juice, onions, peanuts, chillies and a variety of spices.

Drink *lahpeq ye* (tea water) poured from the cup and drunk from the saucer at the Sei Taing Kya Teashop or any one of Yangon's teashops.

Do have a go at rolling a *cheroot* (like a cigar) and, if you're up for it, try the 2cm-thick variety.

Watch an impromptu game of *chinlon* (cane ball) on any street at any time of day and watch the players perform gravity-defying pirouettes.

Buy a *longyi* (the Bamar version of the sarong) from Bogyoke Market.

After dark wander barefoot along the cool stone floor of the Shwedagon Paya and watch the many-coloured jewels sparkle at its tip.

Yerevan

DATE OF BIRTH 782 BC: WHEN KING ARGISHTI BUILT THE TOWN FORTRESS OF EREBUNI ON THE ARARAT PLAIN **ADDRESS** ARMENIA (MAP 8, E1) **HEIGHT** 990M **SIZE** 210 SQ KM **POPULATION** 1.1 MILLION **LONELY PLANET RANKING** 178

Yerevan is the cultural heart of the Armenian people, one of the surviving ancient peoples of the Near East; it is a proud, cultured and enterprising city stunningly situated in the mountainous realm of the Caucasus.

ANATOMY

The centre of Yerevan sits on the east bank of the Hrazdan River. Streets are arranged in a strict grid system, and the heavily trafficked Opera Sq where Mashtots, Marshall Baghramian and Sayat-Nova Aves meet is often patrolled by female traffic cops in high heels. The city itself is surrounded on three sides by mountains. To the southwest stands Mt Ararat, holy mountain of the Armenian people, in full view, yet poignantly sited just across the Turkish border. Yerevan has tonnes of public transport, including buses, minibuses, trolleybuses and a metro.

PEOPLE

Yerevan is populated almost entirely by Armenians; there are some Russians, Kurds (including the little-known Yezidis, a Gnostic sect sometimes mistakenly called devil-worshippers) and nationals from other Caucasian republics.

TYPICAL YEREVANI

The typical Yerevani is hospitable and eager to help visitors. They are likely to be adherents of the Armenian Apostolic Church (Armenia was the first nation to convert to Christianity – in AD 301). They are resourceful, industrious and resilient, if a little melancholy, in the face of hardship (to which Yerevan, and Armenia as a whole, is no stranger). Members of a nation of stonemasons, philosophers and poets, they are fiercely proud of their culture and artistic traditions. Yerevanis tend to linger over meals and have a relaxed attitude to work, happy to stay out late at night, turn up at work around 10.30am and then take a long lunch. In fact, attitudes to time are pretty relaxed. Punctuality isn't de rigueur in Yerevan.

THE PEAKS OF MT ARARAT ARE A STRIKING BACKDROP TO THE CITY.

DEFINING EXPERIENCE

Visiting Matenadaran, a repository of the country's literature and home to thousands of manuscripts in elaborate Armenian script; heading to Echmiadzin, the spiritual heart of the Armenian church; pondering Armenia's past at the Genocide Memorial; climbing the Cascade for the view over the city and watching the sun set over Mt Ararat; then following your nose to a sizzling *khoravats* (barbecue) along Proshyan Poghots.

STRENGTHS

- ◢ Thriving heart of Armenian art and culture
- ◢ Hospitality and generosity of the locals
- ◢ Intriguing atmosphere – a city poised between East and West
- ◢ Proximity to all of Armenia's attractions – it's a small country!
- ◢ Long lunches and dinners

WEAKNESSES

- ◢ Vodka toasts – fine, but it's poor form to reveal any sign of drunkenness
- ◢ Power shortages
- ◢ Bitterly cold winters
- ◢ Earthquakes
- ◢ Soviet-style customer service (or lack thereof)
- ◢ Corruption and local mafia

GOLD STAR

Art and culture – a city of museums and galleries in a nation of writers, poets and artists.

STARRING ROLE IN...

- ◢ *The Crossing Place* by Philip Marsden
- ◢ *Among the Russians* by Colin Thubron
- ◢ *Imperium* by Ryszard Kapuscinski
- ◢ *Calendar* (1993)

See the East and West meet at the National Folk Art Museum of Armenia.

Eat *khoravats* (barbecued lamb or pork).

Drink Armenian cognac – smooth and potent.

Do visit Sarian Park on the weekend to see the gatherings of contemporary artists who critique each other's work.

Watch a performance of the Yerevan Ballet Company.

Buy local handicrafts and lacework at the market at Vernissage.

After dark check out the casinos at Argavand, slightly seedy and very garishly lit, or visit Giza, Yerevan's ground zero for dance music.

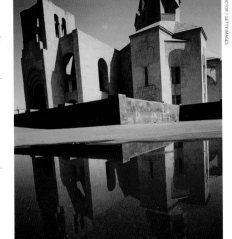

SURP GRIGOR LUSAVORICH CATHEDRAL.

YEREVANIS TAKE PLEASURE IN THEIR HISTORY.

ARMENIANS ENJOY A HEIGHTENED SENSE OF CULTURE.

A DANCER PREPARES TO PERFORM THE RAMAYANA, A TRADITIONAL HINDU EPIC.

Yogyakarta

NICKNAME YOGYA **DATE OF BIRTH** 1755; WHEN PRINCE (LATER SULTAN) MANGKUMBI BUILT THE KRATON OF YOGYAKARTA **ADDRESS** INDONESIA (MAP 10, A2) **HEIGHT** 106M **SIZE** 33 SQ KM **POPULATION** 388,000 **LONELY PLANET RANKING** 129

If Jakarta is Java's financial and industrial powerhouse, Yogyakarta is its soul. Central to the island's artistic and intellectual heritage, Yogyakarta is where the Javanese language is at its purest, Javanese arts are at their brightest and Javanese traditions at their most visible.

ANATOMY

Jalan (Jl) Malioboro, named after the Duke of Marlborough, is Yogya's main road, running from the train station to the *kraton* (walled palace). The tourist office and souvenir shops are along this street and most of the budget places to stay are west of it, in the Jl Sosrowijayan area near the railway line. The walled *kraton* is the centre of old Yogya, where you will also find the Taman Sari (Water Castle), Pasar Ngasem (Bird Market) and batik galleries. It is impossible to go to tourist areas without being greeted by *becak* (auto-rickshaw) drivers. Regular taxis are metered.

PEOPLE

With a mix of Javanese, Sundanese and Madurese peoples, the main languages spoken in Yogya are Javanese, Sundanese, Madurese and Bahasa Indonesian. While the predominant religion is Muslim, there are Hindu, Buddhist and Christian minorities.

TYPICAL YOGYAKARTA CITIZEN

Living in a cultural centre crammed with universities, the Yogya citizen is used to living in a city enduring a Westernised puberty. As the town swings moodily between fast-food joints, malls and satellite TV, locals have a traditional focus, centred around the family, the 'village' and piety.

DEFINING EXPERIENCE

Scoffing down a street-stall *gudeg* (Yogya's signature dish: it's sweet and made with jack fruit, coconut and eggs among other ingredients), meandering the grounds of the *kraton*, then being enchanted by one of the many *wayang kulit* (shadow-puppet) plays at night.

839

STRENGTHS

- The *kraton*
- The Gerebeg festivals
- The Dutch-era fort Benteng Vredeburg
- First-class Javanese art
- Museum Kareta Kraton
- Sumptuous spices
- The Affandi Museum
- Purawisata amusement park
- Kota Gede
- Museum Sasana Wiratama

WEAKNESSES

- 'Last chance' batik scammers
- Copycat batik painting galleries
- Bag snatchers and bike bandits
- Pickpockets

GOLD STAR

Location – aside from being Java's premier tourist city, Yogya is an ideal base for exploring nearby attractions, including Borobudur and Prambanan Temples.

STARRING ROLE IN...

- *Agung Gives Ivor a Haircut* (1991)
- *Becak driver – Superimposed* (1998)

See budgerigars, orioles, roosters, singing turtledoves and pigeons, all in ornamental cages at Pasar Ngasem.

Eat anything from nasi goreng to greasy-spoon fry-ups at the atmospheric FM Café on Jl Sosrowijayan.

Drink a pick-me-up from Civet Coffee, a coffee shop that offers more varieties of bean than just the type that has passed through a civet cat's digestive tract.

Do marvel at the restored 1760s bathing pools in the Taman Sari, and imagine the sultan and harem members relaxing in this one-time pleasure park.

Watch the spectacular Ramayana ballet held in the open air at Prambanan in the dry season.

Buy exquisite leatherwork, batik bags, *topeng* (masks) and *wayang golek* (wooden puppets) from all over the archipelago in Jl Malioboro.

After dark *wayang kulit* performances can be seen at several places around Yogya every night.

PICKING UP A NOCTURNAL SNACK.

SHAKING TO THE BEAT AT PURAWISATA AMUSEMENT PARK.

COLOURFUL KITES ARE FLOWN OVER TAMAN SARI.

York

DATE OF BIRTH AD 71; PRIOR TO THE ARRIVAL OF THE ROMANS WERE THE BRIGANTINES, A LOCAL TRIBE WHO MINDED THEIR OWN BUSINESS **ADDRESS** ENGLAND (MAP 4, F7) **HEIGHT** 17M **SIZE** 272 SQ KM **POPULATION** 198,000 **LONELY PLANET RANKING** 076

York is a the kind of place that makes you wish – if only for an instant – that the Industrial Revolution had never happened.

ANATOMY

Compact and eminently walkable, York has five major landmarks: the wall enclosing the small city centre, the minster at the northern corner, Clifford's Tower at the southern end, the River Ouse that cuts the centre in two, and the train station to the west. Just to avoid the inevitable confusion, remember that round these parts *gate* means street and *bar* means gate. York is easily walked on foot – you're never more than 20 minutes from any of the major sights.

PEOPLE

Traditional York has a very traditional demographic: almost all of the locals are white Brits. Although the University of York (established in 1963) heralded a 'return of the young people', York has an ageing population, with a higher proportion of elderly folks than anywhere else in England.

TYPICAL YORKIE

Possibly employed in the tourist industry (as over 9000 Yorkies are), the typical York citizen is a proud expert on their city's heritage, unfazed by the four million tourists that trod the narrow *snickets* (alleyways) each year. However, the newer breed of Yorkie might well be a person of science, as York's R&D laboratories steam full-speed ahead in the city's reinvention as a 'Science City'.

DEFINING EXPERIENCE

Marvelling at the tennis court–sized stained-glass Great East Window at York Minster before enduring the claustrophobic climb of 275 steps to the central tower (the heart of the minster), then following the city walls clockwise to Monk Bar, York's best-preserved medieval gate.

BUILT BETWEEN 1220 AND 1472, THE MINSTER IS STILL YORK'S TALLEST BUILDING.

RENT A ROWING BOAT TO EXPLORE THE RIVER OUSE.

STRENGTHS

- Oodles of history
- York Castle Museum
- York Minster
- Museum Gardens
- The Shambles
- Clifford's Tower
- Narrow *snickets* (alleys)
- Jorvik Viking Centre
- Castle Howard
- Easily negotiable on foot
- National Railway Museum
- Medieval churches

WEAKNESSES

- Summertime traffic congestion
- Severe flooding from the River Ouse
- Demented tourism in the high summer season
- Cold, dark and grim winters

GOLD STAR

Resilience – garrisoned by the Romans, rampaged by Vikings, besieged by Parliamentarian forces in the Civil War of 1644 and blitzed by the Nazis in 1942, at almost 2000 years old York stands strong as a living museum – a true gem in England's crown.

STARRING ROLE IN...

- *Elizabeth* (1998)
- *Harry Potter and the Philosopher's Stone* (2001)
- *All Creatures Great and Small* by James Herriot
- *Behind the Scenes at the Museum* by Kate Atkinson
- *Possession* by AS Byatt

LIVING HISTORY – YORK'S PAST IS TAKEN QUITE SERIOUSLY AT JORVIK VIKING FESTIVAL.

See Castle Howard, the palatially Palladian Vanbrugh/Hawksmoor creation surrounded by the rolling Howardian Hills, acres of terraced gardens, landscaped vistas and a scattering of monumental follies and obelisks.

Eat sandwiches and high tea, old-school style, at Bettys, a Yorkshire institution – a pianist tinkles Bett's ivories after 6pm (for added class).

Drink an ale or few with the old blokes at Ackhorne on St Martin's Lane, a locals' inn that's as comfy as old slippers.

Do visit what is easily Yorkshire's most important historic building – the simply awesome York Minster.

Watch well-regarded productions of theatre, opera and dance at the York Theatre Royal on St Leonard's Pl.

Buy unusual secondhand books from the Worm Holes Bookshop in Bootham, with a far-reaching selection of old and new titles.

After dark join the 'ghost hunt' of York, an award-winning and highly entertaining 75-minute tour beginning at the Shambles.

Zagreb

DATE OF BIRTH 9TH CENTURY; WHEN SLAVIC SETTLEMENTS WERE FOUNDED **ADDRESS** CROATIA (MAP 5, O3) **HEIGHT** 163M **SIZE** 631 SQ KM **POPULATION** 792,000 (CITY); 1.2 MILLION (METRO AREA) **LONELY PLANET RANKING** 125

Vibrant, cultured and laid-back in equal measure, Zagreb is the gateway to the Balkans, an often overlooked melange of Slavic, Central European and Austro-Hungarian (understated) grandeur.

ANATOMY

Upper Zagreb sprawls across the hills of Gradec and Kaptol, the sites of the city's original settlements. Dolac Market is the hub of the upper city, just near the Cathedral of the Assumption of the Blessed Virgin Mary with its twin spires. The central square of Trg Josip Jelačića is the heart of Lower Town. Crisscrossed by tramlines, this is where old men meet for morning coffee and where teenagers congregate on Friday evenings. The tram system is an effective, if overcrowded, way to get around, although the city is so compact you can walk anywhere.

PEOPLE

Zagreb's citizens are uniformly Croatian; the era of Yugoslavian multiculturalism is now sadly passed.

TYPICAL ZAGREBIAN

The typical Zagreb local is resolutely Western in outlook – they feel distinct from their Slavic Balkan counterparts – and staunchly Catholic. They are elegant, but casually so – although Croatia was the birthplace of the necktie, no self-respecting Zagreb habitué would be seen in anything other than an open-neck shirt. Remaining well dressed at all times is paramount: they will forgo other extravagances to ensure that they can be suitably dressed for all occasions. Relishing the culture, history and artistic heritage of their city, Zagreb locals are given to conviviality and amiable chatter and enjoy the outdoor café lifestyle.

DEFINING EXPERIENCE

Wandering through Dolac Market and choosing grapes as big as plums, watching the changing of the guard at the Banski Dvori, contemplating

TRG JOSIP JELAČIĆA, THE HEART OF THE CITY, IS FILLED WITH FLOWER MARKETS, SHOPS AND CAFES.

THE NEO-GOTHIC BELL TOWERS OF THE CATHEDRAL OF THE ASSUMPTION OF THE BLESSED VIRGIN MARY WATCH OVER TKALČIĆEVA

PERFECT DAY – COFFEE, A CIGARETTE AND A GOOD BOOK.

CHEQUERED HISTORY – THE TILED ROOF OF 13TH-CENTURY ST MARK'S CHURCH.

the airy interior of the Cathedral of the Assumption of the Blessed Virgin Mary, taking your time to ponder Zagreb's long and eventful history and lively arts scene at the city's museums and galleries, and then bar-hopping with the crowds along Tkalčićeva after dark.

STRENGTHS
- Cobbled streets
- Elegant squares and gardens
- People-watching from cafés on spring afternoons
- Streets not fouled with traffic
- A compact and conveniently walkable city
- Few tourists – Zagreb is generally overlooked by travellers
- Meaty cuisine

WEAKNESSES
- Bad coffee
- Shortage of reasonably priced accommodation
- Pockets of Soviet-era architecture
- Steep streets in Upper Town
- Meaty cuisine

GOLD STAR
Central European elegance (if somewhat faded) and architecture, without the hype and crowds of Prague.

STARRING ROLE IN...
- *The Zahir* by Paulo Coelho
- *How We Survived Communism and Even Laughed* by Slavenka Drakulić
- *Black Lamb and Grey Falcon* by Rebecca West
- *Café Europa* by Slavenka Drakulić

See the view from Lotrščak Tower, a 360-degree vista of the rooftops, spires and squares of Upper and Lower Towns.

Eat *čevapčiči* (meaty, garlicky Balkan sausages) with sliced onions or *ayvar* (capsicum paste) and flat bread.

Drink *slivovica* (plum brandy) or locally brewed Ozujsko (beer).

Do visit Zagreb's museums and galleries for a view of a little-known, but surprisingly rich, culture.

Watch any of the free performances of the Zagreb Summer Festival.

Buy embroidery in cheerful red-and-white geometric patterns.

After dark head for the bars on Tkalčićeva, or around Trg Petra Preradovića.

Zanzibar Town

DATE OF BIRTH 8TH CENTURY; WHEN SHIRAZI TRADERS FROM PERSIA ESTABLISHED A SETTLEMENT **ADDRESS** TANZANIA (MAP 7, G3) **HEIGHT** 15M **SIZE** 1574 SQ KM **POPULATION** 1 MILLION **LONELY PLANET RANKING** 074

Zanzibar's old quarter, Stone Town, could have been lifted out of a Persian fairy tale, bringing together a mesmerising mix of influences from the Indian Sub-continent, the Arabian Peninsula and mainland Africa.

ANATOMY

Stone Town juts into the Indian Ocean on the western side of Zanzibar Island. Mizingani Rd runs along the waterfront from the ferry terminal to Stone Town. Here is a magical jumble of cobbled alleyways where it's difficult to get your bearings. The best approach is to follow your nose – you'll either emerge on the waterfront or on Creek Rd on the east edge of Stone Town. There's no transport system (and no need for one). *Dalla-dallas* (minivans) connect the town with the rest of the island.

PEOPLE

The residents of Zanzibar mirror the melting pot that is their Swahili culture: they trace a mix of Omani, Shirazi and African ancestors in their bloodlines. There are also sizable Asian (Indian) and Arabic communities. You may also encounter a few Maasai tribesmen, conspicuously clad in blue, unlike their red-robed Kenyan brethren.

TYPICAL ZANZIBARI

Zanzibar is a Swahili town, hence it retains a Muslim atmosphere. Most Zanzibaris are modest, yet welcoming and gregarious. The *baraza* on houses' outer walls exemplify the social nature of Zanzibaris – these benches are where people catch up on gossip. Zanzibaris are given to elaborate greetings, love to discuss politics and take life at a languid pace.

DEFINING EXPERIENCE

Passing through the carved doors of the House of Wonders; pondering the horrors of the past at the Anglican Cathedral built on the old slave market; wandering the Darajani Market and inhaling the scents of spices and dried fish; strolling aimlessly and endlessly in Stone Town, getting deliciously lost in the maze of streets, discovering children chanting Koranic verses, or a mansion with overhanging balconies, or a coffee vendor clacking cups to

A SCENE UNCHANGED OVER THE CENTURIES – DHOWS MOORED AT SHANGANI POINT.

ON THE TRAIL OF FEATHERED BARGAINS AT THE POULTRY MARKET IN STONE TOWN.

BETHUNE CARMICHAEL / GETTY IMAGES

drum up business; sampling the delights of the foodstalls in the Forodhani Gardens in the early evening.

STRENGTHS

- The scent of cloves
- The twisting, turning alleys of Stone Town
- Overhead lattice balconies, ornate doors and window frames
- Wandering barefoot on the cobbles
- Games of football on the beach
- Breakfasts of mango, pawpaw and chai
- Lateen sails of dhows bobbing in the harbour
- Hearing the lap of the bay as you sleep
- Nearby beaches – azure waters and pristine white sand
- Diving the crystal seas
- Seafood, grilled or cooked with coconut milk

WEAKNESSES

- Humidity and monsoon rains
- Political tensions
- Security after dark (an issue in some parts of town)
- Street touts, known locally as *papasi* (ticks)

GOLD STAR

Tropical enchantment – it's hard to think of a more evocative place name than 'Zanzibar' and the reality doesn't disappoint.

STARRING ROLE IN...

- *Admiring Silence* and *By the Sea* by Abdulrazak Gurnah
- *Zanzibar* by Giles Foden
- *Revolution in Zanzibar: An American's Cold War Tale* by Don Petterson
- *Zanzibar Stone Town: An Architectural Exploration* by Abdul Sheriff
- *Zanzibar Style* by Javed Jafferji and Gemma Pitcher

See the Festival of the Dhow Countries (every year in July), a film festival whose participants come from around the Indian Ocean.

Eat savoury pilau at the Passing Show restaurant.

Drink chai, milky and sweet.

Do a Spice Tour and learn all there is to know about the spice trade.

Watch the moon rise over the Dhow Harbour and the House of Wonders.

Buy spices, silver jewellery or fabrics *(kangas and kikois)*.

After dark head for any of the bars overlooking the bay.

Tony's Best
10 Additional Cities

It's easy to love cities like Paris and San Francisco – I've lived for a year in each of them, written guidebooks to them and am a total enthusiast – but there are lots of things to like about cities that don't pop up on anybody's favourites list. Here are 10 cities, in alphabetical order, that didn't make the cut but where I've still managed to leave a piece of my heart. - TONY WHEELER, COFOUNDER, LONELY PLANET

Mandalay

DATE OF BIRTH 1857; WHEN IT WAS ESTABLISHED AS A NEW CENTRE FOR THE TEACHING OF BUDDHISM **HEIGHT** 74M **ADDRESS** MYANMAR (MAP 9, D6) **POPULATION** 1 MILLION

Kipling never actually took the 'Road to Mandalay'; the road to Mandalay is really a river, the mighty Ayeyarwady, but this is still the heart and soul of Myanmar. Quite apart from the huge Mandalay Fort (gutted during the closing phases of WWII), there's a host of temples and assorted Buddhist sites around the city. Plus it's the home of street theatre (pwe), and no visit to Mandalay is complete until you've caught a performance by the subversive Moustache Brothers. Nevertheless, it's outside Mandalay where the real surprises lie: the abandoned royal capitals of Inwa (Ava), Amarapura and Sagaing, and the massive Mingun Paya (pagoda), all a short boat ride north up the Ayeyarwady. Further afield there's the British colonial-era hill station of Pyin U Lwin (formerly Maymyo), or you can jump aboard a river ferry and head downriver all the way to the amazing ancient city of Bagan.

LEFT AN ANCIENT TEMPLE IN MANDALAY.

Jakarta

DATE OF BIRTH 22 JUNE 1527; WHEN IT WAS NAMED JAYAKARTA (CITY OF GREAT VICTORY) BY FATAHILLAH, A LEADER FROM A NEIGHBOURING SULTANATE **HEIGHT** 1M **SIZE** 661 SQ KM **ADDRESS** INDONESIA (MAP 10, A2) **POPULATION** 10.1 MILLION

Indonesia's sprawling capital is yet another city considerably overshadowed, in the popularity stakes, by a smaller and more glamorous sister city, in this case tourist favourite and cultural capital Yogyakarta. Nevertheless, Jakarta is, in its own fashion, a mega-city that works from its teeming freeways to its old Dutch colonial capital, the one-time Batavia now known simply as Kota ('city' in Indonesian). No visit to Jakarta is complete without a stroll past the incredible line-up of brightly painted Makassar schooners *(pinisi)* in the old port district of Sunda Kelapa, living proof that the age of sail is definitely not finished. The city is also home to an impressive collection of imposing Stalinist-style socialist-era monuments.

Karachi

DATE OF BIRTH 1795; WHEN THE MIRS OF TALPUR CONSTRUCTED A MUD FORT AT MANORA **HEIGHT** 4M **SIZE** 1994 SQ KM **ADDRESS** PAKISTAN(MAP 8, J6) **POPULATION** 13 MILLION

From my first birthday to my fifth this was home and, like any childhood memories, my pictures of Pakistan's troubled port city are rose-tinted: a melange of camels, sailboats, sandy beaches and exotic colours. Way back then Karachi was going through wrenching changes as India and Pakistan tore themselves apart and floods of refugees propelled the city's rocketing growth. To my pleasant surprise, when I returned to Karachi after an absence of 40 years, the city still had some of the charm I remembered. I could still hire a sailing boat and crew, drift out on the harbour and dangle a line over the side to pull up crabs to be cooked on the deck, just as I had done with my father all those years ago.

RIGHT INDONESIAN WOMEN IN TRADITIONAL ATTIRE.

Detroit

DATE OF BIRTH 24 JULY 1701; WHEN FRENCH
EXPLORER ANTOINE DE LA MOTHE CADILLAC SET
UP A FUR-TRADING POST ON THE DETROIT RIVER
HEIGHT 177M **SIZE** 219 SQ KM **ADDRESS** USA
(MAP 1, P4) **POPULATION** 706,000

Detroit is the Motor City, Tamla Motown and home
to Henry Ford's Greenfield Village, but it's also the
doughnut city, a symbol of urban decay whose centre
was abandoned as people moved out to a fringe of
rich, thriving suburbs, trying to turn their collective
backs on a core that might as well have been nuked.
As a child I spent four great years there, back when
what must have been half the world's chromium
production was rolling down GM, Ford and Chrysler
assembly lines, car fins were flying high, and the
Detroit Tigers were the hottest baseball team around.
It's never going to recover those glory days, but
Detroit is still worth a look and Greenfield Village
remains a truly fantastic museum, incorporating not
only the laboratory where Thomas Edison conducted
his pioneering work on electric lighting but also the
bicycle shop where the Wright brothers built their
first aircraft, quite apart from all the Model T stuff.

RIGHT MOTOR CITY'S MACHINE MUSIC.

Tehran

DATE OF BIRTH 1553; WHEN RAMPARTS WERE CONSTRUCTED AROUND THE VILLAGE OF TEHRAN **HEIGHT** 1200M **SIZE** 1500 SQ KM **ADDRESS** IRAN (MAP 8, F3) **POPULATION** 13.8 MILLION

The Islamic Republic of Iran has a long list of cities that score more highly than its chaotic capital. Sophisticated Shiraz has culture, and gave its name to one of the world's great wine varieties. Nearby lie the ruins of mighty Persepolis (whisper it). Mashhad and Qom far outscore Tehran when it comes to religious piety, Yazd and Kashan are way ahead when it comes to beautiful old traditional buildings and, of course, Esfahan is everybody's favourite and truly one of the world's most stunning cities. But there's no denying Tehran's energy and enthusiasm, with its trendy shopping centres where teenagers raise a tentative finger to the fundamentalist mullahs. And all the time the magnificent Alborz Mountains (if you can see them through the pollution) rise up like a lodestone to the north – a clear reminder that the ski slopes on Mt Damavand are only a couple of hours away.

Stanley

DATE OF BIRTH 1843; WHEN THE BRITISH ABANDONED PUERTO DE LA SOLEDAD AND ESTABLISHED STANLEY AS THE CAPITAL **HEIGHT** 135M **ADDRESS** FALKLAND ISLANDS (MAP 3, F19) **POPULATION** 2100

Some of my neglected favourites are those mega-cities few people can warm to, but Stanley is the polar opposite (and not that far from the South Pole). The capital 'city' of the Falkland Islands may be home to 75% of the 'kelpers' (as outsiders sometimes call the islanders), but that still means it can barely scrape together 2000 people. Despite this small population base, colourful Stanley (the islanders love decorating their houses with a technicolour paintbox) has plenty to see. There's a church fronted by a whalebone arch, a line-up of wrecked or dumped ship hulks along the shoreline, several noisy pubs, an iconic hotel (the Upland Goose), and a world-class garden-gnome collection in one front garden.

LEFT WOMEN AT THE WHEEL IN TEHRAN.

Papeete

DATE OF BIRTH 1824; WHEN THE LONDON MISSIONARY SOCIETY (LMS) SETTLED HERE **HEIGHT** 2M
ADDRESS TAHITI (MAP 10, T4) **POPULATION** 26,000

The capital of Tahiti and French Polynesia has a reputation as an overpriced, shonky Pacific disaster zone, a mere jumping-off point to the much more beautiful (though equally overpriced) attractions of neighbouring islands such as Bora Bora. Yeah, sure, but this is still a great place to buy a baguette, sip a glass of wine, sit by the harbour and watch the pirogues (six-man outrigger canoes) charge across the harbour. Meanwhile those dramatic green-draped mountains rise up right behind you, cruising yachts drift in from all over the world, catamaran ferries surge out to nearby Moorea, cargo ships steam out towards the exotic Marquesas (Gauguin's final retreat), the *roulottes* (vans) set up to turn out bargain-priced food beside the docks in the evening, the towering *mahu* (Polynesian cross-dressers) totter off in their high heels and it's all done with a certain French style. What's not to like?

Tunis

DATE OF BIRTH 814 BC; FOUNDED BY PHOENICIAN SETTLERS **HEIGHT** 4M **SIZE** 346 SQ KM
ADDRESS TUNISIA (MAP 6, H1) **POPULATION** 728,000

The sprawling Mediterranean capital of Tunisia is not going to win any beauty contests – although there's a fine World Heritage–listed medina (the ancient walled city) and some great restaurants. But Tunis also has one attraction that alone makes the trip across the Mediterranean from Europe worth the fare: the Bardo Museum. Even if you've never had an enthusiasm for Roman mosaics you will be a convert after you've wandered this treasure house. The Romans left mosaic treasures everywhere they built, from the frigid north of England to the warm Turkish coast, but it was in Tunisia where the art reached its apogee. The glowing artwork, which studs the Bardo's walls, underlines the fact that the colony's rich Roman settlers clearly knew how to build with style.

Oslo

DATE OF BIRTH AD 1048 (ACCORDING TO THE NORSE SAGAS); HOWEVER, ARCHAEOLOGICAL RESEARCH HAS UNCOVERED CHRISTIAN BURIALS DATING FROM BEFORE AD 1000 **HEIGHT** 629M **SIZE** 454 SQ KM **ADDRESS** NORWAY (MAP 4, L4) **POPULATION** 586,000

Cold, conservative and mouth-droppingly expensive, it's hardly surprising that Norway's capital and largest city doesn't feature on the city hit parade. Choose a sunny summer day, however, and Oslo can still charm you with leafy parks, busy cafés and restaurants, plenty of outdoor sculpture (Gustav Vigeland is the big name) and a simply dazzling collection of museums and art galleries. The Viking Ship Museum with its collection of longboats is my favourite, but ship lovers can also visit the Kon-Tiki Museum with Thor Heyerdahl's balsa raft and the polarship *Fram*, which carried Roald Amundsen down to Antarctica for his epic journey to the South Pole in 1911. Of course, walking out of an Oslo art gallery with a Munch masterpiece under your arm seems to have become a Norwegian tradition.

LEFT THE VIKING SHIP MUSEUM IN OSLO.

Warsaw

DATE OF BIRTH 13TH CENTURY; IN 1413 IT
BECAME CAPITAL OF THE DUCHY OF MAZOVIA
AND, IN 1596, CAPITAL OF POLAND **HEIGHT** 106M
SIZE 512 SQ KM **ADDRESS** POLAND (MAP 4, P9)
POPULATION 1.7 MILLION

Poland's capital city, the 'Big Potato', ranks
nowhere in the country's glamour stakes – as a
tourist attraction Kraków gets all the votes. In fact,
this is a city that has clearly gone through hell, and
come out the other side throwing high-fives. The
Old Town Sq was totally destroyed by Hitler's storm
troopers during the closing days of WWII and so
flawlessly rebuilt you'd have trouble telling where
medieval Europe segues into the reconstruction of
the 1970s and '80s. Weep at the poignant reminders
of the Warsaw Ghetto; rage at the incredible story
of the Warsaw Uprising, meticulously detailed in
the Museum of the Warsaw Uprising; laugh at the
'Elephant in Lacy Underwear', the USSR's unwanted
gift and for years the tallest building in Europe
outside Moscow. And then hit the city's clubs and
bars, where the Poles party as though they've got 50
depressing years to make up for.

LEFT THE ROYAL PALACE IN WARSAW'S OLD TOWN.

The Maps

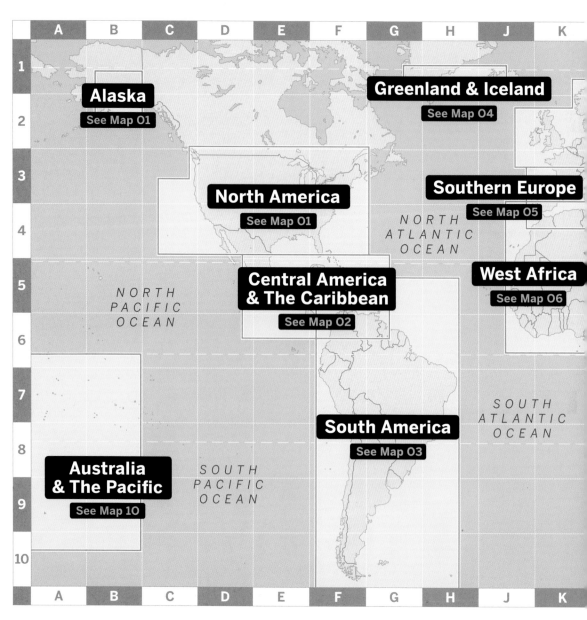

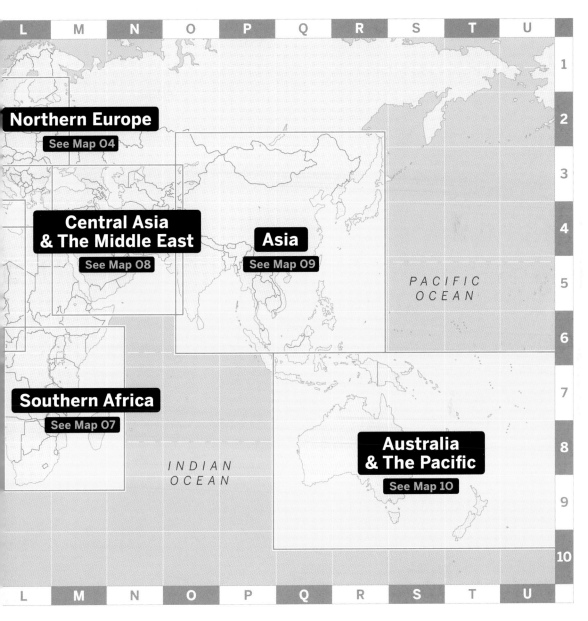

Map O2 **Central America & The Caribbean**

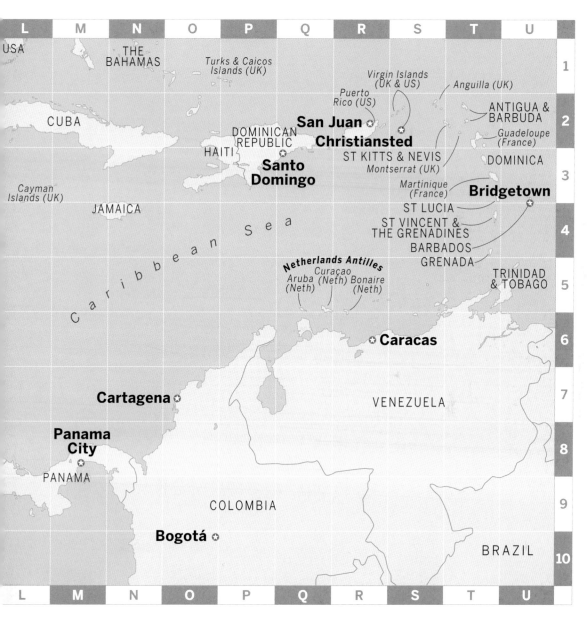

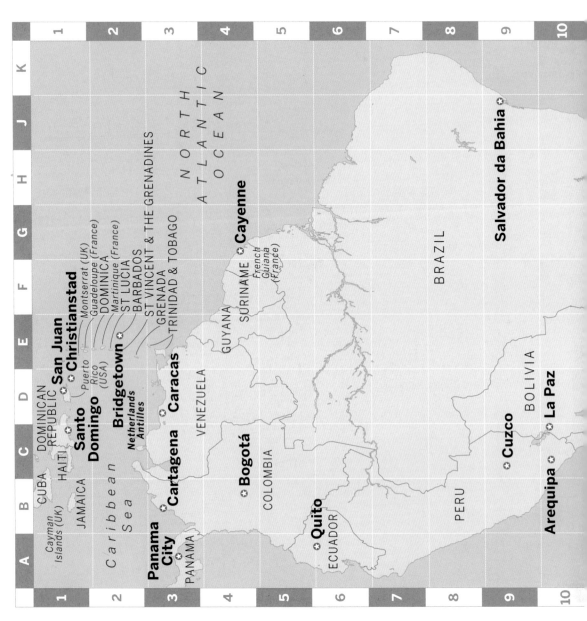

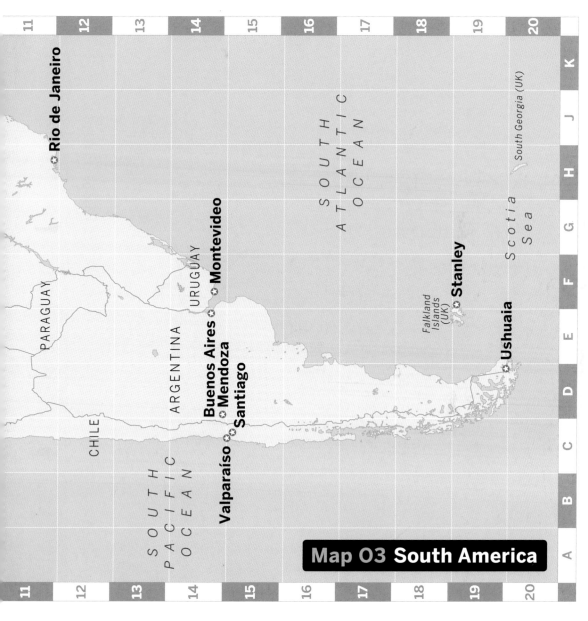

Map O3 **South America**

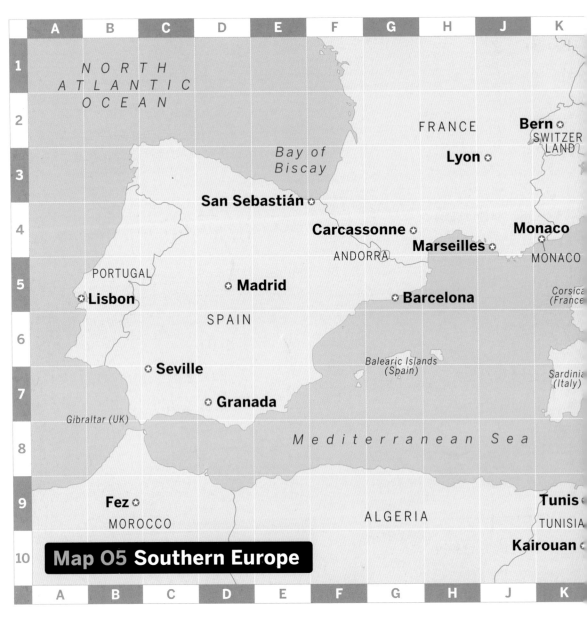

Map O5 **Southern Europe**

Map O6 **West Africa**

Map O7 Southern Africa

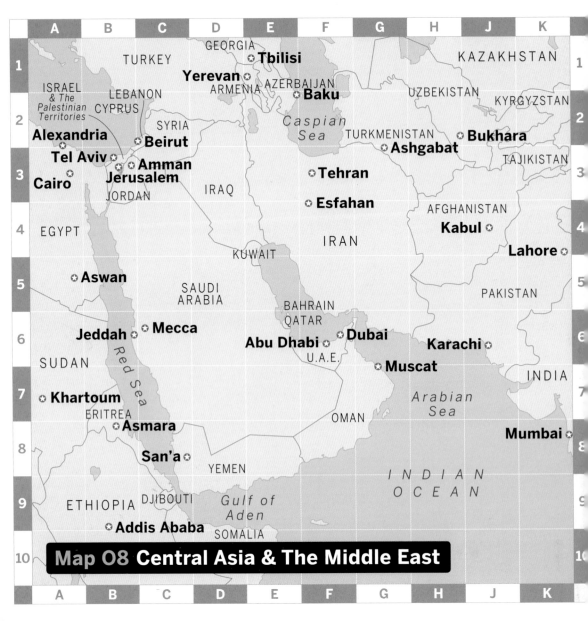

Map 08 **Central Asia & The Middle East**

Map 09 Asia

Map 10 **Australia & The South Pacific**

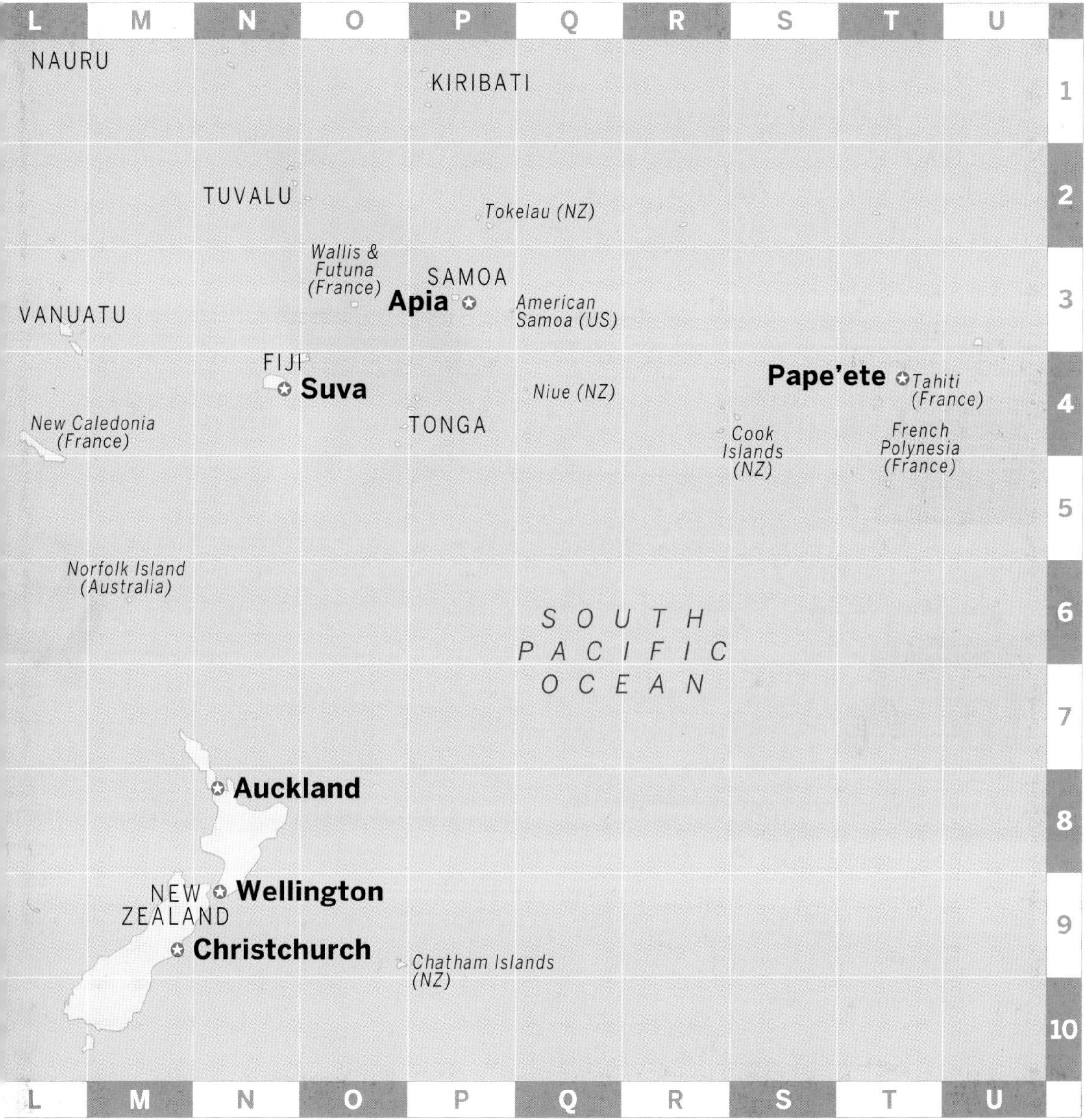
L
M
N
O
P
Q
R
S
T
U
1
2
3
4
5
6
7
8
9
10
NAURU
KIRIBATI
TUVALU
Tokelau (NZ)
Wallis & Futuna (France)
SAMOA
Apia
American Samoa (US)
VANUATU
FIJI
Suva
Niue (NZ)
Pape'ete
Tahiti (France)
New Caledonia (France)
TONGA
Cook Islands (NZ)
French Polynesia (France)
Norfolk Island (Australia)
SOUTH PACIFIC OCEAN
Auckland
NEW ZEALAND
Wellington
Christchurch
Chatham Islands (NZ)

THE CITIES BOOK
A Journey Through the Best Cities in the World

Published March 2013
Published by Lonely Planet Publications Pty Ltd
ABN 36 005 607 983
90 Maribyrnong St, Footscray, Victoria 3011, Australia
www.lonelyplanet.com

Publishing Director Piers Pickard

Publisher Ben Handicott

Project Manager Robin Barton

Art Direction & Design Mark Adams

Designers Frank Diem, Lauren Egan,
Joe Spanti, Clara Monitto

Image Researchers Mark Adams, Sabrina Dalbesio,
Jane Hart, Naomi Parker, Aude Vauconsant, Rebecca Skinner

Editors Alison Ridgway, Trent Holden, Ali Lemer,
Erin Richards, Louisa Syme, Kate Whitfield,
Christopher Pitts, Gabrielle Stefanos

Cartographer Wayne Murphy

Print Production Larissa Frost

Pre-press Production Ryan Evans

Front cover images (left to right) Hendrik Holler / Getty Images; Getty City
Commission; Felix Hug / Getty Images; Anders Blomqvist / Getty Images;
Terry Carter / Getty Images; Jonathan Smith / Getty Images.
Spine image Ricardo Gomes / Getty Images.
Back cover images (left to right) Dan Herrick / Getty Images;
Eddie Gerald / Getty Images; Neil Setchfield / Getty Images; Getty City
Commission; Krzystof Dydynski / Getty Images; Jon Davison / Getty Images.

ISBN 9781743217047
Printed in China
10 9 8 7 6 5 4 3 2 1

© Lonely Planet 2013
© photographers as indicated 2013

Statistical information including population, area and
official languages for each country was sourced from the
Central Intelligence Agency.

MIX
Paper from
responsible sources
FSC™ C021741

Paper in this book is certified against the
Forest Stewardship Council™ standards.
FSC™ promotes environmentally responsible,
socially beneficial and economically viable
management of the world's forests.

Lonely Planet Offices

Australia (HEAD OFFICE)
90 Maribyrnong St, Footscray, Victoria, 3011
Phone 03 8379 8000
Email talk2us@lonelyplanet.com.au

USA
150 Linden St, Oakland, CA 94607
Phone 510 250 6400 **Toll free** 800 275 8555
Email info@lonelyplanet.com

United Kingdom
BBC Worldwide, Media Centre, 201 Wood Lane
London, W12 7TQ **Phone** 020 8433 1333
Email go@lonelyplanet.co.uk